W9-AMX-739

Gramley Library
Salem Academy and College
Winston-Salem, N.C. 27108

Black Mountain Days

Gramley Library
Salem Academy and College
Winston-Salem, N.C. 27108

Also by Michael Rumaker

The Butterfly
The Bar
Gringos and Other Stories
    (published in England as *Exit 3 and other stories*)
Schwul (Queers)
A Day and a Night at the Baths
My First Satyrnalia
Gringos and other stories: A New Edition
    (the Collected Stories)
To Kill a Cardinal
Robert Duncan in San Francisco
Pagan Days

Black Mountain Days

by Michael Rumaker

Black Mountain Press
Asheville, North Carolina

© 2003 Michael Rumaker
All rights reserved

Second Printing

Published in the United States
by Black Mountain Press
an imprint of the Black Mountain College
Museum and Arts Center
P.O. Box 18912
Asheville, North Carolina 28814

Acknowledgements:

Letters of Robert Duncan
© by the Literary Estate of Robert Duncan.

Letters of Charles Olson, Robert Creeley and
Michael Rumaker, Archives & Special Collections,
Thomas J. Dodd Research Center,
University of Connecticut Libraries.
Used with permission.

Portions of this book have appeared in the
following publications:
Boundary 2
North Carolina Literary Review
Minutes of The Charles Olson Society

Library of Congress Control Number: 2002101510
ISBN: 0-9649020-8-7

Cover design by Jon Jicha
Cover photo of Black Mountain College
by Gregory Masurovsky, 1948

For George Butterick,
the inspirer

Preface

Although I have tried to be as factual as I can here, I have been more focused on the "psychological truth," which Jung says is the most important, rather than the factual truth, given memory's turnings, much as that is a strong consideration. There are for any past occurrence as many takes on it as points on a circle. This book is my particular take as a student at Black Mountain College in North Carolina from 1952 to 1955, from my own personal point on the circumference.

1952

My mother was Irish-English, confessing to a "taint" of French, hence, her maiden name Marvel, the root of it probably stretching back to Merville, in northern France. Her mother was Katie O'Connor, several generations removed from County Cork; her father, Robert Marvel, was a South Philly cobbler and occasional Delaware River pleasure and fishing boat captain who sometimes disappeared weeks at a time on benders, leaving Katie to fend for herself (mainly scrubbing floors for others) with their nine surviving children.

My father was Lithuanian-Polish. His father left Lithuania for America to escape conscription in the Czarist armies of Russia; his mother grew up on a chicken farm in Gilesia, Poland, and both came to the United States in the late 19th century at about the same time, each settling, then meeting and marrying, in Philadelphia.

Since my grandfather couldn't write, Ellis Island immigration officials, as one version goes, changed the Lithuanian name Romejko to Rumaker, how it sounded to them phonetically; the other version says it was changed ("Americanized") by a nun in a parochial school in the Richmond section of Philly, where my grandparents first settled and my father first went to school.

My grandmother Sophia tried to raise chickens in her tiny South Philly backyard, just as her family had done for generations in Gilesia, till the Public Health nixed that. Thrifty and shrewd, after a number of years she ended up owning several working-class row houses. My grandfather Paul worked all his life in the Franklin Sugar refinery on Delaware Avenue near the river, where they changed his name again: all his pay envelopes read "Paul Remark." He died, as did my grandfather Marvel, before I was born.

I was born in South Philadelphia in the midst of the Great Depression in a Preston Retreat charity ward on March 5, 1932. My mother helped pay for her keep and my getting born

Gramley Library
Salem Academy and College
Winston-Salem, N.C. 27108

by peeling potatoes in the kitchen of the Retreat, a maternity home for poor married women of "good moral standing." I was the fourth son. Later, the family grew to include another son, a daughter, all born in Philly, and three more sons, born in New Jersey—eight sons and one daughter in all, the same number my grandmother Marvel had raised.

Because my mother went only to the fifth grade in parochial school and my father to the seventh, when we moved across the Delaware to then-rural Gloucester County, New Jersey—my long out-of-work and hard-drinking father was looking for better prospects—my parents considered it quite an achievement when I became the first in the family to graduate from high school. Not only that, but upon graduation I also won a half scholarship to the School of Journalism at Rider College in Trenton. However, once there, I soon saw that I would not be able to work, go to school full-time, *and* pay off the other half of the tuition, I realized I'd have to quit after my freshman year. So, in my last term, I received permission to take all the advanced courses in writing and modern literature. By then I'd decided I wanted to be a "real writer," not a journalist. But I was baffled as to where to go to learn how to become that; and if I found such a place, how could I afford it, since I was totally broke?

In the meantime, when I was 18, my father, with my mother's silent assent, had kicked me out of the house for not going to church and for being queer; I moved to a $7 a week room in Philly in the then semi-redlight district behind Independence Hall and worked in a factory. By chance, in the winter of 1951, a friend and I heard Ben Shahn give a lively lecture at the Philadelphia Museum of Art in which he extolled the unconventional and innovative virtues of a place called Black Mountain College in the western hills of North Carolina, where he had spent the past summer teaching painting. He was especially enthusiastic about a giant of a man, a poet, named

Charles Olson, who was the writing teacher. My ears pricked up. It sounded like the place for me. The only person my friend and I knew in Philly who might know something about this Black Mountain was a young woman named Mary Reed, who taught painting at Moore Institute of Art up on North Broad Street. She said: "Oh, yes, Black Mountain, I hear it's a hotbed of communists and homosexuals."

Hearing that, in the oppressive McCarthyite years, my young, queer ears really pricked up. It *definitely* sounded like the place for me.

I wrote a letter of inquiry to the college, noting my poverty, and received an invitation from the then-registrar Connie Olson, wife of the above-mentioned "giant." She said there were "work scholarships" available and invited me down for a three-day visit.

Three others who also wanted to look the place over went down with me: two other gays (we always managed to find, and cling to, each other in those dangerous days), Roger and Marge, who were students at Rider, and Mary Ann Fretz, who was a student of Reed's at Moore Institute. Fortunately, Marge had a new green Chevy and loved to drive.

Early in June 1952 we set out on our 600-mile journey south.

Once Marge got behind the wheel there was no stopping her. Ever silent, her eyes stared straight out the dusty windshield, spattered, after several hundred miles, with smashed corpses of moths and other insects, ignoring our incessant chatter in her fierce concentration (particularly Roger's dry acerbic comments on the passing scene). Her left arm, resting crooked on the sill leaning out the driver's window, was black from the sun, the other arm inside the car negligently holding the wheel was snow white because Marge took a lot of long drives—What was a lesbian to do at Rider College in Trenton, NJ, USA in

1952?—and so got us there in good time. It was the early hours of the morning west of the little sleeping town of Black Mountain ("altitude 2,400 feet" read the road marker) nestled in the Swannanoa Valley, when we spotted the hand-painted BLACK MOUNTAIN COLLEGE sign with its directional arrow along the county road. We pulled over and parked in a dark, heavily-wooded area near the road leading up to the college. Worn out after our almost non-stop trip, we scared ourselves silly with imaginary phantoms surrounding us in the dark and, after rolling up the windows and locking the doors, with even the usually taciturn Marge joining in, hysterically laughed ourselves into a few fitful hours of sleep sitting up in the car.

After breakfast in a roadside restaurant on the highway leading into Asheville, we turned back toward Black Mountain and made our way up the mountain, the dust-streaked Chevy steadily climbing the steep narrow asphalt road which led past vast stretches of hilly farmland and cow pastures to the place that was to be my home for the next three years.

It was early, perhaps around 9 a.m., when we drove past a creosote-shingled gatehouse and under the black-lettered sign on a white board up on posts with the college's name painted on it. We drove along the bend of a yellow dirt road with broad flat fields of grass, covered with acres of tiny blue flowers and rambling wild rose bushes stretching far away on either side. Just ahead, to the left, was another, much larger dark creosote-shingled building with a high red tarpaper roof, fronting on a small lake which we glimpsed through a sparse stand of trees on the edge of it. Behind this sprawling building was a small circular structure of fieldstone with windows all around.

To the right, across the road from the large building, was a tiny fieldstone cottage, almost hidden in the dense pine trees and mountain laurel bushes surrounding it. Beyond that could be seen the roofs and upper stories of two huge, rambling lodges, their wide clapboard walls also darkly creosoted.

Directly behind the lodges, which had a worn, shabby air like the other buildings, the lush green hills, which I learned later were named the Seven Sister Mountains, rose steeply, their tops still shrouded in early morning mist.

Beyond these, higher hills ringed the valley, pillows of cloud sliding over their crests, the wide green valley where other, out-lying and far-flung buildings and cottages of the college nestled on 600 acres of mountainous woodland, as the brochure Connie Olson had sent me stated. The place was in many ways just as I had envisioned it: steep mountains with isolated build-ings along the slopes, a sense of vast wilderness-like space and isolation.

Marge parked by a huge flat millstone lying by the walk lead-ing up to the steps of the large building on the right. Near the millstone was a rickety, weather-worn park bench under an apple tree. We sat in the car and peered about. Not a soul to be seen. The chirr and thrum of insects filled the air. Bird cries everywhere.

After several minutes of waiting, a mangy-looking orange dog sauntered across the dusty road and disappeared around the corner of the building, our first sign of life.

"There's hope," I said, and we all laughed. But it was a real letdown to have driven so far in such high enthusiasm—at least on my part—only to arrive, tired and almost sleepless, to find a drowsy, deserted place that looked as if it would never show, and had never shown, any spark of life.

"Maybe it's because it's between sessions," I said, trying to give some kind of explanation. "There's probably not too many people here now."

The others appeared unconvinced. Their faces seemed to say I'd taken them all off on a wild-goose chase.

We were uncertain as to what to do, whether to go into the cottage-like building on the left or the larger, sprawling one on the right and try to find someone and make known our arrival.

Feeling inexplicably shy, we tacitly decided to just sit and wait.

The mangy-looking dog, oblivious to our existence, reappeared, padding slowly back across the road. Our heads turned equally slowly in unison to watch its unhurried progress as it finally vanished among the pine trees surrounding the fieldstone building across the way.

Through the dusty, bug-splattered windshield the place looked so isolated and rural—a sense of primeval forest, really, there was so much overwhelming lush greenery standing up high on the steep towering hills that pressed around close on all sides. The buildings had such a rough-hewn, rundown look about them. It just didn't look like a *real* college, or had even the semblance of one, like Princeton, which I'd only glimpsed from a distance from a Greyhound bus window on one of the trips to New York City from Rider with Roger, Princeton with its thick ivy-covered Romanesque-gray architecture and spacious neat lawns and its distinct but subtle smell of old money, all jumbled in my raw, impressionable head with the glamorous irresponsibility and silliness of F. Scott Fitzgerald's *This Side of Paradise*.

Black Mountain was certainly not like Rider College, from which I'd just escaped, whose richly dark wood-paneled entrance lobby, then located off State Street in the capital of New Jersey, with gleaming metal nameplates on huge solid polished desks and heavy, forbidding doors of dark wood, was like, with no efforts of concealment, the sacrosanct interior of a posh bank or an exclusive *nouveau riche* men's club, all quietly bespeaking that money, not education, was the main object of worship. (Princeton at least gave the pretense of offering a liberal arts education.)

That first cursory glimpse of Black Mountain was that of a run-down summer camp with hastily constructed, temporary-looking lodges and outbuildings, what the place had actually been before the college moved there from across the valley in

1940-41.

Perhaps we had traveled 600 miles for nothing.

Then, each of us stiffened in our seats, eyes alert, as a small-boned woman, an apparition in white, emerged from behind the same pines the dog had wandered into, and began crossing the road in the direction of the large building. Her delicately-featured face had a slightly puffy, sleepy look, as if she had just awakened. Her fine dark blond hair was drawn back tightly over her skull and fastened behind in a long ponytail down her back. It shone in the sun with a glossy, just-washed gleam. She wore a man's much-too-big cotton shirt tied at the middle and knee-length, cream-colored wraparound Mexican pants. Eyes cast down, a king-sized cigarette clenched between her teeth, bare-footed, she picked her way carefully among the stones in the road. In one hand she held an empty mason jar.

"Grab her," snarled Marge over her shoulder at me. "She might be the last live one we catch all day."

I scrambled out of the car and hurried up to the woman, introduced myself and told her the reason for our being there. She took the cigarette from between her small, perfect teeth and smiled, a smile that seemed to well up from some deep and private place, one of the warmest I'd ever seen. Close up, she really had the most sensitive face, with dark eyes that had an edge of sadness and inward contemplation. Everything was fine about her, not only her facial features, but her hands, her slight body as well. She was like a finely proportioned and delicate bird. Dropping my eyes in accustomed shyness, I noted her thin feet, their long delicate toes in the dust.

I felt a pang of hope.

She spoke with a calm sureness, a faint hint of New England in her voice. "I'm Connie. We've been expecting you."

I apologized, motioning toward the car, that there were more of us than expected, three more, in fact. I explained as best I could that Mary Ann and Roger wanted to check out the school as a possibility for future enrollment, and that Marge had come along because, well, Marge had the car. This didn't seem to bother Connie, or at least she didn't show it.

"I was just on my way to the dining hall to pick up some milk for breakfast," she said, indicating the large building on the right where we'd parked. "Have you had breakfast?"

When I said that we had, she said, "Well, bring your friends along and come in and have coffee. And then I'll show you around. We probably won't find too many people up and about." She gave me a rueful but impish smile. "We had a party last night."

There was no one in the dining hall, for that's what the large building turned out to be. The place had the most deserted air; I figured it must have been *some* party. While Connie delivered her jar of milk (I was already wondering when we would meet her giant poet of a husband), we drank coffee in thick white mugs on the screened-in dining porch and had our first look at the lake. In surprising contrast to the old ramshackle buildings we had seen so far, at the far side of the water the trim modernist lines of what the brochure had called the Studies Building gleamed whitely like a pylon turned on end. Beyond that, miles away in the distant northwest, snowcapped against the sky, was the hazy blue peak of Mount Mitchell, at almost 7,000 feet the tallest of the Appalachians. I began to feel better, getting a wider, less hemmed-in perspective as I took in, through the screening, the valley stretching away to the north and west with its broad pastures and grazing cows and furrowed farmland marking the rounded hills rolling lazily away under a sky at last clearing itself of morning mists.

The lake, Connie told us upon her return, was called Lake Eden.

Leaving the dining hall, she led us past a large round dinner gong supported on wooden posts just outside the back kitchen door. Beyond the gong, where the road made a circle ("Dinner

Bell Circle" it was appropriately called), was a small, rambling shingled cottage, its sides and front porch covered with dense wisteria and other hanging vines, which was, Connie explained in passing, the home of Hazel Frieda Larsen, photography instructor and secretary-treasurer of the college. With her recent interest in photography, Mary Ann gave me a quick look.

We walked up the narrow dirt road running alongside Lake Eden on the right, with tall marsh grass growing at its edge, while to the left one of the Seven Sisters swept up sheer and tall right from the edge of the road, its high slopes covered with timber, while lower down grew a thick, wide-leafed vine I was later to learn was called kudzu, cuttings of which had been imported years earlier from Japan to keep the slopes from avalanching onto the road; we also later discovered the kudzu vines were ubiquitous and so vigorous everywhere you could almost watch them grow. Connie pointed out to us the small, fieldstone Quiet House, hand-built by a faculty member and a student as a memorial, for anyone seeking solitude or meditation, almost hidden in the shadow of the hillside foliage; and further on the almost-completed science/chemistry-lab building, also student designed and student built, a tri-level, open-decked, all glass-fronted construction of even more modern and advanced design than the older Studies Building. The bulk of its trim, linear shape was supported only by what looked like two very slender metal poles, the whole of it jutting out from the boughs of tall pine trees high up on the mountainous slope to our left.

Connie told us, pleasantly, conversationally, that the building had been designed for science workshops and labs, but when Natasha Goldowski, the physicist and head of the science programs at the college, took one look at the nearly-finished structure, she refused, and refused to allow any of her students, to set foot in it, or to use it for classes or for the purposes for which it was built, insisting that the precariously perched structure, on its two skinny metallic legs, was sure someday to tumble down the steep mountainside and crash onto the road. And neither she, nor her students, were about to be maimed or killed for the sake of such modernist architectural folly. (Having taught at Princeton briefly after immigrating to America after the war, perhaps she was pining for some of those solid Romanesque edifices I'd seen from the bus.)

So the brand-new, aerie-like structure gracefully nestled among the pine boughs went mainly unused, except occasionally for a language or writing class held there.

Hearing this bit of eccentric information, my heart really began to warm to the place.

However, with a bit of alarm, I noted metal snake-bite kits nailed to the occasional gray-rotted, rusty-shaded lampposts we passed and cast a wary eye at the tall, thick vegetation growing either side of the road. I wanted to ask about snakes, particularly the poisonous variety but, beginning to feel good about the college, decided not to.

Connie, no doubt sensing my uneasiness as I gazed at the kits, assured us in her quiet voice that no one, so far as she knew, had ever been bitten, and the snake-bite kits had never been opened. "There are rattlesnakes and copperheads," she smiled back at us, "but they mind their own business."

We gave each other looks, but I felt reassured—there was something calming about this woman—particularly when I noted rust spots on the kits, reinforcing Connie's observation about their lack of use.

By now, the mists were beginning to burn away from the hilltops and the sun shone down with a burning edge. Down to the right, on the far edge of the lake, almost hidden in the lush growth, Connie pointed to a long, white barracks-like building, the library. The morning was turning hot and humid as we walked up to the flat concrete entrance of the three-tiered Studies Building adjacent to the library, Connie explaining that here, "just as at Princeton," each student had his or her own private study. Inside, the long narrow upper level hallway was cool and dark, with most of the study doors closed. There was still that air of desertion and silence everywhere; we had yet to encounter another human being. She took us out on the sundeck at the far end of the long, slender structure, its floor covered with green roofing, and another spectacular view, this time back across the lake toward the dining hall we'd just left. Miles off to the south were more ridges of high mountains rearing up mistily against a now almost cloudless sky, Connie pointing out the tall white columns of sprawling Lee Hall halfway up a mountain far across the valley, the first site of the college before it moved to Lake Eden.

We walked down a back flight of stairs to the lower level where there was another long hallway lined with studies, about a hundred in all, I calculated (the school had a full capacity for only 99 students). At the front of the building again, we descended a wide metal stairwell, and down at the bottom level we came into a big cool white room with gray-painted floor and large windows running along either wall, a room Connie explained was then being used as a painting workshop. Outside one bank of windows, on the shady side, I heard the loud roar of a mountain stream rushing close by. Looking out, barely visible in a jungle of brush and vines, at angles to each other, were two more long, white-painted barracks-like buildings Connie said were called the Eye and the Stables and were painters' studios.

She spoke of Robert Rauschenberg, a painting student who'd left Black Mountain that spring and done a painting called "Black on Black" (followed by "White on White") which had caused a stir in avant-garde art circles up in New York City. She also mentioned that "abstract-expressionists" Franz Kline and Willem de Kooning (names unknown to me at the time) had taught at the college. Kline would be teaching again that summer she said, and both he and de Kooning had strongly influenced the painting students, "As you can see by the canvases around the room," especially "Kline's influence."

I kept looking around for evidence of paintings but could see nothing that resembled, to my eyes at least, even the hint of one. I figured the students must've taken them all back with them to their studios or studies and left only a lot of odd-sized canvases leaning against the walls, canvases that strangely enough seemed to be used here only to serve as palettes, their surfaces were so daubed and streaked and smeared with dribblings and smudges of every color of oil paint imaginable, along with wipings of turpentine and linseed oil.

Connie was pointing to a smaller-sized canvas propped neglectedly in a far corner of the room. Glancing at it, wondering whatever was she drawing our attention to it for, since I honestly thought an apprentice artist, using some dark mixture of oil and grease, had used it for cleaning his or her brushes, I heard, to my amazement, Connie, in her quiet and utterly serious voice, describe it as a *painting* she particularly liked, one in which she felt the student had achieved some dynamic and interesting shapes, didn't we agree?

We all stared at it politely, murmuring inaudible murmurs. It was then I learned my first lesson at Black Mountain even before I ever became a student there: When confronted with objects of creation beyond my comprehension to keep my mouth firmly shut and my eyes and ears open. I also recognized, with a delicious excitement of my well-hidden but naturally rebellious heart, that there was something going on in this isolated backwoods called Black Mountain College that I had never conceived of in the world outside.

It was at that moment I knew I must get to this seemingly abandoned place in the wilderness, by whatever means.

Just then, by coincidence, the artist-student whose grimly splotched work Connie admired, wandered in through the rear wide double doors of the room leading to the outside open area beneath the building. "Phyllis Franklin," Connie said, and indicating us, explained to the artist that we were visiting from up north. She mentioned parenthetically that Phyllis was from Kansas, giving a suggestion of a sharp and perceptive intelligence in which I began to hear even more distinctly the slight flint-edged tones of New England.

Phyllis smiled at us shyly, a thin-lipped smile, skin tight over broad cheekbones, and in her big black luminous eyes, a mystical hint of inner absorption. We greeted her in turn, avoiding any mention of her painting, myself anyway. Shy in my own way, I was determined not to be phony or pretend to understand and enjoy something I didn't, so I kept still.

Connie told her we'd been looking at her work, and all Phyllis said was "oh," neither a question nor a statement. Those large dark eyes then riveted on the canvas with an intensity of absorption that startled me. She appeared for the moment lost to us in her scrutiny of it, as if she were taking swift and accurate mental notes for future changes to be made.

The seriousness of that gaze, the aura of this spare young woman from the plains of Kansas standing transplanted in the middle of the mountains of western North Carolina as she soberly examined a work of her own making that was incomprehensible to me, caused my reserved attitude to the place to thaw even more.

I looked at the painting again, trying to see what Connie saw. I knew that this, and similar works, would take some looking at before my eyes could adjust to seeing what the painter was up to, but in that second look I could perceive a power and boldness of energy, a certain muscular force, however "chaotic" and random the dark abstractly swirling shapes appeared to my unaccustomed eyes.

Connie said to us, "Come on, I'll take you up to Roadside, where you'll be staying."

Leaving the coolness of the Studies, we stepped out into a blazing molten early spring day. I began to understand in the dizzying heat why greenery grew so lushly here.

We passed what looked to be an abandoned cottage, its wooden shingles weathered with age, most of its windows gone—just beyond the front of the Studies Building, a curious anachronistic contrast to the sleek modernity of the latter; Connie said it had once been used as a painting studio. Then we crossed a wooden footbridge over a deep ravine, passed another wood-shingled cottage or smaller lodge, that Connie said was a faculty residence called "Streamside," so named because the same mountain stream that I'd heard rushing past the Studies Building rushed past here as well. We walked up a gentle slope under tall pines with a deep carpet of dried needles underfoot and came to Roadside, another small lodge or cottage, obviously so named because it was built close to the road which wound further on up the slope with the scattered roofs of several more cottages either side of it visible through the trees. The college farm, Connie said, was not too far beyond the brook and the woods stretching past Roadside.

She showed us our rooms, Roger and I on the first floor, Marge and Mary Ann on the second, in the traditional segregation of sexes, for appearances' sake, I guess, although, ironically enough, Mary Ann was the only predominantly nongay member of our party and might've been thought to be "safer" sleeping with either Roger or myself.

The rooms were pine-walled enclosures, unpainted and furnished austerely with only the bare necessities: beds, whose mattresses had a soury smell, an old chest of drawers, a cane-bottomed, straight-backed chair or two. A smell of damp and mildew permeated throughout despite the open windows, an odor I have ever since associated with Black Mountain where because of the Seven Sisters encircling the campus, many rooms in many buildings never saw sunlight—not to mention, as I later learned from former student and then faculty wife Mary Fitton Fiore that Black Mountain also had the highest rainfall in the region.

There were several students also staying in the house, to whom we were introduced outside under the pines once we'd gotten ourselves squared away. One in particular was Mark Hedden, who in later years was to play an important part in my life, an anthropology student from Westport, Connecticut, a dark-blond, solidly built youth in khaki shorts and wearing horn-rimmed glasses and a hearing aid, whose quiet, unassuming manner I found instantly appealing, increasing my growing affirmation of the place.

Lunch was at twelve Connie told us. We'd hear the dinner bell and to just come down and sit at any table and make ourselves at home. "I won't be there, but I'll see you at supper tonight."

We thanked her for her attentions and for showing us around and went into our rooms to rest and get ready for lunch.

I was feeling a growing excitement about the place, one which I knew Roger didn't share.

"It's the place for you," he said, prophetically. "Me, I'll finish up at Rider. I need that sure thing of a degree."

It wasn't until Saturday evening, the second day of our visit, that Charles Olson put in an appearance. I was anxious to meet this man I'd heard so much about, not only earlier from Ben Shahn's Philadelphia lecture but now also around the Black Mountain campus, his name being spoken more often than any other, and with a respect that bespoke his influence. Connie had told us we would eventually meet him, that he was then preoccupied with his own work, often well into the small hours of the morning, and slept late.

In the meantime, the four of us went off to do some sightseeing, Marge driving us into Asheville, with the main purpose of making the pilgrimage to Thomas Wolfe's Old Kentucky Home on Spruce Street, the actual and fictional boarding house his mother ran in his first novel, *Look Homeward, Angel*. I don't think Marge ever read the book and just came along for the ride, and to please Mary Ann and me who had devoured all the novels of word-drunk Wolfe like any greenly romantic teenagers, devouring his logorrheic romanticizing of those hills—Wolfe obviously a most seductive writer to those in their teens. Roger, cooler, more jaundice eyed, not so easily seduced, also, like Marge, went along to please us. I was later to learn what Olson thought of Wolfe, calling him "a big sentimental galoot," Olson showing no empathy that Wolfe and he were almost as tall as each other, the only trait they shared as I came to learn, their visions and work galaxies apart.

But that day, my head still reeking with romantic notions of the South, as we drove through Asheville's Pack Square and I saw the actual shops and business buildings, the Pack Library Wolfe had written about and where he bragged he as a kid had devoured just about every book on the shelves, I felt like a kid myself with my nose pressed up against the car window.

It was the first time I'd ever been inside the home of an actual writer, and one who, still at that time, was so famous; in a home that was the actual setting of a book that had, for better or worse, helped ever more to confirm my own determination to be a writer, so that, as we went through the old boarding house with its wide front porch and its high-backed rockers, all of it kept exactly as it was when Wolfe's mother died, I thrilled at every stick of furniture, at seeing the room where brother Ben died of pneumonia, in actuality and in the novel, thrilled even at Wolfe's father's large spidery handwriting of names and phone numbers scrawled on the wall around the antique telephone—all details Wolfe had so lavishly and lovingly written about in *Look Homeward, Angel*; all the while I was trying carefully to conceal from the aloof and sneering Roger the intensity of emotions all such details aroused in me, unwilling to risk one of his jeering, sophisticated wisecracks had I expressed any of those feelings. And if that weren't enough, Mary Ann and I convinced Marge to drive us to the Riverside Cemetery on Birch Street, where Wolfe was buried back in 1938, and where the two of us stood secretly reverent reading the inscriptions on his stone, "Tom, son of W. O. and Julia E. Wolfe . . . A Beloved American Author . . . 'The last voyage, the longest, the best . . .,' " the latter quote from *Look Homeward, Angel*, while Roger stood around wisecracking, and Marge, in her mannish, short-sleeved sports shirt, looked bored.

He was, I believe, the first *total* person I'd ever glimpsed, or what I understood to be total at that time anyway. I'd never met anyone like him before, and now, years later, as I write this, I can say I've never met anyone quite like him since. He was truly one of a kind, and this even in a place such as Black Mountain, as I came to learn, where genius was not exactly scarce.

My first glimpse of him was at supper on the dining hall porch, with its dozen or so tables lined up single file down the long length of it, roast chicken being served, a Saturday night tradition at the college, cooked up by cooks Malrey and Cornelia, with student help. (The students, we were discovering, had a hand in everything, from working in the kitchen, including washing dishes, to mending the roads, to keeping the lush kudzu on the mountain slopes in check with bolo knives, to working on the farm that produced all the college's milk and much of its meat and vegetables.) Connie Olson invited Mary Ann and me to sit at a table with her and her husband, Charles, and the composer in residence, Lou Harrison. (Marge and Roger, either uncomfortable or deciding the place wasn't for them, had taken off that afternoon in Marge's Chevy to see some local sights and didn't return till the next day, Sunday, the time we were supposed to leave.)

Saturday night was also "dress-up" night, we learned, and Lou, his thick dark-brown goatee in sharp contrast, was decked out in a sparkling suit the dazzling shade of vanilla ice cream. Connie was dressed in a subdued blue blouse and skirt of denim with a light, bright, loosely knit shawl thrown over her shoulders, and simple leather sandals, Grecian-looking in design, held on her slender feet with thin thongs.

But it was Olson, up to that time the tallest man I'd ever laid eyes on, appearing close to seven feet tall, with a large head, who immediately impressed me, and not only because of his size, impressive as the length and width of him was—including an appetite to match, as I soon learned as I watched, amazed, as he tore into the platter of chicken. Wearing a long, loose-hanging, brown seersucker jacket, a faded blue workshirt with a shrunk, out-of-shape, nondescript necktie twisted around his extra-large neck, chino work trousers, the cuffs of which came well over the tops of his high-topped worker's boots (it must have been almost impossible for him to get off-the-rack trousers in his leg length), Charles was all charm and courtliness, attentive to Mary Ann and me, especially to Mary Ann who, besides her dark-eyed, exotically attractive face, with a subtle Asian suggestion in her eyes and features, was, as always, in her quiet, unobtrusive way, instantly likeable and winning. Unaware of it, she exuded a strong and attractive personal appeal, modest, vulnerable, that, time and again, I saw both men and women succumb to, as did I myself and as did, I could see that evening, both Charles and Connie.

I don't believe that either Mary Ann or I said much during the meal except in monosyllables in response to Charles' questions (he was graciousness itself), both of us being shy in these unusual surroundings and not yet quite able to figure out what the place was all about, or if there was a place for us in it. I felt an immediate pull to Olson. His presence lit up the place for me in a totally new and appealing light. I'd never met anyone before who radiated such healthy animal spirits, such exuberant great humor and enticing charm, who made me feel—as I'm sure he did Mary Ann, too—that, in his beaming and affectionately owlish eyes behind thick, horn-rimmed glasses, I was a very special person. He awoke a strong desire in me to be in this place and to be near him. I cannot more adequately describe the hope this man inspired in me within only the first minutes of having met him.

We had no need to be concerned about our shy reticence, however. Except for an occasional quiet and astute comment from Connie, Charles and Lou dominated the conversation (Olson obviously had a high regard and a jocular affection for Lou), entertaining us with rollicking banter. Although a lot of it, consisting mostly of "in" jokes, went over my head, it was bantering that brought grins from the diners at nearby tables who were apparently familiar with these boisterous exchanges.

Sitting at the table, I recalled that Mary Reed, the painting instructor at Moore Institute, had jokingly called Black Mountain "a hotbed of communists and homosexuals." If not a communist, Lou Harrison easily fit the other side of Reed's whimsical definition (although the FBI, I subsequently found, did not take it so whimsically), for he was obviously gay, with a highstrung nervous energy and a quick and energetic wit along with a loud rippling laugh that shook the roofbeams of the dining porch (later I learned Lou enjoyed getting "high" on numerous pots of strong tea—the liquid kind—in the Gatehouse where he had an upright piano to compose on). That Olson, whose own merrily booming laugh could be heard quite a distance, obviously enjoyed the witty sparring and company of this out-and-out gay man, and that in the friendly and amusing banter of each there was such obvious affectionate regard (I later learned Charles held Lou's exotically ingenious musical compositions, with their Asian resonances, in high esteem also), were other seductions, wearing down in me any resistances I might've had to the place.

Perhaps I had found a safe place—a rare enclave in America of that time—for my own queer self.

There were several more seductions to occur that evening to make my surrender complete. What finally clinched it for me was the ride into Asheville after supper with Connie and Charles in Charles' old blue beatup Ford convertible, with the leather driver's seat smashed far back from the wheel by the weight and pressure of his huge frame.

I don't recall the purpose of our trip into Asheville, but I believe it was to get something at a drugstore for their first baby, Kate, who we were told had been born eight months before, and I think also to stop and have some ice cream at one of Charles' favorite drive-in shops along the highway. Whatever the reason, Mary Ann and I were invited to come along. We were more than pleased to do so since we both felt at ease with and were captivated by this incongruous couple: the small-boned, soft-spoken, incisively intelligent woman with the delicate, bird-like features; alongside her towering, big-framed, highly vocal and forceful figure of a husband. But the latter, in spite of his bluff voice and gigantic physical size, which dominated every presence he was in, had, I immediately perceived, a delicate, somewhat "womanly," and for that reason, very appealing sensitivity.

By chance, there was a full moon that night, and riding in the back seat of the convertible with the top down, Mary Ann beside me, we drove down into the valley and headed toward Asheville 12 miles away. Charles, a fast driver, one big hand laid casually over the wheel, talked easily, relaxedly to us over his shoulder. I scarcely heard what he said, not only because of the wind rushing past my ears, but because I was held spellbound by the powerful glow of the moonlight flooding Swannanoa Valley—the light of the moon of a quality and strength, its huge size and closeness, such as I had never seen before. It had just risen above the distant hills as we set off, and all the way into town my eyes stayed riveted, looking out the left side of the car, excited by the prospect of the vast light-golden moon, its wide luminescence silhouetted against the pitch-black hills.

That did it. Mingled with our visit to the Old Kentucky Home in Asheville the day before and my excited memories of Thomas Wolfe's lush and verbose descriptions in *Look Homeward, Angel* of his mountainous home-country which I'd gotten intoxicated on at a green 18 (the perfect age for Wolfe, as for Swinburne, "all sound, no sense," to quote another Black Mountaineer, poet Jonathan Williams) was now the real thing, and a more intoxicating presentation of it couldn't have been better imagined. Perhaps it was my having grown up in the flat, once-under-sea yellow sands of South Jersey that made me yearn to live in this different, hilly, inland terrain. If it was that, it was also combined with the powerfully seductive sense of Charles and Connie, both of whom emanated such vital and attractive energy, although in different ways: Connie, the quieter strength, the more pointed intelligence; Charles, I could already sense, with curiosity and enthusiasms sprawling and darting over enormously wide fields. With his flattering attentiveness I, despite my habitual guardedness, found him totally irresistable.

But mainly it was the feeling that maybe here I could finally learn to write; equally as important, maybe here I could find a place to be.

It was late when we got back from Asheville, but even so Charles said he'd like to take a look at some of the writing I'd brought down with me. After he'd parked under the pines surrounding the office cottage across from the dining hall, Connie went back to their apartment to check daughter Kate, whom someone had been looking in on while we were away in town, while Charles walked Mary Ann and me back to Roadside so I could pick up the manuscripts I'd been requested to bring down to show as examples of my work. Charles, walking between us, talked and talked, mainly about Black Mountain, the kind of place it was, the kind of place he envisioned it could be, interjecting at times questions about ourselves. The twisting dirt road that skirted Lake Eden was bright with moonlight, an extravagance of light that made every leaf and blade of grass distinct, every wrinkle and fold of the nearby and far-flung hills clearly visible—the earlier golden light now changed to a curious clear blue light filling the vast valley such as I had never seen, certainly never in New Jersey.

There's no doubt, in that spring of 1952, eager as the college was to have more students, that much of Charles' talk was artful and seductive sales pitch (he was after all, as I came to discover, an authentic American, not only as a poet but also when it came to hype). But the substance of his talk went well beyond that. The possibilities and vision he expressed about Black Mountain took on the excitement of an adventurous crusade, a sacred vision, that he intimated Mary Ann and I (Mary Ann hadn't yet expressed her decision not to apply to Black Mountain that fall) would be privileged to participate in if we would only apply and were accepted to the school—if our potential and our work met the standards. There was also about him that immediate sense of friendliness and openness, that he seemed so in tune with Mary Ann and me and treated us from the first moments of meeting him as intimates and equals. It quite turned my head. Later, after my own struggles with him, I was to learn when Charles liked you there was no escaping him and, as in my case, there was no desire to. It was like my chance to have another father at last, a beloved and loving master to serve and learn from. At that moment, I would have done anything to become his loyal and willing apprentice.

I ran quickly into Roadside, to the room Roger and I shared, and grabbed the batch of manuscripts from the battered old suitcase my mother had lent me when I first went off to Rider, and rejoining Charles and Mary Ann, we retraced our steps back down the path to Olson's place.

Although Charles and Connie's apartment was on the first floor at the far end of South Lodge, above the photography workshop and storerooms in the basement at that end, the land sloped down so steeply there that the apartment was quite high up on the hill and a long flight of steps was needed to get up to the place. Branches of tall trees pressed in around the lighted windows where the largest moths I'd ever seen, luna moths they were called, were batting against the panes. On the small back porch, I was surprised to see their new baby sleeping soundly under mosquito netting in a basket in, at that altitude, the now-chill air. One glance up the steep side of the mountain, rising almost perpendicular just beyond the railing of the high porch, the moon-washed and densely forested slope with its dynamic loud thrum of insects and the occasional cry and rustle of animal night-life, gave me visions of the infant being snatched from her basket by some predator in the middle of the night and dragged away up the hillside to disappear into a hidden lair in the thick brush, never to be seen again.

When I whispered something to this effect, trying to make a joke of it, that weren't they afraid Kate might be "stolen by bears" (we'd been told there were black bears in the surrounding mountains), Charles said only, "Outdoors is healthier for the child."

Up on the porch, he leaned his great frame over the basket and peered down through his thick lenses with a quiet, pleased smile. "My daughter," he said grinning, and turning to us, "Still new to me."

Mary Ann and I tiptoed up and looked in the basket, but because of the heavy white netting and the dim light through the open window, we could only barely make out the form of a child lying peacefully on its side.

"You don't need to creep about," Charles said. "Nothing

wakes her. The most amazing thing."

He pulled open the screen door and we entered a large, light, bright-painted room, sparsely furnished with an odd assortment of furniture: low comfortable chairs and pallets covered with colorful throws. In one corner, near the door and two of the large windows that opened out with handles but were screened on the inside, was a big stout table littered with heaps of books and papers, a black Royal typewriter jutting up in the midst of it all, that I took to be Olson's work desk. The walls were covered with abstract paintings and drawings similar, and indistinguishable to my unawakened eye, to those we'd seen in the art workroom of the Studies Building on our arrival. Also on the wall was a broadside on orange paper, one of Olson's poems, "This," which he proudly pointed out to us, saying it had been printed by one of the students, Nick Cernovich, in the print shop across from Roadside: "Ain't it a smart job?"

I had never before seen a poem printed that way; but not wanting to be constantly giving away my greenness, I nodded my head in agreement, which wasn't a total untruth: It was an attractive broadside, with a free-form sunburst/sunflower design, and I liked this, to me, novel idea of hanging a poem up on the wall, although glancing cursorily at it, I couldn't make any sense of it at all.

We could hear Connie moving about in an adjacent room where the door was closed and there was light showing through the cracks around the doorframe and between the wide wallboards (solid in appearance though the lodges and other houses were, you could see, once inside them, they weren't built for winter dwelling; even so, the college was open year round). She made no further appearance again that night, leaving us to Charles who went into the small kitchen and puttered about making us tea and chatting with us through the open doorway.

I felt relaxed and comfortable, sitting in one of the cane-bottom chairs (another of the locally handmade chairs, exactly like the ones in the dining hall and in our rooms) and smiled contentedly and affectionately at Mary Ann seated across from me. In the way she smiled back, I could see that Charles and the place were also working their magic on her. In spite of the hour, Charles was wide awake and alert, as if the day had just begun. I didn't know then that, in his nightlife schedule, this was "midday" for him.

I had brought down with me a careful selection of what I thought was my "best" work up 'til then: a short story about a young woman undergoing an abortion, and several "poems," dull-rhymed, metrically correct "poems" with the unsurprising lull of a metronome (I hadn't yet read or heard—as I certainly would later from Olson—Pound's famous edict, "By ear, not by the metronome"). Empty of any substantial content or experience of my own other than swiped or watered-down Keats or Shelley, they were "poems" much given to lonely moonstruck adolescent yearnings for a lost, sun-drenched land (in a mild obeisance to Rimbaud, whom I'd discovered, appropriately enough, in a Philadelphia bookstore after my father kicked me out for being a "fairy" and for refusing to go to mass) which Olson zipped through hurriedly, without comment, tossing the pages aside, dishearteningly but, I later realized, justifiably, like so much waste paper.

With the story, though, a different attention came into his eyes; behind the thick lenses they became rounder with interest, his broad brow lifted, and although he also read it hurriedly— I was impressed with the speed of his reading—I could tell by little mutterings and growls and cluckings and shakes of his great head along the way, that the short story was offering him a little more meat than the verse had.

I felt hopeful.

The story, unlike the poems, was, as I remember it, at least *partly* based on experience. In the swirl and confusion of androgynous adolescence, a young woman (in fact the friend who I would later go to the Ben Shahn lecture with at the Philadelphia Museum of Art) whom I'd been going with since my junior year in high school and who lived in the same town in New Jersey where I grew up and with whom I had had my first sexual experience at 17 had, at one point in our relationship, been frightened that she was pregnant. This later proved to be what was then termed "a hysterical pregnancy," but what I tried to capture in flashbacks in the story was the fear and uncertainty of the teenaged couple as they sought out an illegal abortionist (this was the early 1950s) and the young man's guilt and fright (I had actually been prepared, at 18, to marry her, making the decision while working a lathe machine in a Philadelphia factory—Fischer Machine Works off Race Street—where I worked to earn money to go back to Rider, but where I figured I would continue to work once we were married).

But in the story the young woman was set to have the abortion in a dingy room in a back street in some city like Philadelphia (not unlike the seven-dollar-a-week room I was living in on Spruce Street behind Independence Hall), and the story consisted mainly of what was going on in her mind and in the room while the back-alley abortionist was preparing to go about his work. No copy of the story, so far as I know, exists, but it must have captured at least a sense of that ugliness and danger with its undercurrent of anger at the sexual ignorance of young people and the proscriptions forced upon them—the sexual silence of the time and strict laws against abortion—which forced the young woman, like so many other women, to end up in such a shabby dangerous room from which she might or might not leave alive.

Charles was impressed and told me so with a very serious expression. I can't imagine the story as having been anything but melodramatic and very badly written, but perhaps he detected the earnestness beneath the clumsy attempt, a hint, anyway, of a possible ability; and perhaps, too, although I hadn't read him yet, Olson had detected a very vague whiff of Dreiser, particularly *An American Tragedy*, a writer Olson admired as "authentically American" and, along with Sherwood Anderson, "a real American queery," and whom he was later to instruct me to "saturate yourself in."

He said he thought I ought to make application to the school on the basis of the story, that I ought to come down and see what I could pick up. I was, of course, after my contact with him, elated by the prospect, but it was then I brought up my penniless situation, that I wouldn't be able to afford even a fraction of the $1,600-a-year tuition fee. Charles told me that when I got back north to formally apply to Connie, as registrar, for a work scholarship, mentioned in her earlier letter to me, which meant working a minimum of four hours a day, on the farm or in the kitchen or wherever needed, in return for tuition and board. They couldn't promise anything, but they'd see what could be done and that a decision by the committee of faculty and students probably couldn't be made 'til late August or early September.

It didn't matter. I felt extremely hopeful now. I told Charles that I would follow his advice. He seemed disappointed when Mary Ann said she'd decided to continue school at Moore Institute for the time being, but that she hoped to come down for a summer session some time in the future, especially for the photography workshops, which she did the following summer.

I thanked Charles for his time and attention and, perhaps to put the seal on my resolve or maybe to try again to convince Mary Ann to apply to the college, he walked us back up the road to Roadside. The moon was highest now in the topmost arc of the sky and everything was filled with a bright ashy light. I felt very tired but pleasantly elated and, clutching my poor manuscripts as I looked around at the mountains, now silvery under the moon, knew in my bones this was the place I wanted, and needed, to be, more than any other place on earth.

On the way back from Black Mountain, we dropped Mary Ann off at her home in Willow Grove, Pennsylvania, Marge barely speaking at all now she was so tired and irritated from being so long behind the wheel; although Roger had a license, she insisted on doing all the driving. Then we drove to my hometown of National Park on the Delaware River in Gloucester County in Southern New Jersey. Roger had invited me to spend the summer on his family's farm—his mother would be driving down to Trenton from Jamestown, New York, in a few days to pick us up—and I wanted to tell my mother this and to pick up a few things I'd left at the house, when my father had told me to leave. Since my parents didn't have a phone then, we just arrived unannounced sometime in mid-afternoon, when I knew my father would still be working his shift at the shipyard. My mother was flustered, having been caught by surprise, embarrassed as usual in front of strangers. She kept apologizing for her old housedress and the way her hair and the house looked, until I began, as in the old days, to feel embarrassed too, and, as usual, sorry for her, wishing she wouldn't be like that. I was acutely aware of the worn linoleum on the parlor floor. I felt ashamed that my two friends should see it too, and also see my overly self-effacing mother, and then felt even more ashamed to be feeling that.

When I mentioned to her that we'd just come from Black Mountain, and that, if I could get a work scholarship, I might be going to school there, she was genuinely baffled.

"But why do you want to go to school 600 miles away?" she asked, she who had gone no further than the 5th grade, she who had traveled no further than crossing the river from South Philly to this little town on the Delaware.

I'd been painfully realizing as we sat in the parlor how small the room had become since I'd left; how small all the already small rooms of the house had become. I began to feel the old sensation of being stifled and choked within those walls, where eleven of us had lived cramped together, where poverty and religion had been like a vise clamped tight around the house, where I had felt my spirit and imagination, my very life, suffocating.

After a decent interval, hurrying, taking care not to be there when my father came in from work, I got the clothes and books I had come for and apologized for our hasty visit. Over the protestations of my mother (although I knew she was relieved we were going), we said quick goodbyes and the three of us got back in the car.

I was glad we were going too.

Like a lot of such very old houses, the farmhouse had an enormous, comfortable old kitchen, really a living room-dining room-kitchen combined, with an old-fashioned wood cook stove where there was always a big pot of coffee simmering. This sprawling room at the back of the house was the central gathering place for Roger's family, which included a younger sister, Karen.

Before I got a job at the Automatic Voting Machine Company (besides furniture-making and Lucille Ball, the other product Jamestown, New York, was noted for), I helped Roger pack the lupines and peonies his father grew in a vast field behind the farmhouse and which the father always cut earlier at dawn, before he left for his full-time job at the furniture factory. Down in the ice-cold root cellar, we wrapped the flowers carefully in old newspaper, then packed them in peach baskets for the afternoon train to New York City, over 400 miles east, their final destination the wholesale flower markets in downtown Manhattan.

Roger and I slept in his enormous cherrywood 1860s bed, an ancestral relic from when the house was built before the Civil

War. We slept chaste as some brothers since our tacit under-standing one night while sharing his convertible bed back in Trenton, before leaving for Jamestown, when he had awkward-ly scrabbled at my back and I had firmly, mainly out of fear (the Church's chill hand still clapped firmly on my scrotum), told him to keep his hands to himself.

Roger worked evenings, as he had for many summers, at a drive-in that sold delicious locally-made ice cream (this was, after all, the heart of the dairy country), which meant that I spent my evenings hitchhiking to the Bemis Point cable ferry across Lake Chautauqua to the Chautauqua summer resort some twenty miles away, which Roger introduced me to soon after my arrival—"It's crawling with queers," he smirked proudly—for the concerts and the operas.

With its wide verandaed hotels with their rattan furniture, such as the Atheneum; with its quaint clapboard cottages with their gingerbread front porches—the antique local Browning Society still met in an all-brown one of these cottages; with its opera house and theater and huge refectory, its tall campanile and chapels and churches, Chautauqua, an institution devoted to cultural and intellectual lectures and endeavors with a cozy and serene dollop of American Protestant religiosity spread over all, had the air of an idealized 19th century village. While night-ly keeping an ear cocked to the Beethoven or Tchaikovsky booming out of the orchestra pit of the Amphitheater, I also kept my eyes peeled for the "queers," and spotted what I soon took to be one: a handsome blond crewcut lad who was always in a navy-blue blazer with gold buttons and who was always standing cool and aloof and always alone at the same ramp entrance to the open-air Amphitheater. I had no idea who he was or why he was there, but he was rich—and safe—fantasy material, and I developed a fierce crush on him. I would stand a few discreet ramps away, stealing glimpses his way, love-sick beyond words, too timid (read, terrified) to move nearer, without even a thought of ever having the courage to speak to him. He suggested all that the poor, blue-collar fairy son in me desperately wanted to be and was not: handsome, wealthy-appearing, Ivy League-poised—and seemingly straight.

I hadn't yet come to respect what couldn't be measured by any of that.

I never did get any closer to my secret crush at Chautauqua, but I did lose my gay virginity in a subsequent visit there, this time to one Henry L. Wood, an erect, tight-lipped, middle-aged geometry teacher at Brooklyn Polytechnic High School, in the attic room he rented every season in one of the more modestly priced hotels on the grounds. I got into his bed with my jockeys on, which amused him, and tried, in consideration, after his exquisite prolonging of sensual torture, to pull out of his mouth when I came but he, again amused at my innocence, held on like a lamprey. When it was over I knew that being with Henry was a righter thing for me than being with the young woman who'd been my high school sweetheart.

Through "Woody," I met a number of like-minded acquaintances, young and old, who also summered at Chautauqua. Their prime purpose for showing up season after season appeared to be not only for the cozy cultural and intellectual stimulation Chautauqua afforded (even to those who worked at the place as artists) but rather to keep their eyes peeled for new boys and in a time-honored tradition, bringing them out, then passing them around to one another for additional tutoring in the pleasures of eros. "Did you bring him out?" was a common question. "Remember you owe me one," was often the immediate followup.

Roger was right: Proper, sedate, high-minded Chautauqua, it turned out, was crawling with queers.

My job at Automatic Voting Machine just outside Jamestown was in the huge plating room where I and a gnarled, grumpy old man stood opposite each other over one of the rows of deep troughs, where similar pairs of other workers also were dipping, for plating, at one time, dozens of metal straps hung from an acid-proof loop of wire, dipping them into the bubbling, boiling vats of acid. The whole process only took seconds. The straps—hundreds of which were used in the voting machines—were hung to dry, while we dipped another bundle for plating, thousands and thousands of straps all day long.

In my first week there I went through two pairs of work gloves and dungarees and a stout pair of new workshoes, all eaten through by the acid.

Fortunately, the job paid well, and I could replace shoes and workclothes on a regular basis. And at Roger's father's insistence, after he'd had a few—much to Roger's fury on both counts, since he hated his father's parsimony and heavy drinking (the latter an unspoken and shared reality between us as sons)—I could pay some money for my keep at the farmhouse. I also tried to save as much as I could in case I got good news from Black Mountain College on the work scholarship by summer's end.

It was the summer that I first discovered William Carlos Williams' short stories in *Make Light of It* at the Prendergast Library in town (named for local-born artist Maurice Prendergast, Roger smugly informed me). I was amazed, exclaiming to myself as I read them, "I didn't know you were allowed to write like this!"

I also discovered, with great difficulty, Proust's *The Cities of the Plain* and Joyce's *Ulysses*, for both books were locked away with many other "forbidden" texts, including Faulkner's *Light in August*, in cabinets with heavy brown curtains covering their glass doors down in the vaults of the large basement of the library. When I requested the books, the librarian, a plump, pleasant-faced woman, looked at me carefully, took out a large ring of keys and led me downstairs, saying conversationally, without apology, that "such books are kept out of sight and have to be specially requested, if you're over 21—You are over 21?" Although I was shy a year, I assured her I was and slunk behind her, feeling like I felt when my mother caught me at age 12 with *A Tree Grows in Brooklyn* that I'd nervily borrowed from a perplexed—and Protestant—neighbor who I knew belonged to the Book-of-the-Month Club (Betty Smith's novel one of the numerous tomes in the 1940s on the Roman Catholic Church's Index—nailed to the church door—of forbidden books). I felt now doubly a criminal, as the librarian unlocked the double doors of the stout wood cabinet whose inner shelves were jammed with banned titles.

This was also 1950s America.

It was a summer of drive-in movies, such as *African Queen* (Roger's mother had leased fallow farmland across the road to the builders of a drive-in theater and so the family got in free any time they wanted); drinking Genessee beer at the Mayville Inn, in the county seat, followed by night-time skinnydipping in Lake Chautauqua with Roger and some of his livelier male and female friends, including two gay friends he'd introduced me to; trips to Chautauqua Gorge with one of those gay friends, where in my excitement to see it I nearly fell in; and to Niagara Falls with Roger's mother and father, where I slipped on the wet rocks and nearly fell in there, too; concluding that summer with a hair-raising trip back from Chautauqua one night, where I'd been mooning over my blond crewcut in the navy-blue blazer at my usual discreet and timid distance all through Beethoven's Ninth, the traditional concluding symphony of the summer season; and after, hitchhiking, was picked up by a young man who was also returning from the concert and who put the make on me the moment I got in the car. He was so aggressive and insistent, it turned me off and I turned him down flat, whereupon he was so pissed he pushed the gas to the floor, speeding up to 90, then 100 miles an hour on the back country road, trying to scare, and punish, me. He succeeded in both.

I was never so glad to feel the gravel of the farmhouse drive under my feet as that night, when he finally let me out and, rubber screaming, tore off down the dark road toward Jamestown.

Autumn comes early to western New York. By mid-August there was a distinct chill in the air, and some of the leaves had already begun to turn. It was at that time I also received a letter from Connie Olson at Black Mountain that my application for a work scholarship had been accepted and that they would be looking forward to seeing me in early September, when the fall term began.

I was overjoyed to shed my acid-stained workclothes and head south.

Because I'd saved a little money, I was able to buy a train ticket to Black Mountain. At Union Station in Washington, all trains south switched from the Pennsylvania Railroad to Southern Railways, and I had my first introduction that early September of 1952 to Southern segregation in public transport. A white conductor was standing midway between the sleek, modern, silver-gleaming coaches and sleeping cars at the front of the train and the much older, poky-looking, dusty-dark cars at the rear, shouting, "White folks' coaches ahead! Colored folks' coaches behind!"

Later, once aboard and underway, when I went to the john, I was able to get my first glimpse through the back window of the "white" coach into the first "Jim Crow" coach directly behind, which was more crowded than the one I was riding in. The lights of the much older car were dimmer, suitcases and bags were stacked in the narrow aisle so that the black passengers had to climb over them, because there were no luggage racks. Most of the windows were wide open because there was no air-conditioning or cooling in that car, as there was in the "white" coach, and most of the passengers, their faces shiny with sweat in the heat of a longer Southern summer, were fanning themselves with those paper fans funeral homes gave out in those days, experienced black travelers no doubt bringing them along with evident forethought.

At Charlottesville, Virginia, in the lights of the station through the window, I noted a young blond crewcut youth (not dissimilar in appearance from the lad at Chautauqua) in a blue seersucker suit, alight from the train with expensive-looking leather luggage, evidently also a student like me, but in his case going to classes at the University of Virginia. For a moment, reenvisioning the rundown, backwoods look of Black Mountain, there was that tug, that twinge of envy for that "respectability," that "safety," of belonging to a conventional class, of attending a conventional university. But as the train pulled off again into the night, the lights of small, sleeping towns flashing by, the powerful locomotive pulling me deeper into the dark and mysterious South, the unknown, really, where, in my deep inchoate sense of always going against the grain, of outlawry, not only as a criminalized faggot (in my head I belonged in the back cars too) but in some as yet undefined sense of being a writer, an artist, that I might meet the self who up to then had been eluding me, I knew I was still heading in the right direction.

In the bar car over a beer—no blacks present except to wipe up the puddles on the small round tables—a drunken middle-aged man with deep Dixie accent made even thicker by the number of bourbons he'd been tossing down, confided to me how important it was "ta' keep the niggahs in their place."

At Greensboro, I switched trains to the smaller, less luxurious coaches of the train heading west toward the North Carolina mountains. The Jim Crow coaches behind the whites-only coaches were much worse on this run, more grimy and antiquated. I slept fitfully till dawn in the cramped, hard seat, and then went to the dining car for breakfast. It was surprisingly pleasant, with the tables covered in bright white cloths and laid in gleaming silverware.

Although there was a lineup of black passengers crowded in the corridor leading to the dining car, mostly mothers with irritable, hungry children, I was surprised to see the tables were mainly empty, and was doubly surprised that I was shown to a seat right away at a table all to myself. Then I noticed a group of black travelers jammed together at a single table at the rear of the car, the one table reserved "for colored only." My eyebrows also lifted when I saw the prices on the menu: I suspected the prices were the only things on the train that weren't segregated.

As the waiter brought me my silver pot of coffee, the train had entered the mountains and had begun climbing, a slow corkscrew climb up and around and then slowly down the steep hills that led into the Swannanoa Valley and the town of Black Mountain. It took more than an hour in all, and I sat captivated, staring out the train window as I ate my eggs and treated myself to a second pot of coffee while watching the rising sun over the tall pines up the close slopes burnish with an even deeper fire the red clay earth of the railroad cuts gashed in the sheer sides of the mountains. And as the sun rose higher, brightening the tops of the pines, and the train descended lower into the valley, bringing me closer to my destination, my heart rose too with a hope and excitement beyond words.

When the train arrived at the town of Black Mountain, pulling up around seven in the morning in front of an old gray clapboard station with its separate waiting rooms for whites and colored, I took one of the battered taxis waiting around out front the several miles out the county highway and up the narrow winding road past the Veterans Hospital into the hills, finally reaching the Gatehouse with its Black Mountain College sign at the entry.

I got out in front of the dining hall with my suitcase (the same beatup one of my mother's; my trunk, that I'd shipped down by Railway Express, would arrive later) and, just as in June when the four of us arrived on our visit, there was not a soul around, not even the plodding, orange-colored dog in sight this time. (A dog, I subsequently learned, that had belonged to writer Paul Goodman, who had taught there that summer, and who had been asked to leave.) There was no one in the dining hall, either, or in the little fieldstone office across the way. Dead tired from the trip and emotionally drained from the high excitement of my expectations, still carrying my suitcase, I made my way up the road along Lake Eden to the Studies Building. Everything was silent there too, but on the lower level one of the study doors was ajar. When I peeped in, I was disappointed to see it was empty but pleased to spot a bare mattress on the floor, the only furniture in the cubicle. I stepped in and closed the door, then before putting down my suitcase and sinking onto the mattress, out the broad—and grimy—windows of the study I glimpsed the scene of the lake and across its still waters to the dining porch and the mist-enshrouded mountains beyond. Near the shore in the tall marsh grass, a snowy-white egret was fishing.

I stretched out on the hard, lumpy mattress and closed my eyes, inhaling the same sour, mildewy odor of the beds and room of Roadside as on our visit in June, the smell, along with oil paints and turps, that I would always associate with Black Mountain.

I had arrived at last, in the place where I might find the secret, and direction, of my life, and fell instantly asleep for an hour or so.

Later that morning, Hazel Frieda Larsen greeted me in her wheelchair in her office (she'd caught polio as a child) in the fieldstone building across from the dining hall. A plump woman, with a round genial face and full, black hair, perhaps in her late 20s or early 30s, she was not only the secretary-treasurer but also taught photography in the workshop and dark rooms under South Lodge, which made easy access for her chair. She explained the conditions of my work scholarship, that I'd be working four hours a day, five days a week at the farm, in return for which I'd receive tuition and board. I was very disappointed to learn that Olson might not be teaching until later that fall—he was on a leave of absence up in Washington, D.C., "doing research," she explained. What other courses would be offered for the writing students weren't quite settled yet, but the important thing was for me to get settled. She assigned me to share a room in South Lodge with a painting student from Detroit, Jorge Fick, who'd already been at the college for a year or two.

South Lodge, with the Olson's apartment at the far end, had an enormous high-peaked lobby with a big fieldstone fireplace, its unpainted pine walls darkened with age and smoke. The student rooms were down corridors either side of the lobby, and the room Hazel directed me to was to the left facing the broad front porch.

After I'd unpacked and made up the bed, beginning to feel at least a little easier, the door banged open and in came Jorge, a very pale oval face with jet-black crewcut and even darker eyes, just arrived from Detroit. I smiled and got up to greet him, and the first words out of his mouth were, "What the hell are you doing here?"

I explained that Hazel had assigned us as roommates, and he, storming out, shouting, "That goddamned woman! She promised me she wouldn't put anybody in my room!" clumped heavily down the hall in his boots. Through the window I saw him march across the gravel drive and into the office cottage, only to emerge a few moments later, with the same set, furious expression on his round face (a face, given its Detroit origins, Charles, who also had his run-ins with Jorge, once compared, in a moment of pique, to a "hubcap").

When he entered the room, he muttered, "You're movin' out," and when I looked at him puzzled, all he said was, "Go see that damned Hazel."

She was very apologetic, wheeling up to me with an expression of real concern in her face (an expression I was to see often, mingled with what were probably remnants of her chronic pain of earlier years). "I've arranged to put you upstairs in the men's dorm," she said, "the bed nearest the door."

The dorm upstairs off the lobby was, with its severely sloping eaves, a huge space with perhaps eight or so beds and the same dark unpainted pineboard walls as the lobby. Several of the students were already there when I climbed the stairs; one, a bearded youth with long black hair (most unusual for the time, except at Black Mountain), from New York City who'd been at the college for several years, with extraordinarily sensitive face and eyes and gentle voice, introduced himself as Eric Weinberger (although it could just as well have been "Jesus"); another, a slight, bespectacled, auburn-haired youth, a writer-painter, who spoke impeccable French, Terence Burns, from Providence, Rhode Island, who'd also be working on the farm on a work scholarship; and a third, a somewhat older man, in his late 20s, in sharply pressed army khakis and snow-white t-shirt who was all robust health and orderliness—you could have bounced a dime off the blanket of his bed, it was drawn that square and tight—and who, as he explained, just recently discharged from the army after a stint in Korea, was there as a student on the GI Bill.

I unpacked my suitcase for the second time that day, putting away everything in the little dresser at the foot of the bed, which was nothing more than a mattress on a box spring. I didn't care much for the lack of privacy or sharing the large bath with its open shower stalls and toilets, where the place really showed its origins as a summer camp; but after my run-in downstairs with Jorge, I counted myself lucky to be upstairs in the attic dorm. (Later, I counted myself doubly lucky, when I discovered that a peculiar heavy odor came from the room next door to Jorge's, despite a shared bath intervening, where two long-time students, who rarely made an appearance, roomed: John Grady, a red-haired, pipe-smoking bookaholic who read night and day sprawled on his lumpy, dirty bed where he lived like a mole in a tunnel of books from floor to ceiling, most of which an irate Nell Rice, the college librarian, claimed were never returned to the library; and Harvey Harmon, a genial, slender, droopingly mustachioed lad, who loved to talk and was, in his soft-spoken way, a most pleasant conversationalist; but because, like Grady, he rarely stirred from his room, you had to go to him, finding space to perch amidst the piles of books and litter—neither John nor Harvey were known for good housekeeping, or the frequency of bathing, hence, the pronounced odor in that area of the lodge. Because they slept most of the day and, just like moles, made most of their rare appearances at night, foraging for food in the kitchen, they had the palest skins of anyone on campus. No one seemed quite certain what the two were studying at Black Mountain, but both were liked and so no one seemed to care.)

Before all the faculty and students had arrived and classes begun, I was broken in on my job as a work scholarship student, along with a few others. My first job on the farm was shocking corn, which meant cutting with a knife the withered stalks in the vast field of already-harvested corn and tying them in bundles so they could later be fed into the ensilage chopping machine and blown up into the silo for storage, winter fodder for the cattle. The farm was quite a spread and pretty much self-contained, with a farmhouse for farmer Doyle Jones, a lean, handsome man with the bluest eyes, and his nervous but amiable and attractive wife, Claire, a full-blooded North Carolina Cherokee, and their fourteen-year-old son, Ben. There were also a dairy barn and assorted outbuildings.

Don Jones, no relation to Doyle, a tall stripling painting student from Illinois, who'd been working on the farm for as long as he'd been a student at the college, showed us newcomers, particularly Terence Burns and me, the ropes.

It was monotonous, back-breaking work, bending over row after row, slicing, then gathering the bundles of stalks and tying them with twine, the task somewhat lightened by incessant talk from several of the other students, especially Terence who, having lived in Canada for a spell, would recite poetry in French along the way, like Villon's "*Où sont les neiges d'antan*," or sing French songs, such as "*Auprès de ma blonde*," in between speaking French to one of Flola Shepard's language students, a handsome, sweet-natured youth, with thick black hair and ruddy cheeks, huskily built for farm work, and also named Don.

Eric Weinberger worked a little apart, Christ-like and silent, picking his way among the rows, his bearded face paler than milk, as skinny as I, and just as addicted to tobacco, and occasionally uttering some extraordinary perception in his soft, carefully measured speech.

There was also a student from Vermont, a philosophy "major," with a thatch of greasy, stringy blond hair, wisps of straggly blond hairs on his severely acned cheeks in a vain attempt to grow a beard, black-rimmed glasses that magnified his ice-blue eyeballs, buck teeth, very white, that showed a lot because he grinned a lot; awkward, flailing in his movements, always wore heavy boots and soiled dungarees, who, in an annoyingly supercilious tone, like he was mocking us, was always coyly trying to engage us in philosophical discussions, mainly, I detected, as a "test" of our braininess, and who was always making teasingly coy innuendoes to me about homosexuality, and who I later spied occasionally slipping out of composer-in-residence Lou Harrison's apartment in the rear of the Studies Building early of a morning to go milk the cows. I tried to like him but couldn't. Nobody but Lou liked him.

We were quite a ragtag lot in our ragtag clothes as we bent down, slicing row after row of dead corn till dusk.

But I had a hard time of it, since I was a very skinny 6' 2", weighing in at less than 125 pounds. I exhausted easily, and certainly my heavy smoking didn't help, but I was determined to do my share and keep up with the others. Still, despite the strenuous work, there was, among the furrows, the occasional sudden surprise of extraordinary slithering animal life, such as one afternoon when I spotted a small brilliantly orange salamander with tiny bright blue polka dots, the first of many odd species I'd see in that primeval North Carolina landscape.

The hardest, though, were the milk runs between the farm and the kitchen in the battered navy-blue World War 2 surplus Jeep truck. Helping lift the incredibly heavy cans on and off the truck was a strain.

After a week or so, I began to wonder if I'd be able to last it out.

But the hard physical labor brought a delicious sense of ease and quiet within me, not to mention an enormous increase in appetite. After our work was done, and in the dusk, for the days were already growing shorter, our little band of farm workers trailed single file along the path from the farm through the woods, where we crossed over the cold, rushing mountain stream by Meadows Inn and hiked tired and hungry down the dirt road past the lake to the kitchen and our late supper—kept warm for us on the back of the enormous oil-fired stove by cooks Malrey and Cornelia since, in this busy season at the farm getting ready for winter, we often got back after dark and after the others had eaten. The air was sharp with autumn, the trees on the Seven Sister Mountains beyond the lake—the two most curvaceous hills just across the county road nicknamed "Mae

West" for obvious reasons—stood up in a blinding blaze of color, the intensity of which I'd never seen before. But it was not too chilly for us to have our suppers on the dining porch, laughing and talking easily and quietly among ourselves, Don Jones, with his long legs propped on another cane-bottom chair, cracking jokes in his flat mid-western voice with Terence, and each occasionally interjecting talk about painting, all of us easy and quiet together, drinking Cornelia's hot pan-boiled coffee in the deepening twilight as we peered through the screening of the dining porch out over the lake, myself, despite the laborious work, feeling that inner ease and quiet, realizing more and more I was where I was meant to be.

Not long after those suppers, after a shower, I would drop on my bed in the attic of South Lodge and fall instantly asleep.

One of the greatest pleasures for me that fall was to get up early for breakfast—most everyone else slept through it—and, since the weather was still mild, eat my eggs and grits and drink my mug of Cornelia's strong black coffee out on the screened-in dining porch, a daily ritual. After eating, I'd lean back in the cane-bottom chair and light up my first Home Run of the day, the initial drag of smoke a searing furnace blast in my lungs, the tobacco was that strong. My eyes would travel over the lake, with its early morning mists rising, then over the nearby hills and finally wander far off into the distance to perennially snow-capped Mount Mitchell. That distant view and that first morning hit of nicotine momentarily quieted my anxieties about everything. I liked it, too, because at that early hour there was rarely anybody around except me and the cooks; it was like having the place to myself, a quiet time to sort things out before the day began.

Speaking of tobacco, the cigarettes Carroll Williams stocked in the Black Mountain College store off the dining hall, and pushed, besides Home Runs were:

Picayunes

Gauloises (that Dan Rice and Cynthia Homire smoked, and a few others with heartier lungs)

Sobranie Black & Golds: With their gold paper tips and dark Egyptian tobacco rolled in black cigarette paper, Sobranies were piss-elegant coffin nails that, expensive compared to the other home-grown brands in tobacco tax-free North Carolina, were at least affordable. When on rare occasions I had a few extra coins, I would buy a box, a smart black and gold design, of course, to indulge myself in pretentious elegance, and was about the only one who did. I continued smoking Sobranies on occasion later in Greenwich Village, where a specialty tobacco shop on 6th Avenue sold them, along with Home Runs and Picayunes, just like down home in Buncombe County (from which we get our word "bunkum," thanks to Felix Walker, an old North Carolina mountaineer and congressional representative from 1819-1821, whose district included the County of Buncombe, a name he would drop in the House at every and any opportunity, and who "declared . . . he was bound to talk '*for Buncombe*' " during a debate on the Missouri Question).

Since in that fall of 1952, with a total enrollment of 35 students, it wasn't clear when or if Charles would return from his leave of absence and when or if his writing class would begin, I signed up for other classes: a theater workshop with Wes Huss that met evenings in the dining hall after supper; a class in metaphysical poetry with Hilda Morley, composer Stefan Wolpe's wife, which met in the afternoons in the library; a course in modern physics given mornings by Natasha Goldowski in the lobby of her and her husband (and former student) Eric Renner's apartment in Meadows Inn; and from Natasha's mother, Madame Goldowski, a tutorial in French, mornings in the back sitting room of her apartment in Streamside, Madame, as she was called by everyone, who was in her 80s and had a deceptively frail look.

Wes Huss was tall and lean, with a shock of thinning blond hair; his receding hairline, coupled with his strong, prominent features, made him look all face, the actor's face. He had learned his craft as actor and director at Hedgerow Theater outside Philadelphia, appropriately enough, since he was also a soft-spoken Quaker, but one with, on occasion, a very short fuse. (More on that later.)

With his carefully modulated voice and elegant, rather aristo-cratic bearing, he once said that he'd learned early on that if he ever had to see a doctor, he dressed as shabbily as he could, because if he went in suit and tie, given his bearing, such people invariably mistook him for a man of old money and soaked him accordingly.

With a fine, unnerving intellect, his approach to theater was analytical and experimental—an actor was supposed to understand the play and to understand his or her role in conjunction with the other parts—intelligence and feeling working seam-lessly hand in hand. (He once dismissed our acting class because we hadn't yet thought through what we were doing.)

The emphasis was on mind, but body was included, of course, in the way it moved, in the way thought, feeling, con-sciously or unconsciously, moved it across stage space.

"Stage space" could be anywhere, anything. In Wes' theater class it was the dining hall—all of it.

In the class, we'd do acting exercises and improvisations—"Be a tree, be a reed," he would command us as we stood around the large dining hall area where the class met after sup-per. "Bend! Bend! Be the wind," and we would fling ourselves around the room like Whitmanic atoms of air.

Fee Dawson, a painting and writing student who arrived from Kirkwood, Missouri, in 1949 and who was also in the class, was obstinate, though. (Including in his handwriting—

perhaps, as I later discovered, imitating Olson's own indecipherable hand? Fee mailed out letters that were often returned by the Black Mountain Post Office because the names and addresses were illegible.) He'd fold his arms across the chest of his faded levi jacket and give Wes arguments about why he refused to be a reed, to bend. (Wes later cast him in Brecht's *Mother Courage and Her Children*, and Fee had fierce arguments about how to do that, too—or how not to do it; loudly outspoken, he was always throwing up obstacles.) I was always resistant in my head—always having to go against the grain, too; but, unlike Fee, outwardly went along, afraid to displease, yet also disguising (protecting?) an inner steel resolve. I threw myself into the improvisations, doing my best. Fee didn't give a damn about that—he resisted outwardly as well as inwardly and didn't care at all who liked it. You could see the strain it made in Wes' face; the way Fee threw up obstacles at every turn put Wes' pacifist Quaker philosophy to the test, but Fee usually won out, or occasionally, after getting everything and everybody in a turmoil, would grudgingly go along. It was, exasperating as it could be, just the way he was as a writer, a painter—an artist, really—testing all sides of it before committing himself, not going along just to go along, sometimes of course tipping it over into just plain stubbornness, even to his own disadvantage. But such chafing—as with Olson, as with Wolpe, M. C. Richards, as with Creeley, later, as with most everybody there, what probably drew us to Black Mountain in the first place, knowingly or unknowingly, was shaping, whittling away excess—or more often than not, intrusions—that were no part of Fee (or us), and that he wanted no part of. It was a way he had of *making* himself, with no compromise. In all, it had a kind of ornery purity about it.

It was the same as what Olson once later said about the fierce and peculiar self-protectiveness and resistance of Terence Burns: "He's protecting his *soul!*"

Later that winter Wes cast me—hoping life would imitate art?—in the role of the Bridegroom in Lorca's *Blood Wedding*, a far cry from my one only previous role in my high school senior play: Oogie Pringle in *A Date with Judy* (I even got to sing).

I felt I was coming along.

Hilda Morley's class in metaphysical poetry met for three hours in the afternoon in the open reading area at the rear of the barracks-like library, the marsh grass of the lake pressing up tall against its 6-over-6 windows. Up front, apple-cheeked librarian Nell Rice, wife of the college's late founder, John Rice, her silvery hair up in a stereotypical librarian's bun, padded about among the shelves in her tennis sneakers. Despite her age, given her sturdy, upright, gym-teacher stride, she had the most muscular calves on campus.

Hilda, who was brought up in England and as a girl spent time in Jerusalem where, to Olson's pleased amazement, just at the thought of someone that age reading such a forbidden text, she spent afternoons reading Joyce's *Ulysses* lying in the grass in the Jerusalem hills, was knowledgeable and congenial, with a droll, offbeat sense of humor, a compulsive smiler and talker. Beneath her Dutch-girl bobbed hair, she had merry blue eyes and pleasant broad features, and from her generous mouth came a ready wit that saw wry humor—and absurdity—in everything. She was often playfully girlish, even, with her ever-present smile, flirtatious, and since she was some years younger than her composer husband, Stefan Wolpe, a German with heavily seamed basset face and dour, heavily browed eyes, when they were together (which was most of the time, including working away in their rooms up in Black Dwarf) she more often appeared like his little girl of a daughter than his wife.

She also wrote poetry, precise and subtle, which she rarely showed, perhaps sensing that Olson's commanding voice had already staked out that particular claim at Black Mountain.

There were maybe four or five of us in the class, including Terence Burns, and a tall, heavyset young woman with a plump, babyish face from New Jersey, Virginia, who wore her hair in an upsweep à la Betty Grable, and had a prescription for dexidrene, supposedly to help her lose weight and help keep her awake (she narcoleptically nodded off a lot anytime, anywhere). Such pep pills were copiously prescribed in those days, especially for women, and Virginia's stash of amphetamines became the most popular thing about her, since she didn't mind sharing her hoard, for a price. I later occasionally bought a number of those little orange pills from her at 50¢ a pop to pep me up in my subsequent kitchen work and to add to my moonshine highs at the Saturday night parties in the dining hall.

She was physically slow and mainly quiet, and when she did speak lisped in a baby voice. She spent a lot of her time in her room in North Lodge, where the single female students were quartered, washing her hair and setting it in big rollers, making up (lots of jars and bottles of femme lotions, scents, and creams were in her bath), and despite the dexies, napping. No one was ever certain why she was at Black Mountain, or how she ended up there, only that she was one of the few tuition-paying students (hence, no questions asked?) whose pleasant, well-dressed parents visited occasionally from New Jersey and who seemed content to have her stay there for the time being.

Besides Hilda Morley's class, Virginia also took a pottery class from Karen Karnes and David Weinrib in the newly-built pot shop bordering the broad fields of the farm. Cynthia Homire, who was in the same class, over Ballantine ales one night at Ma Peak's Tavern down the road, with wicked, sly humor, drew for us the shapes on the back of a beer coaster that Virginia had designed for several of her pots, all of which were decidedly phallic.

I giggled along with the others but, having been hungrily

chaste since I arrived at Black Mountain, underneath I empathized with her, an empathy that helped get me into a sticky situation subsequently, since Virginia later developed a massive crush on me.

I myself took a brief fling at potting that fall, after being deeply impressed in October with the ten-day Pottery Seminar Karnes and Weinrib hosted up at the Ceramics Studio, and which brought world-renowned potters Shoji Hamada and Soetsu Yanagi from Japan, Bernard Leach from England, and Marguerite Wildenhain from California via the Bauhaus. After the Seminar, I pinched free-form bits of clay under the watchful eyes of Karen and David, who, after a few sessions, I could see didn't hold much hope for me. It was soon mutually agreed that perhaps my abilities lay more with words than with clay—a big perhaps it seemed to me at that time.

At three hours, Hilda's poetry class was too long and the students too unresponsive. She would read metaphysical poems from a thick, broken-back text whose top spine was a rat's nest of tiny bits of paper markers, hundreds of them, which were as much a metaphor for her mind, that also seemed to be stuffed with bits and pieces of poetical odds and ends all jammed together; a mind that veered all over the place at breakneck speed, so that her tongue could hardly keep up with it, nor we with her tongue. She would talk compulsively and with breathless quickness about the poems she'd just read and try to engage our interest, ask questions that she often didn't wait to hear answers to. Maybe the poems of John Donne et al. were too subtle, except perhaps for Terence Burns—I myself, occasionally hearing the subtleties, was still listening for other voices—and Hilda's manner was too hurried and unfocused.

Virginia would nod off in the first half hour.

For me, hanging around the 17th century was like killing time until Olson's leave of absence was over and he chose to start teaching again.

After one particularly dismal session, Hilda, continually distressed about the lack of class response, asked me confidentially if I had any suggestions as to how to perk up interest. Then, before I could respond, she rattled on rapidly, slipping back no doubt to her English roots, her face creased in its usual rapt smile, "*Tea*! Yes! I'll serve *tea*! That should liven things up!"

Teas were big at Black Mountain; for some, the answer to just about anything.

So she brought a hot plate from Black Dwarf next time, and I brought tea bags and lemon slices and cups up from the kitchen.

Serving tea was a pleasant enough break in the midst of the three-hour-long class, but it didn't help.

Hilda taught one course after that, on Henry James' novellas (I was in that one too), and except for posing nude in Esteban Vicente's drawing class in the 1953 Summer Institute of the Arts, that was the end of her classroom appearances.

Virginia once snapped my photo outside the kitchen back door one day after lunch. She took a number of photos at Black Mountain, and when she'd taken the picture, I went burbling on about something or other, as I usually did, full of beans and nervous energy. Virginia, visibly unimpressed as she calmly peered through her baby-blue rimmed glasses winding her film forward, said, in her slow, baby-talk voice, "You exaggerate everything."

That shut me up. It offended me at first but then when I thought about it later in my study, it made sense. She was right, but that's what being a writer is all about (it was also what being a faggot was all about in those days, covering my tracks). That was my job, to exaggerate—Good Liars Make Good Writers, was one of those paradoxes, as in a later thought I came to, "The lie of the imagination creates the truth of reality." Although I had always known how to lie verbally, or "exaggerate," as Virginia put it, I had yet to learn how to put that lifelong practice into my writing.

It was easy to think we knew all there was to know about Virginia, but that remark made me see she was doing more than just curling her hair and napping.

Natasha Goldowski must have been a woman in her 40s when she married Eric Renner, who had been a student of hers at Black Mountain and who was much younger than herself, a solidly built, square-featured, pale-skinned youth with wavy auburn hair and goatee, a quiet, genial humor, with an equally friendly manner, quietly intelligent. He wasn't that much older than myself (I was 20 in 1952).

As a couple, Eric and Natasha were an extreme contrast in many ways. Eric, her boy-son. Physically, she was a strong, hearty figure of a woman with strong shoulders and arms. In summer, wearing nothing but a t-shirt and a pair of shorts, you could see the sturdiness of her legs, the flesh of her tanned thighs pebbled, the skin around her knees purple with varicose veins, legs tending toward fat, as was her whole corpulent body; but the strength still there, like the inherited physique of workers in fields, the muscular substance of a dynamic physical vigor still very much visible. Seeing the solid-fleshed woman before me, it was difficult to see her as the slender ballet dancer and acrobat she said she had been as a young woman in Paris, after she and her mother had fled Russia.

Wonderful hair, glossily raven, crinkly at the roots, the long, bushy length of it streaked with gray, brushed back flat over her forehead and falling in a fan of full-bodied waves far down her back.

A strong, blunt-featured face, handsomely coarse, olive-dark in winter and tanned the color of earth in summer. Black-brown eyes filled with a light of intelligence, humor. A smile that creased her mouth in folds, runnels of flesh either side the mouth, crinkles of crow's feet at the corners of eyes which were themselves as iridescent as crow's wings. That leathery-skinned face that when it smiled—and it smiled often—was like sunlight spreading across a weather-seamed field. It made you feel terrific, and was the same feeling I had when Olson smiled my way, making me feel suddenly, inexplicably, warmed and grateful. In her own way, she was the European version of Olson's American charm.

Since, as Connie told us during our visit in June, Natasha refused to use the, to her, dangerous new science building built by student design and labor high up on one of the slopes overlooking Lake Eden, she taught her physics classes in the lobby of Meadows Inn where she lived with her handsome young American husband. As we half dozen or so students reclined on throw-covered pallets in front of a huge roaring fireplace, Natasha lectured with wit and brilliance about modern physics and other related matters, and after class often served tiny glasses of Grand Marnier, if the autumnal morning was crisp, and it usually was. She was so vivaciously interesting, so intensely passionate, her two-hour classes were over before we knew it.

Her mother, Madame, was something else. She had silvery hair piled up in a tiny loose bun, was very short and usually wore a black close-fitting cap with a curled peak and a black knit shawl. She was a White Russian and along with her family, including daughter Natasha, had been booted out of the country in the Communist takeover in 1917, after her capitalist husband's two chemical factories were confiscated by the new Bolshevik government. The family escaped to France, where daughter Natasha, in between dancing ballet and being an acrobat, took a doctorate at the Sorbonne, and lived there till the invasion by the Nazis in 1940, when, the father now dead, Madame and young Natasha made their way on foot through the *Luftwaffe* bombings and strafings of the French countryside, heading for the southern port cities to try to get a boat to

Morocco. They walked most of the way across France, Madame, according to Natasha, getting through the almost daily strafings and bombings by carrying close to her stomach a fancy hatbox containing her best hat, carefully preserved from better and richer Russian days, shielding it in her folded arms, her focus on the care and worry in protecting the precious hatbox distracting her from the horrors going on around them. They stayed in Morocco through the early war years, then emigrated to the United States in 1942, where Natasha worked on the Manhattan Project at the University of Chicago and the Palmer Physical Laboratory in Princeton, before coming to Black Mountain in 1947 as instructor in physics and chemistry.

Madame kept about a half dozen ravenous stray dogs in her apartment at the back end of Streamside, vicious, snarling brutes with razor-sharp ribcages, mongrels that had wandered onto the campus and been taken in by her. When I would knock at her door precisely at 10 a.m.—Madame insisted that I be punctual—the beasts would set up such a clamor of shrill barking to give even the boldest thief pause; then they would all hit the door at one time, jumping and snarling to get at whoever was on the other side, which meant me, since I was the only student Madame had. Presently, I would detect amid the screeching howls Madame's soft geriatric voice murmuring, "*Allez, allez*," and, even though she knew perfectly well it was me, the door would open the merest crack, then, with a look of feigned surprise, she'd open it further and there she stood, all four feet of her. "*Silence!*" she'd sternly order the dogs, pointing her bony finger to a corner of the room where they'd all slink off, casting murderous glances at me over their scrawny shoulders, resentful not to have had the chance to leap at my throat.

"*La Leçon*" was an hour, the first half of which consisted of Madame, over cups of tea, pumping me for campus gossip, particularly who was who and, more particularly, who was sleeping with whom. During this time she was bright-eyed and alert, asking her questions *en anglais* and demanding I reply in kind, "*s'il vous plaît*," since my French was still so rudimentary she didn't want to miss a morsel of any of the news, such as the plumply voluptuous blond student from New Jersey who, it was hotly rumored, within the first week of her arrival, slept with, in her study, most of the available heterosexual males, married and unmarried, on campus.

Madame would nod and wink, smiling slyly at such delicious revelations—besides avant-garde art, gossip, I quickly discovered, was the other main staple at isolated Black Mountain—and egg me on with the most shameless flattery, calling me "*Michel l'ange*," and asking the most artfully "innocent" questions.

Despite her diminutive size and great age, she could be quite commanding—the only one at the college not intimidated by her was her daughter—and sometimes when there was nothing juicy to report, rationalizing it as practicing my writer's imagination (again, Good Liars Make Good Writers, etc.), I would invent little salacious tidbits to appease—and amuse—her. You could see that she thoroughly enjoyed the gossip, but if it was of a too bawdy nature, once she'd heard enough, she would cluck her tongue and wag her peaked cap in a most morally disapproving but charmingly hypocritical way.

Once she'd pumped me for all the news she could get, real and imagined, we had the second half of "*La Leçon*" (she'd given up practice conversation with me in French after I spent most of the second half of one session trying to figure out what Madame, speaking in an English that was as faulty as my French, meant by "noots" served at Natasha's Christmas dinner; in my incomprehension, Madame got quite exercised, her voice growing shriller and shriller as she began to scream "*Noots! Noots!*" over and over, as if sheer volume would overcome my obtuseness, until it finally dawned on me she was talking about "nuts"). From then on the last half hour consisted of me reading aloud my translations from the ancient textbook Madame had assigned me, which included excerpts from Jules Vernes' 1873 *Le Tour du monde en quatre-vingt jours*, a textbook so old she had probably brought it with her in that hatbox when she escaped White Russia, so that I was learning an antique form of very formal 19th century French.

As I read, Madame would at first nod approvingly, except to respond annoyedly to my mispronouncing the French *et* like the Latin *et*, a hangover from my altar boy days, then she would nod off completely, along with the beasts slumped in the corner, and would not awaken until I had finished, when she'd murmur drowsily, "*Très bien, très bien.*"

And that was the way my tutorial went with Madame Goldowski several mornings a week.

I never learned much French, of course. When I tried to speak to Terence Burns or to language teacher Flola Shepard's students (precise Flola with whom I later took a much more useful French class up in the science building), particularly to Don, the handsome, husky student of hers who worked on the farm; or sat at Flola's French Table in the dining hall, I discovered to my dismay that no one could comprehend a word I said because I was speaking not only an antiquated version of the language but also French with a Russian accent, and a White Russian accent at that!

I decided Madame called me "*Michel l'ange*" because only someone with the patience of an angel would've studied with her.

The first poem I read of Charles', "A Po-sy, A Po-sy," was in Cid Corman's No. 2 *Origin* of Summer 1951, which I bought in the college store off the dining hall from printer-artist Carroll Williams, a slim, handsome, mustachioed youth who ran the store and who lived with his wife, Canadian painter Dorothea

Rockburne, and their new baby, in a second floor apartment in North Lodge. The poem baffled me totally. "aw, piss, and sing, be / robert burns . . ." I read it several times and still didn't get it. It was like reading something in a new language (and so it was). Although I could appreciate its reckless energy, I began to wonder if my intuition had led me astray in thinking this was the man for me. As I confessed to him a few years later in a September 30, 1956 letter just before I hitchhiked out to San Francisco from Philly:

> Dear Charles,
> Four years ago or so when I first read your work
> (mostly in Origin) I thought you were straining
> after an impossible chaos - that it was whimsical,
> meaningless, sensationally tricky.
>
> But what was necessary was a correction of my ear.
> I didn't see the form, I didn't hear the limpidity of
> your thought and feeling, your rhythm - what you
> were always after me for, limpidity, telling me that
> night over the dishrack to go to Williams, as I did,
> and found, and as I find now the same in you, in all
> I've read of you. I read you and I read you with
> pleasure. I now fully understand the meaning of
> limpidity . . . .

That fall of 1952, several of the older writing students, such as Joel Oppenheimer, Fee Dawson, Jorge Fick and Duck Daley (the last, tough good looks and tough-talking Boston-Irish, one of Olson's "fair-haired boys" I was told), seemed to be only hanging around, waiting to see when, or if, Olson returned. In order to hurry things along, a few students, including Mary Fiore and her painting teacher husband, Joe, collected among themselves a hundred dollars (which in those days went a *long* way at the college) as supplementary pay at money-pre Black Mountain to try to lure Olson back.

In the meantime, my days were filled with going to classes, working on the farm, and writing and reading in my study in the lower level of the Studies Building, a cubicle with the entire wall by the door of frosted glass. In imitation of some of the paintings I saw hanging about the place, I painted each of the other three walls a stark white, black, and yellow, with cheap paint I bought from Carroll in the store. Working inside an abstract painting, à la Albers and Kline, was hard on the astigmatism, I discovered.

But I felt like I was only marking time till Charles returned. I was bitterly disappointed that the man, despite his incomprehensible poetry, whose overwhelming magnetism had pulled me to the college in the first place, continued to be absent, was still holed up with his family in wealthy patron and Black Sun Press publisher Caresse Crosby's apartment in Washington, D.C.

How was I ever going to learn to write without the man, who, despite "A Po-sy, A Po-sy," I still deeply sensed could show me the way?

Meanwhile, concerned that students weren't getting to know each other and were holing up in their rooms and studies, especially the newcomers, Mary Fitton Fiore, writer from Hamilton, Ohio, an ex-WAC, or U. S. Women's Army Corps, which she joined while she was still back in Hamilton in World War 2; challenging, blond, blue-eyed Mary, who very much resembled, from a reproduction of a painting she once showed me, her Elizabethan ancestor Mary Fitton, gave lovely late afternoon teas in the lobby of North Lodge, with platters of butter cookies she baked herself in the college kitchen. She also suggested I organize a Sunday night reading in the lobby of North Lodge, which I was shy about doing, being so new to the place. But with Mary's encouragement I did it, asking Joel

Oppenheimer to read William Carlos Williams poems; painter and jazz trumpeter (he'd played with Stan Kenton in the 1940s) Dan Rice (no relation to John or Nell) to read an essay of his on architecture; and finally a rather intense, dogmatic student named Ed Stresino who shared our attic domicile in South Lodge and who was an Ezra Pound fanatic (who developed an equally fanatic passion for David Weinrib's newly-arrived and good-naturedly nubile younger sister, Betsy), to read a few of Pound's *Cantos*, which he did in grim, stentorian voice. (On Ed's way to Black Mountain, he'd stopped off in Washington to visit Pound at St. Elizabeth's Hospital where Pound was still incarcerated for his "treasonable" broadcasts in Mussolini's Italy during World War 2; student Jonathan Williams who also visited Pound at that time found the poet "surrounded by spooky fascist-type Jesuit priests.")

It all helped, but there was that sense of something missing, especially for those students who'd studied with Olson in the past, and for those like me who were eagerly waiting his return.

Also during that time, Mary and Joe would pack as many of us as they could into their Jeep stationwagon and drive us all into Asheville to the Pack Library for the library's afternoon program of showings of classic films, such as Marlene Dietrich in *The Blue Angel* and Buster Keaton's *The General*, both of which I saw for the first time there and both of which knocked my socks off.

Occasionally on other nights, they'd invite two or three of us along in the Jeep to see a movie in Asheville. (Another campus vehicle available for trips the rare times he chose to leave his den was John Grady's 1938 wood-paneled Ford station wagon, that was less popular in winter because it had no heater, few windows and a habit of breaking down at the most unlikely times and places.)

On one of those nights returning late from a movie in Asheville, we spotted a tall, lank mountain man in overalls and wash-worn plaid shirt and carrying a baby in his arms, standing on the road several miles from Black Mountain.

Joe stopped and offered him a lift, and he squeezed in up front with the child next to Mary. "Much obliged," were the only words he spoke. He sat tight-lipped and stiff-faced clutching the child and got out when we came to the cut-off road up the mountain to the college.

"Trouble at home," was all Mary murmured, troubled herself by the man and the child out so late on the lonely roads.

The strenuous farm work continued to be difficult for me, and it was finally a foolish accident that got me kicked off the job.

In times of harvest or getting ready for winter, there was a long tradition among the farm folk in the valley of helping each other, and so when it came time to chop up the several tons of corn shocks we'd amassed over the past few weeks for ensilage, four or five of the farmers whose land bordered our own came to help. They were mostly red-cheeked, quiet talking men with floppy, sweat-stained hats, who were marvelous gabbers, since talk, in the oral tradition handed down from forebears, was the main form of entertainment and news, at work and at home. Few, if any, had phones (even at the college the only phone on campus was the pay phone in the Studies Building lobby) or radios or even certainly TV sets. (Newly-appointed farm manager Doyle Jones' television at the college farm house, with its telephone pole-high aerial on the roof to pull in weak signals over the mountains, was a rarity in the valley). They turned everything, like most Southerners, into a story and a figure of speech, usually slyly humorous and earthily crude. These hill-folk, from the farms scattered over the valley, some of whom had been there for generations, were no exception.

Besides the work-scholarship students assigned to the farm, there were other students there as well, female as well as male ("men's work" was also women's work, and vice versa, at Black Mountain), since each student, as I've mentioned, had to do a few hours of work each week around the college on the farm or in the kitchen or on maintenance. The job was to have several students pull the tied bundles of corn shocks from the back of the trailer wagon hooked onto the farm tractor and feed them onto a metal conveyor belt where, either side of it, a half dozen of the rest of us stood with penknives ready to cut the twine as the bundles rapidly moved by on the feeder belt. They were fed into a chopper operated by farmer Doyle and then blown up into the top of the open slot cut in the side of the concrete silo, for winter storage. Ben, Doyle's fourteen-year-old son, a very husky lad who had a speech impediment and was somewhat slow of thought, was inside the silo with another student, Fee Dawson, I believe, jumping up and down, packing down the ensilage as it was blown through a thick hose high up over the edge of the open-topped silo, the two rising higher and higher as the level of the ensilage rose inside, each taking turns tucking boards in the slot as they ascended, to keep the ensilage from leaking out.

Everything was going well, all our hands busy, including the lazy, honey-measured tongues of the farmers, as they exchanged yarns and gossip and, merrily amused, made sly but courteous observations about the young "city slickers," meaning me and the other new students, getting a taste of farm work—"*real* work"—for the first time in our lives. (Probably they'd never tried to write a short story, or worked in a shipyard, as I had.)

Doyle, like my father, an energetic, highstrung man, was eager to get as much ensilage stored away before dark, so at one point, noting the sun lowering toward the mountains, he speeded up the conveyor belt. With that, I, who'd been doing okay till then, slicing my bundles as they sped past, had a harder time keeping up with the cutting, and as I was slashing away as quickly as I could, suddenly dropped my penknife into the metal innards of the belt, where it promptly disappeared.

The clattering belt came to a sudden screeching halt. Doyle, a perpetual cigarette butt hanging from his lips, leapt down from the ensilage blowing machine, his face red, the muscles in his neck straining, as he hollered, "What happened? What happened?"

Everybody looked baffled and shrugged his or her shoulders, except me, which of course drew everyone's attention.

"Did somebody drop their knife?" shouted Doyle. "Huh, did somebody?"

With head hanging, I raised my hand, like a naughty student in class, and in a low, shamed voice confessed that I was the culprit.

"That does it! That does it!" shouted Doyle, his face getting as blood-red as the sun setting over the mountains, as red as my father's got when he was angry, the bulging veins in his scrawny throat looking like they were about to bust.

"Get up in the silo with Ben," he ordered me, and cupping his hands to his mouth, shouted up at Fee, "And you up there, get on down here and take his place!"

Doyle was fit to be tied as tight as the corn shocks at this loss of precious time—and daylight (as valuable to a farmer as to a movie director on location)—but after awhile he, with the help of the other farmers, soon located the mangled penknife and with much soft, easy chuckling and wisecracking about "city boys" from the others, managed to wiggle it out from where it was jamming the works.

In the meantime, I climbed the metal rungs cut in the board-ed-up part of the silo slot after Fee had climbed down, not a high climb at that point, and joined young Ben, who being a simple soul, greeted me with the foolish grin that was always on his still sun-darkened face.

We hadn't been working long before the accident occurred,

so the level of ensilage inside the silo wasn't very deep. But after Doyle and the other farmers got the conveyor belt moving again, the machines rattling at a greater speed, as the afternoon light bled from the sky, the ensilage level grew steadily and quickly higher. At first, it was great fun, jumping up and down and all around with the big grinning Ben over the chopped corn stalks, which still had in them a fragrance of summer that stung my nostrils, along with the chaff and dust of dead corn leaves blowing down over us, packing it all down to discourage mold and make room for more. Ben and I made a dance of it, facing each other, our arms out and flapping, like cranes in a dance whooping at each other as we jumped around and around, starting first at the edges then moving in ever-tightening rings as we galumphed to the center of the silo, packing down the ensilage, making that space for more, then dancing around and around again back to the circular tiled wall as the fresh successive waves of chopped corn blew in from above and rained down over our heads in a constant storm, each of us taking turns jamming in a panel of wood in the side slot as needed, to keep it all in.

After an hour or so, before I knew it, I was aware that I could see over the lip of the silo's rim. To my amazement, we were several stories high, and I could see for miles around the valley, the patchwork quilt of the other farms rolling off in the distance toward the far mountains in the deepening light. I had a queasy feeling in the pit of my belly being up so high.

When, as the sun slipped below the hills, the silo was finally filled to the brim, I felt suddenly dizzy looking around the vast expanse of the valley from what seemed to me a great height, a height I hadn't experienced since working with my father in the shipyard that summer of 1950, just after graduating from high school, saving to go to Rider College. I'd had to climb a narrow ladder up a steep mast of the oil tanker we were working on in drydock, with my face mask and grinding machine and yards of rubber air hose slung round my shoulder, to grind a large oval slot for the overhead mast cables to pass through, at the very top of the mast standing on nothing but shaky, foot-wide planking serving as scaffolding, the whole of Camden, New Jersey, and South Philly across the murky Delaware River spread out before me, as the Swannanoa Valley was now stretched wide before me. I had panicked then. "You're white as a ghost," my boss at the shipyard, who'd climbed ahead of me up the ladder, had said. "This your first time?" When I nodded curtly it was, he, very sympathetically, murmured, "Just don't look down. Keep looking out over the river. Do your job, grind out your slot, but don't look down."

I did as he told me to, and got the job done, and he, bravely, climbed down first, saying, "I'll be here, just take it one rung at a time. You'll be OK."

I felt the same panic now, having to climb down the rungs in the steep narrow slot of the silo, as steep and narrow as the ladder on the oil tanker's mast, and almost as tall as the mast had been.

"Come on down, you two!" Doyle hollered up from below. "We still have to cover it up, case it rains!"

Ben, for all his size and awkwardness, was over the top like a squirrel, grinning at me, his big head disappearing from sight as he scrambled agilely hand-over-hand down the rungs.

I wanted to stay where I was, but since that was foolish, and I would rather have died than to look foolish, I remembered what the boss at the shipyard had told me up on the ship's mast: "Don't look down, just keep looking out over the river." I did that now, making the valley the river, and looking out over it in the thickening dusk, swung my leg over the edge, and keeping on looking out over the broad expanse of darkening green land, one slow rung at a time, made it down all right.

The next morning I went into Hazel Frieda Larsen's office and asked her if they couldn't use me better in the kitchen.

Meanwhile, while awaiting Olson's return, there were other diversions:

Just after I'd started working in the kitchen that fall of 1952, a fierce forest fire broke out on the slopes of the Seven Sister Mountains directly across the valley from the college just beyond Snake River. In the night you could see the flames billowing halfway up the slopes. The situation was so dangerous, for the college as well as for the surrounding homes and farms, forest rangers came to the campus that evening looking for volunteers to help fight the fire, coming upon a group of us in the kitchen. They looked us over and passed me by, I suspect because I looked so miserably skinny, and anyway with my new job to do in the kitchen and dining hall, it would be difficult to go. Eric Weinberger and Terence Burns, not exactly heavyweights themselves, along with a few others, offered to go, marching off with heavy Indian Pumper tanks of water on their backs, red hoses in hand. They were gone overnight and into the next day, when the fire was finally brought under control. They trooped into the kitchen for the food Malrey had kept hot for them on the back of the stove, reeking of smoke and streaked from head to toe with soot, but even so chattering excitedly about their night on the fiery mountain.

Pat Nelson was coolly intelligent with a sly sense of humor, a subtle, seductively attractive smile, and equally cool blue eyes that were even more subtly alluring. She had fine-spun hair so blond it bordered in the Carolina sun on platinum, and the whitest skin of anyone on campus, even hermit night-creatures John Grady and Harvey Harmon. When you talked to her, she listened with all her attention, yet with an expression in those eyes that manifested, at once, not only a playful intelligence but a playful flirtatiousness as well, the latter invitingly there as only another subtle trace, but there nonetheless, something very much a part of her, yet something you sensed she was self-mockingly unaware of. Lingering after meals in dining hall conversation, that old custom at Black Mountain, she would rest her chin on her arm at the table and listen to you in that intelligent and flirtatious way of hers, particularly to the males on campus, and as a result turned quite a few heads. (She also had a wonderfully logical mind, with a clarity of reasoning. One day, crossing a street in Asheville, she got a jaywalking ticket and was perplexed—used to now (spoiled by, perhaps) the freedom at Black Mountain—why the cop was so insistent over such a trivial matter, unable to understand his—and the city law's—"reasoning," because of its *illogic*, telling us all about it angrily when she got back to campus.)

Rumors about her abounded: It was said she had slept with several guys (married and unmarried) in her study her very first night on campus; it was said she was a hopeless "nympho," insatiable. She had that kind of round, smooth-featured face, white as a movie screen, that you could project anything onto, any fantasy, any dream, so that what was true and what imagined—or envied, perhaps more to the point—about Pat was hard to pin down. She had a wonderful laugh, spontaneous and clear and light—and a way of carrying herself that had in it, especially when she sat or reclined but even when she walked, a subdued and unconscious ease and invitation.

We were both in Wes' acting class and took to each other immediately, not only because we were both "newcomers" and had that special early bond of still learning the Black Mountain ropes, but also because we were both from New Jersey, she from the northern part near New York City. An even more special bond, though, was that both of us were refugees from the Catholic church, Pat, especially, being an escapee from parochial schools which I, blessedly, only managed to escape because my family had moved to a Jersey town without any.

Perhaps—more like *probably*—because of that early religious repression, we both shared a hidden—maybe not so actually hidden, if those rumors about Pat were true—defiance and rebellion and a rather goofy sense of humor. And you could talk to Pat about anything, and those listening, nonjudgmental blue eyes seemed to understand everything (maybe that was why after Black Mountain she went on to medical school and eventually became a psychiatrist). It was probably that goofiness we shared plus the Roman Catholic experience, that prompted us to decide to go to the Black Arts Ball, got up by potters David Weinrib and M. C. Richards the following summer for Wes Huss' 45th birthday, Pat dressed as a nun and me as a monk.

Early in that September I took my first long walk outside the grounds of the college, hiking several miles past the farms in the surrounding hills and valley. Since it was an early Sunday morning, the only living things I saw were the livestock, each farm, no matter how poor-looking, always had a cow or two or a horse standing out in the pasture. But there were plenty of vicious, barking dogs who fortunately were more interested in barking and snarling than biting. I suspected I didn't see any of our farmer neighbors because of its being the sabbath and being in the Bible Belt, it was a day of rest and everyone was in church. But every farmhouse I passed, I had the creepy feeling eyes were carefully scrutinizing me behind curtains.

Dark-eyed Ellen Georgia Schasberger from New York City was another of the new students at Black Mountain that fall of 1952. She was no more than 17 and had a child-like sweetness and a way of glancing sideways at you with her shy smile and those darkest of brown eyes that was most appealing. Her earth-brown skin turned even browner in the late summer sun of the mountains, her loose, long dark hair that reached down to her waist gleamed even more shinily dark. There was a freshness and openness about her that everyone responded to, and while the weather was still warm, she often shed her city shoes and walked barefoot in the fields and along the roads, herself like an earth creature newly sprung from the grass, like a child raised on the earthy closeness of a kibbutz, which she actually expressed a wish to go to after Black Mountain, there was about her such a clean-limbed, radiant health of a daughter of a new nation—a new world, really, very much at home at Black Mountain.

She studied German with language teacher Flola Shepard and took potting with Karen Karnes and David Weinrib, her lean fingers made to shape clay—as were Betsy Weinrib's, David's kid sister, who in spiritedness and teasing humor was very much Ellen's twin. Ellen had a clear-eyed intelligence and, perhaps because of her being raised in Manhattan, was not afraid to speak her mind, but did so in a firm, sweetly-pitched voice that had a wonderfully inviting music in it. She was so full of quiet energy and laughter, and sometimes you could hear her playing her recorder alone in the tall grass and sometimes you could catch her dancing barefoot by herself in the dining hall or along the road, sort of solo folk dances or variations on such, very much like the ones in the Jewish folk dance program she later took me to at Cooper Union one night over the fall 1954 break, when, after she'd left the college, we reconnected again in Manhattan. That evening she introduced me to several of her friends she'd gone to school with in New York and, seeing folk dancing for the first time, the dances moved me greatly, so light and airy and full of life, especially in the handkerchief dance, so much like Ellen and her own spontaneous dancing at Black Mountain.

Ellen's sun-browned face was a stark contrast to Pat Nelson's silvery moon-like countenance, but she, like Pat, but in another way, a more fresh and openly appealing way, had a face on which one could also be stirred to project one's deepest desires, visions. Several of the young men, particularly Fee Dawson, projecting their own fantasies onto her, were after her. But just as she had the skill to slide away in her eyes in any situation, so, too, she seemed able to sidestep the most ardent suitor, deftly dance away, not as much of an innocent pushover as some thought her to be. I was so taken with her that, later in the spring, I myself thought we might get together, although I was erotically only half pushed to it, since by that time it had become more and more clear to me where my impulses lay. Still, one deliciously fragrant evening I asked her if it were possible. Smiling her smile that anything could be read into, her dark eyes sliding away in a night as dark, she said only that she would be in her room later. Perhaps she meant it, for that was part of her nature too, child-like, to impishly tease, but if that were so, the night hid that. I wanted to think she meant it, but I saw the way she danced away from the others, and later, when I crept up on the porch of North Lodge and tapped on her window, there was no answer, and when I leaned into the darkened room, softly calling her name and saw it was empty, I felt tricked. That was that other part of Ellen, her playful mischievousness, never mean-spirited, never meant to hurt, but perhaps her way of protecting herself, of slipping away, of perhaps slipping away that very night in the dark, perhaps watching me from a safe distance, perhaps giggling to herself, perhaps even dancing alone in the shadows, till she saw me come down off the porch and walk slow-footed up the road to the Studies Building and the safety of my study, my pride hurt more than anything, whatever erotic desire for her only half-hearted anyway, I consoled myself. I loved her for all those other qualities that most everyone else saw in her and loved her for; and probably that, more than anything, was what I needed to know.

It wasn't only some of the males who had their eye on Ellen. Another new student that fall was a young woman recently discharged from the Women's Marine Corps (SPARS I believe they were called), perhaps only a few years older than Ellen, who took quite a shine to her. Snub-nosed and sturdily built, she had short-cropped pale blond hair and pale blue eyes behind her glasses. I'm not sure exactly what she came to Black Mountain to study—perhaps, like so many of us, she was another stray, another outcast, looking to fit in—but it soon became apparent her main interest was Ellen, and she focused much of her energies on being with her as much as she could.

She had a blunt, forthright manner and seemed somewhat out of sync at the college because you got the feeling that although she'd gotten her discharge, she hadn't yet left the military, which was apparent in her no-nonsense bearing and manner, just as it was true with a number of students recently mustered out of the service and at the college on the GI Bill. One telling sign was that their neat-as-a-pin living areas were in stark contrast to the more casual living conditions of some of the more boho students who'd never been in the service.

She enjoyed driving the jeep truck on the milk runs to and from the farm and could haul milk cans around better than anybody. She also had a quick temper and, although she apparently tried, didn't seem to get along with anyone, except Ellen. Whether her obsessive attentions to Ellen were becoming a problem, since Ellen seemed not to encourage them, or whether she wasn't enrolled in any meaningful way in any of the classes, perhaps a combination of both, she was asked to leave.

The day she left, Ellen was nowhere in sight, had slipped off, had danced away again, no doubt, and the ex-marine scrawled in blue chalk across the blackboard in the conference room below in the Studies: I'M COMING BACK FOR YOU, ELLEN!

But she never did. Ellen, when she reappeared, kept tight-lipped and nobody ever said anything to her, but some made jokes about it, about the tough ex-marine and her bravado, her uptight manner and intense focus—in *that*, she was very Black Mountain. But I felt for her and could certainly understand,

thize with, her fierce attraction for Ellen. Like so
us, she seemed to have come to Black Mountain
, and she *had* found what it was she was searching for,
at ... n her eyes. Maybe it just wasn't the right time for her,
the right woman—the thing was, in that time of the dark
1950s, Black Mountain existed as that rare, that almost unbelievable place where one could come looking, and maybe find.

Tommy Jackson was a student in graphic design and printing
who spent most of his time at the print shop on the road to the
farm, where he innovatively designed and printed programs
and announcements for Black Mountain concerts, plays, and
other events, as well as poems by Black Mountain people on his
Grapnel Press. Other times he was locked away in his study,
where he finally kept his own printing press, listening to music
and tinkering at something or other, sleeping through the day
and working during the night, so that one rarely saw him,
except occasionally when he was breaking into the food lockers
in the kitchen late of an evening, like a clever human racoon.
He had long blond hair down to his ass and kept a blue nylon
hairbrush tucked in the hip pocket of his levis to compulsively,
lovingly, brush that mane. I never saw him with shoes on, he
being another Black Mountaineer, like Cynthia Homire and
Ellen Schasberger and a handful of others, who trod the roads
and trails of the campus barefoot from early spring to late fall.
On the streets of 1950s Black Mountain town and Asheville, he
lifted many a shocked eyebrow.

His most prized possession was an auto he'd shipped back
with him after a stay in England, a long, low-slung, pre-World
War 2 MG two-bucket seater sports car, pitch black with
big spoked wheels. A few months later, on one of Tommy's
occasional disappearances from the campus for several weeks
(not unusual for him), it came back in a heap on the back of a
flatbed truck, along with a bruised and black-eyed Tommy who

one night had rear-ended at high speed an apple truck where on a back country road in Tennessee.

His home was his jam-packed study on the lower level of the Studies, which I glimpsed on rare occasions when the door was left ajar and could see was crammed with his press, his books, a phonograph and records, the walls all but papered, when he could get the paper, with examples of Tommy's ingenious printing jobs, his pallet covered in a bright-striped Indian-style throw or rug, plus scattered disassembled bits of electronic equipment and auto parts, so that there was barely space to move around. Sometimes there would be a sign he'd designed and printed himself in bold-faced orange type hanging outside on the doorknob: DO NOT DISTURB—FUCKING. Tommy once confided to me with that boyish grin (he had a blue-eyed boyish face that could be most deceptive): "I love women so much I want to come back as a lesbian." His own sister, Alice, had been a former student at Black Mountain and along with several of the women students at that time, wore leather jackets and, in order to get to New York City the cheapest way possible on breaks, hitched freights out of the town of Black Mountain, till they were caught once by the railroad bulls and someone from the faculty had to drive a long distance to pay the fines and reclaim them; that incident creating one of the very few rules at the college: students shall not hop freight trains. After she left Black Mountain, Alice and several of her female cronies climbed up the steeple of an old church in lower Manhattan and hacksawed off the statue of an angel on top; later, she transported it across country with her to San Francisco, and when she opened a lesbian bar on the waterfront Embarcadero in the 1950s, she hung the angel outside the door and called the place, appropriately enough, The Tin Angel, which I was introduced to by ex-Black Mountaineers Paul Alexander and Tom Field when I hitchhiked West from Philly in 1956.

Tommy riled administrative tempers at the college, not only for breaking into the food lockers at night (easily busting the locks that had been installed in the first place because of his illicit food raids), but, among other rule breakings, for sending printed poems out to the world as if they had the imprimatur of the college, which particularly incurred Olson's wrath; so much so that, after a row with Charles, Tommy changed the name of his printing outfit from The Grapnel Press to The Terrified Press, becoming an outcast nonconformist even among the nonconformists.

Tommy, who except for his long blond hair, occasional strawberry-blond beard, blue hairbrush always riding on his hip, and barefeet, in physical appearance—he had a well-proportioned body I daydreamed over on occasion my first celibate months at the college—could, given a haircut, shave and a change of clothes, resemble the All [White]-American Boy stereotype of that time. In spite of all that, he had the most curious romance with one of the students that fall of 1952.

Dorothy (Peggy) Darrell was a friend of Pat Nelson's—they'd gone to school together—and Pat, who often talked about her brilliant friend, finally persuaded her to come down and give Black Mountain a try. Dorothy you could see right off was indeed brilliant, a good talker, most articulate, a wonderful cheerfulness about her, with a wonderful laugh to match, radiating good spirits in a leanly lovely face with large, beautifully expressive brown eyes, leanly sensitive fingers, and a cascade of hair, when she left it free, that was brown-blond waves falling about her shoulders. In face, hands, in her feet (which one could plainly see, since she, too, chose to go barefoot), she was proportional in every way. But something had happened perhaps in her growing in the womb, or maybe it was because of some genetic accident, for she was severely humpbacked, her midsection squashed in misshapenness, her legs spindly, the stick-like legs of an undeveloped child, a beautiful face and beautiful hands on a deformed, dwarfish body, like a creature in fairy tales. At first, I wondered if this squeezed-together body hurt her, made her uncomfortable—or bitter. But if it did, she never complained about it; in fact, she always appeared unself-conscious about herself, was out-going, quite assertive and radiated that energy noted earlier, not only in her face and voice, but in her manner as well. Although she walked with a bit of an awkward, draggy gait, she always strode, in her man's khaki shirt and shorts, with a fast pace, like someone who was going somewhere and knew where she was going—as if nothing would hold her back. So, expressions of pity—that one-way street, where the pitier always places him- or herself above the pitied—or treating her like an invalid, not that any-one ever tried it with her, were out of the question. You just knew instinctively she would have none of that.

Like Pat, having a scientific and philosophical bent, Dorothy was interested, among many other subjects, including Einstein and his theory of relativity, in psychology, and was particularly curious about the then-popular increasing use of hypnosis as a psychotherapeutic tool. Very sure of herself, she boasted she could "hypnotize anyone," including me.

One night in my room (by this time, I'd been moved down-stairs to my own room, first floor rear in South Lodge), while I sat on my bed surrounded by Pat and a few other observers, Dorothy, quite expert in her technique, tried to put me under. As the repetitive phrases of her silkenly seductive voice mur-mured in my ear, soporific rings of light began to dance across my eyes, and I was just about to lose consciousness when, by sheer force of will, not to mention fear, I pulled myself bolt upright on the bed and forced myself awake. My hands, my entire body shook for a good several minutes after, while high-spirited Dorothy, first checking to see if I was okay and then calming me, laughed that good-natured laugh of hers, perhaps more to save face, since she'd admitted I was her first "failure," exclaiming delightedly, "But I *almost* gotcha!"

Needless to say, the experiment was not repeated.

So it came as a surprise for some of us when Dorothy, vivacious and outgoing, began spending time with Tommy in his study (how he managed to fit another person into that crowded space was a mystery), Tommy, the night-creature loner, given to few words. It wasn't long before we began to see less and less of Dorothy as she, over time, more and more adapted to Tommy's topsy-turvy schedule, sleeping through the day with him in his study and working through the night. Sometimes when I passed by outside in the hall I could hear them laughing and talking together inside Tommy's study. And Dorothy, if it were possible, seemed even more radiantly happy and content when we did get a chance to see her; and there was something about Tommy, too, a pleased quietness in his manner, in his face, as he sometimes darted about in daylight, either on foot between Studies and print shop, or tore off on mysterious errands out in Buncombe County in, before the apple-truck accident, his MG, Dorothy sometimes in the bucket seat beside him. But you rarely saw the two of them together, mainly because they spent so much time behind the locked door of Tommy's study, his personally printed DO NOT DISTURB sign hanging on the knob. Although I'm sure Pat was pleased for Dorothy, I also suspect her nose was a bit out of joint, deprived as she was of her closest friend's company. I know I was a little jealous of Tommy myself, missing Dorothy's presence, too, as much as Pat or anyone else who was taken with her.

Lou Harrison spent time off to himself—unseen for days sometimes—down at the Gatehouse by the county road, getting "high" on endless pots of tea brewed on a hot plate and composing on the battered old upright piano inside, even slept nights there; flush-faced, eyes sparkling, laughingly telling everyone about it, when he resurfaced. Or he worked in the little student-designed and -built Music House, with its one wall of window panes and nothing in it but a Steinway grand piano and a seat, off in the middle of the woods near the cooks' quarters (an old faded-green, tar-shingled shanty). Inside the Music House there was also a small pot-bellied stove, so Lou or any of the music students could practice or compose there in chilly weather. Sometimes birds used to fly in through the metal chimney pipe and get trapped, drop into the unlit stove, and then fight their way out through the stove door and bat frantically against the wall of windows, till one of us, as I did one morning, came along and swung open the door to shoo them out to freedom.

Lou wasn't ever very friendly to me, although I tried, since I'd liked him so much that first meeting in June at Saturday night supper on the dining porch. Maybe he smelled the threat his own openness was to me. Or maybe smelling one of his own kind, and still tarred, as most all of us were in those days, with internalized homophobia, kept his distance. And of course I was no musician. But more than likely he simply considered me too callow and hidden to be of interest—or of use.

Nell Rice, that fall of 1952, continued a long tradition, perhaps started by her and her husband, John, when he was running the school, of inviting two or three new students to her apartment under the attic eaves of Black Dwarf Sunday evenings to eat our cheese and Malrey's home-baked bread suppers, since Sunday afternoons were the cooks' days off. Nell provided tea or coffee and perhaps a dessert of some kind, but the main idea was for her to get to know us, to exchange ideas, and incidentally to tell us something about the library. I suspect the main reason was, besides her genuine liking of and caring for the students, that long having been first divorced and never remarrying, and then the "widow of John Rice," she was simply lonely.

There was also, paradoxically, a disconcerting look of pure blue madness in her eyes, eyes that had the intensity of having stared too long into cold, empty skies, who became finally, in the last years of the college, an avenging woman, a furious woman. First perhaps because lost in the shadow of her husband, then cast off by him; then, as cast off again under Olson's regime, she helped bring Black Mountain down in lawsuits for back pay, along with Natasha Goldowski, old Johanna Jalowetz (another recent widow living alone on the grounds) and some of the other women. Sometimes I think that pure blue madness burning coldly in those bluest of eyes helped destroy it all, that she would be avenged, destroying that which she had helped create with her husband and all the early founders of the college, which had in it the seeds of its own destruction perhaps long before it ever began.

But all that's later on down the road in my story.

Glenn Lewis wore a brush cut, butch badge of the day, along with chinos and brown suede athlete's jacket, underneath which were the lineaments of a husky build. No one would take him for the stereotypical gay of the day, or suspect that he was struggling with that persuasion within himself. Born and raised in Santa Rosa, California, whose claim to fame, he informed me, was as the place where Hitchcock shot *Shadow of a Doubt* in 1941 when Glenn was a boy, and a graduate of University of California, Berkeley, in math and music, he had once been a Black Mountain student during Paul Goodman's stay. He had returned that fall of 1952 for a visit on a break from his recent appointment as a mathematician at the Institute for Advanced Study at Princeton, where Einstein, who once gave a lecture at Black Mountain in 1941, was also in residence. (Later, on a lovesick trip to Princeton, since I'd developed such a mighty crush on him, Glenn gave me a tour of the Institute, including a peek at Einstein's office, and at one of the world's first work-ing computers, the huge, punch-card hungry UNIVAC, which filled the length and breadth of one large room from floor to ceiling with its thousands and thousands of humming, blinking orange lights.)

Glenn, with his formal education, his Ivy League connec-tions, his knowingness and articulate speech, right down to his elitist collegiate mode of dress and brush cut, was an embodiment to me of the "safe," the "respectable" and the "acceptable" (in disguise at least)—the same as I had glimpsed in the mien and figure of the youth in the smartly tailored blue seersucker suit alighting that night from the train in Charlottesville, home of the University of Virginia, who also, in my uncertainties on my way to Black Mountain, embodied that "certainty" to me—a powerful seduction against those gnaw-ing uncertainties and the consequent struggling against what was more and more becoming the certainty of my destiny at Black Mountain; all that, plus the fact that Glenn had once been a Black Mountain student (that gave me hope and helped still a little any lingering fears that I might've made a mistake coming to such a ragged, impoverished, far-out, experimental college); then too that he knew a great deal about music, especially classical music, and with his incongruously nimble and sensitive fingers played the piano beautifully, made me really fall for him.

And always, underneath, in our long talks seated side by side leaning against the wall on the pallet in my study on the lower level of the Studies Building was a tone of superiority in the onslaught of Glenn's self-appointed "tutoring," in which he was often talking way over my head and that only reinforced my own deep sense of inadequacy which I chose to ignore, I was so besotted with the complexity of all that told me he was every-thing that I was not or could not ever be.

Wolpe made no bones of his dislike for Glenn's "preten-sions," particularly his "tastes" in music, but I was too gaga to listen.

While a student at Black Mountain, Glenn had come under the tutelage and strong influence of Paul Goodman who was frighteningly uninhibited, particularly to many of the old Quaker and European hands at the college (one last straw that led to his expulsion was his openly taking a piss "behind a tree" during a softball game before the assembled college, including children). He was openly queer, despite his traditional paterfamilias accommodation (he had a wife and kids), an "accommodation" Glenn himself later reached in New York where he continued to see Goodman in his capacity as "lay" analyst, Goodman helping Glenn adjust his gayness to Glenn's (and I suspect Goodman's) own paterfamilias inclinations. I first met Goodman during the1954 winter break at a gathering Glenn took me to in a loft across the Hudson in Hoboken, New Jersey, where a number of Manhattan artists were then moving because of cheap rents. Goodman, dressed like a laborer, with flushed red face, pipe perpetually clamped in his broken, tobacco-stained teeth, was bemoaning to everyone that he'd "dry-fucked" a virgin youth that very afternoon and was worrying that he might have hurt him, not using lubricant, so hasty was he in his eager desire to have the boy, Goodman's face flushing even redder as he nervously repeated his worries over and over, so much so that I whispered to Glenn that Paul "looked like a devil." Later in the evening, Goodman, who I hadn't formally met yet, came right up to me, puffing wreaths of pipe smoke, and, without preliminary, his first words were, "So you think I'm a devil," his expression quite serious. I didn't know what to say, and was so thrown by his abrupt manner, and irritated at Glenn's treachery for telling, I left the party and returned alone by bus to Manhattan and Mary Ann Fretz's apartment on Minetta Lane in the Village, where I was staying during that winter break.

To Glenn's credit, he let me stay at his East 96th Street apartment in New York when I returned from San Francisco in 1958, and later lent me close to $200 when I badly needed it, money I never repaid, perhaps unconsciously rationalizing that I'd "earned" it, since by that time I was deeply troubled, drinking heavily and capable of any rationalization. But during his brief return to Black Mountain in 1952, I was kept so on edge by the unfulfilled tightrope of desire and of the tension of unacknowledged admission between us, I was both saddened and deeply relieved when he left to return to Princeton.

In that fall of 1952, Wes Huss held auditions and early practice sessions in the lobby of Roadside, where he and Bea and baby son David lived on the first floor, for a production of Lorca's *Blood Wedding*. I was surprised when he cast me as the Bridegroom, but perhaps not so surprised: Even so early on working with Wes, I was beginning to get a sense that everything he did was designed for a careful, calculated psychological effect or outcome. In this case, I suspected, perhaps a bit paranoically, that he cast me as the Bridegroom to stir up some latent heterosexuality in me.

Once the play was cast—his actor wife Bea was to be my mother—we moved down to the dining hall where we rehearsed for weeks at the far end of the hall before the huge fieldstone fireplace, with a dark, austerely lit setting by Wes, with no scenery but with various levels of platforms to indicate place (not dissimilar to the set of Lorca's *The House of Bernarda Alba*, which we performed at a later date). Costumes were severely black, the whole look of Wes' vision of the play matching the brooding and somber formality of Lorca's language. The night of the performance (given the small on-campus audience, only one performance of any production was ever given at Black Mountain), face smeared with pancake makeup, hair slicked down in the Spanish mode, wearing a white shirt with black string tie and dark trousers for the day of my wedding, my belly was dancing a thumping flamenco I was so jittery, about to give my first performance at Black Mountain before what I knew was a severely critical audience.

My first brief appearance in the first act over, I was so relieved I abruptly realized I had to relieve myself. Rather than passing the audience to reach the restrooms at the other end of the hall, figuring I had plenty of time till my next appearance onstage, I slipped out the side door and hurried down the road to use the locker-room-like bath in our upstairs dorm in South Lodge. Determined to keep calm for my next entrance, I deliberately took my time (Black Mountain slowdown had really begun to work in my life), so much time that, after I'd done my business and was carefully checking my pancake makeup in one of the mirrors over the sinks, who should suddenly and unaccountably appear in the john doorway but Wes Huss.

"Everyone is waiting," he said rather evenly. "Are you ill?"

I looked at him blankly.

"I've been hunting all over for you. Your next entrance was some time ago."

He was remarkably calm, considering I was holding up his play, an exacting director who was a stickler for timing.

I felt like a fool and was told to save my apologies till later, as we raced down the stairs and back over the road to the dining hall, where I paused a moment to catch my breath before I stealthily entered the side doors again and stepped up on my designated platform while the rest of the cast, still in their formal poses, stared at me curiously, particularly Cynthia Homire who stared at me most severely. Bea Huss, however, still deep in her role as Mother, wore a subtly amused, more empathetic expression.

In early winter darkness 1952, with so few of us, the sweet brightening of spirit to walk into the dining hall for supper and hear Bach being played in pure pitch on recorders by three or four students gathered regularly by the dark windows overlooking even darker Lake Eden—Mark Hedden, Mary Fitton Fiore, Ellen Schasberger in particular.

Coffee was another comfort that winter. At Black Mountain we'd make boiled coffee in a big, open cook pot—"pan coffee" it was called by cowboys and miners—to get coffee quick and simple, often after the kitchen closed and the regular coffee urns were empty: When water boils, toss in coffee, lots of it, let boil a few minutes, then sprinkle cold water on top and bang the pot down hard to have grounds settle to the bottom, let sit a minute or two, then pour.

Some swore by it, and it did always seem to taste even better than Cornelia's pretty delicious urn-made brew. Cynthia Homire taught me how. Another vital part of one's education at the college, as important as learning to write a clear sentence or paint a clean brush stroke.

I first saw music student Merrill Gillespie, the back of his head at least, at a gathering in the lobby of Meadows Inn early in the fall of 1952. Since the event was held where Natasha Goldowski and Eric Renner lived, perhaps it was a rare talk by Natasha on modern physics, since, like some of the other hermits on campus with their special interests, Merrill would have shown up if it were that, or if it was something musical or on music, so little else at the college was said to interest him.

He was sitting next to Herb Roco, his lover, whom I'd seen innumerable times, especially when Herb was hauling the milk cans in the old Jeep truck on the daily noon milk runs from the farm before lunch. As I mentioned, I soon had to retire from milk runs for lack of muscles, but Herb, pallid-skinned and with a dark crewcut, who appeared deceptively soft and delicate, easily wrestled the heavy cans into the walk-in cooler behind cook Malrey Few's huge old coal stove, which had been crudely converted to blast-furnace oil power. Occasionally, he'd show up in the kitchen late at night, where there were always a few late-owl students, including night-hawks Harvey Harmon and John Grady, the latter puffing on his pipe, all gabbily holding forth under the pots and pans that hung atop the huge metal-surfaced work table in the center of the room, Herb come not to loiter but to pinch some Sunday-lunch cheese or leftover cornbread or milk from the cooler. That, as noted, was against one of the college's few rules (besides that and no hopping freight trains, no possession of guns was the other), but most everyone did it, until an even stronger padlock was put on the freezer door, which of course clever Tommy Jackson, who I suspect had a criminal bent, naturally soon learned to pick. Herb never hung around to shoot the philosophical or artistic breeze with the regulars, but did occasionally put up with some good-natured ribbing over his quiet aloofness, before heading back to Merrill, since the pair kept mainly to themselves up in their rooms in Next-to-the-Last-Chance, one more of the barracks-like buildings on the farthest reaches of the road to the farm. (The other student-couples barracks next to it, where Joel and Cissy Oppenheimer lived, was called, appropriately enough, Last Chance.)

Herb and Merrill rarely appeared in the dining hall for meals either, Merrill especially. He was from Kewanee, Illinois, and having been at the college for several years, ostensibly writing music—his last formal studying was music composition with Lou Harrison—seemed to have mostly withdrawn from the community and did little more, rumor went, than hole up in Next-to-the-Last-Chance, smoke Pall Malls, play the upright piano installed there, and read. From what I could gather in the brief times I saw Herb, he was from Houston, Texas, where his father owned a car repair garage and where, no doubt, Herb got his mechanical knowhow—he could fix anything, including the World War 2 milk Jeep, and was a real asset to the college for that alone. Also earlier, as did students Robert Rauschenberg and Carroll Williams, he made an experimental three-minute 16 mm film without a camera, by hand-painting each frame.

No matter what, he always appeared quietly courteous and unruffled, centered in the Zen readings and meditations, the ideogrammatic calligraphy he'd been introduced to at Black Mountain, perhaps primarily through Lou Harrison's Asiatic interests and music—eerily (enviably, in my own unbalanced, distracted eyes) on an even keel. He also had a quiet, affectionate listening nature. I never once heard him raise his soft-spoken voice, get angry, or impatient (virtues I learned later from personal experience undoubtedly stood him in good stead with Merrill who, I found, had a short fuse and was demanding and self-centered as often an only-child can be).

In a letter to Robert Creeley, dated "tuesday jan 29 52," Olson exasperatedly referred to Herb, among other students, including Robert Rauschenberg, as "these sexually marginal girls and boys . . . of the sexual continent, of that geography I know in the other hemisphere of itself . . . ."

Merrill and Herb were sitting two or three rows ahead of me that night at Meadows Inn, in the ubiquitous cane-bottomed chairs which were lined up across the crowded lobby. The first thing that struck me about Merrill's sandy-brown, closely cropped, crewcut head was his ears, which, from behind, looked first like a bat's ears, then were transformed in my mind's eye into a faun's, then a satyr's ears. A shudder of repulsive fascination went through me, I couldn't take my eyes off those ears, something pre-human, something almost animal-like about them. "I could *never* be attracted to someone with ears like that," I thought, and shivering again, forced myself to look away, little realizing what a trickster Eros is in the tricks it plays on us, discovering as I would in a few short weeks how wrong I was; discovering also, coincidentally regarding those ears, that Merrill was also partially deaf, just as my older brother Bill was.

In those early months at Black Mountain, I was so caught up in getting used to not only the wildness of the terrain but to the equally wild ideas of creation and thought that were also new, exciting ground. Between working on the farm and later in the kitchen, attending classes and spending hours holed up in my study struggling not only with my writing but with reading the spread of newly recommended books that were required reading if I wanted to know what was going on around there, I had little time to think of sex, which was a good thing, given how few we were and my prospects anyway not of the best. Once, though, after a month or more at the college, it hit me right between the eyes one Saturday evening in the huge bathroom shared by us male students in the attic dorm of South Lodge.

To look at him, to listen to him, his Philly wiseguy charm, you'd never guess he was interested in composing serious music, particularly the wildly atonal contemporary modern music he was learning from master Stefan Wolpe, whom he and a friend of his, who had arrived earlier with his wife, had studied with in Philadelphia. He had finally come down to the college at this friend's urging to pick up studying with Wolpe again, a month or so into that fall 1952 term.

Another ex-army vet who was friendly enough, with a quiet, watchful humor, he bunked with us up in the attic dorm but spent most of his time, when he wasn't studying with Wolpe or working up at the farm, with his pal and his pal's then-pregnant wife in their room in North Lodge. Older, and having had some experience in the world, he seemed amusedly bemused by Black Mountain, and by most of the rest of us, I think, as if he were at some sort of summer camp, and complained, *sotto voce*, at the lack of women—a not uncommon complaint among most of the few single straight males (including a few who weren't single)—annoyed that he had to take to driving into Asheville of a Saturday night to get laid.

I never thought much of him one way or the other; he was a likeable enough guy, as familiar to me as one of my South Philly cousins, except he was a puzzling contradiction, given the way he looked and talked, which contrasted with what he wanted to do in music. (His navy vet pal, who was just as serious about his composing, still could've been taken for, with his slicked up pompadour, baby boyish good looks and laidback manner, some rising pop star from South Philly.) I guess he felt out-of-place, or maybe the loneliness got to him, because, despite his firm friendship and shared musical interest, he didn't last long at the school.

Anyhow, as I said, I hadn't been too bothered by my own lack of sexual company since I arrived, so it came as a jolt when, after my supper-time shift with the dishes one evening, I walked into our big bathroom in the dorm to take a shower, thinking there was nobody in there, when to my surprise, there he stood, after an afternoon's work at the farm, standing stark naked under the bright bare bulbs by the shower stalls, having just taken a shower himself. He gave me one of his sweetly small smiles which he usually did when we met on the road or else-where, and began toweling himself down. I stood in the door-way for a long moment; despite sharing the same quarters, I'd never seen him nude before.

His thinning, wavy reddish hair, its tips burnished brighter red from the sun in his long hours in the fields (since he was there on the GI Bill, I suspect his voluntary farm work was his way of avoiding campus life, or, for him, non-life), gleamed even brighter now under the bare lightbulbs and the flush of a brisk shower and toweling. His usually fair skin was burnished as well by the sun, his body a reddish-brown all over that, in my startled eyes, seemed to match the fire in his hair—he was all of a fire to me, from his hair to his freckled muscular shoulders down a leanly corded body to his toes, his uncut cock as rubicund as his sunscorched shoulders—a stark contrast to most of the rest of us skinny, pallid denizens of the attic. Since it was Saturday night, he was evidently slicking himself up to go into Asheville. I had a wild impulse to offer my queer self to him—for free, of course, and think of the gas he'd save, etc., etc.—but was too tongue-tied, too frightened by how he might take it, cautious because not sure yet of how those things went at Black Mountain; too paralyzed, really, by his beauty.

It was only a glimpse of him, but a fiery one that burned into my brain, stayed with me for days, weeks even. I stepped quickly into the nearest shower stall as if to escape a too bright heat, even the hot water from the shower head a welcome coolness.

Upsetting the rhythm of my work, my concentration, eros leapt in with a vengeance. I was kind of glad when he left the college, since ever after that incident I was uncomfortably aware of him sleeping on another of the box spring mattresses under the sloping roof across the dorm—his area always army neat—not more than 20 feet away; or seeing him in the dining hall now at his Philly pal's table, or on the road to the farm, always envisioning him as I saw him that night in the shower room, and still do after nearly 45 years.

Later, in looking back, after we'd read the books in Olson's class, I saw that Stendhal was right in *The Charterhouse of Parma* and *The Red and the Black*, that the romantic pursuit of or fantasizing about the beloved is more enlivening than the reality of the capture—a realization I was bitterly to learn more deeply in my final summer at Black Mountain.

Glimpsing him that night made me realize it had been a long time since Chautauqua, and that other attic room in a hotel there with elderly geometry teacher Henry L. Wood. But as things turned out, I wouldn't have long to wait before a genuine prospect appeared, and in the most unlikely person.

Not long after, late on a cold night in December as I was heading up to the Studies to do some writing, I saw someone standing near the road in front. As I drew nearer, I was surprised to see that it was Merrill Gillespie, I so infrequently saw him anywhere, especially at that hour. In fact, we had seen even less of him the past few weeks since his lover, Herb Roco, had gone back to Texas to help his father out in his auto repair garage. Merrill started toward me, and I had the curious feeling he'd been waiting for me, although I couldn't imagine why, he had such a cold and distant manner and intimidated me more than a little; I was sure he didn't even know I existed. In the dim light from the entrance, I could see, as he approached me, his pasty complexion even more ghastly pale in the night, that he wore a crooked, hesitant smile, but in his cold blue eyes was an expression of firm resolve that chilled me a little. Later, when I got to know him, I figured what it must have cost his pride to approach me that night, how desperately needy and alone he must have been.

He didn't mince words: did I want to sleep with him? My first thought was, But what about Herb? Won't he be returning soon? What would he think? My second response was an image, really: the still powerful memory of first seeing the back of his head in Meadows Inn a few weeks before, still revolted yet fascinated by those bat-like ears, ears that now in the faint light thrown from the Studies entrance I could see were joined in straight lines from lobe to cheek, such earlobes always striking me, fancifully, for some unknown reason, as being "aristocrat-ic."

They weren't quite as frightening that night, but I was so startled by his totally unexpected proposition, my first at the college, from someone to whom I'd barely spoken, I didn't know what to say and confusedly mumbled, "I'll think about it," and when he cocked his head quizzically as if he hadn't heard, repeated it louder, as I'd learned to do as a child with my own deaf brother.

"When will I know?" Merrill persisted. He was quite deliberate, his cool blue eyes on me, his head still cocked in that alert listening of the deaf.

I shrugged, not knowing what else to say; felt gawky, nervous; felt something dangerous. All I wanted now was to get into the safety of my study and bury myself in my writing, where perhaps I'd already been burying such troubling emotions, although I already suspected any writing would be out for the rest of that night. What I really wanted was to be alone to think about this sudden turn, this out-of-the-blue offer which I never expected to occur so soon in my stay.

"I'll ask you again in a few days," he said, very sure of himself, very determined, his face unsmiling now. But there was a persuasive softness in his voice that I hadn't heard before—indeed, if I had ever heard him speak as much before.

I had been unaware he had his eye on me.

I only wanted to get away—I would never have sought him out, I would never have chosen him, even in my fantasies, where the majority of my choices then lay. I nodded quickly, mumbled again something in farewell, and hurried into the Studies Building, clattering down the metal steps to the sanctuary of my study on the lower level, where I locked the door behind me to try to think through this surprising offer, this perplexing opening of another door.

During the next few days I was very jumpy, expecting Merrill suddenly to appear out of nowhere to demand of me if I had made up my mind about his proposal. One evening not long after, as I was going out the back door of the dining hall after I'd finished my dishwashing stint, glad to get out into the clear, cold night air after the steamy kitchen, Merrill was waiting for me in the shadow. My heart gave a jolt, I realized there would never, for all Black Mountain's 600 acres, be any way ever to avoid him.

"Well?" he asked in that soft but firm voice of his, his breath cloudy in the nippy air.

"I was going up to the Studies," was all I could manage to say, although I had really planned to go back to South Lodge, as usual, for a shower after my sweaty job with the dishes.

We began walking up the dark road, not saying much of anything, kind of feeling each other out. By the time we passed the Quiet House in its dark grotto of winter leaves, I could see Merrill felt as awkward as I did, sensed a shyness in him too that I identified with and was beginning to find appealing. When we got to the Studies I thought, Oh, to hell with it, and just kept walking beside him, staying on the road past the stream at the print shop, and on past the houses of Mrs. Jalowetz and biology teacher Victor Sprague and his wife, then finally Minimum House where the road turned sharply to the right at the Next-to-the-Last-Chance, where Merrill and, lately, Herb, I thought guiltily, lived, the road then wending around to the farm. Next door, there were lights in the windows of Last Chance where, to the relief of some, the Oppenheimers were back together again, Cissy having moved back up the hill after sharing a brief stay with painter-farm worker Don Jones in his room in North Lodge.

Residents at this distance from the center of the campus were told to be extra sure to keep their outside garbage can lids on tight so as not to attract the bears in the hills, but the racoons always found a way to pry them open. I followed Merrill up the rickety front steps and in the door, entering a spartan, military barracks-like front room where he'd left a light on, glad now to get into the warmth from the army-surplus oil heater glowing against one sheetrocked wall. As he closed the door behind us, he smiled and said, "Like some green tea?"

My heart was really tripping in my chest by now. I nodded, too nervous to ask what green tea was, never having tasted it before, watching as Merrill brewed it on a hotplate in the alcove kitchen. Warmed by the tea (which I later discovered was made popular at Black Mountain by acting and ceramics student Cynthia Homire, of pan coffee fame), Merrill took my cup when I'd finished and put it in the sink, came back and with that same lopsided smile, looked me in the eye, placing his hands on my shoulders. I looked back, looked away, knowing what it all meant, no need for words, no need for that in the oldest body language in the world. Since he said it was so cold in the bedroom, the door to which he—he actually said "we," conjuring up for me Herb's presence again—kept shut till bedtime to save on heat, he dragged a single-sized mattress out from where he and Herb slept.

In the shadowy bedroom, I glimpsed a huger mattress taking up most of the space of the floor, and troublingly thought again of Herb, worried if he would know about this on his return, and wondered, too, was Merrill, for now, in deference to Herb, keeping sacrosanct their "marriage" bed?

"It'll be warmer here," he murmured, a glancing brightness in his eyes, those faun-like ears of his becoming less, and more, threatening.

He slowly undressed me, which surprised me, looked me over quickly—which made me shrink a bit in the glaring light, made me suddenly remember too I hadn't showered after dishcrew. Then, with that crooked grin still on his face as seeming encouragement, he led me to the bare mattress and laid me down, in my nudity the closeness to the floor chilly despite the nearness of the stove. Next, he undressed himself, sliding off his well-worn plaid flannel shirt, his t-shirt, dungarees, a surprisingly lean muscular body, milky-white skin as bright as Herb's, I noted with a twinge, his lean chest and strong legs dusted lightly with the same shade of sandy-brown hair as his crewcut. I looked in shy uncertainty, pretending not to look, that curiosity, that discovery, as always in seeing a totally naked body in first-time intimacy, an undiscovered continent of possible sensuous delight and fearful newness.

As when he first propositioned me, he wasted no time and like someone famished for it, got right down to business. We kissed. I was glad to see he was a good kisser, his lips on mine like eating the juiciest peach, his body pressed close so that I no longer felt the chill of the floor. Then without warning, he had expertly switched himself about, and was kissing now down between my legs, his own crotch slung over my mouth—It was all too quick, too abrupt—I could barely get my breath with the size of him, the musky uncut odor of him, so swiftly slipped down my throat—I gagged a bit. Then, to my astonishment, since no one had ever done it to me before, he ducked his head, lowering between my thighs and began tonguing me there, so astonished I barely had a sense if it were pleasurable or not. He then tucked his sandy-haired buttocks forward over my face, with no words needed to convey he wanted the same, and I, with some hesitancy, finally obliged, wanting, as always, to please, wanting to know that, too, what it was like, rimming for the first time another male there—a faint swampy scent like marshlands in summer.

It was over quickly, our coming synchronous, which I took as a good omen. I felt flushed all over now from the quick heat of it. As I lay beside him on the mattress, his arm lying lightly across my chest, I wasn't sure I liked it; I wasn't sure I would stay, I would have to think about it, not able yet to trust "the evidence of my senses"; in fact, was only thinking of heading back to South Lodge and a hot shower. Perhaps Merrill wasn't so sure either. He didn't ask me to stay over, that first time. He did say he'd heat up the hot water heater for a shower if I wanted. I said no, not to bother, thinking there might be some hot water left in South Lodge, got dressed and left.

Walking back down the road, breathing steam in the cold night air, I figured that was that. But a few evenings later, Merrill was waiting outside the kitchen door again.

It wasn't long before I was spending so many nights up at Next-to-the-Last-Chance, I rarely slept again that winter in my bed up in the attic dorm of South Lodge.

In the beginning, as on any honeymoon, as his body (not to mention his ears) became less foreign to me in the night, the hidden delights of it increasingly discovered, the thoughts of him in the days grew larger; his body was in mine, I began to feel a happiness I hadn't known before. In the evenings, he played his Lou Harrison-inspired compositions for me on the old battered upright in the front room. They still sounded jarringly alien to me, but I kept mum, listened hard, a habit begun since I first entered that strange place called Black Mountain. Or he worked scribbling on music composition paper on the music rack of the piano and pounded out the notes he heard in his head, while I sat reading John Donne or George Herbert (one of Merrill's favorite poets) for Hilda Morley's metaphysical poets class, or Brecht's *Caucasian Chalk Circle* for Wes' acting class (never writing in our barracks nest, that was saved for the privacy of my study), glancing up occasionally and smiling, gazing around the room with a feeling of contentment, a cozy, homey scene.

I even took to smoking his brand of cigarettes, king-size Pall Malls, even their bright red packs, because they were connected to him, eroticized in my eyes, giving up my cheap but lung-searing Home Runs, not only because I wanted to be part of everything he thought and did, but because, not quite as poor as myself, he was able to order cigarettes by the carton (an unheard-of luxury at hand-to-mouth Black Mountain) from Carroll Williams at the college store. (Having a stash of butts was another ploy that enabled Merrill to stay holed up for longer periods in Next-to-the-Last-Chance and not have to go down into the campus.) And it was easier for me to buy a pack from him when I was out, or even, since I was always broke, to get a pack on credit, wisecracking to him, "I'll pay for it later, in bed."

As the physical intimacy improved, other intimacies grew as well. In those cold nights, after lovemaking, we lay close in each other's arms for additional warmth under the heavy featherbed (something I hadn't slept under since I was a child sleeping with two of my brothers in the same bed in our freezing clapboard bungalow in Gloucester County, New Jersey, during the Depression—those hard economic times at Black Mountain not much different, come to think of it). The musty, pillowticking featherbed protected us from the chilly room with its thin barracks walls, and the even chillier bare floor with only the ground beneath just under the bare mattress (simpler at Black Mountain College dispensing, for most of us, with the nuisance of sheets). We talked long into the night, told each other our stories, physically eased, hence, at ease with each other, gazing up into the dark, the darkness evoking in us the narratives of our lives—I wanted to know everything about him, about his rather solitary boyhood in Kewanee, Illinois, about his mother and factory worker father, about what it was like to be an only child (incomprehensible to me, coming from a large family); fascinated and incredulous, aware of his lean body beside me, to learn that at 15 he'd been fat; and that, also at 15, his first piano teacher, a man in his 40s, on a trip the teacher took him on to a concert in Chicago, had, once back in their hotel room, given Merrill his first blowjob, his music teacher his first queer experience, their secret continuing once back in Kewanee; and how Merrill had come to Black Mountain a few years back; and the litany into the night of all those he loved there, with reasons why: M.C. Richards (for her lively Zen intellect); Bea Huss (for kindliness, sensitivity); painting student Dorothea Rockburne (for her wit and talent) and her husband, Carroll (for his vast reading and his lovely eyes); Natasha Goldowski (for her brilliance and energy) and her husband, Eric (for his sweet good looks, and perhaps a fantasized sense that he was *really* gay); and mainly Lou Harrison (for his innovative genius and knowledge of music). Then there was the longer litany of those he detested (sounding then, in my ears, despite my suspension of criticism, I was so besotted with him, like someone who'd overstayed his time), with concomitant resentments: Olson heading the list, as an arrogant windbag who was wrecking the school; Wes Huss, because Merrill perceived him as being cold and mean to and, hence, unworthy of Bea; Stefan Wolpe, another arrogant windbag to him, this one with a heavy German accent, who—his main crime—would shortly replace Lou Harrison as music instructor when Harrison (at Charles' prompting) was let go.

And on and on, the resented far outnumbering the respected.

I lay beside him listening to it all in the dark, uncritical, unjudging, ready to take his side, to defend, to protect, in that way only early love can bring, that rapturous blinding, like pollen flung in the lover's eyes.

In my heart, though, I particularly disagreed with his assessment of Olson (who'd made such a powerful impression on me back in June and who I resented only because of his absence); and of Huss, although that was mainly based on my being in his theater course, in which I was learning a lot; not to mention the others, especially Wolpe, who, though he could be unnervingly blunt, was obviously a brilliant composer and loaded with Old World charm.

But I kept silent, not wanting to start something so early on, not wanting to risk angering him and possibly turning him from me.

And he would listen to my stories, loving to hear them, like bedtime stories, when you think of it (like when, again as a child starting at the age of 4 or 5, lying between them under that old featherbed, I told stories to my equally young brothers, Bill and Bob), of how I grew up poor and Catholic in a large family, and what that was like; and even though he came from a working-class family and they were not as poor (in fact, his parents still managed to send him a little money now and then, which went a long way at Black Mountain), my family's poverty, my numerous brothers and my one sister, were especially exotic to him, an only child. Sometimes in those early days of being together, we talked till the windows brightened with dawn, telling each other our stories, another act of love.

My days now had a bounce to them, and my nights, the hike up the mountain road to Merrill's place put a spring in my step. And although Olson hadn't shown up yet and I was struggling along in my writing, everything had a lightness in it, even my mopping and dishwashing duties in the kitchen, so that in the afternoons as I swept up the dining hall and set up the tables for supper, I turned the music on the old Magnovox phonograph up to full blast and danced with the broom around and around the wide floor, I was so full of him.

At first, I overlooked the "small" things, however—warning signals that I willfully chose to ignore (the blinding love-pollen again): a perfectionist in everything, he angrily refused to drink my coffee after my first attempt at brewing it one morning to please him, calling it "terrible"; and how pissed he would be when I pronounced his native state, South Jersey- and Philly-style, with an "s" ending, as in "Illinoise," snottily quick to jump on me every time to correct me, which baffled me as to why he made such a big thing of it; or when, the first time I penetrated him with the cheapest lubricant available at Black Mountain, spit, I solicitously asked if I was "hurting" him, he murmured from the depths of the pillow, a bit sneerily, "I had to take a *lot* more from Herb," which is kind of funny now but wasn't then, given my shaky ego.

My mother, who I learned later, not knowing where I lived, had gone blindly searching the streets of Philadelphia in hopes of finding me after my father had kicked me out, now wrote me letters, wondering if I were coming home for a visit at Christmas. But the last thing I wanted to do then was leave the college, leave Merrill, actually, and hitchhike hundreds of miles north to spend time with a family I was still deeply conflicted about, particularly with my father, then hitchhike all the way back. I felt a twinge of childish guilt, that still powerful seduction of *home*, the surrender—the dying back into—and sentimentality of it, especially at that most seductively sentimental time of the year. But I resisted it, pushed it from my mind whenever it crooked its finger in allurement, knowing my path, knowing how little help there was back there, knowing there was much I had to learn to do on my own, and wrote my mother some excuse, some lie. I was content to stay where I was, my affection for Merrill deepening as winter deepened, the bare trees, now exposed, standing up smokily on the hills of the Seven Sisters, the air sharp with cold, and with the first heavy snow or two (no matter how deep, in that quickly moderating climate, much of it would be melted by noon next day), Merrill and I were snug under our featherbed, breathing in the scent of the sweetly aromatic oranges stuck with cloves Cissy Oppenheimer next door had given each of us for the holidays.

Another reason I didn't want to leave the college that winter were rumors circulating that Olson might be returning any day, and I certainly wanted to be there for that.

Malrey roasted beforehand, because of course she and Cornelia had the day off, an enormous turkey for Christmas day dinner, to cheer up those of us who'd stayed on over the holidays, Mary Fiore and several other students and faculty helping her in the kitchen. I spread clean white sheets from the linen closet in North Lodge on the tables in the dining hall that day to serve as tablecloths, and managed to scrounge up enough stubby candles for each table, all special for the occasion since we never used tablecloths or candles, not even for our dressup

Saturday night chicken dinners. Someone had gone out into the woods and gathered laurel and holly and pine boughs and cones to put along the mantle of the fieldstone fireplace and around the candles on the tables. And wire-rim bespectacled T. J., the newly-hired handyman, managed, despite his scrawniness and age, to haul in the hugest yule log anyone said they'd ever seen—it was the *first* I'd ever seen—which completely filled the mouth of the great hearth at the far end of the dining hall. He had lighted it at dawn so that by dinner time it burned ingot-red throughout the meal and for long after into the evening. How he got it to do *that* was another one of his many mysterious talents.

There was wine and all the trimmings. It was like a family all together, more so than I felt with my own family—I knew that day this was my home now. Even Merrill deigned to show up, which pleased me as we sat side by side, and he even managed, after a few glasses of wine, to be pleasant to the others at our table. The room glowed in the light of the candles and the blast-furnace gleaming of T. J.'s yule log and our own high spirits, as the cares of the problems and future of the college were forgotten for the day.

Merrill even helped me on the dishcrew afterward, his usually pallid cheeks flushed not only from the wine but the steam from the dishwasher, helped me so we could get back to Next-to-the-Last-Chance faster, which we did, hurrying up the hill in the cold dusk, our steaming breaths trailing after us. Once inside the barracks I now thought of as my home within the larger home of Black Mountain, we quickly undressed, tossing our clothes about the bedroom and tumbled onto the feather-bed to enjoy another delicious feast.

I was never so happy.

1953

Just prior to Olson's return, Wes Huss began holding an evening class in drama writing in the Conference Room downstairs in the Studies. Even though my main impulse was to write stories and poems, I was so eager to get started writing in a classroom setting and get some feedback, while awaiting Charles' imminent appearance, I joined the course with a handful of others sitting sparsely spaced around the huge conference table that took up most of the room.

Wes had a dry, utterly serious, intellectual approach to teaching, with an occasional subtle flash of humor. We discussed Brecht, Lorca, Molière, Ibsen and other playwrights and how they put a play together, or rather Wes and the others did, since I was all ears to learn. Particularly vocal was Duck (Donald Francis) Daley, there, I believe, on the GI Bill. He looked like a stereotypical Boston-Irish thug, with his close-cropped crew-cut, perpetual 5 o'clock shadow and toughly handsome Irish face with its cleft chin, his short but sturdily-built body perpetually in tight-fitting chinos and a worn brown suede jacket. Actually, he had an assertive and energetic intelligence in his darkly-lashed, sensitive blue eyes, was extremely well-read and articulate. Curiously enough, he was married to a baroness whom he had met in Austria after the war, a lean, intense chain-smoker, who loved to read English novels, particularly 17th century writer Samuel Richardson's *Pamela: or, Virtue Rewarded* and *Clarissa: or, The History of a Young Lady*, in nice weather sitting, and looking very American in her tight levis, on the lawn across from the dining hall. Duck, as I was to learn first-hand once Olson got back, and envied him for it, was truly one of Olson's "fair-haired boys," an apprentice writer whom Charles hoped to make into "an American Dostoevsky."

Coincidentally, after Olson's return, one of the number of writers he pushed as essential reading was Dostoevsky, whose novels in the library I immediately plunged into and became captivated with, particularly with the hot idea to make a one-act play for Wes' theater writing class from "The Grand Inquisitor" chapter in *The Brothers Karamazov*. Caught as I was then in the struggles of my own religious and spiritual doubts (Charles was fiercely fond of quoting Dostoevsky's saying, "My faith was forged in the fires of doubt"), I was quite taken with, and as shaken as, the saintly Alyosha (with whom I completely identified) when his brother Ivan inventively pits the Grand Inquisitor against Christ in questioning God's permitting human suffering to go on in the world. It was a complex theological question in, for naïve me, a seductively simple dramatic setting: a one-set Spanish prison cell at night, only two characters, and the ironic twist that Christ, in a second coming, is such a danger with his promise of the hope of freedom, especially to the masses of people who, the Grand Inquisitor cleverly posits, once losing their chains, would be so terrified of that freedom, they would beg for them back again. No, says the Grand Inquisitor to Christ, his Church of benevolent tyranny will continue to give the people bread and miracles, that's what they want, the fatherly hierarchs know that as Christ does not, and at dawn he will put Christ to death again to be rid of his threat to this orderly arrangement.

Pretty heady stuff, and in the hands of someone with pretty sophomoric insights and inabilities, a threat in my own right—and writing—since my conceit was simply to transcribe literally from fictional drama to set-piece drama Dostoevsky's great cynical and spiritual discourse between the utilitarian Inquisitor and the visionary Christ, making, finally, for no drama, and certainly no change for the better regarding the original. But so intoxicated was I with my puppy-like "understanding" of Dostoevsky's paradoxical underlying subtleties, I was too naïve to see this.

Wes, on the other hand, who gamely read the "adaptation" aloud in class one night, *all* of it, was not. Nor was the sharp-eyed, quick-witted Duck Daley. With looks of pitying tolerance,

Duck bluntly put down my approach, suggesting that merely to transcribe wasn't enough, that there was no advance or insightful variation on Dostoevsky, what drama there was was all still in *Dostoevsky's* prose, no thanks to me, and that I needed to learn more about what made drama drama, what made a play a play—and where was I in all this? Wes pretty much reiterated Duck's perceptions, a non-committal flatness in his eyes, a quiet, passive politeness from him, as well as from most of the others in class that night, in respect for my greenness, my wrong-headedness, I suppose, seeing it for what it was: a keenly enthusiastic but misguided, and misused, appropriated appreciation of a great 19th century novelist.

Singed as I was by that first timid outing, I learned from it, saw even more vividly my vanity and arrogance. That I had a lot to learn is what I learned that night.

Olson, when he heard after his return I'd taken on "The Grand Inquisitor," wanted to see what I'd done. Tremblingly, I handed it to him. After taking a quick look at it and seeing what little I'd done to change anything, he promptly handed it back saying that for it to be discussed in *his* writing class would be like "throwing you to the wolves."

Another lesson learned.

Winter barely gone and women in poke bonnets and long flour-sack dresses, living in the nearby mountains, stooping with gunny sacks to gather "simples" (wild herbs) growing along the roadside outside the college, to eat raw and to make their tinctures and tonics, their herbal medicines.

Opening the door to the sun deck at the rear of the Studies one afternoon to read in the sun, I saw a black king snake at least 9 feet long looping itself again and again up and over the left-hand railing, shedding its skin, the scales on the new skin shining sinuously in the sun, as the sheets of dead gray tissue floated to the ground several stories below. I came upon several more king snakes after that, engaged in the same graceful ritual, which I was told by Mary Fiore occurred every early spring. Another afternoon, walking down the road by Lake Eden, a car passed me heading in the direction of the county road. A few yards ahead of the slow-moving auto, stretched from head to tail across the road, lay another of the ubiquitous king snakes, drowsily sunning itself. The driver appeared not to see the snake, and after the car wheels rumbled over it, the snake stirred, its fat length even longer than the other king snakes I'd seen shedding their skins on the sun deck railing. It slithered slowly down into the marsh grass by the edge of the road, moving in the direction of the lake, its undulating, yielding body obviously unhurt by having just been run over by the four wheels of a huge sedan.

When Charles returned in early spring 1953, the spirits of all of us who were eagerly anticipating his coming back rose, as if the winter gloom that was lifting from the earth all around the Seven Sisters with the early return of spring was the same gloom lifting in ourselves as well.

The first few classes met in the afternoon in the back meeting room, because it was the warmest, of the office cottage, with its paintings by former painting instructors Jack Tworkov, Franz Kline, and Willem de Kooning hanging over the fieldstone fireplace and around the gray walls. With most of us students puffing away on our Home Runs and Picayunes (at 18 cents a pack—no cigarette tax in the Tarheel tobacco state—the cheapest butts available in Carroll Williams' little college store), and Charles all but chain-smoking his Camels, the air was soon thick with smoke. We were not permitted to open a window even so much as a crack since huge, rugged-looking Charles had the sensibilities of a newborn infant and could not abide even the slightest draft. Often, looking like a potentate, he sat in class with a ragged, out-at-the-elbows gray cashmere sweater balled up on top his large, balding head, to keep his brains warm, I imagined.

It had been well worth the wait. Charles, expansive, garrulous, all over the lot, did most of the talking. Listening to him was like riding a magic carpet anywhere in the imagination or the world (including his recent trip digging among the ancient Mayans in Yucatan with wife Connie on a shoestring archeological grant) or the universe, for that matter. But the old hands—Fee Dawson, Joel Oppenheimer (the fierce-featured poet from the Bronx and refugee from Cornell, whose father owned a luggage shop in mid-Manhattan), Dan Rice, Jorge Fick, Jonathan Williams (descendant of New England's Roger Williams and from a well-to-do Highlands, North Carolina, family and another refugee from the Ivy League, this time Princeton, and who was later to publish the first two volumes of Olson's *Maximus Poems* while stationed as a soldier in Stuttgart, West Germany), Donald "Duck" Daley, the future "American Dostoevsky," Boston-Irish variety, and Mary Fitton Fiore (Mary, a rarity in the class on two counts: (a) being the only female; (b) being the only non-smoker)—these Olson vets interjected on occasion their own energetic and argumentative questions and comments, talking about writers I'd never heard of (I took quick mental notes) and speaking about writing in a way that was more often than not so new and startling to me as to be incomprehensible. They all seemed to know a language I, and a few other newcomers, would have to struggle to learn. As a result, with Nell Rice helpfully supplying the locations on the shelves, I spent hours in the back of the library reading the books mentioned in the class, trying to learn the lingo, cramming on everything I could get my hands on by Pound and especially the poetry now, after first reading his prose in Jamestown, of William Carlos Williams, plus Frobenius' anthropology and folktales in *African Genesis*, and Jung's psychology—borrowing where I could what the small college library lacked, usually from the well-stocked bookshelves of generous Mary. And so, not only intimidated but shy in this boisterous, hurlyburly bunch, I listened hard and kept my mouth shut, becoming a sponge, soaking up as much as I could; listened hard even though I hardly understood anything Charles, or the others in the class, was saying; still sensing, even so, somewhere in some instinctive, knowing part of me that he had what I needed to know, that he had the answers for me, and the secret to my directions, going it on the intuitive trust of that alone.

One of the strict requirements for Charles' writing classes was that you had to bring a manuscript, otherwise you couldn't come in. I had stacks of them, not only those I'd brought down with me in my trunk, but also those I'd been busily accumulating on canary-yellow second sheets—the cheapest paper in Carroll's store—in my study after my stints in the kitchen, while waiting for Charles' return to the college.

Since he'd made some favorable comments on the story I'd shown him on the visit in June, I of course was looking forward to the same. I couldn't have been more trusting. I waited eagerly for his comments on the first story I handed in, and when he handed it back to me, his hasty, idiosyncratic scribblings in the margins in pencil were so indecipherable I had to ask Mary to help me interpret most of them. Mary was the expert decipherer on campus of Olson's handwriting. It took me some time to learn how to do it.

I was sorry I'd asked her help.

Olson's slangy comments were so snotty and scathing (and yet so accurate, as I came to see later), I was crushed. He found not one thing to praise in the entire piece. He even jeered at my spelling "cigarette" "cigaret."

Appraisals of my adolescent writings up till then had been

largely uncriticial—a few English teachers at Woodbury High School back in New Jersey, where I had my first published work, a serial, in the *White and Gold*, had been largely encouraging, tilting toward lavish praise. Although I must say when I shyly showed my oldest brother, Joe—who in World War 2 narrowly escaped torpedoing off Iceland while still in his teens—one of my stories written when I was still in grade school, a story filled with the palmettos and scrub oak of Marjorie Kinnan Rawlings' *The Yearling*, flora as foreign to South Jersey as giant sequoias, he sneered at it as heartily as Olson had this latest effort; needless to say, Joe never saw another story of mine. Olson, unfortunately, did. In the second story I handed in, the assault of his sneering hieroglyphics stayed pretty much the same.

Olson's initial response humbled me, but it also made me more determined: I listened harder in class; I read even more than I usually did, which was a lot; I worked harder and longer holed up in my study. But each canary-yellow manuscript came back filled with the same cryptic, disparaging remarks.

I'd never learn to be a writer after all.

Yet I stayed stubborn. I joined, unwittingly, the other handful of hardy hangers-on, who wrote and wrote, it seemed, in order to write something to please the master.

I don't recall any of my stories being read aloud in class by me or by Olson in those early days. (Everyone loved Charles to read his work aloud; since he read so magnificently he made, like any vocal artist, bad writing sound good.) That was a mercy I see now on Charles' part.

He was right: criticism, not only from Charles, but from all the older, more hardened student veterans, was unsparingly and brutally direct.

It took me some time to understand that that old saw, "Sometimes you have to be cruel to be kind," was operant in Charles' method; that I was being tested.

It also took a talk from Charles in the kitchen one afternoon to dishearten and tear me down some more, and yet curiously enough to inject in me more spine to succeed with him.

In the meantime, there were other messages, especially from Jorge, the painting and writing student from Detroit who'd got me kicked out of his room in South Lodge my first day at the college, and who after some time spent earlier in Mexico had returned to Black Mountain with his first name now spelled spanishly and ambled around wearing a sombrero, a serape (to stave off, he said, malarial chills he'd gotten South of the Border), faded Wrangler's jacket with levis stuffed into the tops of stout motorcycle boots, and sporting a jet black bebop goatee and a pair of large, very opaque cool jazz-style wraparound shades. He looked like a hybrid cross between Emiliano Zapata (whose recently released movie life, *Viva Zapata*, starring Marlon Brando, Jorge had raved about) and early American hipster out of his hometown Motown. As rumors spread about my awful writing, he used to secretly leave copies of paperback novels by Edna Best and Kathleen Norris (once even one by Fanny Hurst), all writers of popular sentimental romances (torch songs of victimized women without conscious aware-ness, "women novelists," in all that implied then, especially at male-dominated Black Mountain, as a macho slur), would leave such paperbacks on the writing desk in my study as a sneaky and sneering evaluation of my work.

"Enjoying your Fanny Hurst?" he'd smirk knowingly to my face, not caring that I knew it was him doing it.

Even so, when Jorge read one of his poems in class one night, his influences including not only William Carlos Williams but more recently Creeley, Olson asked which were the best lines in the poem, and when there was a long pause as everyone pondered it, I, who rarely opened my mouth, said without hesitation:

What do you want
that you would break
your head your heart
to learn

Given almost 50 years intervention of what the poem actually looked like, regarding line spacings and exact wording, I give
it here as closely as memory serves, with apologies to Jorge.

What has stayed vividly clear, however, was Charles' quick
look of surprise and grin of agreement. That was worth all the
nerve it took me to, for once, speak up.

Speaking of romance novels, those first months, there was a
guy named Dick Bishop, a slightly-built, bespectacled, ex-ser-
viceman living at the other end of Last Chance with his wife and
child, who dropped out of Olson's class, telling Olson he'd
decided to try his hand at writing romances that "made
money." Charles sneered at this, and even more so when
Bishop told him he'd bought one of the new-fangled electric
typewriters, the only one on campus, to help him in his new
ambition. Olson told him flatly: "That electric typewriter
might make you *type* faster, but it won't make you *write* better."

Like a handful of others, Bishop more and more retreated
into his living quarters up the hill, banging away on his new
machine. Not long after, he packed up and left with his family.

Fast takes on Olson's comments in and out of his writing
classes:

Charles' many useful tips. On Hemingway's spare use of dialog, using, in paraphrase, " 'Gimme two beers' " as an example.
"You can't beat it," he insisted, making the point H's prose, as
in a poem, wasted no time, no word.

Also helpful: Olson quoting William Carlos Williams saying: "not to copy nature, but to imitate nature."

In another class, Olson reading aloud Archibald MacLeish's poem "Ars Poetica," its title a bow to Roman poet Horace, and asking us what we thought of it, if we agreed MacLeish knew what he was talking about. The class hemmed and hawed but Olson wasted no time sneeringly dismissing its "definitions" of what poetry is, voicing particular scorn for the line that a poem is "dumb as old medallions to the thumb."

Another evening Charles read several of the new just-published *Pisan Cantos*, which Pound was continuing to compose in St. Elizabeth's Hospital in Washington, where he was locked up, and which he'd started in 1948 in the prison camp outside Pisa. Charles was especially amused by Pound saying "the moon is my pinup," chuckling that was just "Ez' " using World War 2 GI slang to "sound hip," and wasn't buying it. Then he held up one of the Cantos that had a large bold black Chinese ideogram amidst the text, which Pound spelled out as LING. Charles, pronouncing it loudly, asked us could we "read" it. As picture, as image, it looked so balanced I blurted out "harmony," Olson gesturing at me for more, till I finally said, "Sensibility," and Olson said, "Bingo!"

During that same class, we also discussed several Pound lines:

> Awareness
> restful and fake
> is fatiguing

with Charles emphasizing how phoniness in others robs you of energy.

Olson saying in another class, regarding a putdown of one's work (thinking of his own no doubt): "Well, if you don't want to dance with the writer, you don't want to dance. Nothing you can do about it."

Consolation for what lay ahead.

He was always generous about reading our writing aloud in class, did a credible job, intuitively bringing out the best in it, acting too no doubt out of the slab of ham in him, his love of performance enlivening all his classes, shamanic, really, enlivening all.

Charles telling us one night in class how he and Connie, hearing a mockingbird as they were out for a late-night walk in the streets of Washington. Charles was so entranced he plonked himself down on the curb, "Listening to this damned bird singing like crazy up in the tree at one in the morning!" With Connie beside him, the two of them listening delightedly for a long time.

Charles disliked the word "inexplicable," stumbled over it once in writing class, disgusted—said it was "a word should never be used."

Charles distastefully referring to radio in class as "that disembodied voice."

Olson, who pushed me, pushed all of us, to read Stephen Crane, but limiting it by asserting in class one night that Crane's "The Blue Hotel" was his "best" work and that the "opening waves scene" of "The Open Boat" had "merit." All the rest, he implied, we could ignore. I got so hooked on Crane, though, another spirit kin, I, disobeying the master as I often did (including with that other Crane, Hart), read everything, learning the use of careful eye, particularly taken with the sharpness of his detail in "An Experiment in Misery," notes Crane wrote when he, practicing his belief, after *The Red Badge of Courage*, of experiencing first-hand what he wrote, posed as a bum for a couple of weeks and panhandled and drank in the rotgut bars and slept in the fleabag flops on the 1890s Bowery. That scene was pretty much all still there in February 1954 when, on a work break from Black Mountain, I first wandered the area under the girders of the el, seeking traces of Crane—and Maxwell Bodenheim, 1920s bohemian poet and novelist who later peddled his poems for drinks, then eventually ended up murdered there, along with his third wife, by a one-time mental patient.

Charles and I teamed on a Saturday afternoon work crew hacking at the overgrown kudzu and bamboo weed with bolo knives in front of the Stables, where recently widowed Johanna Jalowetz's book bindery and painters' studios were, Charles asking me in one of our pauses in the hard, sweaty work, what I was reading, what writer I particularly liked. It just so happened I was reading The *Heart Is a Lonely Hunter* by Carson McCullers, whom I'd recently discovered, and when I told him, he sneeringly dismissed her as "*Saturday* night," and went on hacking away at the tall weeds.

I, while blushing at my naïveté, secretly agreed. However, once more disobeying the master, I just as secretly continued to read her, having some strong sense of kinship with her dark, twisted root of queerness (which I also felt pulled to in Tennessee Williams and Truman Capote, whose stories I had begun to read just before I came to Black Mountain, the only obliquely "gay" writings of the time passed by mouth and hand to hand on the underground gayvine). But at the college, I read such writers in secret since they were not "approved of."

Jonathan Williams, having recently spotted Capote sillily tipsy on a wrought-iron balcony in the French Quarter in New Orleans, was particularly mocking and sharp-tongued regarding that fey writer. (Curious that, as I write this, the late Carson McCullers' vanilla ice cream-white Victorian sits tall in the next yard, a house, by pure chance, I've lived next to now in South Nyack, New York, for 22 years.)

Reading at Olson's strong urging: Andre Malraux's powerful novels *Man's Fate* (1933) and *Man's Hope* (1937), and in conjunction with the latter, Edgar Snow's *Red Star over China*, and absolutely bowled over by the expert mix of powerful narrative and powerful ideology (I experienced the same mix later when Olson recommended D. H. Lawrence's 1923 novel, *Kangaroo*). What developed even more for me at Black Mountain was an enormous open, although often uncritical, hunger for reading, to know, to learn, to take it all in (just as images had always vividly flooded and fixed in my eyes, the "greedy eyes," as Lawrence once put it, accumulating clouds of images needing the discharge of lightning in writing or go mad), devouring all the words of those writers Olson particularly directed my way and said I should "saturate" myself in. Olson opening me, learning like lovemaking.

Man's Hope, which recounts Malraux's experience fighting for the Republicans in the 1936-1939 Spanish Civil War, came up in class one night with Olson, movingly, passionately, telling us "many American young men" of his generation in the late 1930s were caught in the dilemma of whether to chuck everything and go join the American Lincoln Brigade to fight fascist Franco in Spain—the fate of the world seen teetering on democracy vs. fascism—an agonizing and defining moral dilemma over whether to go or not, including himself, suggesting he was long troubled, as were others of that time, because he did not get to go.

n had high praise for his early mentor Edward Dahlberg, especially for his first novel, *Bottom Dogs*, which also had, most impressive to me, a cranky introduction by the critically fastidious D.H. Lawrence himself. It was a grittily told tale right out of Dahlberg's mid-western growing up, with a mother who ran a beauty parlor and struggled to support them both. Olson recommended we read it, especially, which I did, relishing the hard realities depicted that were written in vivid and colorful language.

But Olson sang even higher praises for Dahlberg's critical study *Do These Bones Live*, which he even more strongly urged everyone to read and which became, like D.H. Lawrence's *Studies in Classic American Literature*, something of another literary holy relic passed from student hand to student hand.

However, Charles had harsh words for Dahlberg's *Flea of Sodom*, which Dahlberg had been working on during his brief two-week teaching stint at Black Mountain back in 1948 (finally unable to stomach the student disrespect, he abruptly departed, recommending Olson as his replacement). With amused disgust in class one night, he said Dahlberg had finally retreated to a biblical paradise of "goat's tits and honey," and there was in his voice a sense he'd by this time given up on Dahlberg as a writer of any vital importance.

He then related, in his merrily venomous way, an anecdote about Dahlberg, whose satyr-like impulses with females on campus quickly spread. Dahlberg, as was his habit, had taken one of his more zoftig women students for a walk to "discuss" her writing, a student who'd been attracted to Black Mountain in the first place because of rumors she'd heard of its "loose" reputation, and who in fact lost her virginity at the hands of Dahlberg during the stroll, somewhere down in the marsh grass by the library, making it the high point—by whose report Olson didn't say—of her stay at the college.

Charles, continuing to feed me tips, intuiting my reading needs, suggested I look at Anzia Yezierska's 1925 novel *Bread Givers*, which I immediately got out of the library and read right through. I was deeply impressed with the struggles of Sara Smolinsky, Yezierska herself, a Jewish immigrant woman fighting to survive in the New World on the teeming, poverty-ridden Lower East Side of Manhattan in the 1890s, youngest daughter of a tyrannical rabbi father whose problems with him I could heartily empathize and often identify with:

". . . Only if they cooked for men, and washed for men, and didn't nag and curse the men out of their homes; only if they let the men study the Torah in peace, then, maybe, they could push themselves into heaven with the men, to wait on them there . . ."

I also powerfully understood her grinding poverty and her fierce ambition to make something of herself, her driven need to be a writer, to become independent from her domineering father and the constricting male-dominated traditions of Judaism, an overwhelming need to find work, which she did as an ironer in a laundry, to be able to find a room, and room, for herself, to live and grow and write in, away from the smothering influences of father and religion; experiences tracking similarities in my own young, father-dominated, Catholic life, so that my immediate identification with her and her writing was certainly understandable, Black Mountain the "room" I found as my escape from a stultifying homelife, that had been, finally, as with Yezierska herself, no life at all.

I read everything in Nell's library by Yezierska: *Hungry Heart and Other Stories* (1922), *Children of Loneliness* (1923), *Arrogant Beggar* (1927), and *All I Could Never Be* (1932); and when Charles suggested I write to her telling her of my appreciation, I was hesitant at first, wondering whatever could any of my words hold for her. But Charles was persuasive, and I did write to her in New York City where she still lived, and received several letters back, written in her large, bold hand, about how she had almost "killed" herself writing those early works, works that despite their eventual immense popularity in the 1920s and a Hollywood film deal with Samuel Goldwyn, were now out of print and largely forgotten.

Discovering her writing through Charles was yet another thread I needed to know in my own writing, the directness and simplicity of a prose style, with its complexity of content, open and honest, direct from experience and right from the heart—this, thanks to Charles, is what I learned from Anzia Yezierska, one of the many intuitive suggestions from him, as with Sherwood Anderson and Stephen Crane, that nudged me in directions I needed to go.

Olson telling us in class another night about a letter from Creeley in which Creeley related how he and Robert Hellman (who later replaced Creeley as writing instructor in 1955) had come by chance upon Picasso sitting at a sidewalk table at *Les Deux Magots* in Paris one afternoon. Creeley described "Picasso with owl eyes" and how their eyes locked, a mystical connection, the piercing eyes of Picasso boring in on Robert's one eye. Olson admitted it was a good story, but pooh-poohed it, wondering if Creeley was making more of that look than it really was, suggesting it might've all happened in Creeley's imagination, perhaps under the whimsical influence of the name of the cafe itself. He further suggested he'd "trust" Hellman's version (whatever that was) more than Creeley's, implying Creeley would make it more a "Creeley experience" than the occurrence warranted, trusting Hellman, the "realist," over Creeley, the "fantasist."

Charles telling a group of us on the dining hall porch that spring of 1953 about his uncanny, and finally scary, ability to read tarot cards, and how, full of himself, he would in the past read the cards for anyone on campus who asked him.

But one day he divined in the cards of a student who'd asked Charles to read for him death by suicide, and Charles prudently withheld that information from him. When, a year later in 1950, Olson learned that this student had indeed killed himself, he gave up the cards forever.

Charles in writing class on another night describing how male inmates in Nazi concentration camps (information he'd got from artist Corrado Cagli who, with his U. S. Army artillery unit, helped liberate Buchenwald) slept pressed 3, 4, 5 tightly together in their tiers of wooden bunks. Olson looked at me quick, direct, as if I would understand the levels of that. I was so startled, hit by the homoerotic implications, I looked away just as quickly.

He then countered the popular notion promulgated by English historian Arnold Toynbee et al. that the Holocaust was truly evil because of "how many potential Beethovens, Bachs," etc., great artists, thinkers, etc., "were lost to the world because of it." Olson insisted that that wasn't the point, that a handful of potentially "great" perished—it was in the lives, the human lives, regardless of that alleged hierarchical and cultural "importance." To him it was a perverted, elitist notion as wrong-headed as the myths of racial supremacy at the root of the Holocaust, at the root at that very moment of all that lay beyond the Gatehouse of Black Mountain College, guaranteeing another.

"How do we defend ourselves, any of us, from what's just over the hill?" he asked.

Roadside, the cottage around the bend on the road to the farm, just beyond the footbridge, where we'd stayed on our visit back in June, burned one evening while we were all at supper my first winter at Black Mountain. Joe and Mary Fiore lived on the second floor, while Bea and Wes Huss and new baby David occupied the first. Joe and Wes took turns tending the furnace, and it had been Wes' turn that night. In banking the fire before going down to the dining hall for supper—Bea and the baby and the Fiores had gone on ahead—Wes either left the damper or the furnace door open, or both, which was believed started the fire. By the time it was discovered, we all raced up from the dining hall but because there were no fire hoses or hydrants or fire-fighting equipment of any sort on campus, there was little we could do but stand and watch as the old, creosoted, wood-shingled building went up in a ball of flame, smoke and sparks billowing into the surrounding pine trees, illuminating the darkness in a fierce orange glow. There was fear the fat sparks might ignite the pines and then the roofs of nearby cottages, Meadows Inn up one slope and Streamside down the other.

At one point, Natasha came by carefully but quickly leading her mother, tiny Madame Goldowski, by the arm over the tangle of tree roots, Madame murmuring excitedly, "*Dépêchons! Dépêchons!*" hurrying away from Meadows Inn where she'd been dining with Natasha and Eric, fearful it, too, might catch fire.

By the time the Swannanoa and Black Mountain volunteer fire departments, miles away down in the valley, got there, the place was engulfed in flames, and with no pumper and no hydrants there was little they could do but stand by in their asbestos gear and watch helplessly like the rest of us.

The Husses and Fiores lost everything, of course; Mary and Joe a number of wedding presents from their recent marriage, Mary more annoyed at the loss of a batch of new clothes she'd just purchased.

Wes looked taller and gaunter than ever, as the flames he was watching flickered over his stricken face. He was so broken up, and you could see in those eyes the responsibility for what had already been whispered as common knowledge by now among us, that his mistake had caused the fire. Bea and the baby stood near him, and directly behind him loomed Olson, his hand comfortingly on one of Wes' hunched shoulders.

When the fire had finally burned itself out and I'd returned with my dorm mates to the top of South Lodge, all of us talking desultorily about the fire, Olson suddenly appeared in the doorway, surprising since I'd never known him to climb the stairs to our dorm before. He ducked his great head to get through the door and then went from one to the other of us, saying in a quiet, urgent voice, "Wes is in a bad way. Do you have any whiskey? It might calm him down."

With money so scarce, nobody did—except me. It just so happened that a few days before on a trip to Asheville, with Mary probably, I plonked down the few bucks needed for a fifth of County Fair bourbon, the cheapest booze, Dan Rice had told me, you could get in the state-run liquor store.

It was now hidden away under my underwear in the bottom drawer of my dresser, for future Saturday night parties.

But for some reason, I kept mum, feeling a rush of confused guilt but still murmured not a word, thinking, cheap as it was, how much that bourbon had cost me, but mainly wanting it only for myself. An ominous sign I didn't comprehend then, my silence baffling to me, not wanting to help a man in pain by simply fishing the bottle out of my drawer and handing it over to Charles, in an act of simple generosity I would have done immediately had it been any other request.

Charles left empty-handed, still looking grim and troubled like the rest of us over the loss of Roadside, which was even more catastrophic given the school's financial problems; and obviously worried about Wes as he ducked out through the door again, while I stood frozen with guilt but yet quietly glad the bottle was still safely hidden—a sign that was to haunt me for a long time after and to reach finally a bitter realization in the years to come.

Fortunately for the Husses, biology teacher Victor Sprague, soured by now on Black Mountain, and perhaps by too much sour mash whiskey, soon departed with his wife, which enabled Wes and Bea and baby David to move into the Sprague's white clapboard house with dark green trim just beyond Mrs. Jalowetz's place. Mary and Joe were soon able to move into the student-designed and -built sizable one-room Minimum House (built at a minimum cost of $1,000) at the turn in the road to the farm, its one wall of glass overlooking the mountain stream that rushed down throughout the campus.

The kitchen was hard work too, but unlike the work at the farm, I could manage washing dishes, sweeping and mopping floors, taking out the garbage, and setting tables. Besides students working on the college farm and the roads, the grounds and buildings, another part of the work program was students taking turns on the dish crews as well, and that was part of my job too, to see that people signed up on the schedule posted beside the kitchen door, and that they showed up on the days assigned. The latter part was no easy task, and the hardest part of the job sometimes at free-spirited and lackadaisical Black Mountain: the monotony of trying to track down helpers and hearing "Oh, I didn't know it was *my* day for dishes," and "Are you sure it's my turn?" got pretty wearing. Some of the students who'd been there awhile were the worst offenders at trying to weasel out of the job by ducking out after meals and hiding in their studies.

So, twice a day, after lunch and supper (and occasionally in a pinch after breakfast, if the crew didn't show), with my rubber spatula, I scraped the leavings of dirty plates through the stout black rubber ring built into the wide stainless steel drainboard by the huge sink, underneath which was a large garbage can to collect the leavings—and my job to empty—and fed wooden racks stacked with dirty dishes and cutlery through the steam and boiling spray of the World War 2 army-surplus automatic dishwasher. It was hot, sweaty, dirty work, like the farm labor, but at least this was work I could handle.

After washing the lunch dishes, I mopped the kitchen and swept the dining room, set the tables and arranged the chairs in the dining room for supper, while I played classical records on the old floor-model Magnavox phonograph down beside the great stone fireplace. In the beginning of my days on the job, I listened to Beethoven, Brahms and Bach (romantic resonances of Chautauqua still reverberating in my ears), then later switched to Telemann, Ravel, Mozart, Scarlatti, whatever was there in the stacks of old 12-inch 78 rpm classical albums (LPs hadn't hit Black Mountain yet) stored in heaps near the phonograph. I also played music I hadn't heard before, Prokoviev and Bartok. As I rolled my trolley cart of dishes around the tables or pushed my long broom over the wide expanse of floor, I had the Magnavox going full blast, the music booming out over the lake on one side and out the screen doors to the road on the other. Sometimes as it played, I'd drop everything and, thanks to Huss' theater class, jump around the room in a free-form dance.

Connie Olson used to like to bring baby daughter Kate down of an afternoon, and they'd sit in the grass across the road in front of the wild rose bushes and listen to the music pouring out the open doors and windows of the dining hall. Sometimes Mary Fiore, or Bea Huss, bringing her little son, David, or the painting student Dorothea Rockburne, carrying her infant daughter, would come down from her and Carroll Williams' apartment in North Lodge, and they would all socialize while listening to the music, which pleased me as I worked and danced about inside, that we were listening to the same music

oying it, like an informal concert, a small brightness for
he work routine.

nie told me several times how much she liked the music
and thanked me for playing it. But Charles, who had an opinion
on everything and was never shy about vocalizing it, once hearing her say that in my presence, sneered, critical of my choice of
music (which was often no choice at all, since I stuck on the
turntable whatever album was at hand). He pointedly implied
that I had much to learn about music, which was certainly true.
It was even truer that Olson had a gigantic need to be an
"authority" on everything, even that which he knew little
about—but this I only came to learn later.

But there was also in it, in his tone, a tinge of jealousy, that
Connie had paid me a compliment for some inconsequential
thing I did but which gave her enjoyment, and Charles seemed
to resent this. As always, wanting to please him, I had wished
Connie had not thanked me while he was around, giving him
the opportunity to shoot me down yet one more time.

Some time later, when we were returning from a movie
which starred William Holden at the Roxy in Swannanoa,
Connie casually remarked that she found Holden "sexy," and
Charles, jealous of a celluloid fantasy it seemed, had to instantly
put him down, muttering Holden wasn't so hot as an actor.
There was, I was beginning to see, a tremendous need in
Charles to always call the shots, to always be on top, a sugges-
tion of his contrariness with her in his poem of this time (1953)
"Common Place": ". . . And I, to be irritable, had corrected
[Con] . . ."

Then too: One pleasant twilight in summer, after supper, as I
was coming down the road from the Studies Building and
approaching Lake Eden, I could hear Charles' booming laugh,
even from that distance, echoing over the water from the
screened-in porch that jutted out over the south side of the
lake. He was sitting at a table with someone, long after supper

and the dishes had been washed and the kitchen closed, as was often his habit. What he was laughing at, I saw as I got closer, was Connie standing in the prow of the old weather-beaten, splintery community rowboat a few yards out in the lake, trying to pole it ashore with clumsy difficulty, as it had no oars. Kate, who was around two then, was sitting solemnly in the middle seat, her earnest dark eyes focused on her mother's awkward maneuverings to steer the boat in shore; no easy trick for anyone inexperienced (as I had found out myself), since the reeds grew thick there and made the cut of water to the landing spot very narrow and hence chancy.

Charles' laughter continued to ring out. As I got closer I could see him now through the screening of the porch, head thrown back, tipped back in his cane-bottomed chair, long legs spread, huge hands plonked on his kneecaps, thoroughly amused at Connie's lack of even the barest "seamanship," he who at 26 had gone to sea for three weeks on the swordfishing schooner *Doris M. Hawes*, 190 miles off his hometown, Gloucester; he who had once beamingly noted with pride how well Connie "took to sailing" with him off Lerma on the coast of Yucatan during his recent Mayan digs. The face of the person sitting beside Charles was a dark scrutiny behind the rusty screening, probably Wes Huss, who sometimes had one-on-one talks with Charles after supper, but Charles, in between shouting instructions to Connie, was sharing his merriment in sly asides to whoever it was.

As I approached nearer, I wanted to help her but something stopped me. Then Connie, exasperated, her slender fair throat reddening, hitched up her skirts to her thighs and leapt out of the boat and into the muddy water, standing kneedeep in it a little ways out from shore. Bending over, she tried to pull the awkward rowboat ashore—as I've said, she had one of the most sensitive faces I have ever seen, registering even the barest nuance of emotion, and now her features were a mixture of

ınd fear and bent pride. She was fearful with good rea-
nce in that particular marshy area of the lake copperheads
ater moccasins, not to mention the odd cottonmouth,
which in the past few years had begun to make an appearance in
the region, were seen swarming daily.

I don't know why this image of Connie stays so clearly in my
mind when a thousand other images of Black Mountain are
gone forever from memory. It brought to the surface a conflict
in myself regarding Charles, obviously a powerful influence on
many of us students (especially the male students), whose own
attitudes about women couldn't help but affect each of us in
some way or another. And I think it was that, why I hesitated to
help Connie, fearful of appearing to take sides, of arousing yet
one more time the displeasure of Charles, whose favor I needed
at that time more than I did Connie's.

Connie, after much pulling and heaving with the pole—the
water in Lake Eden was shallow there, the keel of the boat
scraping along the lake bottom, and the mud being like viscous
sludge made it even harder—finally got the bow on a piece of
dry shore, enough of it so that it wouldn't drift into the water
again. Picking up Kate, who had toddled to the prow, she carried her off in her arms through the tall marsh grass, heading
toward the Olson's apartment in South Lodge, in no way
acknowledging Charles' taunting laughter, eyes set straight
ahead, her cheeks hotly flushed, not even looking toward the
dining porch.

I could hear Charles' laughter dying away as I passed by the
back door of the kitchen, watching Connie marching off ahead
of me, still clutching Kate.

The hysteria of kitchen cleanup whenever the Buncombe
County health inspectors showed up in a surprise visit. Malrey
Few, as head cook, her glasses slipping down her bridgeless
nose, was the one who often confronted them. She was very

polite and helpful, showing them around, with just a tad of impish gleam in her eye, while Cornelia, her helper, took a powder into the storage room to hide her homemade peach brandy, and to quickly tidy up behind the scenes whatever she could, during which time Malrey stalled the inspectors in the kitchen. If they came while I was washing dishes, I made sure to put more elbow grease into cleaning up, putting an extra spit and polish on everything, scared out of my wits I'd be blamed if the place was shut down and I'd be sent packing back to the farm.

They *always* found a number of offenses to cite us for, generally overall lack of A-1 cleanliness (an impossibility where three meals a day were prepared with primitive equipment and with student work crews whose main object was to get out of the kitchen as quickly as possible, as I'd discovered when I took over that job). But there were often specific unsanitary citations, such as the rough stone cylinder in the potato peeling machine not being clean enough, or unsanitary drains or lids missing on some garbage cans, the grease traps in the sinks not emptied, stove hood greasy, or, given the abundant wildlife population in the surrounding mountainous wilderness, numerous rodents in the food storage rooms. The inspectors would always give us a few days to correct the problems, threatening to close us down if they weren't.

The first time such an inspection occurred when I'd first started working in the kitchen, once the inspectors left, Cornelia had a snort of her homemade brandy to relax her nerves, and then, along with Malrey, was quite gleeful, with relief no doubt, the pair of them laughing about the whole thing so merrily, as if there was nothing to worry about, they'd been through this terror so many times before, I began to relax and join in their laughter.

Everyone, students and faculty, including Malrey and Cornelia, pitched in with high good humor, and for several days we scoured and polished and mopped, even washed the windows. You never saw the place so spotless, at least by Black Mountain College standards. When the health inspectors returned, we all held our collective breaths until, grudgingly it always seemed, they would issue the kitchen about the lowest rating you could get, I suspected, short of a shutdown, similar I imagined to the "C" rating that I often saw, because you publicly had to post it, in the sleaziest, most vermin-infested greasy spoons along the rural roads of North Carolina when I hitchhiked.

None of us cared about that, though; we were always so relieved we'd scraped by one more time and could get on with our work and our lives, not to mention our meals, at least till the next inspection.

Olson's table in the dining hall was the most popular, and many students, as well as some faculty, jockeyed for a chair at it. Except for old-line faculty, such as biology teacher Victor Sprague, dour-faced as if always sitting in judgment (and always appearing a little soddenly drunk), and his overly chirpy wife (another woman on campus with dread not far beneath the surface of her dark eyes); and physicist/chemist Natasha Goldowski, on the rare occasions she did make an appearance in the dining hall, who wanted a more academically structured Black Mountain, and saw Olson's vision for a vital arts-centered college as a threat. It was also a popular table because it often ended up, even in lean times, with the most food. Charles' gargantuan appetite has been well-documented, and it is no exaggeration. Food was extremely important in his life, and he ate copious amounts of it, keeping up a steady stream of conversation as he ate. Despite his appetite, his eating habits were quite restrained, refined, even, as was much else about him. He often managed to get refills for his table by personally going into the kitchen, meat platter in hand, and charming cook Malrey, a woman, given her nickels-and-dimes food budget, not easily swayed. But when Olson turned on the full suavity of his charm, you were as good as a goner, and after Malrey would put up a mock protest, wagging her finger up in his face as her glasses slid down the bridge of her tiny nose from the kitchen steam—she eventually took to holding them in place with a Bandaid stuck to her forehead—Charles often came away with what he wanted. (As finances got leaner, there were increasing meatless meals, which meant the "lentilburger" was cooked up by ingenious Malrey.)

Between the eating and the talk, meals usually lasted longer at Olson's table than at any of the others. Often, I and my dish-washing crew were almost finished when the dirty dishes would arrive from Charles' table. One night, the animated talk and prolonged dining went on well beyond the usual time. My crew and I had finished cleaning up and were only waiting now for the soiled dishes from Olson's table at the rear of the dining hall (one of the kitchen and County Health Department rules was you couldn't leave dirty dishes in the sink), so I told the crew to go and waited patiently at first, eager as I was to get cleaned up and back to my study to continue working on a story I was writing. Finally, others at Charles' table began to notice me waiting by the dishwashing machine through the large serving window and remarked on it. Charles, still chewing and talking away, suddenly stopped and boomed out in a voice loud enough so I'd be sure to hear it, "I'm more important than any fucking dishwasher!"

His inconsiderateness pissed me off at the time, but I later came to agree that he was right. What I should've done was left the dirty dishes and said to hell with it, because my story was more important than any dirty dishes, even Olson's.

But I had to finish my job.

I wasn't so clear about it then, and I have to admit, fear, often unadmitted, ran my life at the time. Starting at home, I'd done everything double, everything just right, especially to please my demanding father, for fear of being thrown away, for fear of being thrown out if I didn't, but nothing I did was ever right enough to suit him, and I was tossed out in the end anyway. Irrational as it was, that fear was still very strong in me at Black Mountain: I was very hung up on—very meticulous about—doing my job just right, because I was afraid they were going to send me back to the farm, or worse, take away my work scholarship and kick me out. I'd begun to feel that I'd really found a home, difficult and frustrating as it was at times, and those same fears of my childhood were just as strong here in this second, more meaningful home.

More often than not, I buried my pride and my anger for fear of getting thrown out if I wasn't a good boy—a good little queer child, really, who knew he'd better watch his step.

Charles didn't seem to know what to do with me. His exasperation with my, to him, all but nonexistent progress in my arduous, confused and often painful apprenticeship as a writer could be measured by the increasingly scathing remarks he scrawled on my manuscripts and the fact that he had not yet seen fit to have me read any of my work aloud in class.

Outside the back screendoor of the kitchen in Dinner Bell Circle one sunny afternoon, his eyes boring in on me, Olson spoke bluntly about my early callow writing: "Rumaker, you gotta stop sucking the cock of your own experience!"

I was stunned by the image (with its mighty queer, not to mention autoerotic, resonances), a right-left punch to all the ambiguities it struck in me. Yet I knew what he meant and later realized he was right, regarding pathological narcissism, and the need to move out of my fearful solipsism—ego, in short: move out, show what I had, pass it around, be nervy, open—all the things he had that I so desperately wanted, was willing, trying, to learn.

What he said that day really shook me up, another crucial

shaking from the master shaker, jolting me onto my path.

An even more severe tremor, however, was not far along the way.

One day after lunch, as I was tying on my apron, getting ready to turn on the dishwasher, Olson came into the kitchen, trailed by Fee Dawson. Leaning his massive bulk on an elbow on top of the metal dish shelves, he pulled me over to have a talk, the gist of which was what I already knew: that I was a green sprout, totally ignorant and naïve as a writer and I needed to smarten up.

"You don't even know *how* to write *English!*" he exclaimed, and in the next breath, in one of his dizzying shifts, "But I'd give a million bucks for your innocence—I wish I had it!"

Then he said I needed to read, what did I read? And when I told him, besides most of the books mentioned in his class, I'd most recently read the writers I'd discovered at the Prendergast Library in Jamestown, New York, that past summer, Proust and Joyce and William Carlos Williams—his eyebrows shot up when I mentioned Williams—he was impressed, even though Proust and Joyce were not writers who "fed" him, to use Olson's own word. He seemed even more impressed when I told him I'd read Rimbaud's *A Season in Hell* and *Illuminations* which, as noted earlier, I'd discovered when prowling the midtown book stores in Philly while I was living in a $7-a-week room in the redlight district behind Independence Hall, after my father kicked me out of the house.

Still, he said he felt stymied, that he didn't know what to do with me. "Saturate yourself in Dreiser," he said, no doubt remembering my story on abortion from the summer visit. "Saturate yourself in Sherwood Anderson for the limpidity of his style, and Stephen Crane." He emphasized again Crane's "The Blue Hotel," "the best thing he ever did."

Then, lifting his arms and shrugging, looking me straight in the eye, he said, "I can't help you because I don't love you."

That took me aback. But only for a moment. I said to myself fiercely, still remembering the exact words to this day, "*I'll make you!*"

I wasn't giving up. I knew what I had to do, and Charles knew what I had to do, even if he was losing patience that I'd ever get to do it.

But I wasn't giving up.

Then Charles turned to Fee, one of the old hands at the college and one of Olson's on-again off-again fair-haired boys, and turned me over to him, saying, "Fee'll help you get hip, Fee'll smarten you up."

Then he walked out, with Fee in tow, leaving me to do my dishes.

But I didn't want substitutes.

Although quieter about it, sneakier, really, I could be just as resistant as Fee in fending off unwanted intruders and intrusions, as Fee himself showed so strongly in Wes' theater class; and although Fee's intentions were good, his loud and bossy attentions offended my sensibilities, driving me deeper into my hole. Over the next few weeks, his attempts to take me in hand and make me a real Black Mountaineer were a nuisance more than anything. Fee just didn't know the way I needed to go. I spent a lot of time ducking him.

And as for Charles not "loving" me, I had already lost one father, and although I hadn't the words for it then, I knew instinctively that Olson was a "father-spirit," whether he liked it or not, the seasoned wise man who had much to teach me, and being spirit kin, as the Native Indians know, he was more important to me than my own biological father, who had cast me out.

It wasn't going to happen a second time; I wasn't going to lose him.

With so much reading of Jung (and later sharing my dreams

for interpretation with Jung's associate, Maria von Franz, who'd arrived from Zurich for Olson's three-week seminar, the "Institute of the New Sciences of Man," in that winter of 1953), and hearing Olson talk so much about Jung in class, I had a dream which, urged by Charles to write down our dreams in order to remember more of them, as Jung directed, showed clearly what was going on downstairs in my unconscious at that time:

"A door opens and an aged black woman ushers me into a long dingy corridor. She motions for me to follow her and leads me down the hall to a flight of steps. We climbed the stairs and at the top, standing before a dark door, he stood, tall and large. He wore a long voluminous black robe and on his head was a black turban with a gold crescent moon. He stood solemn and erect, a quiet dignity. He did not speak. The ancient black woman bowed to him, then, backing away, nodded to me, motioning I should approach him."

This Wise Man, one of Jung's archetypes, as I later learned through talking with von Franz and listening to Charles himself in studying Jung, was, of course, Olson. He was Fee's spiritual father too, as he was to so many of the lost sons who had wandered into Black Mountain, strays looking for a way, and a place, to be, many of us not unlike the stray dogs that wandered onto the campus from the surrounding hills, whipped curs, fiercely angry and—as with the pack of snarling dogs Madame had taken in up at Streamside—just as fierce to find a home.

But I didn't want to settle for a mere "sibling" like Fee to teach me the ropes, I wanted the real thing—we all wanted the real thing. And admission, I was beginning to learn, into that charmed inner circle meant losing a lot—for starters, the crumbs in my eyes and "getting the wax out of your ears," as Olson always said. It also meant getting a skin, getting toughened, tempered. It meant waking from the sleep of my mother and to quit running from my father.

But I was learning, learning what Charles already knew, that I had a lot of crap to lose before my eyes and ears would be cleansed enough to see and hear clearly, with "limpidity," that favorite word of Olson's, before I would be able really to write.

Much of my early time at Black Mountain was spent in this process of elimination.

One thing I really needed to learn was to slow down.

After the precise regimentation of Rider College, with its strict rules and regulations, its attendance requirements, exams, grades, its classroom bells going off at the precise beginning and end of each 50-minute class; with all this ant-like activity, plus the easy distractions and quick pace of even such a small city as Trenton—not to mention my earlier time spent in the even more distractingly larger city of Philadelphia—the slower, surer rhythm of Black Mountain took some getting used to: Where the dinner/fire gong out back of the kitchen door, that Cornelia the cook banged on with a hammer to call us to meals, was the only bell on campus; where there were no grades or exams to fret over and where a student went to classes only when and if he or she chose; where, as noted, the only three rules of the school were that students couldn't carry firearms, hop freight trains, or if an unmarried female student got pregnant, she and the male student involved had to marry or else leave campus (that particular 1950s propriety didn't, of course, apply to faculty members, given, for example, Charles and Connie's unmarried state, which few knew at the time).

One of the most precious things at Black Mountain was *time*—time to do one's work, and the space to do it, time and space to take risks, to succeed, or fall flat on your face with no opprobrium. (No wonder the place was so attractive to genius, to an Olson, to an M. C. Richards, to a Wolpe, a Buckminster Fuller, to all the others pulled to those mountains.) But for some students, after being told what to do for years in conven-

tional classroom settings, it was hard for them to adj
to developing the responsibility and discipline of working on
their own, and those who couldn't adjust, left, defeated and
sometimes embittered, unable to get used to the freedom, the
almost anarchic freedom, really. Despite my having to work, as
it sometimes turned out, five to six days a week in the kitchen
and dining hall, and my going to classes, often *long* classes, several times a week, I still had plenty of time to write and read and
even socialize. The days, like space, had quite a stretch at Black
Mountain.

But early on, I, too, had to give up expectations of being told
what to do every minute of the day. I knew I had begun to succeed at this when one sunny afternoon, after my chores in the
kitchen were done, I sank down on the pallet in my study and,
folding my hands behind my head, stared out the wide windows, just enjoying the clear autumnal blue of the sky—and *not*
feeling guilty about it, and *not* feeling that I had to be up and
doing something, that I had to be somewhere, out of the old
habits up North of doing just to be doing.

Away from the northern antheap of Rider and the cities, I was
learning not only the slowed pace of the school itself but also
the slow time of the Seven Sister Mountains, so that my movements, even my heartbeat, became slower, yet, paradoxically,
my eyes and mind became sharper; began to perceive—that
heartbreakingly blue sky, or a foxglove in a shadowy glade up in
the hills, or one of those orange blue-spotted salamanders
that I mentioned earlier amidst the corn stalks, the rugged rock
and heave of the mountainous earth itself as I hiked over it and
began to receive—the new ideas, the new ways of seeing
and thinking about things that streamed from Olson's mouth
and huge cranium (talk about "containing multitudes"!), and
from the mouths of the others, Wes Huss and Lou Harrison,
Joe and Mary Fiore, and Stefan Wolpe and Hilda Morley, M. C.
Richards, ideas and visions that seemed to stream everywhere,

tumbling and echoing from ridge to ridge over all of the hundreds of acres of land that was Black Mountain, ideas and ways of seeing and being that would in years to come stream everywhere beyond its borders.

After my unsuccessful tutorial with Madame, learning antiquated but crude 19th century French with a White Russian accent, I, along with the other students, took my turn being called into the meeting room in the rear of the registrar's cottage to be interviewed by the faculty for signing up for prospective classes in the next term. Olson, Huss, Wolpe (who had replaced Lou Harrison, much to Merrill's bitter disappointment), and Hazel Frieda Larsen were there, perhaps a few other faculty, including Flola Shepard, the language teacher, who when I said I wanted to study French with her, asked me why. Confronted by her habitual and unnerving skeletal grin, her cold, precise articulation and steely, intelligent gaze, her spare, ascetic manner and dress—she was most always clothed in Puritan-gray, as gray as her severely cut bobbed hair, in cotton jackets and skirts that she appeared to have made herself—I got tonguetied. I had always found her more than a little intimidating, and no less so at that moment under her direct questioning that day in the meeting room. It threw me, and I was unable to put into words what I really wanted to say, which was that I wanted to study proper French, not Madame's antiquated French with a White Russian accent (although I was reluctant to "rat" on Madame), wanted to learn properly so that I'd be able to read, however limitedly, in the original, my first French loves, Rimbaud and Baudelaire (besides Rimbaud, I'd also picked up George Dillon and Edna St. Vincent Millay's translation of *Les fleurs du mal—Flowers of Evil—* in my Philly wanderings), plus Stendhal, whom I'd grown to love when we read his novels in Olson's class, not to mention Molière, scenes from whose plays we were doing in Wes' acting workshop. And another deeply-rooted impulsion, if a trace of heritage had any-thing to do with it—I'd always been drawn to all things Gallic—perhaps, learned via my Great-Aunt Ida, that "taint" of French blood my mother always whispered about on her side of the family, as if it were an obscenity, the English Marvel side through her father, Robert (a name which, years later, a family-tree obsessed student of mine traced back to Merville in north-ern France).

But faced with Flola's probing cross-examination, her precise, flinty directness, her overly scrupulous articulation, I got flus-tered and stumbled and stammered.

Charles suddenly cut in, coming to my rescue. "Perhaps," he said flatly to Flola, "he wants to take French because he *wants* to take it."

Flola, her straight bobbed hair bobbing as she rapidly nod-ded, grinned her bony-skulled grin and backed off.

I was most grateful for Charles' intervention.

Saturday night parties were as much a tradition at Black Mountain as Southern fried chicken for Saturday night supper, where for that one night in the week everybody put on shoes and dressed up: the women in dresses and stockings, the men in ties and jackets. Booze for the party was supplied, with help from painter Basil King, by the student home-brew master on campus, Bert Morgan, another work scholarship student on the farm, who'd turned his study into a mini-brewery, cottage industry-style, and did a brisk business with rows of Mason jars fermenting away on every available square inch of bookshelf space. At two bits or so a jar, more than competitive with Ma Peak, this illegal little enterprise helped pay for cigs and his stay at the college.

A collection, though, was taken up for the hard liquor, moonshine provided fresh from the still at five bucks a gallon by the farmer down the road, whose brother was the local sheriff in dry Buncombe County. The sack of nickels and dimes and crumpled dollar bills would be tied to a fence post down from the Gatehouse, and the moonshining farmer would tool along in his old Ford, snatch the money off the post, then toss the cork-plugged jug of moonshine in the tall grass of the ditch, for us to run out and retrieve, once he'd banged off down the county road.

Moonshine punch, mixed, as discovered by M. C. Richards, in a base of strong, cold tea, cut the diesel-fuel flavor.

One afternoon during one of Olson's writing classes, a horrendous explosion boomed throughout the Swannanoa Valley, rattling all the windows in the Studies Building. We all thought at first it was the dining room across Lake Eden must have blown up, but we found out later it was our moonshining farmer's still had exploded. Tragic news, not that anyone was killed, but that our source of illicit hooch was cut off. Not for long. The still was back in business a few days after.

Practically everybody living on campus showed up at our Saturday night parties. The music—Miles Davis and Charlie Parker and Bud Powell and Stan Getz (whom Ed Dorn didn't like)—blared away on the Magnavox phonograph in its walnut cabinet, or on one of the new LP record players borrowed for the occasions, and everybody danced to it or listened, really *listened*, to the music in a very serious, if stoned, way—so typically Black Mountain, so typically the attentions of most of the people there, at the cutting edge, ahead of what was being broadcast in the rest of the land.

Charles, though, rarely ever showed up. He and Connie stayed home with baby Kate, and often, returning tipsy to South Lodge after a party, I could look up and see him in the big lighted window of their apartment among the pine boughs, reading or scribbling or hear the furious tapping of his big Royal typewriter. The first party I recall him being at was in 1953, the first time he heard the Miles Davis record Jorge Fick had brought back with him from Detroit. (Jorge also later introduced us to the smoky-voiced singer Chris Connor.) Olson stood hunched low over the phonograph, long arms lifted at his sides, the huge bulk of his body held absolutely still, great head cocked to one side, eyes snapped wide, ear down to the music, leaning in, listening intently to Davis' squeezed sound, a serious and wondering look on Olson's face, like a child or a deaf person hearing recorded music for the first time. When the record hissed to an end, he demanded in a breathless, excited voice, "*Who is that? Who is that?*" When Jorge, happy to be in the forefront of things and deliver the information, sidled up in his black leather biker boots to tell him, Olson insisted Jorge play it again.

I never saw Charles drinking at our parties, I think he hardly drank at all then, and I say that because that was the only night I ever saw Charles dance. When that spare, muted horn sounded once more, Olson grabbed painting student Arlene Franklin who, with sister Phyllis, was from a farm on the Kansas plains and who happened to be standing close by. He danced with her over and over, one cut after another, to the Miles Davis record, hovering several feet over his timidly smiling partner, holding her lightly and at a measurable distance in a big but loose bearhug, shoulders crouched, moving around, in spite of his size, with surprising deftness and grace, bent over Arlene in a high, loose crouch, shuffling his steps, not terrifically varied in footwork, dancing in a small space, small steps, keeping close to the phonograph, close to the music, his movements as spare and to the point as Davis' horn, his head, as I said, way above Arlene's, still cocked to that pinched, dry trumpet as Davis noodled away, a very new sound then, utterly fresh to us, like no other jazz trumpet before, singular and personal in a sound which Charles was obviously experiencing for the first time, and as with all new experience with him, attuned to it in every nerve and fiber of his body, his whole being totally absorbed in this innovative and then unheard-of jazz artist.

Next noontime, I was sitting on the dining hall steps before lunch when Charles came around the corner of the building and started up the steps to check out his mail in the mailboxes on one wall in the entry porch. We talked a little, about the party the night before, he, mostly about Miles Davis and how excited he was by the sound. Suddenly I remembered the look of him dancing and, reckless, filled with a generous but nervy impulse, with impish affection, blurted out naïvely, "Charles, you danced last night like . . . like a whale!"

I meant no harm, meant no *conscious* connection to his spiritual father's *Moby-Dick*, was not that clever, but it didn't come out that way.

The eyebrows shot up well above his glasses. For an instant that hard, amazed look of his came into his eyes and bore right through me. I knew instantly, in my silly babbling, I'd offended him by comparing him to a whale! I had only wanted to pay him a compliment, but it had come out all wrong, of course. I guess he thought I was making fun of him. It was no wonder I kept my mouth shut in front of him most of the time, the wrong thing, or the right thing said wrong, always on the tip of my tongue.

But he was, as usual, quick to take care of the situation. With a small grin that was part amusement, part annoyance, his long heavy right arm shot out and punched me square in the biceps, a rabbit punch of such force it almost knocked me off the steps and left the flesh stinging.

"Oh *you*!" he jeered and stepped past me to the screendoor and into the mailboxes, leaving me to massage my arm, and my far more deeply injured ego, realizing how much I deserved that sock.

A *whale*! Shades of his beloved Melville. It's a wonder he didn't knock my block off. Looking back, though, it wasn't a silly or inaccurate thing to say. A whale, certainly, is a graceful and

mighty dancer in the waters; Olson himself, in his own sound-
ings, a powerful dancer in spatial seas.

But it was another lesson learned: to watch my mouth, watch
my language, really, what Olson was always insisting on in his
writing classes.

Early that spring, painters Franz Kline and Philip Guston,
along with the owner of the Egan Gallery in New York City,
had some business in the area, an exhibit or to give talks, or
more probably for Kline, as later outside examiner for Fick's
graduation, to look over some of Jorge's paintings, and so paid
an overnight visit to the college. There was some hope, especially on Fee's part, that Kline might return to teach. Kline was
short, stocky, with thick pitch-black mustache and hair and
crinkly, heavy-lidded, sharp but genial eyes. He talked and
looked like a regular guy, a blue-collar air about him, a steel
worker or a coal miner (he was actually from the coal fields
around Scranton, Pennsylvania).

Guston, on the other hand, had sparse gray hair brushed flat
over his forehead and the classic face of a Roman senator, tense,
darting eyes, but spare in his words; while Kline, as he and
Guston sat by the kitchen stove drinking coffee that chill, gray
afternoon they arrived, was more relaxed and open, turning
everything into a quiet but incisively (slyly, really) observant
story. Those of us, including taciturn Dan Rice—who, months,
even years, after, could repeat, word for word, Kline's shaggy-
dog stories—who were seated around on the metal-topped
table hung on his every word, avidly listening to this master
raconteur, who was already something of a Black Mountain leg-
end as he became an increasingly well-known action painter in
New York City.

Olson later liked to tell the tale of seeing Kline in
Provincetown in the red Thunderbird convertible he bought
from the first big sale of his big abstract black and white paint-

ings and how like an excited teenager he was with his first car, a poor kid from the coal country owning such a snappy model.

Kline's company was so enjoyable and he so engaging, funny, warm, honest and down to earth, I was hoping he'd come back to teach too.

But he never did. The next day he, with the others, was on his way, moving on, the last time he was ever at Black Mountain.

As the weather turned pleasanter that spring of 1953, we climbed the steep hill to hold our writing classes out on the open deck of the science building. Since Natasha Goldowski still refused to set foot in the place, Charles thought we might as well use the space, and also perhaps to show her how groundless and silly her fears were that the modernist-designed building, propped on its slender pilings, would come toppling down the hillside onto the road.

It was a welcome change from the smoke-choked back room of the office cottage, as we sprawled on the slats of the open decking. With the fat boughs of the pines pushing in all around the deck, it felt like we were meeting in the tops of the trees, the heavy scent of pine in the open air offsetting the smoke of our Home Runs and Olson's Camels, as most of us still addictively puffed away.

It was on a gloomy, rainy afternoon that Charles really pounced on me for the first time in one of his writing classes, this one, because of the weather, held inside the science building, in one of the classrooms on the upper level with its wide wall of window glass.

I had written some godawful story based on anecdotes my mother was fond of telling about South Philly, stories that she herself had heard as a girl from her own mother, Katie O'Connor. There was one in particular that I put in the story, about an old Irish woman who had run a boardinghouse in a street in the neighborhood near where my mother lived as a child, whose laborer tenants were mostly drunks. The rent included meals, but what the shrewd, penny-pinching old lady would do was, during the night, when a boarder would fall into a drunken stupor, she would creep from bedroom to bedroom smearing the mouths of the sleeping drunks with daubs of egg yolk. When they awoke in the morning and came downstairs demanding their breakfast, she'd say, "You've only to look at your mouth to see you've already eaten!" Then she would direct the befuddled and hungover boarder to the mirror, where he would look and see the dried crumbs of yolk on his whiskers and believe it must have been true, he'd already eaten and been so drunk he'd forgotten, and so was tricked by the miserly old lady to go off to work with an empty belly.

Maybe because we'd gone through everybody else's manuscript and there was nothing left to read, Charles, for the first time, asked me to read what I'd brought. I read it—in that hypercritical class—in a timorous voice, thinking they might find it "amusing."

Charles was not amused.

What mainly incensed him—aside from my slow progress in "wising up"—as he tore the story to shreds was that he knew the stories within the story, anecdotal to begin with, were a rehash of a rehash, about the about, experience two or three times removed from my own. What he had been trying to pound into my head—into all our heads—was, for starters, to write, simply, what we knew from our own experience, what we had seen with our own eyes, what we had heard with our own ears, to write it in our own tongue, "like Pausanias," the ancient Greek traveler and geographer, he'd instruct us, "go out and see for yourself and come back and tell what you saw and heard, first-hand." And this I found was the hardest thing to do for a variety of reasons: fear of exposure, of plunging into the imagination, the main ones; fear of facing not only the world but myself, another. The gist of it was to get the cataracts out of my eyes, unplug my ears, and speak direct with a singular voice— "the many in one"—rather than mouthing the stolen, second- and third-hand banalities of others, including my mother's.

What struck me most was the impact on me of the vehemence of Charles' anger, but one phrase in particular cut deep: "I'm not here to be a psychologist to you!" Charles echoing what my mother had shouted at me two years before, just before my father kicked me out of the house, when I told her I wasn't going to church anymore: "You better see a psychiatrist!" —she, wanting me to conform; Charles, now urging me most powerfully not to. My mother's will thwarted—she'd gone into the parlor after that, our first, and only, explosive fight— "Stop blackmailing me!" I'd cried out at her—and she had gone and hunched in her chair by the window, looking out, troubled, silent. I had had to pass through the parlor on my way to catch the bus to work at my factory job in Philly and left her there without another word. She later, I found out, from one of my sisters-in-law, had gone down to the rectory to talk to the priest who had advised her to be patient and not to do anything for awhile about her renegade son. "It's only a phase," he'd comforted her, "he'll soon return to the fold."

The second separation, then, from my mother—from "boy-angel" in cassock and surplice to long-haired, barefoot rebel of 1950s Black Mountain, with strong remnants still, as Madame rightly named it, of "*Michel l'ange.*" Yet Charles, more strongly and convincingly, was showing me, in no uncertain terms, I had not cut that invisible psychological cord—"Quit bein' so much on the side of the angels, Rumaker," he exhorted—that I must cut it, to be born into the world, a part of, yet apart from my mother. Charles would have me join the fathers, the root of my conflict with him because, a queer son, I was resistant to the fathers, hid from them and their world rather than identify with them ("I hold what the wind blows, and silt./I hide in the

swamps of the valley to escape civil war,/and marauding soldiers ," lines of a poem Charles had written that past summer of
1952, "Merce of Egypt," and that I did strongly identify with),
a world I knew very well, a world that, not long after, would,
however glancingly, surface in my writing. On the surface, for
survival, I feigned a loyalty and obedience that was not there,
deeper down, where was rooted a tongue in a collective voice
that had been silenced for centuries, but that would begin to
speak aloud in years to come.

I loved Charles for his shifting sensibilities, the unpredictable
androgyny in him, the flashes of tenderness and strength, of
swift and brilliant illuminations and perceptions, the Jungian
male and female cojoined—more that, than the "father" in
him. (And what, too, was *he* struggling with, or any male of that
time, of all that was forgotten?)

I squirmed in my seat under his tongue-lashing, my head
drooping lower, my spirit along with it. I had no words to
defend myself; I was without protection, exposed, without skin.
The heart went out of me, and with it the lovely airiness of the
afternoon, up there in the pines outside the spacious windows,
the broad expanse of valley and mountains in the distance—I
felt myself shrinking, felt I could barely breathe.

I had failed again. I would never get the hang of it. I'd be cast
out once more, this time by the man I wanted to please more
than any other.

"I can't help you because I don't love you."

Despite my fierce determination, perhaps he was right.
Perhaps it was hopeless.

As Charles berated me, I sensed the others staring at me; in
the eyes of some was a look of pity, the worst to see; in others a
look of contempt.

It was the first time Charles had been so furious with me, in
or out of class, verbally worse than his scathing screeds on my
manuscripts. He tore apart that piece of writing about the

deceitful old Irish landlady at great length, before he started in on me, much of it justified.

Although I thought it was cruel at the time, his thunderous wrath was really an awakener bringing me into a badly needed awareness. It woke me up.

But at supper that night in the dining hall, I was still so stunned by Charles' wrath that I talked to no one and had no appetite. I dared not sit at his table, didn't even try to get a seat. Charles was sitting a few tables away, and once I stole a glance his way and could see when he caught me looking his face was set in an angry frown, that his anger with me was still working in him.

Occasionally, others from the class who were sitting at his table were looking too. Perhaps they were talking about me. I felt more humiliated, baffled.

Hard as Charles' fury was, his verbal slaps that afternoon awakened me into a second birth, for they marked the beginning of my writing life. That lacerating day commenced my leaving the coma of the amniotic sac of an unborn self I—not my mother alone, not my father alone—had up until that moment encased myself in. It was Charles who broke through that self-imposed protective fluidity of unconsciousness I had tried to drown myself in out of fear and timidity, taking comfort in comfits, the uncontested sweet waters of the overly familiar, his voice, again, the same as thunder that raises drowned bodies. It was his—I can put it no other way—beneficent fury that freed me into the world, a second spiritual "mother" and, in time, a second and most important spiritual "father."

The old knowledge in folk tales that once we start on the path our helpers—our familiars, our spirit-kin—appear, to help us along our way, was new again for me.

Of course, I wasn't the only one, student, faculty or otherwise, who had at one time or another encountered Charles' wrath. As with most geniuses, he did not suffer fools gladly, and, except for Mary Fiore perhaps, he had a notoriously short temper with some of the women in his classes. But after that day, things began to change for the better with me—as if his rage had been a cruel but necessary baptism of sorts. As a result, I was really now beginning to be a part of Black Mountain College. I was on my way, and Charles would be my mightiest helper.

If Charles could explode in exasperated impatience, he was also wonderfully patient. I look back now and marvel at his patience, and the generosity of his inexhaustible energy. What a drain I and some other slow growers must have been on him. How lonely at times he must have been in his own teeming necessities I can only imagine, but I'm sure they occurred, there were so few of us, and fewer still to give anything back in any way resembling or commensurate to recharging his own vast and unquenchable reservoir.

No wonder his feedings through the mail, with Creeley in particular but with countless others, nourished and sustained him, and the occasional visitor to the campus up to his measure.

I was beginning to see that Charles was the most open, the most honest of men. Painful as it could be, you always knew where you stood with him; you may not have liked it, but you knew where you stood—and most definitely where *he* stood, always: upfront, nonhypocritical, exactly as he was, where he was, virtues, warts and all.

Still, in spite of Charles' mighty influence, I knew I had my own instructions, amorphous as they were as yet. And like a creature in myth, who stumbles awkwardly and infantilely along to the jeers of everyone, from father, mother, one's other blood kin, from many other doubters one encounters on the way, while others his age have moved on (the old Mali myth of Sundiata comes to mind), there is always a deep unconscious sense of his time coming, of a wordlessly powerful sense of spirit kinship with other unseen fields of energy despite his own as yet meager and undeveloped abilities—a strong undercurrent that propels and keeps him on his way, in spite of false turnings, false dawns; in spite of more conscious, often daily doubts, confusions, torments, including those doubts and jeers and taunts of others—the old myth of the Yet Unseen who, through such trials, is tempered, is made ready, is, finally, in all readiness, for when his time has come to do what he must do.

When Olson fervently quoted in class Dostoevsky's "my faith was forged in the fires of doubt," he was speaking, it sounded, as much of himself as of Dostoevsky.

I sensed that Charles, who saw himself as a great delicate babe in his huge body, and as, to borrow his word, "retarded" somehow in many areas of his growing, especially regarding his sexuality, slow in his growing away from his own mother ("As the Dead Prey Upon Us"), from his own father, growing and going on and out, the singular self among many, a part of and apart from, that he knew this too about himself.

One of those visitors up to Charles' measure arrived shortly after Olson blew up at me, perhaps just in the nick of time for him, for me, for us all.

To look at Maria von Franz, who appeared before me late one afternoon in the kitchen shortly after she arrived for the winter 1953 Jung Institute, was to see a small, sharp-featured, somewhat dowdy woman in a plain blouse, plain dark woolen jacket, plain gray woolen skirt that matched her dull, slightly crimped gray hair, and with plain stout brown hiking shoes, most unusual to see on the feet of a female at that time. But when she spoke, in her breathy, precise Swiss-German accent, there was such energy in her voice, and, later, in her talks to us in the dining hall, such obvious intelligence and keen insight, such passion for the work of Jung and the unconscious, the analysis and roots of dreams and fairy tales, her unprepossessing appearance was belied. It's no wonder Charles referred to her as one of "Jung's vestal virgins," a modern version of those ancient keepers of the hearth, of the fires of knowledge and mystery, of the sacred.

She arrived in mid-March for her several-day participation in Olson's abbreviated three-week "Institute of the New Sciences of Man," focusing on mythology and archeology, scheduled February 2 to March 23. Charles had tried to induce Jung himself to come, but Jung couldn't make it because of illness, and since she was already in the United States lecturing, he sent Von Franz instead, his closest associate at his Carl Jung Institute in Zurich. We were all very excited over her visit, since Charles had been preparing us for weeks in advance with lectures and class discussions of Jung's work—particularly on mythology, on the collective unconscious and its archetypes, such as The Wise Old Man (my dream on Olson as such noted earlier), plus Von Franz's own specialization: archetypes of fairy tales and interpretation of dreams, the latter of which, prepped by Olson's enthusiasm, I was avid to hear from her own lips.

Every bit of material on Jung, either in the library or floating around campus, was read eagerly and passed from hand to hand. Olson even appropriated my paperback Penguin of selected writings of Jung which Mary Fitton Fiore had given me, and never returned it—a habit of Charles', as previously noted, with other books that he took from the college library, to Nell Rice's despair, and insisted on keeping for his own uses.

Charles was deeply fascinated with dreams and, even long before Von Franz's appearance on campus, he discussed Jung's take on them, in and out of class. As an example, a dream in a letter he later wrote to me from Fort Square, Gloucester, dated "Tuesday Feb 3-4/58 . . . I forgot to tell you I once dreamed of you (with a woman I know, a priestess) as with me in a visit to a temple of Black Isis, no less (sort of like Hitchcock's The

Man Who Knew Too much [sic], original version [1934], with Peter Lorre, and Edda [sic] Best and her husband (was the Man), in which they end up their search for their daughter in a temple of the Sun, or something, in Limehouse. Terrific (I mean the dream too . . ." He was particularly preoccupied with the problem, the puzzle, of how one could dynamically and structurally assimilate dream content into a poem without its "being boring, like when we simply tell our dreams," as he put it in class. He later demonstrated how to do this in poems, such as "As the Dead Prey Upon Us," which he considered a break-through, written April 13-16, 1956, and "The Librarian," a copy of which, because of our ongoing discussions of the matter, he later mailed to me in San Francisco on the very day he wrote it: "Mon Jan 28/57 . . . I write at the moment abt yr dream poem (the person and the bird). [Dream 5 in "8 Dreams," later published as prose in John Wieners' *Measure* No. 2, Winter 1958, out of Boston.] It raises the whole problem of how one gets dream material to avoid its own obviousness. And I take it the rule is the turning of it - drying of it out, shifting it into the real - has to be done by a means of the poem itself, not by exterior devices: such as, in this one of yrs, the coffeee [sic] afterwards. That is, you are merely placing it over arbitrarily into the real. Carrying it across. But not changing it, by the act of writing. Thus it too stays description: doesn't get reanimated in another form than the dream-form (the hardest form, I suppose, to force writing to undo, and recreate its own.

"That is: I shld think any success there is in that mother poem of mine ["As the Dead Prey Upon Us"] is whatever transposition it does succeed in. And I have done another (a Maximus) ["The Librarian"] which maybe does something of its own in the same direction. I enclose a copy to you in case it may throw light.

"In any case, it's a tricky thing you are involved in, and do let me see anything you come up with. I don't know anyone else except us who seem interested in it, and I shld like to watch what you do with it. As I shall let you see anything I do . . . ."

His preoccupation with these matters, then and, as his just-quoted later letters show, continuing through the 1950s, only intensified in the weeks before Von Franz's visit, and he often spoke in class about how poets could make use of dreams in their work and, as noted, also spoke of it a great deal to me personally, since, myself also a heavy dreamer, he picked up on my own lively interest in the subject. Charles encouraged us to write down our dreams, and this I had been doing for some time, struggling to read these night letters from the unconscious, striving to get a clue, a handle, on my baffled and fractured self, reading their symbology, often wittily punning, I was discovering, for omens as to what I needed to be doing, as to where I needed to be heading. I suspected other students and faculty wanted to know this as well, since Charles recommended not only that I share my dreams with Von Franz and get her angle on them, but also suggested that others do the same.

Much of the content of the events at Black Mountain have been erased with time; I reach back through a kind of dream time, remembering Jung's injunction, as I note in my preface, "so long as it's *psychologically* true." (My emphasis.) But certain details stick: that late afternoon in the kitchen, for instance, moments after Von Franz's arrival. She was looking none the worse for wear, and after being shown to her room in Streamside, she reappeared in the kitchen asking me when supper would be served, and when I told her in about half an hour, she nodded curtly, saying she would take a hike before dining. I followed her as she strode out the kitchen back door and watched as she began, without fuss or preliminaries, to stride off across the road in her stout hiking shoes and to march straight up one of the rather steep Seven Sister Mountains behind North Lodge, walking erect with a brisk, purposeful stride until she was lost in the trees. On her return, precisely a half hour later just as Cornelia banged the dinner gong, she was rosy-cheeked and smiling merrily, saying she felt invigorated, the mountains were beautiful and she was ready to eat.

I attributed her energy and ease with mountains to her Alpine upbringing, and loved her on the spot.

Coincident to Von Franz's visit, Wes was then directing a cast of practically the whole school in Brecht's *Mother Courage and Her Children*, for which I operated the lighting. Cynthia Homire, with fat pigtail down the back of her worn levi jacket, played Mother Courage, while Fee Dawson, with some resistance, played the role of the airplane pilot. Fee brought up his role in a question-and-answer period after Von Franz's initial talk in the dining hall, and she confessed, with a roguish twinkle in her eye, that as part of *her* Jungian "animus" she had to beware of in her "shadow," "The young pilot in blue uniform is one of my archetypes," implying said archetype could easily seduce her away from her true path, her purpose, if she did not watch out.

After that first talk and after she had settled in for her brief stay, I, feeling a bit sheepish and nervous, frightened, really, made an appointment with Von Franz as Charles had suggested, to which she cheerfully and readily assented, to show her my dreams, a few selected recent ones. She was kept busy with a steady stream of appointments in her little room under the eaves on the second floor of Streamside, as each of us came clutching our dreams in hand for her to have a look at.

In late afternoon at the appointed hour, I made the climb, with pounding heart, to her room. My head was aswarm from the past several weeks with reading and hearing Charles talk about mystical (and realistic) Jungian archetypes and the collective wisdom and experience of that vast unknown self within the universal psyche; all of it, as Charles exclaimed conjecturally in awe in class one night before Von Franz had got there, pinching his thumb and forefinger together and pressing them around at the base of his skull, "residing in this little pea in the back of the brain, the hypothalamus." I felt like a modern-day descendant of those ancient ancestors who sought the prophecies of the sibyl, the plain wooden steps up to the attic of Streamside becoming the wide marble stairs leading to the sacred temple of the prophetess herself, Von Franz's small, pine-paneled room, with the waning light over the mountains slanting in through the window by which we sat, becoming the inner sanctum of the temple of mysteries. I just knew this small, frumpy, plain-faced woman with the steel-rimmed glasses and the breathy voice, was the seer herself, an anima archetype who appeared in all complexions and in many guises in my own dreams—and whom she soon quickly spotted when I recounted them— knew that she had much to tell me, just as in my dreams such female figures, if I could read their message, had much to signal to me, which was the main reason I had come to see her, hoping she would help me interpret the signs, to set my shaky feet firmly on the one of "many paths to the godhead," as Jung had put it, that I needed to be on, that Olson's wrath in class had recently jolted me in the direction of.

At that time I was also having dreams of my mother, and in my dreams were always broken bridges over the river and the river was always the one flowed past the Southern New Jersey town in which I grew up, the Delaware; and its waters were black and fuming ("write from there," Olson had pushed me, when I related the dream to him), and I had to get to the other side, to the city, and sometimes my mother was in the little boat and sometimes she was not, but there was only the broken bridges and I didn't know how to go over the river.

With each dream of mine she read, including the river dreams, she read quickly, all concentration, all business, with little shakings of her head, little gutterals in her throat, rapidly, incisively responding to each with interpretations and associations that went too fast for my ears and mind to catch, my apprehension muted also by the fluttering beat of my heart in my ears, too timid, too fearful to ask the big questions, which I could never bring myself to ask of Charles, the Father: Was I on the wrong path? Was my queer self a wrong way? Where was the secret to Right Path for an outcast? What was the Secret of the Golden Flower?

One of the dreams was the earlier related dream of Olson as black robed and black turbaned and the ancient black woman who bid me to approach him. The figure in the turban with the crescent moon in this formal, ceremonial dream Von Franz was quick to point out was the archetype of The Wise Old Man, whom the helper in my shadow, the old black woman, was leading me to, he who had much to teach me, and to whom I must give myself up.

She could only allow each of us a certain number of minutes, her time was growing short at the college and so many wished to see her. But despite all that, I left her room—it had by that time indeed become a sanctuary—with a curious, excited sense of communion, of deep and previously unshared aspects of my unconscious, of impersonal self taken seriously by a woman whose brief visit energized my mind and imagination for months, even years, to come, as it did with many of us, including Charles of course, since what she brought enlivened our work and discussion for a long time after.

Most important, her interpretation of my Wise Old Man dream clinched my further resolve to surrender myself to the one who could continue to help me on my way.

Not long after that, the first piece of writing I did that genuinely pleased and excited Charles came out of one of his classes on Melville, a critique I wrote of "Bartleby the Scrivener." It was actually a course not only on Melville, his long poem "Clarel," and his short prose works ("Bartleby," "The Encantadas," "Benito Cereno,"), and his novels—*Typee, Omoo,*

Mardi, Redburn, White Jacket, The Confidence Man, and "the blonde-brunette novel," as Olson termed it, *Pierre; or, The Ambiguities*—Charles at one point grinningly referred to Melville's work, particularly *Moby-Dick*, which threaded through all of his talks, as "a great stew of everything stirred in together"—but also on other novels, such as Hawthorne's *The Marble Faun*, with Shelley's *The Cenci* tossed in for good measure, Stendhal's *The Charterhouse of Parma* and *The Red and the Black*, D. H. Lawrence's *Kangaroo* (the novel where I had my embryonic socialistic ideals and my innocence of charismatic leaders shaken), as well as William Carlos Williams' *In the American Grain* and Lawrence's *Studies in Classic American Literature*—the latter another Black Mountain "bible," the one tattered copy of which was passed from hand to hand like a sacred relic. Since it had long gone out of print and the Doubleday-Anchor paperback hadn't appeared yet, Carroll Williams typed copies of it—yes, *typed* the whole book, making carbons—for others to read. Charles chided me in class over a paper I wrote on *The Marble Faun*, saying I sounded "too Laurentian," noting, with amusement to the others, Lawrence's singular voice was hard to resist, calling D. H. "an American, not English."

More to the point was my pondering Stendhal's romantic love, the pursuit more important than the attainment—the richness of fantasy the imaginative root of making, the thrilling pain and ache of hunger and longing, like loving at a distance—my aloof blond lad at Chautauqua, for starters—the dazzling accretions on that bare root within like Stendhal's image of a bare branch tossed in a salt mine that soon grows encrusted with gem-like salt, which he likens to love, stinging salt in the bare wound and yet unspeakably gorgeous, which illuminates the caves of creativity in self in painfully burning but sparkling light.

Charles met me on the road by the lake one afternoon after

he'd read my piece on "Bartleby"* (which I'd connected up with the biblical Job). Startling me, he exclaimed that he was so excited by it, "It makes me want to go back to Melville, to do something on Melville again! That story is talking about Melville's soul! That story's talking about the writer-artist—the scrivener—in America! Bartleby *is* Melville!" Ideas came tumbling out: we could print a broadside together, or a pamphlet, we could set it up at the print shop—He would write a new piece on Melville; he'd get others to contribute, and of course he would include my piece on "Bartleby."

"Mike, you must stop hiding your talents under a bushel basket!"

He went on and on. But the magical word in my ears was "*we.*"

I was dumbstruck and stuttered some incomprehensible sounds meant to be murmurings of gratitude. If I was bewildered by his earlier anger, I was equally baffled now by his overwhelming enthusiasm, which seemed to me to be so much more than what the piece warranted. More than that, I was deeply gratified to have him at last praise something I'd written. That praise, for Olson lauded my Bartleby piece skyhigh in class, also signaled a kind of acceptance by the others, who looked at me now with at least a wary respect.

Maybe it was a one-shot fluke, but for days I walked on air. But more important than the grudging respect of a few of the others, important as that respect was to me from those seasoned Olsonian vets, was that this marked a change in my relationship with Charles: having now offered him something with at least a hint of substance, he could offer me something in return, truly accept me as a student, an apprentice, show me the ropes, teach me a trick or two, "the shortcuts," as he phrased it,

*Published as "Bartleby the Scrivener by Herman Melville" in *Kulchur* 10: N. Y., Volume 3, Number 10, Summer 1963.

steer me along the path he intuited for me, which meant—wonder of wonders, starved as I was for it—the lavishment of his attention, generosity and praise, all of it far in excess, still as far as I could see, of any insights I might have had into Melville's story.

But I had broken through to him, he now noticed me, perhaps had begun to love me, if only a little.

A mark of this was that on occasion he now allowed me access to his personal library. Olson did not lend books, ever, but he would let a very few select students read a book, if it was not in Nell's library and if he felt it was important to their "direction," their "path," from his extensive library in his study in the Studies Building, which he rarely used, preferring to work late into the night up at his house (he and Connie had by this time moved to the student-built, compact modernist house where the Jalowetzes had lived, just beyond Meadows Inn), where in his living room and bedroom-study was more of his vast collection of books stacked in floor-to-ceiling shelves.

His study in the Studies Building was one of the larger ones, the only one as far as I know that was kept locked, the wall shelves of which were crammed, as in his home, with volumes, many of them first editions and quite rare; many of them, too, lifted—or "appropriated"—by Charles from the college library and simply never returned—as noted, a constant sore point with librarian Nell Rice, who waged a constant but losing battle to get the books back but never did. To Charles, he just *had* to have them, they were, as far as he was concerned, more important to him for *his* work than to anyone else's, so why shouldn't he have them, at hand and ready to use whenever he needed them? He was also not averse to "borrowing" books from students: as I mentioned earlier, a paperback selection of Jung's writing that Mary Fiore gave me also later ended up in Olson's personal library. (Genius has its own laws.)

You had to promise Olson to read the book in his study and

nowhere else, to not let anyone in while you were there, and to make sure the door was locked after you were finished. It was in his study that he let me read his copy of *Lady Chatterley's Lover*, one of the 1,000 unexpurgated copies D. H. Lawrence had printed himself in Florence in 1928, and whose trusting the "evidence of the senses" spoke most powerfully to Olson. Apropos of the above, hanging on the honey-colored paneled wall just inside the front door of Charles' house was an original water color by Lawrence of a nude man pissing in a bed of daffodils, presumably D. H. himself, that Olson had somehow gotten hold of in some kind of trade—as always secretive in certain matters, he didn't say how.

I browsed through as much as I could in Charles' private collection, including getting my first introduction to the Jung works he had, in the brief time allotted, and took it as a great honor that he permitted me into this inner sanctum, for however brief those periods. Charles subtly intimated that it was indeed an honor, and even more, that he trusted me—not only with his precious books but also, after the "Bartleby" piece, in my writing as well.

From his earlier work on Melville, Olson had become close friends with one of Melville's granddaughters, Eleanor Melville Metcalf, who lived in Grey Gardens East in Cambridge, Massachusetts. She was rather elderly at the time, but even so he invited her and her husband, Harry, for a visit to the school. I don't know which I was more impressed with, the fact that she was a living relative of the great Melville (whose *Moby-Dick*, at Charles' wondrous urging, I'd just read and lost my head over), a relation who, as a child, had actually seen Melville in the flesh; or the fact of her rather impressive garb: a voluminous purple plaid tartan suit with short cape, *very* purple, with purple plaid military Scottish highlanders cap to match, her crimped silvery hair peeking at the brim.

Charles was all courtly fuss with her, like she was a favorite aunt. Indeed, he seemed so much spiritual kin to Melville, as his guide and illuminator, that back in the 1930s, this had prompted Mrs. Metcalf to share not only her family's home but also her grandfather's papers with the young, questing, and impoverished Olson. So it was no surprise to see him treat her as family, or himself to appear to assume anyhow that he was related, since she was, despite her formality, as familially affectionate with him.

Charles, ever persuasive, induced the gentle Mrs. Metcalf to share her memories of her grandfather, and one afternoon in the dining hall before dinner, enthroned in her full purple plaid regalia on one of the cane-bottomed chairs, she told about the house in Lower Manhattan that the Melvilles lived in and, with a pleasantly impish smile, how her grandparents had separate bedrooms, a snow-white coverlet on Grandmother Melville's bed (one thought of the Moby-Dick implications of that!), a pitch-black one, at his own request, on Grandfather Melville's bed (more food for symbolic and allegorical thought). She recounted how Melville would often take her and her sisters for a walk to a nearby park, he all the while often deep in thought, so preoccupied he rarely spoke to the children or even seemed to notice them. Once, while they sat on a park bench, Melville deeply pondering, he got up and began walking home, leaving the children there. When he arrived back at the house, as it was later told to Eleanor, Mrs. Melville exclaimed, "Herman! Where are the children?" Melville looked about him, baffled, then suddenly remembering, raced back to the square to reclaim the tots.

She also told us there was a painting of the Bay of Naples that Melville was especially fond of, hanging in the entry hall of the house. Invariably, when they came in from their walks, Grandfather Herman would lift his walking cane, point to it, and wagging his stick back and forth, repeat in a singsong over and over to the grandchildren, "See how the little boats swing to and fro, to and fro . . ."

After her talk, Charles proudly introduced me, telling her with a big smile that I was the composer of "a wonderful piece" on Bartleby. I blushed to the roots and she smiled graciously. Olson suggested I send her a copy of my paper when she got back to Cambridge, and a week or so after I mailed it off, I received a letter on pussy-willow gray paper from her in response, thanking me, a letter that was as gracious as her smile.

Charles laughingly hooting in a writing class about Marianne Moore, "When she starts to have an emotion, run for the hills!"

Moore in her day perhaps "accepted" more readily by male poets and critics for her "objectivity," her "rational" approach, because she wrote "like one of the boys," even was an ardent fan of the old Brooklyn Dodgers. (Years later, Rachel Blau Duplessis in her essay "Manifests" argues for Moore's—unconscious?—influence on Olson's 1950 "Projective Verse" via William Carlos Williams' 1925 "Marianne Moore" essay.)

Olson speaking about Isadora Duncan and her autobiography, *My Life*, in class one night, recounting stories of her love of display and of long, gossamer scarves, that they could trail and whip in a breeze as freely and spontaneously as her own dance movements. And how, a speedy, carefree driver, as Charles was, her long scarf caught in the rear wheel of her convertible as she sped along in France, snapping her neck and causing her instant death.

He told us how earlier in the book, he was most impressed with her walking on a beach by the ocean, alone, pregnant, torn between love, motherhood, her art, agonizing over whether to keep the child or not.

His sympathetic account took me to the library to read the book, to introduce me to a singular and innovative woman,

another of the ghost-dancers, perhaps, among Charles' w
he spoke that movingly of her.

Also about that time he strongly recommended I read
Dreiser's *Sister Carrie* (1900) and *Jennie Gerhardt* (1911), for
Dreiser's own sense of women, which had also fed his own
sense.

Charles may have had regard and respect for those "non-
erotic vestal virgins," as he called them, those "hearth goddess-
es," Maria von Franz, Ruth Benedict, and Jane Harrison (note
that none were poets), hearth-meets for his own poetic and
intellectual ignitions, because, at root, Charles couldn't seem to
get beyond seeing most women as anything but sexual and as
house-meets for his own convenience and comfort, essentially
wives and mothers, especially useful to himself in either capacity, much like Olson's mother, Mary, he as an only child the
apple of her eye and hence used to being spoiled and waited on.
They were to serve him (including the epistolary stimulus of
intellect, source and artistry via Frances Motz Boldereff from
1947 to 1950, another hearth-meet and Olson's mental equal,
though their passionate intellectual relationship tipped over
occasionally into the passionately carnal) and be secondary in
his own life, common male notions still as much alive then as
they are now, even, for all its progressive thinking and attitudes,
its daringly adventurous avant-gardism, at innovative Black
Mountain College.

So, in 1953 when Marilyn Monroe wiggled across an
Asheville movie screen in vivid technicolor in *Niagara*, "her
first big part," he, to put it bluntly, had the hots for her. You
could plainly see it in the admiring yet lascivious flicker in his
own eyes as, more animated than usual, he talked about her
with gusto in class one night to Jorge Fick, Joel Oppenheimer,
and the other guys who'd seen the flick.

Later, he would comment, "What did she ever get but has-beens? Look at who she got stuck with—Dimaggio—most boring ballplayer—Arthur Miller—all has-beens—Nobody up to her." (Meaning except possibly himself?)

How Marilyn, like the slyly witty celluloid visitation of a carnal angel, all winking smile and promise (perhaps of redemption?), fit into Charles' acknowledged cosmogeny of muses — Von Franz, Benedict, Harrison et al.—is uncertain. But it's safe to guess her luminescent image must have fed him *something* in the dark, fed something in his work, he was so taken with her. How much, as with the other women, this acknowledgement was on an equal exchange is unclear, however. As Florence Howe said in *No More Masks*:

> . . . The [male poets] need to name their source of inspiration woman or muse. The naming is not a sharing of power, but an extension of power: it codifies a patriarchal relationship. Women may be mysterious sources of energy, but as muses they are designed to feed their powers to poets.
> But what if that poet be a woman ? . . . (31)

Good question, given Charles' oft-repeated advice to us guys, and to himself: "Take what feeds you." Maria von Franz might've said to Florence Howe: "Feed your own animus," with Jungian pun intended.

That same year around this time, Charles in a lecture in the back room of the office cottage, asserting, "I'm sure that's why the cloacal and the genital are so close a triad in us," intimating the bare separation of the generative and the eliminative, creation and disposal (death?), impulsions of our making, and unmaking. Coldly, passionately logical Flola Shepard in the front row, as often with Charles' wilder statements, grinning

170

skeptically, but Olson stuck to his guns, reaffirming his point. And that statement stuck with me, as did so much he said, stuck for years ("like adhesive tape," as Mary Fiore put it, "till you understood it"), rising up in a visionary scene in a 1977 novel of mine, after a brush with drugs and alcoholic death, *A Day and a Night at the Baths.*

Then, Mary Fiore told me around the time when Charles and Connie were later having marital troubles, of the period in the 1940s when the Olsons were living in Washington, D. C., and Charles had one of his early poems published. He proudly, eagerly, showed the magazine opened to the poem to Connie at the breakfast table and Connie said, "I'll look at it later," with a touch of indifference in her voice, and put the poem aside. Charles was crushed, and never forgot that moment of Connie's lack of shared enthusiasm (and obeisance to his talent?), it still rankling in his chest when he told Mary about it several years later at Black Mountain.

I sympathized with Charles, but vividly recalling that pain behind Connie's eyes I so often saw, wondered was her careless gesture a healthy one of resistance, a shoot up from her netherself that spoke of her own need for self-recognition, for a clear sense of that individuation Olson was always quoting from Jung, apart from Charles' gigantic appetite for his own? Done, not so much to hurt Charles, done more perhaps not to hurt herself, to stop hurting herself. Was it the realization of herself and her own abilities, her own threatened containment, being smothered by Charles' overwhelming needs and energy— a singularity as forceful, and potentially fatal, as an act of nature—his enormous ego the eye at the center of that elemental force he was?

Peter Anastas told me years later in Gloucester after Olson's death in 1970, that he thought second-wife Betty Kaiser's own death, alone in that wintry car crash outside Wyoming, New

York, in 1964, was "no accident," that he strongly suspected she'd "committed suicide." Again, was it the same pattern as with Connie—so early on a hopeless feeling of suffocation in giving up everything for Charles, her putting aside his poem that morning an acknowledgement of that?

Late one morning in the summer of 1953, I came up to the back door of the Olson's house, my heart in my throat, to ask Charles something important, something to do with the possibility of eventually starting plans for my graduation project. It had to be something as important for me to do that, daring to appear at his house uninvited.

Looking in through the kitchen screen door, I could see directly into Charles' bedroom down the hall from Connie's. She and Charles slept in separate bedrooms, mainly I guess because of his night-owl reading and writing habits, and Connie's need to keep Kate's early hours. The house was so quiet, I expected Connie and Kate had gone out, perhaps down to the stream by the print shop. To my surprise, there lay Charles, clearly visible, stretched in his bed, evidently just awakened, with only a sheet down around his thighs. He was staring off into space and absentmindedly running a hand over his stout belly, and below to a protruding great thatch of pitchblack pubic hair.

My knuckles, poised to knock, froze in midair.

It was like seeing my own father naked for the first time, and was in fact the only part of my own father I ever did see closeup, and only once, when I was about 11 or 12, and he had the same deep black shade of dense, tangled groin hair as Charles. It had been dawn when, as happened infrequently, my father had overslept, going back to sleep after my mother had awakened him, no doubt because his hangover was probably more severe than usual. (Often with face gray as death, getting up on time and going to work at the shipyard was a point of pride with him that made it look like everything was all right, no matter how much Schmidt's beer he'd drunk the night before.) My mother had already awakened me at 5 a.m. to ride the running board of paperman Pete Kelly's old khaki-painted (during the war) Chevy truck, down to my crack-of-dawn job selling the Philadelphia *Inquirer* to the grizzled, hacking workmen— many of them as perpetually gray-faced with hangovers as my father—boarding the ferry for the Philadelphia Navy Yard across the murky Delaware. For this I got paid half a buck a morning, but often I didn't make that, since there were always guys that swiped papers when I was busy making change. Pete, a smelly, crusty, old arthritically crippled Irishman who went to the same church we did, and who carefully twice counted every single newspaper he gave me each dawn with his gnarled, paper-shiny fingers, deducted any swiped ones, at 5¢ a copy, from my wages. After my paper-selling duties at the ferry, I walked the mile or so back into town to serve early morning mass at St. Matthew's.

That particular dawn, I was sleepily pulling on my long stockings (boys that young still wore corduroy knickers and long stockings) in the one chair by the windows, my five other brothers still sleeping in the two beds that just about took up all the space in the tiny dark bedroom. There was suddenly loud, repeated car honking down in the dirt road. This was unusual because my father was always out there waiting with his lunch kettle for his ride with his best pal, Joe Harper, and his other cronies to the shipyard further up the river in Camden. But not that morning. I heard my mother exasperatedly murmuring something to my father from the back bedroom, and soon he came stumbling into our front bedroom, skinny-muscled in his shorts. Leaning over me, he flung up the splintery window, the cold winter air freezing on my back, and hollered to the men in the old battered car below he'd be there in a minute. Joe Harper yelled up in his shrill, needling voice something razzing about a hangover, although he was probably suffering one himself since they both drank together every night and gabbed till late in our parlor. He yelled for my father to shake a leg before the whistle blew. My father was leaning close over me, an intimate closeness I'd never had before with him, so close he smelled even more strongly of his usual sweat and cigarettes and beer. The fly of his brown-striped shorts was agape, and I glimpsed, before he ran back to get into his workclothes, his thick black pubic hair exposed in the shadowy dawn through the window, a dark, mysterious forest in my startled eyes, dark forest I sprung from.

That glimpse stayed with me the way, ten years later, seeing Charles sprawled in his bed through the screen door stayed with me. It was that kind of time, the hidden mystique of the male body, the generative part anyway, unlike the exposure of women, in movies, in magazines, in ads, women's bodies, all there, suggestively revealed, all there for the taking. And that morning at Black Mountain, there was Charles, naked on his bed—vulnerable, his hands calmly, casually, combing his belly, his great head propped on the pillow lost in thought. I stood for a few moments staring indecisively in through the screen door, across the tiny kitchen and into the sanctum of his bedroom, the most private room in the house, knowing if I knocked, he'd know I'd seen him. I didn't want to think about that, what he might think. Anyway, although it was late in the morning, he was still in bed (noontime often dawn in Charles' time). I couldn't disturb him, and no matter how important the business I had to ask him about, I couldn't move my fist to knock, losing nerve totally by this time, realizing how bold I was to even approach the house let alone knock uninvited, breaking one of Charles' tacit cardinal rules about intruding on his privacy.

So, I turned and left quietly, leaving the great man to scratch his belly, the image of him at that moment vividly with me then and forever. Secretly seeing him naked, seeing his black thatch, made him even more human to me than ever, more a balance of what he was, something I needed to see, just as it did when I had seen my other father.

Not long after that incident, one night in Olson's writing class in the Reading Room in the Studies, I found myself absentmindedly, or perhaps not so absentmindedly, staring at Charles' gaping fly—his clothes were often in disarray with rips in them, buttons missing. I only became conscious of it when, catching me at it, as he sat in his customary broken-down arm-chair in the corner, I sensed him glaring at me sharply, our eyes meeting for a fraction of a second, confused embarrassment in mine, huffy irritation in his, as if I were taking liberties in spying on forbidden territory.

There was nothing I could say aloud, even if I had had the nerve, in response to that accusatory look, but to myself I said: *It isn't what you're thinking.* Having a clear shot at my eyes, per-haps it was that other he saw in them, so deeply unconscious it was beyond words.

Speaking of my other father, the only letter I ever received from him was a brief note written in pencil in his careful, paro-chial school-boy hand on lined notebook paper that arrived late in March 1954, telling me my mother had given birth to a baby boy, David, her ninth child. That was it, simple and direct. Her cigar-puffing physician of many years, Dr. Campo, in Westville, New Jersey, who always carried an enormous wad of bills in his side pocket and with whom I suspect my mother was uncon-sciously in love, since he showed her, as doctor, more care and respect than my father, who was often very much like another child to her, ever could. Dr. Campo had assured my mother, I learned later from one of my sisters-in-law, that she was well past menopause—she was actually 48 at the time—and that she

father, who were having their usual ongoing marital ups ↓ wns, mainly because of my father's boozing, and who ...., t again reconciled during that time with the help of the parish priest, and especially Dr. Campo, didn't need to worry about her ever becoming pregnant again. After the baby was born, my father, after he'd had a few, always snidely referred to David as "Dr. Campo's son." Other times, if he were really tipsy, he'd call him "the priest's son."

After I'd read my father's note, I knew that my mother, simple and unprotesting heart that she was, would accept the new baby as God's will, just as she accepted, with silent sorrow and anger, my father's drinking (not to mention my own baffling behavior). And yet reading that brief letter I felt a great sadness for her, that at her age she would have yet another child to care for. I got angry, at Dr. Campo, at the priest, especially at my father. All the past came rushing back too: the grinding poverty of the Depression of the 1930s, and my mother's misery with too many mouths to feed and a husband out of work who struggled to provide as best he could but drank every chance he could—her gnawing shame, her daily fears for all of us, all came back with a deep burning fury in my gut.

For some time after that, whenever I saw a pregnant woman, I wanted to kick her in the belly.

The two of us were sitting in his Ford convertible, parked in front of the dense shrubs outside the fieldstone office cottage. We had returned from a movie at the Roxy in Swannanoa, one of those rare occasions I went anywhere with Charles, especially just the two of us. I can say in light of what follows that it wasn't a result of too much beer because I'm pretty sure we hadn't stopped at Peak's after the movie, since Charles wasn't at that time going much, if at all, to the tavern. In fact, he complained loudly and angrily that students were spending too much time there, just as past faculty members had complained and then

bev

decided that the tavern, built years back and run by Mountain students to have a place to socialize, must be ¦ get the students back on campus. Actually, the only thing that changed as a result of the sale was ownership by Ma Peak—students still hiked the several miles down the mountain to the tavern for their 3.2 beer and spent long hours there.

That night stays vivid in my memory as being one of the first and few times that I was alone with Charles in the privacy of his battered blue Ford convertible with its mashed-back driver's seat. Why it's also imprinted in my memory is that it was the first and one of the only times Charles was intimate and open with me about his sexual self.

As we sat parked in the shadows under the rhododendron and mountain laurel bushes that surrounded the office cottage, Charles began speaking of the "difficulties" he had with certain women at Black Mountain. He mentioned several by name, especially Natasha Goldowski, the physics and chemistry instructor, that vital, assertive and strongly opinionated woman, outspoken, and not shy in standing up to Charles. She was one of Olson's chief combatants in the never-ending confrontations over which direction the curricula and educational thrust of the college should go, and what the structure of that educational spirit should be.

"The trouble with Natasha is," Charles had said to me earlier, with a sly smile and confident air, "she's like a squirrel who always wants to take the nuts home with her," referring to the growing exclusive use of her own apartment in Meadows Inn to hold her classes (she had still adamantly refused to step inside the science building students had designed and built for her after her lab burned down in September 1948). As well, over time, she and her youthful, ex-student husband, Eric, and her mother, Madame, made rarer and rarer appearances at meals and public functions in the dining hall, becoming all but recluses in the community, until their eventual move to a small rented farm outside Asheville.

As I've already intimated, Natasha had, in many respects, besides bringing to Black Mountain her enormous vitality, intelligence, curiosity and generosity, also brought Europe along with her. And it was her Old World sense of things—in spite of her radical spirit—of what education, especially, should be and her desire and need to impose higher academic standards and structures to make the college more "respectable," stable and attractive, hence, attracting more students who could pay tuition, that brought her into direct, headlong conflict with Charles, who resisted the seduction of "that pile, Europe," as he called it. With equal vigor—they were certainly a match—he struggled to impose, as I've also earlier suggested, his own visionary design of a spatially open and more variously-rooted American shape on the school, a place that would challenge all the old concepts and practices and be a space to make, anew, the latter vision certainly well under way by the time I'd got there in 1952.

Completely different in their visions, they were, in will, defiance and stubbornness, twins. At times it seemed like a neo-classic struggle of European-trained Scientist and free-wheeling American Poet of Space—the questing and disciplined academic sciences pitted against the imaginative and visionary arts—for control of the future focus of the school. At other times it appeared an irreconcilable conflict between the old hermeneutic and class-structured, European-based teaching of Natasha, centered on private tutorials; and the wide-ranging, more grubbily democratic, open-arena hurlyburly approach of Olson; in short, the shift to Lawrence's "evidence of the senses" as opposed to hierarchical academic intellectuality. At the nub of it was a conflict over those academic standards which Natasha read in Olson's far-ranging methods as too slipshod and without cohesion; whereas Olson saw hers as too one-sided and restrictive, elitist, in fact, even though each believed in maintaining Black Mountain's doing away with traditional academic requirements, such as grades and tests and final exams. Even so, Natasha continued to complain that "there are no measuring devices at Black Mountain College."

Raw to the intricacies and machinations of political infighting going on around me, and still more or less frightened and baffled by Olson, I found myself, in the beginning, after taking Natasha's modern physics class in 1952, siding more with Natasha, since I had yet to "prove" myself in Olson's classes, had not yet written the piece that would *show* him, that would make him love me; whereas Natasha, with her "European bag of tricks," as Olson might have said, was all smiling flattery and robust cordiality—an Old World sophisticated and seductive charm. Hungry for any scrap of affection, attention, however artful, I was easily seduced.

But now that I'd written my piece on Bartleby, and had had Charles' enthusiastic response, my old fear and bewilderment regarding him had tipped just this side of total awe. Now, I would have done anything he asked me to do, even, improbable as that was, going back to work on the farm.

So that evening as we sat side by side in the darkened car as Charles spoke of women and sex—and how he began speaking of it, what started him off, as often with him, arose in the moment out of some urgent need to give voice to some inner connection—he talked in a low and intimate voice, the way lovers do after lovemaking, about the complexity of Natasha, and his struggles with her. I also had a strong realization of seeing myself again, in that moment, as I had long ago begun to feel as a child with the struggles between my mother and father, caught once more between the pull of differing affections and loyalties, the same as I felt also between Connie and Charles, and between Natasha and Charles, that I was once again strung out on a precarious tightrope, being extremely careful to veer neither to one side nor the other, feeling the need for each on either side of me to serve as surrogate props, for balance, utterly aware of the riskiness of dropping one at the expense of the other, trying to keep both—mother-father/Natasha-Charles/Connie-Charles—in an evenness of balance, in a torsion of suspension and still-childish need.

Charles was leaning very close in the darkness of the car, his physical size still a threat to me, though becoming less so. But it was especially a threat now in the close space of the front seat of the convertible as he continued to speak in that low intimate voice, that voice that you felt spoke only to you, speaking of Natasha, speaking of several other women. I was on my tightrope, holding myself less in balance than in rigidity, in fear of falling; swarming with a conflict of feelings, flattered on one hand that this man who I so admired and respected was airing confidences to me; uncomfortable on the other that he was sharing these intimate confidentialities, feeling simultaneously honored and unworthy. I sat silent, listening, staring out the darkened windshield at the pine boughs pressing against the glass. I was embarrassed in a way, too, like I was unexpectedly hearing a confession of the sensual intimacies of my own father, that I was not prepared or equipped to know; that dark, nether side of him which he carefully hid from us, from me and my brothers, even from our eyes, as mysterious and unnerving as my first glimpse of that dark tangle of his groin that early dawn, the same as my first jolting glimpse of Charles' that late morning through the back screendoor—except overhearing, often, after my father had drunk a few quarts of Schmidt's, crude, scatological jokes hoarsely whispered coming up the dark stairs to my alert unsleeping ears (sleeplessly guarding the house against fire till late into the night, night after night), when I was in bed between my sleeping brothers and there was company downstairs in the parlor, his shipyard pal, Joe Harper, and Joe's wife, Toots, my mother's best "girlfriend." But at all other times that was hidden from me, hidden from my brothers too—perhaps most serious of all, hidden from my father as well.

Charles touched easily, unselfconsciously; in the heat [of con]versation, it wasn't unusual for him to place his hand on your shoulder, your arm. But here, in the close and intimate dark, it seemed different. Charles' arm went around my shoulder, his big hand dropped to my thigh, enclosing it lightly, a friendly touch, a lover's touch, my green queer mind still uncertain which was which, as he went on talking, leaning close. I grew rigid inside myself, hung suspended on my interior wire, and since I was not yet always clear between the differences in touch, used only to touches from other males that were only sexual, that led only to that, the thought raced through my mind, Is he queer? And yet he's talking about all these women—What's he trying to tell me? And let slip the flash of a doubt in that dark night, in those dark days of the 1950s, that if he were queer it would have instantly shattered my respect for him, my admiration, the deep need for his acceptance, I was so poisoned. And yet I was so hungry it made me want to snatch up his hand, to squeeze it tight, to cover it in kisses and, remembering his hard, dismissive words in the kitchen that day, echoing the words of my father when he'd told me he didn't want me under his roof anymore, beg him to love me, as that secret self and buried need, still largely unacknowledged in me, had desperately wanted of my own father.

He was talking of Johanna Jalowetz now, she and her husband coming to Black Mountain as refugee artists escaping Hitler's Europe in the 1930s. Her composer-husband, Heinrich, or "Jalo," as he was affectionately called, had died on campus a few years before, his corpse hauled as far as it would go up the mountain on the flatbed wagon pulled by the farm tractor and buried up in the Seven Sister hills under a pile of rocks serving as a tombstone. Mrs. Jalowetz was an old woman now who had stayed on at the college, reluctant to leave (it was into the Jalowetz's old student-built modernist house on the road to the college farm that Charles and Connie would move to, after old Mrs. Jalowetz, realizing she no longer had a part in it, left the college that year, 1953). She had been giving a few voice lessons (to Virginia, in particular; Jalowetz used to rock her head from side to side, bright black eyes wide in astonishment, deeply seamed brow wrinkling even more, "Not much of a voice," she'd confide); or she'd work in her bookbinding shop in The Stables, mending library books for Nell, teaching an occasional student—the Franklin sisters, Phyllis and Arlene, from Kansas—the art of bookbinding in the bindery, and helping Jonathan Williams at one point bind the manuscript of Kenneth Patchen's *The Journal of Albion Moonlight*. Mrs. Jalowetz was nervous that I was there to watch (at Jonathan's invitation), in her fussy, nervous energy, anxious that I not touch anything, making me so uncomfortable that eventually I left and missed the process I was so eager to see: of how a book was hand-bound, especially an original and handsomely hand-written and illustrated manuscript such as Patchen's, one which Jonathan had entrusted to lend me and let me read the night before.

"Even old Jalowetz, even she has that spark," Olson was saying in his darkened Ford. "Even an old woman at her age," he continued, with amazement in his voice, "That spark comes between us, like the spark from other women does. Like with Natasha, too. It gets between us and I can't get beyond it. That spark always stands in the way."

And I began to have an inkling for the first time of Olson's attitude toward women (which had troubled me), that lay at the root of his trouble with Natasha, that he saw her not as a person and an equal with ideas and approaches to education radically different from his own, but as a woman whose "spark" was both a powerful lure and a distraction, a glandular beclouding of eyes and mind, a sexual adversary to be conquered, in deep and ancient biological wiring beyond change—conquest over rather than partners in quest, as were, conversely, his quests, his drives and inclinations with other males—like his voluminous correspondence with the as-yet-unmet Creeley in Mallorca, a correspondence which was in its own way, at an even deeper, unacknowledged level, love letters, eros the taproot of so much human energy and endeavor, as is the ancient-beyond-ancient deep nonrational shrinkage males fear in females, the springing from them and the dying into them.

Charles was a multi-faceted and extremely complex person, but at root, in regards to women, he was no more or less different than any other males steeped in the traditions of a culture that put men first. Woman was sexual, woman was fertile (in womb, in knowing), women cared for babies and cooked, took care of the shelter and kept it cozy for the master, tended the hearth men took fire from. Woman kept the home as a rest-stop and occasional sanctuary for the actionable male, importantly busy in the outside world of competitive power and control and expansion, keeping the darkness of death at bay—women made babies, shelters; men made, and destroyed, worlds. It was as ancient and hoary as Olson's beloved Homer.

Connie, for all her qualities, her incisive intelligence, played just this sort of wife to Charles, her own needs secondary to his. Betty Kaiser, who came down from New York City to study music with Wolpe, and became Charles' future, and legal, wife, and who was of the same slight build and gentle disposition as Connie, played the same sort of passive, self-effacing role, all but blotted out in Charles' huge shadow.

Now, from a perspective of several decades later, and several decades after his death, I suspect Olson seemed never to get beyond seeing women as anything more than creatures created for his own comfort and use. Even the women writers he respected: Sappho; Stein (her "Melanctha" was the only fictional work by a female he recommended as worth it—and Gertrude, who always would rather hang out with the guys—

amusing their gals was Alice's job—always did brag about her "masculine mind"); Greek scholar Jane Harrison, her *Prolegomena to a Study of Greek Religion*, which Olson highly recommended; anthropologist Ruth Benedict, her paperback *Patterns of Culture*, which also passed from student hand to student hand because of Charles' recommendation; and of course Jung's "sidekick" (to quote Olson), folklorist and psychologist Maria von Franz—Charles referred, as noted, to all in an amused and yet amazed tone as "vestal virgins," with its implication of such "asexual" women as keepers of the sacred fires struck by men and maintained for the benefit and ease of men, so that men could do men's work—the *real* work—in the world beyond the hearth; and although they lived apart from men, they lived in service and indebtedness to them (in the alleged Beginning, though long after image, was The Word, a male utterance we are told), as Benedict did to Franz Boas, Von Franz to Jung, even as Stein did in a Parisian world dominated by male writers and painters, a woman who bought and promoted artistic work of males and who, though lesbian, did not wish to speak of artistic and intellectual matters to other "mere" women because of that "male mind." Only Sappho, prime dyke, seemed to burn for a brief time in unadulterated light (till her celebratory singing of and for women was extinguished, only fragments remaining from the fires of time and neglect).

And of course nothing yet was known of the facts and intimacies of Charles and Frances Boldereff, of their love letters, another woman whose spirit and intelligence Charles used as symbiotic sounding board for his own ideas and inspirations, another taproot. She, of all the women who fed him, helped flesh out his insights, his vision; she, of all the women it appeared, was his equal, and then some.

Charles seemed never to question any of this, out loud in his classes at any rate. (My own questioning was hampered by my own ignorance—who is not a product, and prisoner, of his or her own time and space?—and by my need for his approval, by my own rudimentary and inchoate sense of a stirring that had no language yet, just as then, too, songs of celebratory queerness were a long way off in the learning and the making.) Although he had high regard for the work of these women, the understanding and uses he put it to served and furthered his own work, it fed his own purposes, as in "For Sappho Back" (". . . what is rhythm but/her limpidity?"), and "A Newly Discovered 'Homeric' Hymn (for Jane Harrison, if she were alive)"—a subtle ambiguity in that last phrase of the dedication?—and in the "jan 2 53" poem about "Con," and Black Mountain student-wife Libby Hamilton's pregnancy in "Common Place," to cite a few examples. His was a stance that, while "tipping his hat to the ladies," still remained securely anchored in his alliance with men, especially to those males who "fed" him in another way, fed his insatiable hunger, beyond "the trammels," "the nets" of flesh, the "trammels" and "nets" of feeding and breeding, beyond the "spark" that ignites, inflames, and eventually extinguishes all.

Charles respected the intelligence and ability of the above women very highly, just as he respected Mary Fitton Fiore as a student-writer, before she gave up writing after her marriage to Joe, the only woman-apprentice I know of he did respect and treat as "one of the boys," because Mary also displayed a tough and questing mind, a questioning one but one that never appeared, at least, to question Charles' rightful place as master. Giving up writing, she devoted her life to marriage—"It's what she settled for," Olson once said to me, with an edge of annoyed disgust. Mary herself once told me she believed— 1950s America was everywhere, even permeating Black Mountain—it was what a woman should do, "take care of her man and the kids." Just as Constance Wilcock and Augusta Elizabeth Kaiser had done, devoting their lives to Charles, in Betty's case giving up a career in music and acting—and as later discovered, writing, given the extensive and perceptive journals she kept while at the college. Years later, was Betty's death an accident, as some suspect it wasn't? Had she realized, too late, how high a price she had paid? Had she, in despair, in loss of herself in the shadow of Charles, in the hugeness of his over-powering voice and presence, so lost sight of herself, she drove purposely head-on into the approaching auto that wintry dusk near Wyoming, New York?

And yet, and yet . . . amidst the tangle of contradictions, to ring a turn on Creeley's famous dictum on form: Perhaps for males, gnawingly incomplete, short-circuited, women are never more than an extension of self, a totally adored, and feared, completing; a dependence and hold in the very fiber of our being. Perhaps males, like females, need the impulsion of iden-tity, to rise singular, to be a part of and apart from life around us, to vigilantly avoid the undifferentiated dead, like nature raw, "the one mass," who "are drunk from the pot," who "have the seeds in their mouth," who "will deceive you," as Olson wrote in "A Newly Discovered 'Homeric' Hymn," an endless conflict not constricted to gender. As Olson, writing of those "nets," those "trammels," with a knowing beyond societal and cultural inculcations, says in concluding "As the Dead Prey Upon Us":

> the nets of being
> are only eternal if you sleep as your hands
> ought to be busy. Method, method
>
> I too call on you to come
> to the aid of all men, to women most
> who know most, to woman to tell
> men to awake. Awake, men,
> awake

Natasha, the equal of Charles in energy and charisma but

closer to earth; so much alike—except in fields of interest, fields of visions—it was no wonder they became enemies. She was alive and in her element at Black Mountain, and later, on her own farm, a creature of earth herself, yet at times taking great leaps, a woman of the Green Spirit, yet also rooted in it like a wonderful, exuberant ground figure—the mother-ground, which Charles ("Life is not of the earth. /The dead are of the earth. /Hail and beware the earth, where the pot is buried....") sought, as all males must, to fly up from, the real unconscious crux perhaps of Natasha and Charles' conflict, perhaps of any male's. Still, generous, abundant, high-spirited, with intelligent insights and definite opinions of her own, strong-willed, like Charles, who was, in a way her twin—given more of a mutual acceptance, more respectful leeway on both their parts, what a force they could have been for Black Mountain College! Equal partners sharing in strength and responsibility, the equal of himself, the equal of herself.

Too tidy an equation, no doubt, given the orneriness and predictable unpredictability of human nature, the wobbling pivot: the need for the son to leave (flee) the mother (my own torturous journey then darkening my dreams, as Charles himself in his dreams revealed in "As the Dead Prey Upon Us"); perhaps Natasha had that need, too, to murder the mother in her, to put her to sleep, to be free, the fierce mother Madame was, for all her daughter's attempts at flight, holding her earthbound, tethered to an inescapable stake. And what of the fathers? And what of bitch nature? Frances Boldereff in her letters to Olson cursing her enslavement to her female nature, as matrix of generative flesh, while Charles, all males, were not as enslaved by theirs, were freer to make and create, to innovate, to subvert.

And yet, and yet . . .

Yes, what a strength, perhaps, amidst the tangle of contradictions, Black Mountain could have been if these two could have conciled themselves, each to the other, two powerful and essentially imaginative forces allied, yoked sun behind moon, moon behind sun, the one in the other, whole spherical energies streaming from the Seven Sister Mountains out, out into the world.

Perhaps Natasha's determination to "take the nuts home" was to keep her students (and innocents, such as myself) out of Olson's lair. Maybe beneath all the surface animosities and differences of temperament and ideology was a primordial but still strong imprint to keep the young from the possession of what she saw as an increasingly voracious Eater of the Young.

She fought back valiantly, fiercely, with all her strength, wits, intelligence—as undoubtedly did her female forebears, women-warriors battling for balance, battling still. But it wasn't an equal fight. Tradition had not been with her, as it hasn't been with women for many a century, and so she lost.

For all its radicalness and innovation in education and the arts, when it came to relationships between men and women, Black Mountain College was, despite a bit more wiggle room, a replica of the hierarchical and patriarchal order outside the gates, and this was even more so as Olson took over more and more of the command of running the place. With Natasha eventually ousted, he had an open field to do things more or less as he saw fit.

Natasha left the college in the fall of 1953, taking Eric and Madame to a small farm she rented off the main highway to Asheville, just this side of Beaucatcher Mountain. Shortly after they'd moved in, Eric picked up Merrill and me in his car at the college and drove us back to the farm to pay our first visit to them since the three had left Black Mountain.

Natasha was radiant, bustling about showing us the small house which, as I recall now, had a clapboard summer cottage feeling about it, not a house designed for winter, even the reasonably mild winters of western North Carolina.

Madame barely recognized our presence, keeping mostly to her room, where we could hear her clucking and complaining through the thin walls.

"You can see she doesn't like living here," Natasha said, but she herself appeared to love it. She was a different person from the one at the college where, in her long, unabating battle with Olson, her energies had turned negatively inward, mean-spirited and paranoid. Having her own country air to breathe, removed a good fifteen miles from the stifling air at the college over the mountains to the east, restored her naturally exuberant spirits in full measure. Even her mother's constant petulance and complaining couldn't dampen them.

"It's milking time!" she cried gaily and directed Eric, in French, to get the milking pail. "Come along," she ordered and took us outdoors to show us the land, Eric tagging along, proud, eager to let us know how happy she was, how fortunate she'd been to find such a place which, in its lush green growth and high surrounding hills—even in the look of the little white farmhouse itself—very much resembled the terrain and feel of the land at the college.

She had great plans for the place, a huge garden in the spring, some more chickens (she already had a few pecking around the back door) and ducks and livestock. Her idea was to be as self-sufficient as possible, to get from the land as much as they could in the way of food, very much in the tradition of what the farm had been to the community at Black Mountain, and, after the farm closed down, what could be gleaned from Bea Huss' community garden. She and Eric would work together and perhaps in the coming winter months, she would have time to write.

She energetically marched us off some distance from the house, talking excitedly, pointing out this and that feature of the land but mainly to show us their cow, who was grazing out in one of the pastures, a burnished red animal, head down munching in the thick grass.

"*Rouge-ah! Rouge-ah!*" Natasha sang out when she spotted
the cow, her voice cracking with emotion, that appealing and
touching break in her voice I had heard so often, that I had
heard in the voices of other strong women whose lives were
passionate. (In the voice of French film actor Simone Signoret,
making the shadows of the screen substantial with life, Natasha
had some of that same resilient huskiness in her throat that
spoke of inward reserves of banked fires.) She was like a sturdy
peasant figure striding across the grass, very much at home in
this place, unconstricted now, all her enormous energies and
gusto streaming outward again. Here, she could be the self her
conflict with Charles denied her.

Rougea lifted her head to us as we approached, with that
mute, patient gaze of animals, that look of bewildered puzzle-
ment, that each time they see humans anew it's a fresh
rediscovery, a wary perplexity at what strange, unpredictable
creatures these are coming towards them. *Rougea* had that look
as Natasha hurtled over the grass in the thickening dusk, the sky
above the western hills filled with sun but the slopes encircling
the farm already darkening in shade, the mountain air turning
suddenly crisp in early autumn chill.

Natasha kneeled in the grass and flung her arms around the
rich red fur of the animal's neck. "*Rougea, Rougea,*" she
crooned, and crooned other endearments in Russian in her
husky voice into its ear, the ear flicking rapidly as if bees were
buzzing around it. You could tell the cow was her joy.

She stood up, stroking the animal's head and, turning to us,
said, "She's young but she's a good milker. We get enough
from her not only for our milk but for cheese and cottage
cheese, and I'm going to make butter—oh, and we make whey,
too—we feed that to the chickens. And we got her at a good
price, too. O my darling *Rougea*," she cried, hugging the animal again, "You're so precious to me." Looking up at us, she

said, "You can see I couldn't name her anything but '*Rougea*,' 'red' in Russian."

The little animal was precious in more than one way, I was thinking. Since Natasha and Eric's finances were lean (Madame's were evidently nonexistent), it sounded as if they *were* depending on *Rougea* for a large supply of their food, so that, obvious as her affection for the cow was, there was in Natasha's ebullient voice an underlying note of encouragement to *Rougea* not to let them down in the even leaner winter months ahead.

And it was true that it was the most economical of animals as we tasted, at supper later that evening, the cheese and cottage cheese from its milk, with tall glasses of the unpasteurized, unhomogenized milk itself, just like the raw milk from the dairy at the college. Afterwards, we watched Natasha preparing new batches of whey and feeding an already prepared can of it to the chickens after dinner in their coop just beyond the kitchen door.

"But first we must milk the cow," Natasha said, taking the pail hanging from Eric's elbow, which he'd brought along from the house for that purpose.

In spite of having worked a short time at the college farm, with its large herd of cows, I'd never milked one, nor had any of the other student farm-help, as far as I know, had the opportunity (except maybe if the juice went off, as often happened to our rural electric system, around milking time), since the cows were milked by machine as special soothing Montevani-type music, designed not only for contented people but for contented bovines as well, played softly via the local radio farm station from loudspeakers hung up in the barn, while the electrical milking apparatus hummed away.

So when Natasha asked Merrill and me if we'd ever milked a cow, we had to say no. She said she would show us, that we all must take a turn, and did show us in that deft, quick way of hers. It was a delight to hunker down in the cold-smelling grass in the thickening dusk and feel the warm udders silken in my hesitant, massaging fingers, to hear the hot jets of milk ping into the bucket, and feel the surprise of *Rougea's* velvet fur against my forehead as I leaned into her side, squeezing and squeezing, smelling her sweet pungent hide that carried in it the odor of alfalfa and animal-heat and cold mountain air.

So the supper back in the warm kitchen was adequate, simple but filling, with Madame, deigning to make an appearance at table, a little more congenial, especially to me, only because, as had been her habit when she had tutored me at the college, she wanted to find out the latest gossip about the school, questioning me in her Russian-accented French in that artfully sly and oh-so-innocent and indifferent tone that, I'd learned to recognize, concealed so much sharp and greedy inquisitiveness. Much to Natasha's amusement, I answered as best I could in my stumbling French with its heavy Russian accent, learned from Madame, the only one who understood me. That night Madame seemed to need to know what was going on at the place where she had lived for so many years, where the antics and comings and goings of the people had become an amusing and craftily observed part of her life. Now, in a new home and in relative isolation, she missed all the gossipy activity of the college. At the root of her complaining, which Natasha and Eric understood, despite their thinning patience, was the fact that she was terribly homesick for Black Mountain.

But it was Natasha who, as usual, dominated the afternoon and the evening supper table, just as she had in her small, intimate soirées and classes in the lobby-living room at Meadows Inn. Energy burst from her like an uncontrolled river, a kind of fierce erotic energy that enveloped you in a wonderful feeling that activated your own responses; that made me, anyway, as so often in her presence and in particular that day, feel so happily alive. (Much as Charles' own boundless energy did.) She was filled with projects and plans, not only in her own work but for their little farm as well, and she confided to us some of what she had been thinking. Mostly it was the farm and all that she was doing there, and what she was learning and relearning, an abundance of earthlore and local farming information that she passed on to us in a flood of talk over the table.

Like many Europeans, inside and outside of Black Mountain, Natasha could be a crafty and accomplished actor, in the face of our more innocent American experience in which we didn't yet know all the lines. Olson's triangular equation on this, which he excitedly propounded on the spot on the blackboard in class one day, went roughly:

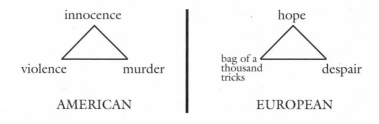

But that day I think Natasha was genuinely, overwhelmingly happy. Being free from Black Mountain and the overbearing shadow of Charles, safe now on a patch of land which, although rented, was still very much her own, where she could be very much her own woman without the threat of dominance or hindrance from Olson, had opened a floodgate of exuberant liveliness in her which I thought was both marvelous and sad to see, sad because I was thinking, despite Charles' own terrific exuberance, how much Natasha's own was badly needed back at the college, at least for balance, as an alternative. But I also knew, equally sadly, that that wouldn't have been possible with Charles' need to be kingpin. It was not to be.

As it grew later and the time came to say goodnight, I felt

very good about the day, as I could see Merrill did, and heartily thanked Natasha for it.

Eric drove Merrill and me back to the college, and that was the last time I ever saw Natasha or Madame or Eric.

Charles saying in class on writing about sex while horny: "Don't *write* about it—Why impose it on us? Go out and take care of it. Then get back to the writing."

Another evening, Charles exclaimed with distaste, "That juice of the world Whitman was all confused about!" throwing me into confusion, it was so much the elixir of communion of the beloveds to me (as well as with Walt), as I knelt before them, anonymous or known, all males beloved in that instant of energetic discharge and infusion.

What was wrong with that? I wondered.

And another night in the Reading Room in writing class, Olson was discussing Inkadoo and Gilgamesh, going on about all the erotic goings on in that ancient Mesopotamian epic, enthusiastically exclaiming at one point, "Who *wouldn't* want all the sex they could get?" But Gilgamesh learning finally to his rue that it wasn't a good thing, Olson repeating that revelation with a great red-faced grin, suggesting it was a hard fact we all come to terms with.

And me sitting there thinking to myself, at (for some of us) sex-starved Black Mountain, "Yeah, who *wouldn't* want all the sex they could get," and ignoring the latter part of Olson's statement.

After I was transferred from the farm to the kitchen, I, at first, after sweeping the vast floor, rigidly followed the tradition of lining up the tables in neat, straight rows. Then one day, feeling the loosening effects of Black Mountain and suddenly sick of the regimented lines, on a whimsical impulse, I scattered them randomly all over the dining room space.

When Charles entered the dining hall that night for supper and saw the free-form arrangement of the tables, he grinned from ear to ear and asked in a loud, excited voice, "Who did it? It's wonderful! Wonderful!"

I owned up, secretly pleased at his pleasure.

"That's what we need more of around here," he said pointedly, still grinning.

However, in sharp contrast to the above:

That day in the dining hall, lunch time, me seated at a table near the fireplace, Charles on his way back to his own table, pausing to talk to someone at another table near ours, and standing directly behind my chair with a cup of tea, some of the hot tea sloshing down my back as he talked and gesticulated in his usual energetic fashion. My first thought was he'd be aware of what he was doing, then I got angry because he didn't notice at all that he was burning me, so wrapped up was he, as usual, in what he was saying. *And me keeping quiet about getting burned!* The weirdest reaction. To show that I could "take it," as I'd had to learn so many times? Or was I afraid to complain, unconsciously believing that Charles could do anything to me—hurt me in any way (even scalding me with hot tea!)—so long as I continued to have favor in his eyes, so long as he regarded me with occasional scraps of praise and affection.

My father all over again.

During one of the 1953 summer institutes there were so many guests I had to set up additional tables from the dining porch itself around to the veranda of the Round House, the fieldstone music room with its Steinway grand, at one end of the dining hall. The additional work was exhausting and I was a little on edge, but I managed. One lunchtime, sitting at table with Charles and Connie, with baby daughter Kate in Charles' lap while he fed her, Kate was dropping and spilling soup and food all over the porch floor (which I knew I'd have to mop up) because Charles, expansive as ever, was sitting too far back from the table. Others at the table, who didn't have to do the mopping, were amused by little Kate's clumsiness, and when I mildly suggested Charles shove in a bit so Kate could reach the table, he took instant umbrage, snarling out, "What's the matter with *you, grandpa?*"

The table was suddenly silent. I, flushed and confused, stared down at my plate, mumbling, "I only meant. . ." but couldn't continue, stung by his reproach, suddenly flung back to suppers at home as a child, with my father seated next to me, reading his Philadelphia *Bulletin*, he forbidding any of us to talk so as not to disturb him, and many a time I got slapped in my nervous babbling, as if that was the part I was meant to play.

"You only *meant,*" he added sarcastically, then stared at me silently, his face set with fury, the hardest of all for me to see, even harder than the grinningly pleased expression on Jorge Fick's face next to me, as he sang out in a voice dripping with mockery "Awwww, the baby's *gonna* cry."

I must've looked that way. It was just what I felt like doing.

Around that time, Merrill's position at the college grew more precarious. He was not enrolled in any classes or studying with anyone since Lou Harrison had left the school, having been replaced by Wolpe, whom Merrill despised. Then, too, some were offended by Merrill's aloofness and cold manner, his supercilious attitude toward them plain in his face. He also continued to refuse to show up for either his work or dishcrew assignments, although, as a favor to me, he once or twice, with Dan Rice and Cynthia Homire also assisting, helped me mop the kitchen floor of a Saturday afternoon. As a result, Jack Rice, big brother of painter Dan, a former student and now newly-hired work coordinator, who'd arrived with his pregnant wife, Barbara, and small daughter, Megan, and who vowed to be gungho in getting and keeping "the plant," as he called it, in shape, came banging on the door of Next-to-the-Last-Chance early one morning to rouse Merrill to come do his scheduled work assignment. Merrill ignored the rapping, while I, still skittish about being caught in bed with another guy, even at Black Mountain, kept mum. That didn't stop Jack. He pushed open the door, catching the two of us wrapped in each other's arms on the mattress we'd hauled from the bedroom close to the stove the night before, so as to be warm in the cold snap at that time when even the featherbed wasn't enough. Jack stared in at us from the doorway, awkwardly hesitant, in his black leather jacket, big-buckled, wide leather belt slung in the loops of his tight, grungy levis (Jack's levis *always* fittingly grungy, hard worker that he was), his freckled, sharp-featured face bird-like, high-cheekboned, his thin-lipped mouth drawn in a severe line, piercing blue eyes severe, even the spiky crewcut of his strawberry-blond hair standing up rigid, all bespeaking the no-nonsense marine he'd once been. He barked out, "Gillespie, you know you're on a work crew this morning?"

Merrill cocked one eye, mumbled something, annoyed at this harsh intruder, then ducked his head under the featherbed. I felt like doing the same, nervous for Jack to catch us that way, but Merrill wasn't the least concerned, about the work detail *or* Jack seeing us.

"You coming?" Jack persisted, his blue eyes flinty now, his thin lips even more tightly drawn.

Merrill mumbled, "Yeah, yeah, in a few minutes." But you could tell he didn't mean it.

Jack stared at the lift in the featherbed where Merrill's head was, glanced sharply at me, then turned and stomped out in his heavy workboots, slamming the door after him.

Sleep was over now for me. I pulled myself up and peered

cautiously over at Merrill, knowing his quick temper by now.

"Merrill, you going to get up?" I pleaded softly.

No answer. I waited a bit, then again, just as carefully: "Merrill, I think he meant it."

Still no answer. I was afraid they'd really kick him out if he didn't at least show up for his work assignments. I couldn't bear for that to happen.

"Merrill . . ."

I shook him gently, but he was fast asleep again, and Merrill once asleep was impossible to rouse.

That was just another incident I knew would guarantee his being asked to leave again, one of many that were to come.

Later that summer, Jack Rice (who, as I've intimated, when he took over the work program, ran it like a drill sergeant), in one of those Black Mountain testosterone fits after a fight with Huss and Olson at lack of what he perceived as support, tacked a six-page ultimatum (challenge, really) to Huss et al. (although "exonerating" Olson), on the cork bulletin board in the Studies entry. Olson, bemused reading it, asked what those of us reading it over his shoulder thought of it. We gave only grins and shrugs in reply, but Charles didn't say much publicly about it himself.

Bea Huss had thick, salt-and-pepper, hacked off-looking bobbed hair, like she impatiently, carelessly cut it herself. Her clothes, always dresses, unlike the worn dungarees and denim skirts that many other women wore at the college, always had a ragtag handmedown look—no doubt because the Husses were as rockbottom poor as other faculty families. Wes, however, with his aristocratic bearing, no matter what he put on, couldn't help looking elegant, even wealthy, which was why he said he always dressed down when going to the doctor, so he wouldn't be overcharged. But I suspect, even if they'd had a few extra dollars, that wouldn't have changed Bea's manner of dress. There was something of the blithe spirit about her that suggested appearances weren't what really mattered to her, even a skin condition that gave her a reddishly blotchy complexion of which she seemed unself-conscious. She also exuded a radiant kindness, with a smile to chase even the deepest blues, and would do anything for you. Her generous spirit was evident in the huge community vegetable patch just off the road above their white clapboard house next to the Olson's, that she had laid out, planted and maintained largely on her own, after the farm shut down. Her baby, David, would toddle right along beside her up and down the rows of corn and tomatoes, the produce of which we all fed on, especially later on when things at the college got even tougher, while, wearing her old straw hat, she uncomplainingly did most of the planting and hoeing and weeding.

She had gone to Beaver College in Pennsylvania and had met Wes at the Hedgerow Theater outside Philadelphia, where both studied acting. Obviously intelligent and with a playful sense of humor, she had the most pleasantly modulated voice that was a pleasure to listen to. She was a good actor and at Black Mountain she appeared in several of Wes' productions during my stay there, playing, as already noted, mother to my bridegroom in Lorca's *Blood Wedding*, and also acting in Brecht's *Mother Courage* (on which I did my first job at lights at Wes' request) and *The Caucasian Chalk Circle*. She was also one of several women who posed nude in Esteban Vicente's drawing class under the Studies Building in the Summer Institute of 1953, and she could always be counted on to pick up necessities in town for anybody on campus, when she drove off to Black Mountain or to Asheville in the Huss' old dark-green Mercury, son David in the backseat.

Merrill, like so many of us, found Bea very appealing—perhaps for her buoyantly Zen personality, a spirituality he, along with his lover Herb Roco and a handful of other Black Mountaineers, dutifully studied but notably lacked, Merrill never big on the Zen spirit end, particularly regarding a sense of humor, subtle or otherwise. Perhaps for him it was also a misguided sense of protection—there was, for all her capabilities, something vulnerable about Bea. One never knew with Merrill, however; he developed a few odd affections among the women, like for painter Dorothea Rockburne, with whom Merrill and I occasionally had tea up in her and Carroll's second floor quarters in North Lodge, along with their new baby; and of course for Natasha Goldowski. But then there were also those odd resentments against just about everyone else on campus, mainly male, especially against Olson, an animosity which really put me in the middle, since I was willing and obedient apprentice to Olson's mastery. I suspect Merrill really felt sorry for Bea because of the way he perceived Wes treated her. Despite his pacifist background in the Quakers, Wes had a fierce temper that was evident in the way he blew up at student Mark Hedden in the late fall of 1952, after a silly, corny skit Mark wrote and directed on Barbara Fritchey's anniversary and put on after supper: "Kill if you must this old gray head but spare your country's flag!," one of those smartass, prankish playfulnesses, of which homebrewer Bert Morgan was a master, that erupted occasionally at Black Mountain. "How dare you!" Wes cried, livid, accusing Mark of willfully and maliciously using the area of the dining hall by the wooden divider—a natural backdrop setting—between the dining area and the kitchen for his skit's setting, the very space Wes had been using to rehearse his own production of Brecht's *Mother Courage*. Wes' argument was that the audience would associate the setting of *his* production with Mark's silly one and thus ruin all of Wes' dramatic effects and diminish the seriousness of Brecht. Mark, the most genial, mild-mannered person, for all his deafness (he wore a hearing aid) couldn't fail to hear every single word and humbly apologized. But Wes was the angriest I had ever seen him, his eyes and neck muscles bulging, his voice hoarse with fury as he loomed menacingly in his tall, lean height over the shorter Mark, who behind his glasses looked very contrite indeed, and not a little fearful.

On another occasion, I again witnessed Wes' cold anger, this time directed against Bea herself, at some gathering in the dining hall when I was seated in the same row next to them. Leaning close to Bea's ear, Wes was guardedly talking about someone—I couldn't hear anything but he was speaking in a way that made it obvious he didn't want anyone else to hear. Suddenly he realized the person he was talking about was sitting near enough possibly to overhear him, and he was instantly furious with Bea, who had evidently been facing the person. I could hear Wes muttering through clenched teeth, his thin lips tight, "Why didn't you tell me they were sitting so close? Why didn't you?" furious with Bea for not warning him the person was so nearby, as if somehow it was all her fault if that person had overheard him.

Bea said nothing, the blotches on her cheeks and forehead turning even redder as she sat there taking his anger without a word. And I wondered after that if those reddish eruptions—psoriasis perhaps—weren't exacerbated by smothered anger, perhaps against Wes and his volatile temper, which I in my naïveté assumed Quakers didn't have, or at least that they prayed and struggled mightily against. But I was surprised at the intensity of the dressing down, and the meek way Bea took it—and empathized with her, since it mirrored so much of my own response, or lack of it, particularly in the face of Merrill's own short fuse, not to mention that first blowup of Charles' over my writing.

It may have been that Merrill did feel "sorry" for Bea, that most cavalier of attitudes, but I'm not sure what he felt about her exactly, no more than I knew what he felt about me, Merrill lived so much in his own head, in his own partially deaf world. I know he disliked Wes, felt that Wes didn't deserve Bea, Merrill having perhaps witnessed a few of those same angrily explosive moments of Wes' with Bea like the one that I'd observed, angry moments that were very like Merrill's own it seemed to me, ambushes that caught me by surprise. Anyway, whatever the reason, Merrill got it into his head to do something "nice" for "poor Bea," and what he came up with was an Asian-style dinner, that he himself would supply the food for and that he would cook himself at the Huss' house because they had a kitchen. Wes, pointedly, *not* invited—in his own house! Merrill saw no incongruity in this. I suspect the main idea of the dinner for Bea was a way for Merrill to get back at Wes for Merrill's perceived mistreatment of her. Perhaps Bea went along with it for similarly deeply unconscious reasons. I, unfortunately, *was* invited and, like a dope, afraid to displease Merrill for fear of losing him, went along.

Merrill, perfectionist in everything, planned the meal for days, even driving into Asheville with Bea in the Mercury to buy Asian vegetables and condiments—I think he was preparing a shrimp dish—and fixing the food himself of course, right in Bea's—and Wes'—kitchen, not trusting anyone else to do it. But what Merrill didn't plan on was that, with baby David already tucked in bed, just as we sat down to eat at the small, nicely laid table (set by Merrill himself, naturally) by the windows in the parlor, as if that were a cue for a stage entrance, Wes himself came strolling in the front door and, without a word, eased himself down in an armchair a few feet from the table, picked up a book on Bertolt Brecht, crossed his long legs, and calmly began to read.

As the dinner progressed, Merrill and Bea made small talk, mostly about the taste and success of the dishes, seeming to be oblivious to Wes' presence. But I was finding it hard to swallow every bite of food, I was so mortified that Wes had been excluded in his own house. I wanted to speak to him, but felt constrained, not knowing what to say. Of course, by his silent reading in the corner he was very much present. Merrill didn't seem bothered at all by that, and Bea, by her pleasant manner, gave no hint, perhaps drawing on her acting abilities. (What happened after Merrill and I left I could only imagine.) But Wes' lesson, very dramatic, to say the least, *and* his victory, slyly, quietly witty, were clear to me: the power of passive resistance which he'd undoubtedly learned as a Quaker and practiced later as a conscientious objector in World War 2 had, that evening at least, paid off.

Merrill never commented on Wes' showing up, as if Wes hadn't been there at all, something Merrill was quite capable of blocking out. Thinking about it later, I wished Merrill cared as much about my feelings as he seemed to care for Bea's. I also wished I had more of the quiet inner strength, and nerve, of Wes. Maybe it was acting, but he had certainly made his point.

Not long after that, Jerry Van de Wiele, handsome, genial, muscular, ex-marine artist with the most heart-brightening boyish smile, who I had once after a drunken party tailed to his studio in the Stables with high hopes but no luck, told me, genuinely baffled yet slyly bragging too, that he'd met Bea by accident alone on the road near the Olson house one night after another party somewhere on campus. He'd never seen her out at that hour and by herself, simply wandering around. She, to his amazement, after an exchange of greetings, suddenly approached him, touched him. It more than startled him, she to whom he'd been nothing more than casually friendly. (But if she had spotted him sunbathing nude, as was his habit, on the deck back of the Studies as I had, it was no surprise.)

The Olsons were still at whatever the gathering was that night, and Jerry, looking back amazed at the foolhardiness of it—"Jesus, it was Wes' *wife*!"—not knowing what else to do, took her into the Olson house (no locked doors to most of the houses and lodges at Black Mountain).

Afterwards, Bea had hurried away in the dark back to the house she shared with Wes a short distance up the road, while Jerry headed back to his studio in the Stables to think, and worry, about what'd just happened, surprised still at the intensity of it.

It never happened again, Bea never alluding in any way to Jerry anything about what happened that night, never attempting an explanation, as if it had never occurred at all.

I thought of Wes, his abrupt angers, especially of his anger with Bea that evening in the dining hall; and later that summer, the night of the Black Arts Ball in celebration of his 45th birthday and his unabashed excitement at seeing Pat Nelson dressed as a nun, their slipping off together. I could see it, could understand it too, in both cases.

When Merrill went off to Houston early that summer to try to woo Herb Roco back to Black Mountain, I missed him a lot. I also hoped he'd be a failure in Texas. My hopes were answered when Merrill returned pissed because Herb, as he sarcastically put it, wouldn't leave "Daddy dear," that Herb didn't have "the guts" to stand up to his father, who insisted he needed his son in his auto garage business because of his own failing health. Merrill, furious, would hear none of that; he only wanted what he wanted.

I nodded my head sympathetically, secretly glad of Herb's filial devotion.

Merrill had arrived by bus back from Houston around lunchtime, and I spotted him as I was coming down from the Studies, just as he was about to go in at the back door to the kitchen. Seeing him again for the first time in weeks, I realized how I'd missed that lean angularity, those bright blue eyes, even, I noted, the newly-trimmed crewcut, missed the feel of it in the nights. I ran to him at top speed, recklessly threw my arms about him in broad daylight for all to see, all those heading around the corner to the dining hall, crying out how glad I was to see him. Stefan Wolpe, with Hilda Morley, going into lunch, beamed at us bemusedly, sizing up everything. I didn't care.

Besides Herb remaining in Houston, Merrill also had reason to be pissed off on another front: the faculty had a meeting to decide whether or not to let him stay. There was strong resistance against his staying. As noted, he wasn't always cooperative, that and his supercilious attitude made him largely unpopular, and since he was still not taking any classes or tutorials (he still flatly refused to study with "Olson's boy" Wolpe) was not regarded as a student, was regarded, really, as someone using the school as a cheap flop, was seen by some, in short, as a parasite (as were a handful of other hangers-on, who some on the faculty were trying to dislodge).

Merrill, stubborn, angrily certain he was in the right, pled his case, that there was music he wanted to write, that he wanted to develop as a composer; he could do that by continuing on at Black Mountain.

During those few uncertain days, not knowing if he'd be kicked out or not, my guts were in a constant turmoil, my heart unable to side with those who were most meaningful to me and wanted Merrill out; Olson, for one, Wes Huss, for another, my loyalties with them as well as with Merrill, although much more decidedly with the latter, given the power of eros at that age, the mind bypass of the hormones that can rationalize anything.

And didn't they know he grew up partially deaf, and didn't they know how that must've contributed to his protectively superior and isolating attitudes?

I've always wondered if my own obvious naked need and open goofy gaiety upon his return, perhaps coupled with my guiltily acknowledged value as an overworked, unpaid peon in the college kitchen, might've had a smidgen to do with tipping the most recalcitrant in Merrill's favor. But I was overjoyed when Merrill informed me they were going to let him stay on a temporary basis, and that, in a move to further economize and to consolidate our shrinking campus, we were offered the two front rooms just off the lobby on the streamside of Streamside, which luckily came with another of those ubiquitous upright pianos in the front room for Merrill to practice and compose on.

We moved in that very day—during Merrill's trip to Houston I'd moved back to my boxspring bed in the attic dorm of South Lodge—and in our new quarters in Streamside that evening, our bed, a *real* bed luckily—two single beds, actually, shoved together, and with real bedsteads—got quite a workout.

With a bed off the floor to sleep in, and Merrill sleeping close beside me, what more could I ask for?

What more indeed.

Being at Black Mountain, where, besides poetry, thanks to Olson, music was also prime and had a powerful influence; and being with Merrill, perhaps because of the even more powerful erotic influence of that, he spending hours a day sitting composing and practicing at the upright in Next-to-the-Last Chance, or later down at Streamside, and my wanting to be like him, to be part of his life, right down to the music; all that reawakened in me a fierce desire that started in my childhood to play the piano. My widowed Grandmother Marvel (née Katie O'Connor) had an ancient upright in the corner of her parlor in her two-story row house on Hoffman Street in South Philly, a dark, handsomely-crafted piece that she kept meticulously polished and also kept locked to keep the naturally inquisitive fingers of her numerous grandchildren off the equally high-polished keys. Neither she nor my Aunt Idy, also widowed, who lived with her, could play—that wasn't the point.

The point was in the pride of owning (on the installment plan) such a handsome instrument, an early 20th Century status symbol, if you will, of the poor and working-class Catholic (my grandmother scrubbed floors to support her large brood, because my Grandfather Marvel, a cobbler and sometime fishing boat captain, was frequently "off on a bender," as my mother later informed me, leaving my grandmother with no money to feed the children). The only person allowed to unlock the piano and actually play it, and that on only special occasions, like Christmas or New Year's, was my Uncle Bert Marvel, who, after a few beers, played wonderfully by ear and had a passing tenor.

Of course, in those Depression years, my family was always too poor to own a piano (even our old Scott radio was a hand-me-down from my father's better-off sister, Steffie), even if my mother and father had wanted one, which I was very sorry to see they didn't. And of course the ones in the various classrooms in elementary school in Gloucester County, New Jersey (where we moved in 1938 for better job prospects for my long out-of-work father), were as off-limits as my grandmother's old South Philly upright. But I found out that one of my 3rd grade schoolmates in the National Park Grammar School, Gerald Gaynor, had an old oak upright piano, as carefully polished as my grandmother's, in his mother's parlor in their house on Wesley Avenue. Innocently and childishly afire about this, intently watching the teacher in school thump away at the keys as we sang "Welcome Sweet Springtime" or "*Frère Jacques*," watching to try to learn how she did it, so eager was I to learn how to play—and even though I was mostly timid and shy, my desire made me nervy. One afternoon after school, I knocked on Mrs. Gaynor's door and to her surprise asked her if I could practice on her piano, convinced from having watched my teacher bang away at the upright that I knew enough how to do it. Mrs. Gaynor wasn't even a Catholic but went to the "red brick church," that is, she was a Protestant, and worse yet, a Methodist, and my mother would've killed me if she'd ever found out how cheeky I'd been.

Mrs. Gaynor, undoubtedly baffled, being a kindly religious woman, amusedly polite, let me in and, much more lenient about her prized possession than my grandmother, allowed me to bang away on the keys for awhile, as I explained to her how badly I wanted to learn to play. I must've made quite a racket and was deeply disappointed to discover I hadn't learned any-thing at all from my carefully watching the keyboard technique of the teacher—I firmly believed a miracle would happen and I would magically play—and so never returned to bother the poor woman again. I'm sure Gerald must've heard about it when he got home, and I don't know what he, a skinny, buck-toothed, good-natured kid, thought; he looked at me oddly in class after that but never said anything.

At Black Mountain, Wolpe, who as a teacher of music com-position was at loose ends after his only two really serious stu-dents left to return to Philadelphia, first the farm worker with the magnificent physique, then the farm worker's friend and his family (Betty Kaiser hadn't yet arrived from New York to study music with Stefan). One day at the lunch table, overhearing me say how much I still had a dream of learning to read music so I could play the piano, he announced confidently, as always: "*I* will teach you."

I wasn't sure it was such a good idea, not only because Merrill detested him for having "usurped" Lou Harrison's place, but Wolpe intimidated me in more ways than one, especially with his blunt way of speaking, as on one occasion, in the presence of Hilda and others, when he asked me very directly what my background was. I was a bit put off but told him, "Irish, English, Lithuanian, Polish and maybe some French." He exclaimed, "Ah! That's why you have such a strange face!" He said it in a way that made me feel like I'd been insulted.

His obvious brilliance also made me feel my own inadequacies, not to mention, even visible to my inexperienced eyes, his innovative genius. I also couldn't understand his wanting to waste his considerable abilities on a raw musical novice like me: he must've been very bored, and desperate, with no students, so at least having me as one was perhaps a way of justifying his existence at the college. But he was insistent: "You come to Black Dwarf at two in the afternoon and I teach you."

So after my dishwashing stint in the kitchen after lunch I walked up the hill to Black Dwarf where Stefan lived with Hilda on the first floor. My heart was in my mouth as I sat down on the bench beside Stefan in front of the open Steinway grand, which at that moment loomed gigantic to me, in their living room.

"Get close," he ordered, the loose folds of his face creasing up into a big grin, amused by my shyness, his heavy beard, always a 5 o'clock shadow, giving him a slightly paradoxical thuggish look. "Don't be nervous—I won't bite you," which made me only the more nervous, but I squirmed a little closer to him.

He began by teaching me the keyboard, and then started me off learning to read music by teaching me the notes to some idiotically moronic children's song about spring, having me play it back to him over and over, patient, encouraging—"Yah, yah, you are getting it!"—which was just about my level of competence.

We met at Black Dwarf for an hour or so in the afternoon maybe twice a week, Wolpe referring to me as "my student," his voice, I was sure, dripping with irony. I could only imagine what the wittily sharp-tongued Hilda, who was usually nowhere in sight when I arrived, shut up in her room reading or writing, I surmised, had to say about my awful playing. But I could see plain enough Stefan himself was pretty much amused at my rudimentary abilities, but was still game to teach me, till, still stuck on that foolish song, we both realized, he long before me, that he was getting pretty bored with it all and that it was useless to continue.

But he left me with one gift: "So maybe you don't learn to read music or play the piano, but I teach you to *improvise!*" And he did, sitting beside me on the piano bench, his voice, as always, making odd musical sounds (which Olson loved to hear, the main reason I suspect why he hired him), his voice another instrument as he chirruped and screeched and squeezed squealings and gutterals and whistlings deep out of his throat and warbled bass and contralto and soprano burblings, his entire body spastic with movement as his powerful arched fingers with their dark black hairs crashed down on the keys or now stroked them whisperingly in discordant notes and chords that electrified my ears as much as his compositions did (you could never *not* hear Stefan's music). He made the piano become a live thing, one with the improvised atonal music of that other instrument, his extraordinary improvisatorial voice, which, like his music, shook sound on its ear.

Whenever I could, all that summer on the Steinway in the dining hall when nobody was around, or out on the Steinway in the Music House near the cooks' quarters, with its wall of glass windows with a view off deep in the woods, I pounded away at improvisations, much of them sounding Wolpe-like, much of them not worth anything, except the freedom it gave me, a freedom into sound, the pleasure of that.

That was the first gift Wolpe gave me; the second unexpected but no less vital one came later that summer after my first public apprentice reading at Black Mountain, and like most genuine gifts, one I didn't at first recognize for what it was.

Later, in the dining room, near the wide open doors leading to the dining porch, on summer nights, alone, after Merrill had once again returned to Houston to win Herb back, still "playing" the improvisational piano on the Steinway grand that I'd learned from the not-so-successful piano lessons I took with Wolpe earlier, my queer atonal chords my love call to any who might hear, loud, plaintive, just like any other love-sick bullfrog out in the mud of Lake Eden, or cricket singing in the high grasses at its edge.

One afternoon that summer, after dishcrew when I was taking out the trash to burn in the big rusty oil drum out back of the kitchen (garbage dropped in the huge can under the sink near the dishwasher went to slop the pigs), I spotted in the ash pit beside it, where people threw excess trash if the drum was too full, a stack of canary-yellow second sheets laying at the center of the pit, evidently freshly tossed there, scattered with gray ash. Looking closer, I saw that they were poems and when I lifted them out and blew off the ashes, I could see they were poems by Olson, lines spaced on the page in his spatially open and inimitable way, some pages marked simply "o," others marked "olson." They appeared to be carbon copy drafts of the early Maximus poems, plus short lyric stanzas. I was very surprised to see them tossed there. Had he thrown them out by mistake? Probably not, since they were the only items in the pit. My first impulse was to tuck them down my shirt and keep them for myself, hide them back in my study. Indeed, I even peered around sneakily to see if anyone were watching before I did, especially, irrational as it was, Olson himself. But then I lost my nerve, thinking that Olson had obviously thrown them out for good reason, either they were superfluous copies or drafts so crude he wanted to get rid of them altogether; perhaps they were even versions discarded in a fit of anger. (I didn't then know, as I learned years later, through George Butterick at the University of Connecticut Library, what an extraordinary pack-rat Charles was, keeping not only, to my great surprise, most of our letters to him but even restaurant napkins scrawled with his notes—not to mention even a sack of marbles from his childhood which George, on my first visit to the Library, impishly showed me.) But then, too, we were all so drilled in it, out of respect for Charles' privacy, even regarding his trash, and also the fact that he'd obviously wanted to throw those copies away, despite the public setting, I guess I mainly acted out of kneejerk respect for that privacy. I knew he would have killed me if he discovered that I'd rescued his personal canary sheets from the ash pit, going against his wishes to have them burned. So I, ever the dutiful "son" with him, grudgingly but carefully placed them back in the pit and set a match to the papers, burning them along with the rest of the trash.

Also years later, I sensed when I told Butterick this story at the University of Connecticut, in the old Wilbur Cross Library where, thanks to George's efforts, Olson's papers were first housed, that he, who was mainly so impassive and mild in manner and voice, could've committed violence to me on the spot. He gasped, his black eyebrows rearing, his eyes growing round behind his glasses, fiercely suggesting I should have saved those second sheets from the flames. He tried to comfort himself again by reiterating, "Olson never threw anything out," but admitted my discovery at the ash pit just might have been a rare exception.

At that time at Black Mountain, for weeks after, I regretted my lack of nerve, my fear of offending Charles in any way, and even to this day am troubled by it: Had I done the right thing respecting Charles' unspoken but obvious wishes or should I have rescued those papers, for future archivists and scholars such as George (just as I kept and carried around with me in old boxes for years wherever I moved every scrap of paper Charles ever wrote to me)?

For Butterick, there was only one answer.

After a Saturday night party in the dining hall, where, at its drunken end, Virginia made a sudden, unexpected pass at me, knocking me off my chair, the two of us ending up on the floor under the Steinway, Virginia's large bulk on top of me, she protesting her love as I gasped for air. Finally wriggling out from under, a dazed Virginia, Bert Morgan, and I swayed up the road to the Studies where, while Virginia gazed blearily on, Bert and I consumed nightcaps of Bert's homebrew in his study, his illegal booze concocted in the Chemistry Lab under the front entrance to the Studies, the only student who made use of the decrepit lab or its rusting and broken equipment. (Besides Bert's still, the lab also housed the potentially danger- ous WW 2 surplus army washing machine with its short circuits and erratic behavior, so that you had to sit on it in the spin cycle to keep it from dancing out the door.)

That night, Bert, in his ripped khaki workshirt with rolled-up sleeves revealing finely muscular arms from several years work on the college farm, his olive skin even darker from the sun, that, coupled with his tight black curly hair, giving him a romantically Mediterranean appearance, was most appealing. Besides working on the farm and making endless batches of homebrew, Bert occasionally got up satirical skits after supper in the dining hall, which were very funny, including one called "Groundhog," to mark groundhog day, Black Mountain-style.

Between the bags of yeast and crates of empty and full mason jars, plus his books, wall desk, a few chairs and the ubiquitous pallet, Bert's study was quite crammed with the three of us, and Virginia was of a size that made it even more crowded, so that our knees jammed against each other. (Virginia, coincidentally enough, played the wine seller in Huss' production of Brecht's *The Good Woman of Setzuan*, while Bert played the waiter.) Bert and I were feeling no pain, but Virginia, except for her brief and clumsy lunge at me moments earlier in the dining hall, was always so solidly steady and quiet it was hard to know if she was tipsy or not. Still, I detected Bert's darkly glazed eyes behind his glasses had an impish gleam, his finely shaped sensuous lips curling in a loose grin whenever he glanced at me, one of his knees on occasion pressing rather casually but pointedly against mine (his shapely thighs tightly encased in his ragged levis also did not go unnoticed). After yet another mason jar of Bert's potent brew went down our gullets, we were both so high we began playfully touching and caressing each other, oblivious to Virginia, who sat stolidly, peering at us through her lopsided, baby-blue framed glasses with puzzled amusement, and who I conveniently forgot had a crush on me. When she finally left, tottering up the hall, Bert kicked the door shut and the two of us fell on each other.

I thought something more would come of it, but he avoided me after that—much to my confusion. I thought I'd found in him (I daydreamed about him for weeks after) the solution to the drought in my life at that time at Black Mountain, with Merrill gone.

In the winter of 1954, Bert and I chanced to meet on MacDougal Street near Minetta Lane in the Village, where I was then sharing an apartment with Mary Ann Fretz during winter break. Bert had left the college the year before to go into the army. He was civil but distant, not much to say. Another Black Mountain happening, done and gone quickly.

Charles was, first and foremost, The Patriarch, Black Mountain his patriarchy with all the attendant, tacit and implied, hierarchical orderings and groupings, starting uppermost with imperative categories of artistic and visionary endeavor, followed by crafts work, then the sciences, with particularly biology, chemistry, and physics taking a backseat according to how they were taught and by whom, at least in Charles' eyes. Then came the favored males, talented writers and painters, preferably the former, who had "proven" themselves, again in Charles' eyes, on down the line through women and children, and, at the very bottom line, Doyle Jones, the farm manager, and his wife, Claire, the animals on the farm and the stray dogs around the place, the last seeming to hold a higher place in Charles' imperious, Vatican-like reckoning than Doyle himself, since Charles disliked Doyle intensely, referring to him once as "a peasant who doesn't know his place." (But Charles also one night in class unaccountably said of Dostoevsky, for all his genius, "What was he, nothing but a peasant," so I figured Doyle was in good company.)

Doyle's Cherokee wife, Claire, was a pretty, fast-talking, chain-smoking woman, always, much like Connie, with a look in her dark eyes of fear, always deferring to Doyle. They would both come dressed up to the Saturday night parties, Doyle in a wide lapel suit and tie, his large, work-worn hands sticking out of starched white cuffs; Claire in lipstick and a tight-fitting dress. They always sat by themselves, looking shy and awkward, uncomfortably out of place and uncomfortably stiff out of their workaday farm clothes, smoking and sipping from a flask of moonshine Doyle brought, Claire's dark eyes darting around more nervous than usual. They came in the beginning to the Saturday night parties at least, till bad feelings between Olson and Doyle developed and relationships with the community soured, then they quit showing up, till Doyle finally quit the farm altogether in 1954.

Even so, one morning, before all that happened, perhaps as a gesture of thanks to Claire and Doyle for letting his class crowd into their parlor to watch, as part of his Reading the Newspaper course, some of the McCarthy hearings on their TV, Olson had us all troop over to wash the windows at the farmhouse, me up on high laughing on a swinging, precarious ladder as I wiped away at the row of back windows—Charles below, grinning up at me, delighted.

In that late spring and early summer of 1953, as the weeks

went by and the letters from Black Mountain to Houston between Merrill and Herb flew thicker and faster, Merrill was becoming more and more irritated and frustrated that the temporary situation of Herb helping his father out in the garage back home was dragging on and on. A part of me went on sympathizing with Merrill's unhappiness but that larger, more selfish part was secretly glad Herb continued with his deeply committed sense of filial piety, which Merrill, in cold fury, rooted in his own interests, termed merely "gutless."

As for my own interests, I began to hope that time and distance away from Herb would improve my own chances with Merrill, that maybe some day he'd come to care about me as much as he did for Herb, such were the green hopes of a queer youth enmeshed in suffering an adolescent crush for another male for the first time, with all the attendant extremes of sappiness. That, plus at tiny-populated Black Mountain where pickings were slim and exaggerations common, I'd already blown out of proportion everything romantic and carnal about Merrill in the already obsessive-compulsive mindset I'd brought down to the college with me.

Therefore, it was a blow when Merrill informed me one evening that the only thing he could do, since his letters, even the occasional long-distance phone call to Houston on the pay phone in the Studies lobby (not cheap in those days), weren't working, was for him to make another trip to Texas to try to convince Herb in the flesh to leave his sick father and the garage and return to Black Mountain with him.

I should've seen then that if Merrill was willing to go that far, his need for Herb was stronger than any need he could ever have for me. But I refused to see it, refused to see that I was only serving as an interim convenience till Herb returned; my pride wouldn't allow that admission. Even so, I continued to secretly harbor the hope that Merrill would fail in his mission, that he'd return to Black Mountain, forget Herb over time, and continue to stay on with me.

Because the college needed all the spare rooms for the Summer Institute guests, I reluctantly moved back to my bed in the South Lodge attic dorm again. While Merrill was gone I missed him a lot, but I kept busy that summer in Wes' theater class and in a movement class that Huss persuaded Merce Cunningham, whose dance troupe was part of the Institute, to teach us to help our acting, which met after breakfast at 8 a.m. in the dining hall several mornings a week. (I don't think Merce was exactly thrilled with the prospect, but he went along with it.) I even tried a few sessions with Merce's advanced class for his own dancers and several of his summer students, which met immediately after our movement class, just for the hell of it, much to Merce's amusement. In fact, my gawkiness in the ear-lier movement class also rather amused him, but no matter, it was all great, freeing fun, a pleasure to be in touch with my body beyond dishcrew, floor sweeping and sex. It was also after one of Merce's classes that Mary Ann Fretz, whose father had driven her down that summer to study photography with Hazel Frieda Larsen and, hence, having a camera always in hand, snapped a campy, "balletic" pose of me perched on the dining porch railing, a nasturtium I snatched from one of the flower vases on the tables held out delicately pinched between thumb and forefinger for "esthetic" appreciation, a pose in a deliberate and probably satirical opposition to the athletically innovative movements we were learning in Merce's class. "Fly across the floor!" he'd cry, in great good humor. "Fly! Fly!" And we'd fly, myself feeling like a fledgling just learning, but a bird for all that as I awkwardly flew across the floor with the others, a floor I'd danced around so many times solo with my broom.

One really pleasant aspect of my work that summer was that Cunningham and his dance company in the afternoons used the huge space of the dining hall with its pitched high-raftered ceiling for rehearsals and for classes in choreography and dance theory. Merce was choreographing a dance, that was to become "Septet," to Satie's "Three Pieces in the Form of a Pear." As I set the tables for supper out on the dining porch, trying to be as quiet as I could with the dish cart, and arranging in the small ceramic cups the Weinribs had fired in the pot shop tiny bouquets of wild flowers I'd picked for each table, it was a delight to hear through the open windows of the porch birdy-thin, bespectacled David Tudor, perpetual cigarette butt hanging out one corner of his mouth, great shock of dark hair bouncing on his brow, as he played on the Steinway the muted, featherweight pieces by Satie over and over, music I was hearing for the first time. Hearing also in counterpoint the other music of the muffled bare feet of the dancers over the wide floor, and Merce's clipped, precise directions, his sharp laughter at occasional glitches.

Sometimes, while his dancers sprawled around him on the floor after rehearsal, Merce would give a class in "theory," his own unique and innovative perceptions of it, and I would listen hungrily through the open windows, trying to catch everything. Once, for some reason I couldn't figure out, he talked at great length about James Joyce's *Ulysses*, which I'd gotten from those forbidden shelves at the Prendergast Library in Jamestown that summer before I came to Black Mountain and had read avidly. Merce was somehow connecting *Ulysses* to dance, a book that was anathema in Charles' writing classes. Olson's opposition to it was as "end," as "closed form," as "done," "deadend," his irritation, too, directed at those critics who were smugly assured that after *Ulysses* there was nothing more to be done, all literary inventiveness accomplished. So, as Merce expounded on Joyce, I listened, all ears, just as I watched, all eyes, when he danced: light, feathery curl of his hair, exotic high cheek-boned face and sharp eyes facing each space as if it were new, newly, surprisingly, come upon; bones of Merce surely hollowed like a bird's, spare flight muscles of arms, legs, a bird's; slim body chiseled by wind as he spread, leapt, flew about the hall, birds his ancestral blood, sky his ancestral space.

Merce, who was punctuality itself regarding his classes, uncharacteristically showed up late one morning for our 8 a.m. movement class. His dance troupe, along with John Cage, had thrown him a surprise birthday party in their quarters up in Streamside the night before, and the rumor was much uncustomary wine had been consumed. It showed in Merce's rather gray face and somewhat hung-over eyes. Still, he strode in briskly with Paul Taylor, then still a student of Merce's and a member of his troupe, and without breakfast, that meal just over, no exceptions made by cook Malrey, even for great innovative dancers. With a sheepish smile he apologized to us and then immediately had us leaping around the room in various exercises. Paul, big, athletic, boyishly handsome, crewcut dancer Paul, for all his superb tall musculature—he'd been a former swimming champ—was the most gentle-mannered, gentle-spoken of young men, with a genial, slyly quiet humor and wit, which soon showed up in his own choreographed dances. He turned quite a few heads that summer, male and female, and not only for his magnificently lithe dancing. Often leaning in the dining porch windows, watching rehearsals, I was pop-eyed at the magical way he moved, his long legs frog-like in their leaps. Paul looked a bit gray-faced that morning-after too, but none the worse for wear and joined in our exercises as energetically as Merce.

Seeing Merce and Paul arrive often together for breakfast sparked rumors around tiny, gossip-obsessed Black Mountain, as to whether they were indulging in a summer romance, despite other rumors of Merce's attachment to John Cage. Such speculations ran around in my own head too, along with, since Merrill was gone, the most feverish erotic fantasies about Paul. But, as with Merce, as with Merce's partner, John, there was no intimation, let alone any public discussion of any of that. Avant-gardists to the core, perhaps even then in the early 1950s, they saw the falsity of such categories in the complexity and fluidity of human sexuality, attraction and affection, and transcended such limitations in their work. "There are no camps," as Olson had said. At any rate, there was no talk outside their own tight camp at least, of who was who and who was with whom. They were a thoroughly professional group, and though friendly enough, kept mainly to themselves, as dancers tend to do, in their long hours together, tight and close-knit. Even so, for Merce, although I recall him lamenting the fact that more things went wrong for him at Black Mountain than anywhere else, that the place was in a way a jinx for him, those times at the college (he'd also been there in 1948) offered him and his troupe rent-free open space to practice and develop his experimental dances of that time, plus temporary freedom from worry about food and lodging so as to develop his ideas.

Speaking of John Cage, when I first clapped eyes on him that summer of 1953, when he wandered into the dining hall while I was sweeping, he, dressed in khaki coveralls, his unexpressive, pallid face suggesting one of the moonstruck hillfolk, I thought he was a newly hired assistant to hired hand T.J., till John opened his mouth.

One Saturday evening after our usual chicken dinner, several of Merce's students, those who had come especially to study with him that summer, gave a program of individual dances Merce had had them choreograph as part of the class. One of the dancers was a plumpish young woman with abundant dark hair and Mediterranean features and complexion who, that entire session, was never out of her leotards (a few wags insisted she even wore them to bed). She spent long hours, after Merce's regular morning student dance class was finished, rubbing her back, much like a cat, up and down one of the posts in the dining hall, while she pliéd, extended her arms in a circle, took turns doing the same with each leg, rubbing herself up and down and sideways on the post, hour after hour, a dreamy, rapt expression on her face, while I worked around her, sweeping the floor or pushing the dishcart back and forth to the dining porch, setting up tables for the next meal. She was mostly unmindful of me, although occasionally, if I swept too close, she'd break the intensity of her concentration and give me a weak smile, almost one of apology. It seemed to say: I know what I'm doing, but can't help myself. Mary Fiore and a few others were especially concerned about her singlemindedness (there was no way to know what Merce thought, if he was aware of it at all), about the narrow range of her repetitive exercises around that post—always the same post. When Mary, her brow crinkling as it did whenever she was concerned, her magnificent blue eyes gazing to the side in worriment, tried to talk to the young dancer, or myself or anyone else for that matter tried, for she was amiable enough, she would speak of nothing but dance and her determination to be a dancer, singlemindedness it seemed as fierce as her daily writhings around the post. All this was doubly sad and disturbing because most of those who knew about these matters (Mary had earlier studied dance with Betty Jennerjahn at the college) didn't think she had a chance as a dancer, Mary finally speculating with great sympathy, that there was something else going on with her, an impossible dream, even an edge of madness perhaps.

Another of Merce's students performed a solo dance that evening that Olson peculiarly enough was quite taken with, "peculiarly" because she in no way *looked* like a dancer (whatever validity that had at Black Mountain, especially in Merce's troupe of mixed physiques). She was very tall and very skinny with unusually long, spindly arms and legs. I myself immediately empathized with her since she so resembled myself, *and*, I'd noted in the morning movement class, she was as gawky and clumsy as I was, which made me wonder why she, like the young obsessed dancer at her post, wanted to be a dancer.

The night of the program, she appeared dressed in an aquamarine leotard with a curious crepe waist that somewhat resembled, given her unfleshed physique, a swimming suit for a prepubescent girl. To top off the "non-dancer" look, she had long black frizzy hair and wore black-framed glasses. The musical piece she danced to was of a spare modernist construction, sound- rather than melody-focused, to match the movements of the dance she'd composed: very small precise movements of arms and legs, so tiny they barely strayed from the trunk of her body, delicate turnings of her hands, her feet, physical shadings barely perceptible to the eye. The viewer had to pay strict attention to observe anything at all. She stood facing the audience through the entire dance, her face a mask of non-expression you could read everything and anything into. She seemed all of a concentrated inwardness, taking care, getting it right. Her eyes behind her glasses gazed straight ahead out over the heads of the audience, her dance, I'm sure, going over the heads of most of us, myself thinking how clever she was to keep her dance small, to not try anything big or splashy like a few of the other student dancers. Working within her limitations, she appeared to open up the illimitable. And perhaps that was why Charles was so enthusiastic about her performance, clapping loudly amidst the modest applause when she'd finished, his grinning face flushed with pleasure, getting it, getting it more perhaps than any one of us, except the dancer herself, letting everyone around him know how much it had pleased him, its subtlety and accomplishment, enthusiastically commenting on her minimal movements, the modesty and precision of her gestures, the pointedness of them.

Something of her in him, I thought, in that vast size of him, in his own dance of words, despite his coming on as the high-roller, something delicate and pointed and small, quiet, that he saw in her—the soul of Connie in him, she, too, like that, and later, the soul of Betty Kaiser.

Olson could be harsh, however, not only on one's writing but on one's acting performance as well, I learned. In Wes' Noh play production of Seami's *Pool of Sacrifice*, performed in the dining hall that summer, Olson came up to speak to the cast afterward and playfully slapping me, sneered about how I acted my formal sacerdotal role, "And *you*—you played it like a *Catholic* priest!"

I was stung, yes, as usual, but thinking, What other models had I, himself included? But the sting was less, because I was beginning to realize that Charles, once he cared for you, had to be an authority on everything you did.

That summer, I even took an additional acting class with writer James Leo Herlihy, a former student, who was later known for having written *Midnight Cowboy*, the novel on which John Schlesinger's 1969 film is based, and who in the 1960s in New York City mentioned casually over dinner to historian Martin Duberman that Black Mountain College might be an interesting subject for Duberman to write a book about. Herlihy had returned for the 1953 Summer Institute, along with dancer Remy Charlip, and rejoined Merce's dance class for that brief time. He also offered an informal class in acting exercises and technique in the basement of the Studies to a handful of regular and summer students. We did scenes from Laurence Housman's *Victoria Regina* (Herlihy pronounced it "Regeena," smilingly saying the other way sounded too much like "vagina"), and he was very good at stage business, like showing the young woman playing Victoria how to screw on earrings to best advantage, and so forth. The young woman was a bleached blond from Sarah Lawrence College with the broadest shoulders I'd ever seen on a female (even wider than Joan Crawford's shoulder pads), her upper torso shaped like an inverted triangle. She spoke very bluntly; was physically contained, erect, straightforward; dressed smartly in expensive summery outfits as if she were always on her way to some country club tennis court; and always gave the distinct impression she was slumming it at Black Mountain, that the place and ourselves were not up to snuff. I admired her strength and intelligence, yet she made me nervous, didn't *behave* like women were supposed to in the 1950s. (Women like her at that time were called "castraters.") Perhaps because she was a psychiatrist's daughter, she felt impelled to tell me, in that crisp, severe voice of hers, as I was saying goodbye to her in front of the dining hall after the Summer Institute ended, while she waited beside her expensive luggage for a taxi to drive her to the train station, "Michael, you are dishonest, duplicitous and a neurotic and should do something about it." I was surprised at the vehemence in her tone, and could readily see why Herlihy had chosen her to play the Queen. I was certainly relieved to see her, and her shoulders, disappear into the cab.

Herlihy had a pale, boyishly handsome face, his glossily thick dark hair swept up in a kind of pompadour. Most unusual, and he was privately scorned for such affectation, considered a phony, a showoff, by the old Black Mountain hands, was his habit of setting up his portable typewriter on one of the tables on the dining porch and pecking away at his latest creation, dressed in skinny silk tie, button-down shirt, and an expensive, narrow-fitting, nattily tailored, single-breasted suit with the buttons covered in the same fine gray pin-striped material as the suit. Nothing like it had ever been seen at Black Mountain, where the more seasoned habitués looked upon writing, or even painting, in public as akin to open masturbation, all acts that should be done in the privacy of one's study or studio. Cage created the first Happening at Black Mountain, perhaps Herlihy unwittingly created the first Performance Artist. Perhaps he got his final sweet revenge when, as noted, he induced Martin Duberman to write his *Black Mountain: An Exploration in Community*.

His summer stay was cut short when, for reasons that baffled some, he fell hook-line-and-sinker for Cockney-born painting student Basil King, a short, curly-haired, round-eyed, blunt-spoken youth who grew up in Detroit (another pal of Jorge Fick's). Basil used to drop in at my first floor room in the rear of South Lodge, flop on my box spring mattress in his levis and t-shirt and talk in his comical, wiseguy way. He eventually married writing student Martha Davis and moved to New York City where they had two daughters, one of whom they named Malrey in honor of the college cook.

When Basil turned James Leo down, Herlihy was evidently so crushed and humiliated, he left the college next day, slipping away without a word to anyone.

In the early 1960s I met Herlihy again by chance at the Actors Studio on West 45th Street in New York City, when I was under the delusion that I might be a playwright. (I had transformed my short story "The Desert" into an alleged play, which the Actors Studio planned to put on, but never did, fortunately.) He was polite but chillily aloof when I reminded him we'd worked together at Black Mountain and seemed to pretend not to remember me.

In the early 1990s, I read in the national gay and lesbian magazine *The Advocate* that he had died, a suicide. No reason given.

The high point of that summer was the previously noted Black Arts Ball, planned by David Weinrib and M. C. Richards to celebrate Wes Huss' 45th birthday. It got to be quite a project, including planned tableaux on, ironically, given the evening's conclusion, Great Lovers in History, featuring most of Wes' acting students, and starring at its finale a nude Karen Karnes, known more for her pottery than as a flower- and vine-draped Ophelia. (No doubt hearing of her posing in Esteban Vicente's drawing class, or spotting her thus, David asked Mary Ann Fretz if she'd be willing to pose nude as Ophelia in the finale of the closing tableau. She, exhibiting yet another desire to display herself, readily agreed to do it. But when Karen Karnes, David's wife, got wind of it, she put the kabosh on it, perhaps suspicious that David was maybe a tad *too* eager to see Mary Ann in the altogether, and insisted she'd do it herself.)

Pat Nelson and I, young renegade Catholics that we were, scraped our meager resources together to make costumes to go as a nun and a monk, respectively. We hitched a ride into Asheville where Pat picked out enough yards of cheap dark-brown sacking at the 5 & 10 to make our costumes. Clever with a needle, she sewed them up herself, including a capacious monk's hood for my outfit, and ingeniously fashioned a wimple for herself from an old torn bedsheet she'd found in the North Lodge linen closet. My contribution was rounding up a length of white cord and knotting it in such a way that it resembled rosary beads to tie around our middles.

As preparations, and endless fittings, continued—most everyone else was also in a tizzy secretly preparing their costumes, including Malrey, the cook—Pat and I got giddier and giddier with excitement of committing blasphemy in our sanctimonious drag, so carried away we even eventually planned to celebrate a Black Mass at Black Mountain—it was, after all, *all* theater, for two theater students—in front of the huge field-stone fireplace at the far end of the hall. We even thought of putting the small, little-played, foot-pumped cherrywood organ beside it to use by having one of the music students pump out a *Kyrie eleison* during our mass. (Black Mountain was indeed proving to be a truly freeing experience for me, even to entertain *that* thought.) But we were dissuaded from doing it by those who thought it would be in "bad taste," and also might "offend" some, not only the summer visitors but all those other still-afflicted ex-Catholics on campus, no doubt. Perhaps the main reason why we decided not to do it was because of our still deeply ingrained fears, both of us maybe not being as ex-Catholic (if there is such a creature) as we liked to believe, still childishly frightened of, if not God's, at least the Pope's wrath in perpetrating a "sacrilege."

On the night of the ball, after supper, and after the dish crew and the resetting up of the dining hall for dancing, everybody retreated to their quarters to get in costume for the big event. Pat and I dressed in her room in North Lodge and despite the few pennies our outfits had cost, we looked surprisingly convincing, especially Pat in her brown sack habit and bedsheet wimple, me in my hooded robes, our knotted rosaries dangling to our barefeet—barefeet essential because we'd decided, in lieu of the Black Mass, to paint our toenails and fingernails pitch black with India ink.

We waited for the right dramatic moment when most everyone was already there, like two good drama students, before we made our entrance into the crowded darkness of the dining hall, which was lit only by candles on the sheet-covered tables scattered around the edges of the room, leaving the center space open for dancing. We caused quite a stir, particularly Sister Pat who, her intensely white face as round and bright as a full moon in her wimple, caught everyone's eye, when, as soon as we arrived, we began dancing together around and around the floor, causing a bit of a sensation, especially among the men, excited at the sight of fair-skinned Pat decked out in full nun's regalia. Many of them, a surrealistic incongruity in their own outlandish costumes, began to crowd around to take her out on the floor one after the other for a spin to the scratchy 78 rpm records on the old Magnavox phonograph next to the fireplace.

I stood off to the side watching Pat, in her long robes, dance from the arms of one to the arms of another of the guys, her radiantly pallid face lifted with the same calm, beatific gaze to each, swirling round and round, myself by now feeling a bit self-conscious, a bit foolish, really, that I was actually there in my monk's costume and black-painted nails. The doing, as always, as I was learning in writing, was the main pleasure.

Suddenly Malrey, dressed as a witch with black cape and tall black pointed hat, and a long orange-colored paper cone nose held on by a rubber band around her head, a costume she later told me she'd decked herself out in once before for a Sugar Hill Halloween ball up in Harlem, grinningly grabbed me to dance. She, considerably shorter, my long arm resting on her chubby shoulder, we foxtrotted around the floor, probably the only black and white couple dancing together publicly at that time in the whole of the South. As we danced, Malrey, her glasses, inside the cone, constantly slipping down the all but nonexistent bridge of her nose, as they did from the steam when she cooked, kept eagerly snapping her head left and right to see who was dancing with whom and what they were wearing, not wanting to miss anything, so that the sharp point of that long cone of a nose kept sticking me in either cheek. I was glad when the record ended, fearing for my eyes.

The costumes for the tableaux were quite campy—slipping out of my monk's robes and into something skimpily toga-like, I posed as Bacchus (appropriately, and ominously, enough, given my future bouts with alcohol)—and the groupings and sets were starkly and simply lighted for sharpest eye appeal, the stage being the raft moored in Lake Eden just off the dining porch. And an impressively sturdy figure Karen was, wearing nothing but a few vine leaves and flowers, standing amazonian in the half light that was just right for the closing of the Tableaux, Karen in no way resembling the addled, suicidal girl-friend of Hamlet, as she exuded the same focused and unruffled calm she did sitting cross-legged in denim skirt and sandals at her potter's wheel up in the slope-roofed Ceramics Studio at the edge of the cattle pasture.

And it was not long after that finale, despite the earliness of the evening, that I saw Pat and the guest of honor slipping off the dance floor, having just finished dancing together, that quiet look of alluring concentration in Pat's eyes as she gazed up at him during the dance, Wes, his movements tense, rigid, his eyes agitated, evidently so excited by Pat in her habit, the two of them, the nun in drag and the descendant of Jan Hus, disappearing from the Ball together by the kitchen back door, where rumor next day was he'd taken her up to the Studies Building to Pat's study, for a more private birthday celebration.

On another ride into Asheville one twilight for ice cream, with Charles and Connie in Olson's blue Ford convertible. Mary Ann Fretz again beside me in the backseat. The top down once more, the three of us listening to Charles as he excitedly spoke about Peter Voulkos, the potter from the West Coast who was learning innovation at Black Mountain while teaching in the ceramics institute that summer, Charles speaking of Voulkos' large head, how impressed he was by the size of it with its thick tangle of black hair, its rugged, darkly handsome Greek face, tossing back to us over his shoulder as the wind whistled in our ears from his fast driving, how "so many geniuses have large heads," his own head sitting enormous on his own broad shoulders.

Through Charles' encouragement, of pushing me back to myself, to what was my experiential truth, I'd begun early that summer of 1953 to write from that experience, particularly about my family. There were moments when there were only sometimes lines, even sometimes just words, that Olson culled out of my prose to remark on favorably. I wrote about my family being on home relief in the late 1930s. For many unemployed, like my father, those years were still the Depression. I wrote about the U. S. Government-surplus rancid butter and wormy flour, all my mother had to feed us, and shoes with cardboard soles that pinched my feet so bad I limped, and how my mother told me to walk as if they didn't hurt since they wouldn't let me in school without shoes. And how unaware my first grade teacher seemed of the desperate poverty in the township, with her admonitions to us to "eat a balanced diet everyday," pointing with her pointer to her glossy food charts at the front of the room, that made me only hungrier, famished for the food we rarely ever had on our table at home. Charles picked up on these first-hand experiences, and bid me to "mine" them.

One particular image Olson seized on was in a piece I'd written on my brother Bill when we were kids in National Park, New Jersey, of Bill's good-hearted, simple nature, about his deafness and his being prone to nose bleeds. I'd recalled one Saturday afternoon in winter in the 1940s during the war returning with my older brothers from confession at little St. Matthew's church. Walking homeward through the woods in the deep snow, Bill's nose suddenly began one of its bleeds, and I was seized with the startling image of the drops of his blood against the white brilliance of the snow. It had been a direct, simply written passage, and Olson scribbled in the margin of the manuscript words to the effect that that was writing, that was the kind of writing I needed to do, that was the direction: direct, clean, and to the point, a precise, uncluttered image.

He had me reread Sherwood Anderson, "for limpidity," a writer whose style he said I could learn from. As a result, I spent days in the back of Nell Rice's library reacquainting myself with *Winesburg, Ohio*, and discovering *Windy McPherson's Sons*, *Marching Men*, *Many Marriages*, *Dark Laughter*, and the story collections *The Triumph of the Egg*, *Horses and Men*, and *Death in the Woods*, as ever, following Olson's injunction to "saturate" myself in my "writer kin," in order to learn to speak in my own tongue, to find my own American speech, pushing what Anderson (via Stein) and William Carlos Williams had long been doing.

It was this kind of writing that Charles suggested I read at my first public reading of my work at Black Mountain that summer, along with old hand Fee Dawson, who privately commented to me how effective the new work was, a turning point. It was quite a surprise, and honor, to be asked, but I was deadset against doing it.

It was one thing to expose my writing inadequacies in Olson's workshops, quite another to expose them to the entire community, including strangers, meaning the summer visitors. But Charles, although still harsh in his judgments regarding my work, approved of this new experiential vein I was attempting to tap. The fact that he now on rare occasions found a nugget here and there in my pages to praise was still a source of wonderment to me, and, ever wanting to please him, I said I'd do it.

Mary, as always, like a strong big sister, understanding, supportive, also pushed me to do it. And so Joe Fiore, a day or two before, had painted a lively, eye-catching poster announcing the event for that Sunday afternoon down in the basement theater room of the Studies (the coolest place), a feathery abstract pattern in various shades of blue behind the black lettering, and tacked it on the big cork bulletin board in the Studies entry. Seeing my name on it, along with Fee's, scared the hell out of me even more, made it "official," so that I couldn't back out. But it also secretly pleased me, gave notice of my presence, that I was part of things (beyond the broom and the dishwashing machine), suggested, at least in some small way, I was coming along, was truly beginning to earn my keep.

The morning of the reading I was so nervous, so filled with childish—meaning self-centered—dread, that I woke up earlier than usual, barely ate any breakfast and sat alone at the dining porch table long after the other customary few early Sunday risers had departed, drinking one cup of coffee after another and practically chainsmoking Home Runs. The rising sun on Lake Eden, the farflung hills, with snow-capped Mt. Mitchell miles in the distance, always such a calming distraction, that morning were none whatsoever. Dorothea Rockburne, the painting student from Canada, sat down across from me and, like Mary, was very sympathetic and tried to be reassuring. She was very practical too. She asked, "What do you need to do *right* now?" "I need to shave." "Well, then," she grinned, "do it." And I did, climbing up to the large bath in the attic dorm of South Lodge. After, I took a long walk in the hills and down along the road past the farms in the valley. When I returned, I met Mary on the road on her way to the dining hall for lunch, and she gave me a good, last-minute pep talk.

I don't recall much about the actual reading itself, except that just about the whole campus was there. Fee read with his usual assurance, in his forceful, slightly stuttering voice. I got through my part of it somehow and only recall a great rush of relief when it was over, relief with the fact that I'd actually *done* it, more than whether anybody liked the writing or not. Of course, I was hoping there might be some praise, of the 100% variety, since the drug of praise is the writer's addiction, especially from the big guns like Olson. And although a few, like Mary, were polite, as usual Black Mountain tradition taking precedence, people tended not to say what they didn't believe, and the lack of any meaningful comments told me I hadn't made much of a splash. At least I'd done it, at 21 my first public reading, but it was especially important because I'd done it at Black Mountain College, where I knew I had to prove myself, and was realistic enough to know that it'd take a long time before I did that, if I ever did, before anyone sat up and took notice.

The greatest news that I was given that day, however, was

something I didn't want to hear, because it struck me as so negative, and something I didn't at first fully understand. It came not from Olson, the writing teacher, but from Stefan Wolpe, the music teacher, who was standing off in a corner discussing the reading afterwards with Charles. Wolpe, just like Olson, always had an opinion, often insightful, on just about everything. I was standing gawkily a few yards away, hoping somebody would say something to me, and, looking pointedly at me so I'd be sure to hear, Stefan said in his high, heavily German-accented voice, "The trouble with Rumaker is he doesn't know how to *lie* yet." And Charles, with one of his bug-eyed grins of delighted and instant perception, stared first at Wolpe and then over at me.

Initially, I was confused at what Wolpe meant, but Charles, in later talks with me, hammered away at Wolpe's insight, which I was finally able to grasp and make use of in a story—the first *real* story I ever wrote—almost a year later in Charles' class. (Years after, I was able to get to the core of Stefan's meaning by putting it thus: "The lie of the imagination creates the truth of reality.")

It took time, but I got it, because that was the beauty of time at Black Mountain, to have it to worry the nub of a problem to a possible solution, to find not necessarily answers, but ways to discover how to do a thing. I look back after all these years, and among so many gratitudes from that time, am especially grateful to Stefan Wolpe for that paradoxical insight that freed me into writing, that gave me the permission of my imagination, once I understood it.

Other useful assists, this from Charles himself:

Olson saying emphatically in class one night, "Keats was stuck with description," saying it with a touch of sadness at what he, Keats (capable of a brilliant insight like "negative capability," which Charles expanded on a great deal in class and in his own writing at the time) might've done if not "stuck" there.

Hearing the "description" crack the first time, I took it as a caveat against my own inclination, which Charles had criticized, the pile-up of adjectives, the standing outside describing instead of being actionably *within* "in the instant of writing."

Desperate to knock off something to read in a class, Charles chiding me for writing a "silly" poem about Billie Holiday, that did neither her nor her singing justice. Showed me the futility of forcing it, just to have a ticket to his class. (Three years later, after I left Black Mountain, one bitter-cold February night, I and a rich lesbian friend and a few of her female pals had gone to hear Billie Holiday sing at the Blue Note, a jazz club in West Philly; ardent Holiday fans that we were, we sat through two sets, wanted to sit through a third, but, our money running low—my rich friend, like many of the rich it seemed, rarely carried much cash with her—we sadly left and rounded the corner where my friend had parked her Mercedes-Benz; passing a neighborhood bar, evidently with a back alleyway entrance to the place from the Blue Note, we stood transfixed on the snow-covered sidewalk as we spotted through the plate-glass window Billie Holiday herself inside on a break, flats kicked off at foot of barstool, but trademark gardenia still in her hair, a tumbler of gin before her, she, chatting amiably with the black bartender who had one leg kicked up against the bar sink, listening, the plain, drab bar—much less glamorous than the plush Blue Note—empty except for the two of them. We hesitated whether we should go in or not, then screwed up our nerve and entered, the women sitting shyly in a booth, while urging me in whispers to go up to the bar to order cheap draft beers and to introduce myself to Holiday so they could meet her. I went, heart pounding, hearing, as I approached the bar, Holiday murmuring to the bartender as she touched her stomach, "I've had heartburn all day and haven't eaten a thing—Gimme one of them Slim Jims," and the bartender pulled down one of the cellophane-wrapped packets of spicy jerky from behind the bar, me thinking *that* probably was only going to give her more heartburn. She saw me standing a few respectful stools down the bar; and, still amiable, playful, asked me, "You a college boy?" while she munched on a bite of her Slim Jim, then washed it down with gin. When I stammered "yes," wondering if I should mention Black Mountain College, before I could, she said to the bartender, as if picking up from their conversation, "Y'know, I've always wanted to add 'My Funny Valentine' to my repertory but don't know all the words," then she asked me teasingly, "You know the words?" Weirdly, it was the only song I *did* know the words to, and when I said "Yes," she had me go put a quarter in the jukebox so she could hear a "My Funny Valentine" instrumental. She followed and stood behind me and when the record began, she said "Sing," and I started, my heart in my throat, but she took over and sang it, sang it sweet in that immaculately-phrased voice of hers right in my right ear, while I stood spellbound.)

Charles saying in writing class, regarding my stories, "Michael has to be *serious* all the time." And added, "You don't know what you're doing anyway when you're doing it," regarding my inarticulateness, meaning, No sense asking you anyway. I was a bit flustered by this in front of the others, but knew he was dead on. (A few years later in "The Use of the Unconscious in Writing," I acknowledged it's crucial not to be *too* knowing.)

And Charles telling me during another of the writing classes "to follow your nose in writing, like pushing a peanut in front of you," that that was the right way for me to do it.

He also warned me "not to always be on the side of the angels," regarding my altar boy naïveté, tacitly encouraging me to take a twirl with the devil on occasion.

The summer sessions sometimes sharply reminded us of the world outside our pagan paradise in the Blue Ridge Mountains. There were occasional incidents that summer to remind us of the then still deeply segregated South (Brown vs. Topeka Board of Education was still a year away). One night around two or three in the morning, a bunch of local rowdies, probably liquored up, drove onto the grounds and furiously rang the fire gong outside the back door of the kitchen, shouting, "Nigger lovers! Nigger lovers!" before roaring off. Another time, when we were all gathered outside the dining hall waiting for supper, a few black guests among us, a big black dusty Cadillac drove up—such an expensive automobile such an unusual sight at Black Mountain, we all stared—with a heavyset white man in floppy felt hat and suspenders behind the wheel, an equally heavyset white woman, no doubt his wife, beside him. They both gaped out the windshield at us, then the driver, with some difficulty, leaned over the woman and shouted out the open passenger side window, "Ahm gonna report all you niggah lovahs!" in a very loud, hoarse voice before tearing around Dinner Bell Circle in a cloud of yellow dust and heading back to the county road.

Another time, several of us, along with a woman visiting from India that summer, went to Peak's for beers late one hot afternoon. But once we seated ourselves at a table, short, stout Ma Peak herself marched from behind the bar and stormed over and announced in her clipped drawl: "I kin serve evahbody but *you*," and jerked her tightly braided head at the Indian visitor. Somebody said, Dan Rice, I believe, sizing up the situation immediately, "But she's from *India*." Ma Peak adamantly folded her arms across her ample chest and snapped, "Look at 'er, black as a nigger." Everybody looked gape-mouthed at each other, embarrassed, wondering what to do, since there was the hard reality of the law on Ma's side. Olson took Ma Peak aside and tried to talk quietly to her, using all his considerable persuasion, but Ma stubbornly refused. "Git 'er outa here! I don' want 'er in here!"

Somebody got some ales to go and we left and went back to the college to drink together and be reasonably safe in our own enclave, my own queer self reminded again of my gratitude for that haven, a haven for the Indian woman, for myself, for all such outcasts in that dreadful time, a time, tragically, in many ways still with us.

Apropos of the above, on another evening in class, Charles saying, "The tragedy of blacks is they just can't play it across the board," meaning they were not allowed to. And: "Between whites and blacks there needs to be a coalescence."

On other occasions, we were brought up sharply to the fact that we were indeed surrounded by the deeply religious conservatism of the Bible Belt. This reminder was brought home forcefully that summer when on a Saturday evening panel on music in the dining hall, focusing particularly on contemporary music, when panelist Stefan Wolpe mentioned in the discussion that he was an atheist, a tall, thin blonde woman in the front row, evidently from the local area, screeched out in shocked disbelief in her deep Southern drawl: "You mine ta' tell me you don't believe in *Gawd*?"

Stefan, as if bored with the question, his basset face ever more frowningly folded in his seriousness, flatly declared, "No, of course not!" in a tone that suggested only fools believed in God.

There was a sprinkle of amused laughter in the audience, mostly from us Black Mountain regulars. Having, as noted, recently done battle in my own family, particularly with my mother, over God and religion, I was very impressed by Wolpe's curt and forthright dismissal, no problem for him. The woman, however, still shocked— "aghast" might be the better word—turned incredulously to the people she'd come with sitting on either side of her and, her mouth agape, sat with a worrying frown for the rest of the discussion, as if she'd wandered into some unbelievably evil place.

Regarding religion, in writing class in the Reading Room one night, Charles was talking about the Church, saying, "Christianity became a deadend when it went after sex in the 1500s."

And: "The Church will continue to be irrelevant until the sacred is restored to the sacrament."

And then he made a crack about the possible demise of the then pope. I quickly said in a low voice, "There'll only be another one."

Olson's eyes darted around, he excitedly asking, "Who said that? Who said that?" and when I confessed, somewhat abashedly, he grinned broadly, looking very pleased—and surprised.

As a white from the North who spent most of his time at Black Mountain insulated within that eden surrounded by the Seven Sister Mountains, I was mainly ignorant of the day-to-day, firsthand experiences of deeply-entrenched traditions of racial segregation that were commonplace just outside our green and hilly paradise (*and* increasing hell, in time to come). That eventually came home to me when cook Malrey invited Mary Fiore and me to attend her nephew Alvin's 8th grade graduation in Asheville on a Sunday afternoon that late spring of 1953. Mary had a strong sense of trying to be as much a part of the place she lived in as she could, and so it was natural she wanted to go. I wanted to go because, like Mary, I was fond of Malrey and also knew her nephew slightly, a polite, skinny kid of few words, who back in August 1948 had played the Page in Erik Satie's *The Ruse of Medusa*, translated by M. C. Richards, that was performed in the dining hall with a cast that also included Buckminster Fuller and Merce Cunningham, decor by Willem and Elaine de Kooning. Alvin spent his summers staying with his aunt down in the cooks' quarters deep in the woods below South Lodge. Going to the graduation was also a good chance to get out of the kitchen and away from the college for a few hours.

Since Sunday was the cooks half day off (after every Sunday lunch, Malrey and Cornelia set up cheese and bread and apples on the rolling table in the kitchen window for us to take with us for our supper that night), Cornelia asked Mary if she could hitch a ride with us to Asheville to visit her family, as she usually did. Malrey, all dressed up in her Sunday best for the occasion, had gotten a ride earlier with family, Cornelia volunteering to clean up the kitchen after lunch on this special day so Malrey could get an early start to her nephew's graduation.

When it was time to leave, Mary and I drove down from Minimum House in her Jeep station-wagon to pick up Cornelia who, like Malrey, also dressed in her Sunday finery, was waiting for us in front of the dining hall. Three could easily sit in the wide front seat, especially with bird-like Cornelia, who was even skinnier than me. So when I got out I motioned for Cornelia to climb in between Mary and me, but she shook her head adamantly and with that wide grin of hers made for the back seat.

"Don't be silly, Cornelia," I insisted, "Sit up front with us, there's plenty room."

But she just kept grinning, saying, "Naw, naw, naw" over and over, "I'll be perfectly fine back here," and shoved her way past me to scramble, quick as a sparrow, into the back.

Of course, I didn't get it and made some joke about how I'd bathed that day and she didn't have to worry. We were always cracking silly jokes with each other in the kitchen while we worked, Cornelia—and Malrey on occasion—had a great sense of humor, fueled at times by a nip or two of her homemade peach brandy from the oddest assortment of bottles that she kept stashed away behind the No. 10 cans on a storage room shelf behind the kitchen. Mary, though, sitting behind the wheel in her usual stolid way, didn't say anything, but looking back later, I could see by her silence she understood what Cornelia's insistence was all about, Mary, less green than I about the peculiar black-white mores of the South, was not as Black Mountain-forgetful as me. Because it didn't hit me till some time after, that Cornelia, in insisting on taking the back seat in a vehicle with a white driver and a white passenger, was only doing what she was supposed to do in the segregated South, what the traditions of segregation and its laws demanded. Driving out into that world from the relative "safety" of the college the thirteen or so miles west to Asheville, she was doing the prudent thing, that which would cause the least amount of trouble and prevent a potential problem, as much for us perhaps as for herself; a black person driving in a front seat with two whites was a parity that was a severe violation of the segregation code. She knew to sit, as ingrained habit, where a black was then supposed to sit, just as she was expected to sit in the back of the segregated buses running down in the valley between Black Mountain town and Asheville.

The neighborhood Cornelia's family lived in I could see, when we dropped her off, was poorer and shabbier than even the poorer white areas in Asheville. I realized, thinking about it afterward, that even though we worked just about every day together in the kitchen and we lived on the same grounds, that we still lived very much apart from each other, that our lives were separate in most vital ways even at forward-looking Black Mountain, that in most ways I didn't know anything much about Cornelia and Malrey's lives—and they maybe not much about mine. Although maybe the latter wasn't exactly true: blacks are usually more sharp-eyed about whites, even now, than whites about blacks—as with queers being sharp-eyed about homophobes, and women about misogynists, you tend to develop a sharp, appraising eye over those who might come after you with a vengeance.

Alvin's elementary school was all black, and off in the backwoods down a country road, a poor enough looking, unpainted clapboard building, compared to the trim, more up-to-date and expensive-looking buildings of the white schools we passed on the way, in some ways as shabby and neglected-looking as the buildings at Black Mountain College. Malrey was so pleased we'd come and fussed over us, introducing us to her family and friends. Everybody was all dressed up, including Alvin, tall and spindly in a black suit and tie, all gangly shyness, much like he was at the college when he stayed with his Aunt Malrey in the summer. Since Mary and I were the only whites, most of those present regarded us politely but cautiously, suspicious, perhaps, of what we were doing there. Blacks and whites did not mingle easily in the South in those days, but it was easier, as at Black Mountain, for example, for whites to mingle with blacks than vice versa, so Mary and I were sensitive to our being in a "privileged" position. And I did take it as a genuine privilege to be invited there on such a special occasion. I didn't know about Mary, but still it was hard for me to shake the self-conscious feeling of being an intruder. I took care to be respectful and kept my mouth shut unless spoken to, like you would as a guest in somebody else's home, and I could sense Mary maybe felt the same. After the introductions, we went and sat on the stiff chairs against the back wall, to be out of the way, and when it was over we waited till all the parents and friends had congratulated the graduates, then we went up and shook Alvin's hand on his getting his diploma and to thank him for the little talk he gave. In turn, he gave us his shy adolescent grin, remembering us from the college.

On the drive home, I thought of how much there was to learn not only at Black Mountain but outside it as well.

One night, not long after, as I left South Lodge on my way to do some writing in my study, I spotted a tall, thin boyish figure crouched down on the porch of North Lodge, peeping into Virginia's lighted bathroom window. As I approached, I saw it was Alvin who, undoubtedly in the hormonal floods of adolescence, was eager to get a peep at female flesh, another vital part of his education, just as it had been for me in my pubescence, only my curiosity veering sharply to the male side.

So as not to embarrass him, I crept by as stealthily as his own movements at the window, both of us in shadow, and continued on my way to the Studies, realizing we were both creatures hidden in the sexual shadows.

One of those shadows was the Quiet House at night, which was the perfect erotic trysting place, since as far as I knew in that particular time no one ever used it for the secluded place of prayer and meditation faculty member Molly Gregory and student Alex Reed had built it for in the 1940s, as a memorial to the Dreiers' son, Eddie, killed in an auto accident on campus. So dank and mildewy a place in all seasons, a small, square fieldstone structure with thick walls and narrow slots of windows, constructed against the mountain in a bower of wild greenery off the dirt road between the dining hall and Studies Building.

Bill McNeil was a painting student from New York City. We'd been quietly eyeing and circling about each other for days soon after he arrived, Bill, a sweet-natured, quiet lad with a quiet humor, coming often to my study to talk; until one night after supper we made our way to the Quiet House, his eyes somewhat shamed by his desire, a worry of guilt there; in my own mind, with Merrill still in Houston, the power of eros overriding a concern of desecration to the memorial. But once inside and the door shut behind us in total darkness, he was as savagely hungry as I, and we fell on one of the damp benches, the feel of the thick, long shaft of him with curiously small snake-like head, a heat of its own in the chill blackness.

We got together several times after that, in the Quiet House (the only ones making use of it for any purpose as far as I could see) or in my study, where it was dry and there was at least light and the pallet to lie on. He didn't stay long at the college— there were other uncertainties in his eyes, and I missed him when he left, especially the ever-hungry animal in me, missed his sweet, shy humor, his brooding quietness.

Years later, sometime in the 1970s, Tom Field told me Bill was now living out in San Francisco, and in the early 1980s, Grey Fox publisher Don Allen wrote that Bill had died of AIDS, one of the first to go.

Esteban Vicente taught drawing that summer of 1953 in the cool and breezy open area under the Studies, using nude models for our line drawings which we penciled in on large sheets of sketching paper gotten at Carroll Williams' college store. A man of few words, Vicente would move from student to student, standing dignifiedly erect, really studying the work, making a few suggestions and comments here and there, often curt, often complimentary, encouraging, before moving on. Hairy bare-chested, in nothing but tight white shorts and sandals, a bull of a chest and head, thick graying hair slicked straight back from his forehead, his craggy, olive-handsome, Mediterranean features were burned an even deeper reddish-brown in the Carolina sun. Unusually shy Mary Ann Fretz, revealing a hidden exhibitionistic streak that surprised me, posed nude in the class, perhaps proving the old saying, "Do anything to a shy person but ignore them"; as did, on another occasion, the equally reticent Bea Huss, who as an actor or as an artist model, showed another side of herself too. Tim La Farge, an appealingly attractive young dancer in Merce's troupe whom I'd seen mainly only in a black leotard that summer in Merce's classes and dances, notably *Banjo*, and who was both shy *and* reticent, also surprised me by stepping one morning through the double doors from the theater room in nothing but a jock strap, to take his place on the posing platform, set on the golden pebbles. Since the women posed totally nude, I was a bit disappointed that Tim had elected to wear an athletic supporter, a conventional double standard regarding anatomies of male and female models practiced then, even at avant-garde Black Mountain it seemed, where the ages-old traditional Mystery of Phallus Size was kept protected and intact, in public anyway.

But despite this drawback, Tim's long, pale, leanly-muscled physique was a pleasure to draw. As was Hilda Morley's, who also unexpectedly one mid-morning, with a shy smile and yet a mischievousness in her blue eyes, stepped quietly through the double doors and onto the tawny gravel in a dark blue velvet robe, slipped it off without a moment's hesitation, to reveal a magnificent Rubenesque zoftig body, a nest of pubic hair as honey-colored as her bobbed hair. Having studied metaphysical poetry in the fall term with her, and at that moment studying again with her, this time Henry James' novellas in the spring/early summer term, I was so accustomed to her as clothed metaphysical instructor, I was a bit thrown to see her standing suddenly physically naked before us.

That wonderful figure instantly seduced the pencil in my hand, and it wasn't long before I was busily trying to capture it. Vicente, who rarely said anything to me because I figured my work was so rudimentary, that morning stopped by my board and, scrutinizing it carefully in his usual manner (I held my breath, fearful of what he might say), for the first time complimented my sketch, which made me feel terrific. (The following summer an abstract ink drawing I had done at the time of Vicente's class and, as a cheeky joke, tacked up in the lobby of Meadows Inn, where Tom Field and I were then living, with a batch of Tom's drawings that Tom had hung up around the walls, as an impromptu "exhibition" for our visitors, was noted by Joe Fiore. Eyeing my drawing with the same practiced care as Vicente, Joe said he liked it, which from Joe was high praise indeed.)

The point is, Black Mountain gave us the scope to try as many avenues to art as were available on campus, and we were encouraged to experiment in all forms, "to play it across the board," as Olson put it. I loved to draw, in clean, incisive lines (in the same way Olson was prodding me to write), to act, even to dance, however stumbly, in Merce's class, and to bang out even cruder improvisations, thanks to Wolpe, on the various Steinways scattered around the grounds. But I knew for a certainty that the written word was where I needed to go—my "direction," as Olson put that too, and never lost sight of that.

There was so much going on that summer, the last of such summer sessions, it would be impossible to cite all of it here. One of the most impressive occurrences for me was when Lou Harrison, shortly before he left Black Mountain, managed to find, since he was always at the edge in music, LP albums of Alban Berg's *Wozzeck* and *Lulu*. He played *Lulu* one evening on a portable phonograph to a small select group of specially-invited regular students and some summer visitors in the front second floor apartment in Streamside, Lou insisting that "only those who are truly interested" could come. Curiously enough, that included a chatty, motherly, suburban blond with glasses, who'd apparently come down to Black Mountain for the summer looking for cultural uplift and knitted something argyle during the whole opera.

I'd never heard Berg's operas before then and to listen to *Lulu*, even on such a small machine with such a little speaker, coupled with Lou's highly animated facial expressions, his grinningly ecstatic comments punctuating the music as he sat hunched on the floor by the phonograph, was a revelation.

There was a great deal of concert music that summer.

Wolpe's first wife, Irma, arrived with her current husband, Hans Rademacher, a mathematician formerly with the Institute for Advanced Study at Princeton. She was a stern-faced, gray-haired woman with glasses and a crisp, no-nonsense, heavily German-accented voice, who came down to play Beethoven and practiced for hours on the dining hall Steinway in a loud, mechanical manner, as if she were attacking the keys with fierce animosity. Even more so than during Merce's rehearsals, I, in my kitchen and dining hall duties, tried my best to work noiselessly around her, for she, like a fierce drill sergeant, would shout complaint at the slightest rattle of a dish while she was hard at it over the keys.

I would never have imagined the loose, whistling, crazily playful, innovative sound- and noise-making, often foolishly grinning Wolpe as husband of the severe, unsmiling woman who sat rigidly upright hour after hour pounding away with a kind of driven brutal energy at the keyboard, in a technically precise but spiritually empty manner.

On the other hand, chain-smoking, tensely quiet David Tudor (who played Webern's spare, micro-brief compositions later that summer in concert, another first for me), a former student of both Irma and Stefan, counting on a quieter time, practiced for his Mozart concert at night in the darkened dining hall. But he didn't count on the blabbermouths hanging out in the kitchen, usually after a few ales at Ma Peak's, laughing and gabbing and smoking according to late-night custom, perched under the hanging pot rack on the huge metal-topped table in the center of the kitchen by Malrey's large, slowly-cooling cook stove. One evening, after stumbling through and repeating a passage several times, the usually mild-mannered David, his face tense and even paler with anger, his eyes blazing behind his horn-rimmed glasses, came storming up to the serving window and shouted at us to pipe down, then stalked back to plonk himself down again at his Steinway. Stunned into silence for at least a moment, because I don't think anyone had ever, perhaps in the whole history of the college, commanded the traditional night-time rebel kitchen gang to shut up, and also probably because no one had ever heard David raise his voice before, after a moment of disbelief, we then resumed talking in quieter voices. But it wasn't long before we forgot all about David, whose brilliant fingers I could hear in the distance at the far end of the dim, cavernous dining hall flying over the keys in Mozartian swift wit, and we were chattering and laughing away as noisily as before. Then, like a stuck record, there came the constant repetition of another passage, finally followed by the slamming down of the keyboard lid, then David appearing even more fierce-faced than before in the window where he glared at us an instant before plunging down the wide rolling window partition with a bang.

Again, there was amazed silence from the kitchen crowd, as if to say, How dare he! followed by a few sheepish grins. But most everyone agreed he should've closed the partition in the first place, and the crowd went on boozily debating the philosophical topic under discussion.

I could hear David begin practicing once more, much fainter now, but evidently thrown by the distractions and perhaps even more so by his own outburst, he kept making mistakes, and it wasn't long before the Mozart stopped abruptly and the keyboard lid crashed down again, followed by a long, unbroken silence, David, undoubtedly admitting defeat, giving up for the night and retreating quietly through one of the dining hall exits, because even the grand piano in the Round House just off the dining hall was maybe still too close to the rowdiness, perhaps heading with the aid of a flashlight to try the isolated but electricity-free Music House, a structure just big enough for a Steinway grand way out in the middle of the woods. Although its acoustics in no way matched those of the vast dining hall where David would be performing, the only competition he'd have in distracting sound would be the hoot owls and the whip-poorwills chugging away monotonously in the surrounding pines.

A young man from Germany came down the same time as Wolpe's ex-wife, a protégé of hers, a taciturn, well-built youth with husky shoulders and mouse-brown crewcut hair, one would never have taken for a concert pianist at first glance. He was perhaps in part shy because he was uncertain of his English, but there was in his large eyes a quiet intensity and watchfulness, in his muscular body a subtle, restless energy. At any rate, at one of the Saturday night concerts he knocked the socks off everybody by playing "*Deuxième Sonate*" by Pierre Boulez that was so deeply felt, so deeply sensitive, it stirred just about everyone in the audience. So much so that, for once, even the low-flying bats careening loose in the hall were ignored, he so drew everyone to listen carefully, to be swept up in his quietly intense interpretation; a completely different experience—it had the raw surge and random energy of the sea in it—than listening to Irma Wolpe Rademacher's mechanically perfect but spiritless march through Beethoven.

Olson, at the conclusion of the Boulez, deeply moved, rose from his seat, exclaiming breathlessly emphatic: "He has *soul!*" and the German youth, appealingly shy, modestly ebullient—one truly sensed an extraordinary talent—acknowledged the genuine applause from the audience with a smile and nod from the piano bench.

Along with the giant moths flapping everywhere, those bats, ingeniously flying in through the numerous breaks in the dining porch screening or when a screen door in the dining hall was opened, were a customary presence during the evening concerts that summer, a half dozen or so of them always zipping up around the high ceiling, skillfully avoiding the rafters, or occasionally swooping low over the audience in our cane-bottomed chairs, with everyone ducking as one. No one was alarmed, at least not among us Black Mountain regulars; you got used to the wildlife, indoors and out, in that near-wilderness terrain. Also, as an accompaniment to the Beethoven or the Boulez, the Mozart or the Satie, the Wolpe, there was, making a little night music of their own, the constant deep croaking of the bullfrogs through the open windows from out in the marshes of Lake Eden, which the musicians were forced to put up with, complain though they may, and competitively play against.

Bats also flew through the upper and lower corridors of the Studies, since in warm weather, the front and back doors were left open for the cross-breeze. One night, as I was going down the long hall to my study, one bat flew by so close I could clearly see the reddish fur on its wing under the ceiling lights as its pointed tip grazed my cheek. And I didn't think anything of it, except to marvel at the lovely color of the wing, I who had, pre-Black Mountain, been terrified of bats.

There was also a string trio that summer, performing both classical and contemporary works, in the latter such composers as Schoenberg, Webern, Stravinsky and Morton Feldman. The cellist was one Seymour Barab, a suave, handsome, sturdily put together young man with the blondest hair and the bluest eyes, originally from Chicago but who then lived in Greenwich Village. Who caught each other's eye first is uncertain, but what is certain is that Black Mountain is where Mary Ann Fretz met Seymour Barab, who would within a year become her lover and eventually her husband, and because of that he would play a peripheral part in my own life in the months ahead, particularly through his friendship with a fellow Chicagoan, composer Ben Weber.

Since Boulez's music had been played at the college, starting in summer 1951 with David Tudor first playing "*Deuxième*

Sonate," when Olson first heard it, up to the German pianist movingly playing the same work that summer of 1953, Olson was in correspondence with Boulez himself, to invite him over from Paris for a future institute at the college. One Saturday afternoon, a number of us were all at Ma Peak's having ales after a work crew; I think Wes Huss was there, Dan Rice, perhaps even Wolpe, who did not often make an appearance at Peak's. Charles had brought along a letter he'd received just that day from Boulez and spread it in the middle of the table, asking for anybody's help in reading it, not only because it was in French, which Charles wasn't all that proficient in, but was also written in the tiniest handwriting you could imagine. Here was my chance to show off my own spotty French, but you needed a magnifying glass to read that microscopic hand. Finally, tiring of the game, after only making out a phrase here and there, everyone gave up in frustration, Olson, I thought smugly, getting a taste of his own medicine regarding his own much larger but equally indecipherable hand!

Speaking of French, Charles, walking with Connie one evening in front of Meadows Inn, stopped me and, knowing I was studying *le français* with Flola, asked me the meaning of the word "*manqué*," in connection with something he was reading or writing. The on-the-spot request made me so nervous that, as always, over-eager to be of service, to please the master, I flounderingly blurted out "mistaken," which Charles accepted even though it was a not quite accurate translation of "failed" or "would-be."

Once I realized my mistake, I rued it for days, fearing Charles, once he discovered my inaccuracy, and I was sure he would, would think what a dunderhead of a language student I must be, so anxious was I to shine in his eyes, even in so small a moment.

The cutting down of the ancient tree and the removal of its

stump at the bend in the road next to the abandoned and win-dowless tumbledown wood shingle building in front of the Studies, that was also being torn down (the building was last used for painting classes), caused an outcry from the older women: the widows Johanna Jalowetz, Nell Rice, and Toni Dehn, perhaps in a fearful identity that their own precarious position at the college could be just as ruthlessly uprooted and themselves tossed aside, along with their deeply rooted service to and love for the college. Dan Rice, Olson, and Huss, among other males, were scornful of "the old women" and their fierce-ly outspoken desire to save the tree and went ahead and had the tree and its stump removed anyhow, along with the falling-down painting studio. Whether there was democratic debate on the conflict, or a vote, I'm not certain, but I can still see Jalowetz's deeply seamed and darkly furious face when her and the other female elders' cause was lost.

When logging rights were granted by the college for money to go on operating in 1953 through and possibly beyond 1954, all day long the huge logging trucks, with countless, tall, thick-trunked trees, shorn of their branches and chained to the long flatbeds, ground bumping slowly in low gear down the dirt road of the college out to the county road beyond the Gatehouse. Also all day long, within earshot anywhere any of us were, working or studying, was the shrill sound of the huge chain saws up on the densely timbered slopes, where once there had been, my first autumn there, only the wind and, in season, in the long nights, "the music of the hounds," as it was called, hounds of local hunters tracking possums and treeing racoons up in those same mountains.

Late fall 1953, with a pittance of money for coal left only for the Studies Building, we went on wood-cutting crews with Olson where we felled trees with a new portable chain saw, of which everyone, including Charles, was a bit nervous. We climbed up on the slopes near the farm and sawed the trees into logs, along with dead trees on the ground, for fuel to stoke the furnaces of student and faculty houses. There were frequent rests for "guy talk" (any work detail Olson was on meant frequent breaks for stopping and gabbing). After her and David's breakup, Karen Karnes' solid, voluptuous, goddess-like figure, on full display for all to see that summer in the Tableaux and, thus, joining the pantheon of female fantasy pulchritude with Marilyn Monroe in the recent movie *Niagara*, was slyly discussed among the others, while I listened, Terence Burns offering he could hear Karen "sighing heavily" nights through the wall of his study from her bedroom in the apartment she used to share with David next door. He said he dreamed of going in and comforting her.

Paul Williams, lean, shy of manner and boyishly attractive, back on a visit to look over the perilous situation at the college and to see what he could do, especially financially, with money from his family's glove manufacturing fortune. He also taught an informal architecture class that fall and organized and ran the buzz saw-cutting operation, where early each Saturday morning in the open area beyond Meadows Inn, we all helped feed logs into the buzz saw to cut sizable lengths to fit the old coal-burning furnaces in the cellars of those cottages that had them. There was that ever-dwindling coal supply in the huge bin outside the Studies, and often several other students as well as myself, when there wasn't sufficient coal for heat in the lodges, on particularly cold nights, slept in our studies. Later, after our move up to the cottages from the south campus, Tom and Terence and I took turns tending the Meadows Inn furnace, located in a tiny, claustrophobic dirt pit of a cellar behind the house under Tom's bedroom. You had to feed it a lot of wood to get the boiler hot enough to force steam up to the radiators;

I was always nervous the damn antique was going to explode. Just tending the furnace was more than enough to warm you up and forget the bitter mountain cold. We used the huge fireplace in the lobby a lot, too, which also helped heat the place.

In 1953 the first out-sized, pale-blue covered copies, with the big black O in brush, of *The Maximus Poems* 1-10 arrived from Stuttgart from former student, Jargon publisher and poet Jonathan Williams, who was stationed in the army there and had used a $1,500 inheritance to publish them in then West Germany. In the grassy area between Olson's house and Meadows Inn, Olson showing us copies in bright afternoon sunlight. Quiet he was, shyly looking at the copy he was holding, then looking at us, not saying anything—but you could see how pleased he was.

The poorest of us managed to scrape together the three bucks (no small amount for most of us in those lean days) to buy a copy, myself scrimping on food and beer money, it was so crucial to have it, so handsomely, so lovingly printed a book on Jonathan's part, so exhilaratingly vital a text on Olson's, the beloved teacher and master, a silent and exciting acknowledging moment there in the sun.

Years later, after getting off booze and drugs, again desperately poor, I had to sell that first copy of *Maximus,* and eventually, later, the second 1956 *Maximus* 11-22 as well. I still miss them.

People were always dropping in at Black Mountain for a visit, especially in the pleasanter weather. This sometimes was a windfall, as it were, for those of us who were single (and sometimes even for those who weren't) because on occasion the odd visitor provided an opportunity not only for fresh talk, not to mention fresh ears, but even possible flirtations, even, wonder of wonders, for sex, a welcome chance for those of us who were short of partners, particularly those of us with queer leanings, for an inordinate number of visitors turned out to be queer themselves. Still, those who ended up in bed with them were sometimes the most macho (and sometimes the most married) on campus. Like one former ex-marine, married with a kid and one on the way, about whom the campus was abuzz with rumors one morning because he had allegedly been gotten soused and was bedded down in his study, by a most persistent, rather chubby, effeminate visitor who seemed more interested in the ex-marine student's muscles than the music program he said he'd come to investigate at the college.

I myself had the rare good fortune, while Merrill was off in Houston that summer trying to get his Herb back, to show around two male visitors from Emory University in Atlanta. One, a pre-med student, quietly, pleasantly mannered, handsome and well-built, with the blackest hair, and the most lovely black-lashed eyes, eyes that signaled interest to me at one point when, after taking him and his pal around on a tour of the grounds, he asked if he could see what my study was like. His friend discreetly disappeared and, my heart racing (Merrill *had* been gone quite a few weeks), unable to believe my good luck, I led him into the study on the second level that had once been Merrill's. The moment the door was closed behind us, wordlessly, he put his arms about me, and I turned and placed mine about him. Also wordlessly we slipped out of our clothes and down onto the pallet against the wall, that was covered with the hand-woven throw that had once draped the Steinway in the dining hall and that Wolpe complained I should return, but I never did because it matched perfectly the Klinesque black and white walls Merrill had painted when the study was his.

Another later time, a group of males arrived in the evening, traveling through the South. They'd heard of Black Mountain and said they'd stopped to check it out, could they sleep in their sleeping bags out on the grounds? They were a very lively, talkative group, always refreshing to hear fresh voices from the out-side, we at the college, in our increasingly diminishing numbers, sometimes got stale listening to each other. They and a bunch of us students all ended up in the kitchen, they doing most of the talking and us answering their questions. Even Merrill, who had returned by now from Houston that fall, *sans* his beloved Herb, much to my secret relief, was there, he who so rarely showed up anywhere on campus, particularly at that hour. But the reason for his interest soon became apparent: one of the youths, lean, strikingly good-looking, with dark wavy hair and in tight t-shirt and snug-fitting levis that displayed his attributes to best advantage, was smilingly, charmingly flirtatious. He was clearly on the make but, despite my success earlier that summer with the youth from Emory, thinking now I wouldn't stand a chance with such a beautiful young man even if Merrill wasn't there, but because Merrill *was* there, there now in bed with me again each and every night, for better or worse, up at Streamside, I was content enough, and never thought to make a move toward the newcomer. Surprisingly, however, the youth kept directing his comments at me, and I answered him as best I could, noting that Merrill, hanging at my side and hanging on the young man's every word, had his lips drily parted in a half smile, his usually pale cheeks faintly flushed, his eyes glittering with excitement. I was envious, wishing Merrill would gaze at me that way, and jealous, too, of his attentions to the visitor, undoubtedly so bedazzled by such beauty, Herb was momen-tarily rendered invisible to his eyes.

It was getting late and the young men made a move to go sleep in their sleeping bags. I believe they also had their own tent, an advantage, given the shortage of space at that time for so many unexpected visitors to our shrinking campus. Merrill, suddenly agitated, pulled me aside, over toward the kitchen door leading to the dining hall and whispered fiercely, "He talks to you—You know how to talk to him, he likes you—"

I stared at him, baffled.

"Go tell him I want to sleep with him. Go ask him if he'll sleep with me."

I was too stunned to say anything. That he had asked me to do such a thing, play pimp for him, really, was the same as if he'd punched me in the gut. When I got my wind back, I said, "Merrill, I can't do that . . ."

In that same fierce whisper he said, "*If you really loved me you'd do it.*"

And such was my insanity, my habitually wanting to please him (just as with Olson), my wanting him to love me so badly, that if this was what it would take, for a fleeting instant I considered the possibility of doing it. But then quickly came to my senses, pulled back.

"Well?" he persisted. "Hurry up, they're leaving."

And it was true, the group of visitors was heading for the back screendoor of the kitchen, the beautiful dark-haired youth, still cunningly flirtatious, still so sure of himself, his beauty, sure of our hunger, playing with it, playing us off each other, tossed back looks our way over his shoulder, as he lingered behind the others.

In Merrill's eyes I could also see his fear, that he wanted me to be brave for him, to have the courage he didn't have to get what he wanted.

What contempt he must have for me, I thought.

"I can't," I murmured, and turned away from him, leaning face forward on the top of the sliding serving table between kitchen and dining hall.

Now that the others had gone, including the flirtatious young man, Merrill gave me an even more furious look and stormed out of the kitchen. I waited a few minutes then left the dining hall and walked, dragging my feet, up the road to Streamside, not knowing what I'd find. Merrill was already in bed when I got there, his body pointedly shoved far over against the wall, his back turned, sleep another escape for him. When I got undressed and slid under the covers, I lay curled on my side for a long time in the dark, thinking about what had happened in the kitchen, my craziness about Merrill and my inability to think still making me wonder if I'd done the right thing, turning it over and over in my mind. Perhaps if I had spoken to the young man, had helped Merrill out—but then where would I have been? The young man would have my place in the bed and I'd be out in the cold. I knew at that moment I had to get away from him, but I rationalized by deciding that what he'd asked me to do for him earlier was only an aberration; that it wouldn't happen again. He knew I loved him—didn't he acknowledge it that night, so sure he could use that love? I knew he'd turn to me again in time, put his arms around me once more.

But the end I couldn't face was already in sight. Trapped in the midst of it, I couldn't see then we were a perfect sadomasochistic match, feeding each other's darkly rooted needs. Very often we do get the "love" we're ready for, and deserve. Looking back, seeing where I was then (and would be for years to come), I know I certainly did.

Merrill reminded me flatly that fall that if his relentless and singleminded campaign to get Herb back succeeded, they would go off together to live in New York City, with the emphasis on the word *together*. Undoubtedly sensing the meaning behind my dark looks, my sour puss, he had also flatly, coolly, reiterated that our being together was only a temporary situation, temporary for his own convenience, I thought bitterly. He, perhaps sensing and resisting my determination to win his love—how could he not love me who loved him so much, how could he not give up Herb in the face of such love?—suggested I could, if I chose, move elsewhere on the grounds. But that was not always, in those economically cramped times, an easy thing to do, given our shrinking campus with its equally shrinking housing space. Also, painful as it sometimes was, I'd gotten used to the day-to-day habits of living with someone, difficult as that often was with Merrill. Therefore, his suggestion I move was one more verbal slap in the face. But, more often than not mistaking passion—particularly erotic passion—for love, and unable to make a decision either way, stuck in that inertia, I stayed on with him at Streamside, in the foolish hope that he would turn around to my way of thinking.

Although we slept side by side in the same bed, we grew increasingly apart, living in our own place, Merrill's mind and heart in Houston, my mind and heart lost in a fantasy of him, of our being together and Herb out of the picture, which I refused to see would never happen. Even my ongoing fierce desire to ever more completely win over Olson was held in abeyance for the time being.

We had long since stopped telling our stories to each other in bed till long into the night after love-making, which I, as lonely as Merrill, had so delighted in in the beginning, stories like the ones I told my brothers under the featherbed when we were kids back in Jersey, Merrill now for me another brother, and I for him, I wanted to believe, since he was an only child, the brother he'd never had, the two of us brothers together, to stand up for and with each other. We had also stopped exchanging ideas or discussing the books we were reading. (I was finally finishing *Moby-Dick* for Olson's class, hating it to end, it so engulfed me, helped by that roiling, overwhelming magnificence of Melville's prose to lose myself and for hours temporarily forget my petty concerns with Merrill.) We often even ate separately, and if we found ourselves in the front room together avoided talking, I, buried in *Moby-Dick*, Merrill, noodling away at the piano or practicing his calligraphy off in a corner; he, as always, better able to shut out the tension between us than I.

And in bed, Merrill, often without a word, pushing me away

when I apprehensively put my hands on him. I would crawl back to my side of the bed and lay there trying to swallow my pride, push down my rising anger, which often kept me awake for hours.

Dan Rice and Cynthia Homire lived in the rooms across the lobby from us, and sometimes in the evening they gathered in the lobby with others to drink beer and talk, sometimes till late. Merrill and I often went to sleep around eleven, I usually waiting till after Merrill had gone in first, the gatherings just outside our door rarely lasting longer than that. Besides, they were never rowdy, a low hum of conversation, rather pleasant actually. We could hear the voices through the thin pine walls of our bedroom, part of which abutted on the lobby wall, with a locked door in it leading out into the lobby, the sound of their talk a welcome counterpart to our own increasing silence. We never worried about making love if Dan and Cynthia and others were out there, since our lovemaking was also never so rowdy, and we were sure no one could hear us despite the thinness of the walls.

I had long since given up reaching for Merrill once we were under the covers. So it was a surprise when one night, one of those times when Dan and Cynthia, I could hear Jorge Fick's voice too, and the quiet tones of the new student from Ohio, David, perhaps one or two others, were out in the lobby beer drinking and conversing, that Merrill reached over and pulled me to him. My heart started thumping, my mind suddenly racing with the wild thought that perhaps now things would change, this sign that he wanted me maybe meaning he really wanted me in other ways too.

I embraced him and moved to kiss him, but he slid away, turning over on his belly, spreading his legs for me to enter, an imperative urgency in him, a blunt curtness. No preliminaries; it was to be all cut and dry. Body language being all in lovemaking, and we having been intimate now for so long, I knew exactly what he wanted— what he had over the months often pressed me to let him do to me. (But, still a virgin in that area, and aware of his enormity, I was more than a little nervous about letting him, irritated with frustration though it made him, and guilty though it made me who would have given him anything to hold him, even that, even more so now, having decided long before that night that if he asked me now, I would, would even suffer the pain of that to keep him.)

I spit in my hand to moisten myself—"Black Mountain vaseline," as we jokingly called it, not as slick but it did the job and, most important to the poor in pocket, was free. It was a way like no other for me, and with Merrill, once I'd learned the habits of it to please him, and he, as in all things, was touchily particular, there was an erotic rightness in it, one more habit of pleasure that made me bask with delight in the afterglow of it long after, and to long for it again as soon as possible, a hope that he would want it soon, as never there was with my high school sweetheart. And then—after so long a time, my hands trembling, my breath dry and short, I entered him quickly.

There was, as usual, no sound from him—there was only, just the other side of the wall, the pleasing, low murmur of conversation, the occasional soft laughter from those out in the lobby, muted beneath the blood-hum in my ears. But I knew he was lying, as he always did, with his head resting sideways on his crossed arms on the pillow, his eyes closed, as I rocked back and forth, in past times often for a long time, but now I ground my teeth, trying to hold myself off because I knew, in that unspoken language again, how much he took pleasure in it, which gave me even more pleasure, knowing how much it pleased him, he, my beloved, he the small sun in my day, this rosy orifice a sun in our dark nights. But it had been so long a time, and I was burning, burning, felt myself ready to explode more quickly than ever before, and pulled out, thinking that I would do other things to please him—and allow me time to cool down—before I went into him again. But Merrill, with a snarl, half wrenched his torso around, his voice in the dark, and by its tone I could imagine the twisted fury of his face, shouted loudly, "*What the hell are you doing? Why'd you do that, you fool!*"

I was so caught off guard, so shocked by the vehemence of his reaction, I was struck silent. Another reason I kept still was I was sure they'd heard it all in the lobby since it got suddenly quiet out there, as Merrill went on angrily shouting at the top of his lungs that I'd spoiled it for him, that I didn't know how to fuck him right, and by implication, that Herb did, that if only Herb were there, that I could do nothing right—interfering with *his* pleasure, when in fact I'd only wanted to prolong it. But he didn't understand that and certainly didn't give me a chance to explain as he continued to blow his top, I wanting him only to stop, sure as I was now with the continuing utter silence out in the lobby that the others were listening, certain of it when I heard Cynthia give a low giggle, ashamed that they should overhear Merrill humiliate me over our most secret intimacies. And I, the meek and shame-filled altar boy risen again, didn't protest, too embarrassed to defend myself, fearing they might hear that too, fearing also if I did it would increase Merrill's ice-cold fury.

Jorge was the only one gave me a sly, knowing grin the next time he saw me; Cynthia and Dan behaved as if they had heard nothing and treated me as before, while David in his shyness intimated nothing. I was glad of that.

That was the last fumbling attempt at sex for Merrill and me at Black Mountain, the real rupture between us I, in habituated denial about most everything most of my life up to then, was no longer able to deny in this instance. What was gone was really all that had ever held us together, a hard enough fact. Although we continued to share a bed and quarters, it was pretty much over. I stayed put, though, simply just too paralyzed to make a move, until a move was finally forced on me.

There was to be a party, as it turned out one of the last to be held in the dining hall that fall of 1953 before the total closing down of the lower part of the campus. I was barely speaking to Merrill at this point, except for brief murmurs or grunts, or a one-syllable "yes" or "no" when absolutely necessary. A master of aloofness and isolation, Merrill dealt with my inwardly turned fury much better than I, easily withdrawing into himself, sleeping till noon, turning to his piano, using his deafness to not hear what he didn't want to hear, also using that uncanny ability I so marveled at, and envied, to shut out of his mind whatever unpleasantness he couldn't or didn't wish to deal with. My ears seemed always turned on, my mind especially on high speed, the switch button of my fear as well always turned up. There was an iciness at the core of Merrill that I envied.

The rare times now we found ourselves together in the front room, we sat not speaking a word, Merrill doodling at the piano or practicing Debussy or Bach. More often than not, however, he was writing long letters I was sure were to Herb back in Houston, letters he wrote deliberately in my presence, just to spite me I was equally convinced, just to toss gleefully more dynamite on my already explosive animosity which I, masochist to the toenails, let implode only within my own vitals.

So, the Saturday afternoon of the party, Merrill spoke the most words he'd spoken to me in days, asking, "Are you going tonight?"

I asked him if he were and when he said yes, I said no I didn't think I would be going, although I wanted to go in the worst way, I was so sick of being alone with myself. But I couldn't bear the thought of being there with him, of trying to have a good time but only pretending, of having to face the others. I would continue as I had been doing: enjoying my misery solo.

There was also the childish belief that I would be, by my absence, "punishing" him.

Merrill merely shrugged, maybe puzzled by my decision, since I'd always looked forward to the parties, but didn't say anything, choosing not to address it in any way. He said he'd gotten someone to get him a bottle of wine on a booze run to Asheville, since he disliked the gasoline taste of the moonshine punch at such parties, even when cut with a cold tea base, and hated even more the yeasty sediment of Bert Morgan's 25¢ homebrew—after each sip you had to wait for the sediment to settle. He casually offered to share his wine with me. I saw his gesture as a tentative peace offering, but because of my wounded pride I was too small to accept it.

"I've got work to do," I lied.

Perhaps he was glad I'd said no, glad to get away from my long puss for a few hours.

When I got back to Streamside after the supper dishcrew that Saturday night, Merrill was in the bathtub, scrubbing himself up in preparation for the party. I went and sat in the front room, pretending to read *Moby-Dick* but actually listening to the water empty noisily out of the tub as he finished bathing, seeing vividly in my mind's eye his glistening body as he toweled off, which caused a sharp intake of breath, since, although we slept side by side, I hadn't touched him in so long now. I could hear him in the bedroom pulling out drawers as he got dressed—thinking, wildly, irrationally, maybe he'll come into the front room and ask me again if I'd like to go to the party with him; even better, *beg* me to go. But when he was ready, he passed through the front room without a word. Out of the corner of my eye I saw he'd put on his dressy red polo shirt his mother had sent him from Kewanee, and a clean pair of dungarees and was clutching the bottle of wine in its brown paper bag. His cheeks, from his bath, were flushed the color of the wild rose petals that grew in abundance by the road past the Gatehouse. I longed to leap up, shout, Wait! I've changed my mind! But pride, again, kept me nailed to my chair, my mouth shut against him, against myself, really.

He went out the door and into the lobby to the main Dutch door without acknowledging me in any way.

I slammed down the useless book I'd been pretending to read and went in and lay fully clothed on the bed in the dark, still sweaty from my work in the kitchen, my work clothes smelling of steam and soap and garbage scraps. Even the thought of taking a bath, of slipping into a tub still warm from bath water his body just moments before had been submerged in filled me contradictorily with both passion and revulsion.

I would lie in our bed, as I had been, really, for the past few weeks, inert and alone. My head filled with visions of the party, seeing Merrill, after a few gulps of wine, becoming sociable, as he had at the 1952 Christmas day dinner, even enjoying himself, as then. I turned my face to the wall to blot out that vision; I would show him.

I was surprised how much time had passed when I heard him come in through the front room—I hadn't slept, just fitfully dozed off, my mind racing. Now, I slid under the covers, not wanting him to see me still in my work clothes, and pretended to be asleep.

He went through to the bathroom; I could hear him taking a piss. When he came back in he was considerate enough not to turn on the light. I could tell he was a bit squiffed from the way he stumbled about undressing in the dark, but like he was trying hard not to waken me. He slid over me awkwardly, to his place in the bed against the wall. I secretly hoped for a wild moment the wine would make him reach for me, but he turned on his side, his back to me, and it wasn't long before I heard his slow, measured breathing as he drifted into sleep. In spite of my resolve, my terrible pride, I carefully lifted my hand from under the covers, tentatively touched his bare shoulder, touched his neck. He shrank away in his sleep, closer to the wall. I withdrew my hand, lay on my back staring up at the black ceiling, my eyes burning. Then I slid over on my belly, loosened my trousers, found the crack between the single mattresses that joined to make up our double bed, slipped myself in, showing him, showing him I didn't need him, stifling my groans, feeling a sad and cheap humiliation after.

I rolled over, my own back to him now, and finally fell into a twitching, restless sleep.

I had begun to enjoy the taste of feeding on my own entrails, had developed an appetite for that bitter flavor, gnawing at myself, no longer speaking to Merrill, nor he to me, no longer able to look at him, not even speaking to anyone of what was going on, not even to Mary, who would have lent a sympathetic ear, so good I was at secrets, so sick with them.

Although the summer session had been an artistic and educational success, it didn't get the hoped-for result of attracting new year-round students, and the financial prospects of the college worsened. Wolpe summed it up by complaining of the transient summer students, "They come and take and leave nothing."

As a result, what delivered me from my own paralysis was a decision by the faculty to close the school for a time in the late fall and early winter in order to save on fuel and electricity, and also to give those desperately poor students like myself an opportunity to go off and earn some cash so we could return to the college for the spring term. There was some notion, too, from Charles, à la Antioch College, of going "out in the field" to work in and learn something hands on about your major study, about "life" out there, but that was mainly just talk. The real reason for the winter break was economic. Charles, when I spoke to him worriedly about my own financial concerns said we'd all have to "make sacrifices," and suggested the possibility of a job at the blanket factory in Swannanoa. But the thought of working long hours again in a low-paying, non-union job in a mill—the textile industry in the South was notoriously anti-union then—while still living at Black Mountain didn't at all appeal to me.

Then, too, there was talk about doing away with the work program scholarships because they were now seen as "undemocratic," nothing but "a source of cheap labor," and that was another cause for worry. So when, in correspondence with Mary Ann Fretz, who now lived in New York City where she was continuing to study photography and lately mime, I was invited to stay at her one-room apartment on Minetta Lane in Greenwich Village while I looked for a temporary job, I saw my way out.

Wes Huss was given the job in the registrar's office down in the administration cottage of taking down all the information about where we'd be over the break (most of the faculty, with no place to go, stayed on of course), and I gave Mary Ann's address. That afternoon, while Merrill was out, I secretly packed my mother's suitcase with what I had of clothes (not many), and hid it under the bed. Before dawn, while Merrill still slept, I crept out of our bed as soundlessly as possible, dressed in the dark, got the suitcase and left our rooms in Streamside without a word to him, left the college too, without saying goodbye to anyone, headed down to the county road to begin to hitchhike east the several hundred miles to Raleigh, there to connect up with U. S. 1 and then hike north the additional several hundred miles to New York City and Mary Ann's place in the Village, with only a dollar or two in my pocket.

There was the fear, still, in the early 1950s, of hitchhiking through the South to and from Black Mountain, the fear of getting picked up as a vagrant by the local police or state troopers and put in jail or on a chain gang. A few of the seasoned hitchhikers at the college had warned us that Georgia was the worst state for that, and as for getting jailed North Carolina wasn't far behind. But getting away from Merrill was worth the risk.

I felt heavy in my chest, my footsteps, as I started down the road past the Gatehouse, wanting fiercely to stay, to try, idiotically, one last time with Merrill. But I knew I had to get away, and thought of him still sleeping soundly, peacefully, unaware of my going, certain he'd be uncaring even if he did know, or would be actually relieved to be rid of me, rid of my long, accusatory face. In those first moments of departure, after my first year-long stay, my heart and mind were as dark as the pre-dawn darkness before my eyes, so early even the birds were soundless still, as I made my way down the mountain.

I traveled by thumb the 600 miles in two days, arriving at the Minetta Lane apartment Mary Ann, after her summer at Black Mountain, had offered to let me stay at. Just across the hall, Mary Ann informed me with sly amusement, first thing, was a male brothel, with a large clientele, from the traffic I later observed trooping up and down the stairs at all hours of the day and night, of U. S. Marines and sailors.

The apartment was on the second floor overlooking a grungy slate courtyard, and with the air in New York at that time so befouled with widespread coal burning, particularly from the ConEd stacks over by the East River, soot blew in the cracks of the two large drafty windows and in no time drifted inches deep on the sills like black snow. The walls were painted a dreary chocolate brown, in imitation of a shade popular with interior decorators at that time, and the only furniture was a large mattress in one corner—à la a Black Mountain pallet—and a large rice mat on the floor. There was a small, crudely painted black refrigerator in one corner that was so noisy we left it unplugged and, since it was winter, used, despite the soot, the outside window sills to keep our meager diet naturally refrigerated (including yogurt, a novelty among the cognoscenti then, which Mary Ann introduced me to). There was a small, adequate bath, and a small fireplace that we rarely used, since the cords of wood sold on street corners were very costly. We could've used the fireplace more often since heat in the building was a sometime thing, so that most of the time we sat bundled up in our winter coats, and on really cold, windy days, with the frigid blasts, and soot, blowing in at the leaky windows, with scarves and caps on too—something we never had to do in winter at Black Mountain, poor as it was. All this for $60 a month, no cheap rent in those days. As a result, Mary Ann spent most of her time over at Seymour Barab's basement apartment on West 12th Street, next to the Greenwich movie house, Seymour back too from his stint as the cellist in the trio that had played classical and contemporary music at Black Mountain that past summer, where Mary Ann had first met him. On West 12th she made use of the warmth not only of his apartment but of a rekindled romance as well.

It was easier, I was discovering, being radical and revolutionary and non-conformist within the safe confines of the grounds of Black Mountain College. But once outside where practical matters like jobs, housing, etc., were a necessity, my radical courage faltered, and I was learning to dissimulate—an acting art second nature to me anyhow, not only thanks to Wes Huss' acting classes but as a queer guy concealed behind my unemotional public face. As a result, I eventually landed a mailroom clerk's and, thanks to my ability to type, teletype machine operator's job at $48 a week at Prentice-Hall, the publishers, then over on 5th Avenue and 13th Street, and was finally able to pay my half of the $60 a month rent for the Minetta Lane apartment. In actuality, the place really became my own, since Mary Ann rarely spent time there anymore.

To save on eating breakfast out, I'd put water on the hotplate for coffee and, while that was heating, run down winding

Minetta Street off Minetta Lane to an ancient Italian bakery on Bleecker that Mary Ann had introduced me to, for a freshly baked roll for a nickel, race back to the apartment, snatch the quarter pound stick of butter from the windowsill, blow off the soot, pour the by-now boiling water into a cup of instant coffee, Medagliadoro, our one luxury, before hurrying off across Washington Square (luckily, I could walk to work and save more money on carfare) to my mailroom job at Prentice-Hall, where on that part of lower 5th Avenue they were just then demolishing the rows of three- and four-story townhouses, one of which, mid-block, contained Mark Twain's last New York residence, and including the old Brevoort Cafe around the corner, to make way for the huge apartment complex that stands there today.

Mary Ann also showed me the cheap Village joints to eat in, the Humpty-Dumpty pancake house on Cordelia and West 4th, Mother Hubbard's on 6th Avenue, the Young China and Hamburger Heaven, across from each other on 8th Street; all places where you could fill your belly for under a buck. At one place we ate so much of the cheap onion soup to get the free bread to fill up on, they finally asked us not to return.

I discovered, on my own of course, those places to satisfy other appetites, the gay bars on 8th Street, Mary's and Main Street and New Colony; and with Mary Ann mainly living over at Seymour's then, I could now occasionally bring home an after-midnight guest, such as a young visiting math instructor from West Point (the male brothel next door I was sure was well out of my price range).

I also reconnected with Henry L. Wood, or Woody, whom I'd first met and lost my queer virginity to at Chautauqua in the summer of 1952, calling on him that winter in his cramped but spartanly stylish (much like his dress, always sharply creased trousers, tweed jackets and silk ties) rent-controlled Brooklyn apartment on DeKalb Avenue, with a fine view many stories below of downtown Williamsburg, and continued with him my apprenticeship not only in matters of the fleshly delights but in Culture with a capital "C." Woody was big on that—the ballet, concerts, the theater, recommended reading—regarding his "boys," so that I got to attend the theater and ballet, with Woody paying the way (my part of the payment coming later in the evening in bed). He also introduced me to the traditional male-only standup Astor Bar in Times Square, at that time the most famous unacknowledged gay cruising area in the city. (For the tonier queer set, the men-only Oak Room bar at the Plaza Hotel on 5th Avenue was the other.)

Woody confessed to me, matter of factly but gleefully, like a pleased uncle, that he often had students of his over from the high school he taught at, Polytechnic High, allegedly for tutoring in geometry, which often ended up in the same tutorings in the flesh he was engaged in with me. He also showed me snapshots of some of the boys that he'd taken in the apartment, a number of them naked, on the Castro Convertible sofa bed, smilingly happy, a few proudly cupping up their endowments for the camera, most of them no more than 15 or 16. They *did* get tutored in geometry, he emphasized, he really did insist on that, and did get sex, and Woody got the pleasure he wanted, introducing them to the pleasures of geometry *and* the flesh; just as he did with me, *sans* the Euclidean approach, however. I not only learned as well a great deal about the joys of male-male sex but, besides the plays and concerts, often got a good meal at a fancy restaurant that I could never have afforded on my own, into the bargain. Perhaps it was my months of freewheeling thinking at Black Mountain, but it didn't seem worth considering he was breaking the law: In the end, the boys, me, Woody, all fed each other, in our own way, with what we had to offer; we all got fed.

As was also at that time the tradition among older big-brother or father-figure queers, lonely boys were introduced to other lonely boys, which is how, through Woody, I met, among others, a shy young pianist/composer from Dallas, Texas, who lived on West 75th Street, the 70s a very gay male neighborhood in the 1950s. Woody was an example of hundreds, perhaps thousands of such older men in New York City then, rich underground networking resources of learning and opportunity, of openings to new vistas, new worlds.

When I first arrived, I poured out my heart—bellyached, more accurately—to sympathetic Mary Ann about Merrill, as the two of us sat crosslegged on the rice mat at Minetta Lane. But now, with so many busy changes in my life, both in Manhattan and Brooklyn, I was gradually thinking less and less of him, a genuine blessing, not only for me but I'm sure for Mary Ann's tired ears as well.

In another kind of artistic networking of the time, Mary Ann and Seymour introduced me to modernist, 12-tone composer Ben Weber, an old friend of Seymour's from Chicago. Ben lived at 230 West 11th Street, also in a basement apartment, where a grand piano in one corner took up much of the space. Short, plump, balding with a fringe of reddish hair, Ben had been suffering unrequited love for Seymour since their teenage years back in Chicago, and was very lonely now after a recent breakup with a lover. So, Mary Ann and Seymour playing possible matchmakers, I, unknowingly, was introduced to Ben by them as a prospective partner to fill the gap in his life.

Once that meeting was accomplished, Ben invited me around to listen to music and drink tall glasses of beer (of which he was inordinately fond), I suspect as a way of getting me tipsily loose and perhaps sensually pliant, since after several meetings, and several huge glasses of beer, he brought out his hidden stash of pornography (possession of which was illegal then), the traditional cartoons of muscular, leather-jacketed motorcyclists caught in the rain and running into a barn for shelter, stripping down to dry off, etc., etc., then other cyclists popping up out of the hay, not to mention a few equally well-built farmworkers, perhaps even the farmer's son, etc. Ben also had a nude photo presumably of a young, quite muscularly sculpted Burt Lancaster, sporting a huge, bell-shaped prick; at least you could see it was Lancaster's head, who the physique belonged to might've been another matter. Ben also often told me long erotic stories about himself, most of which I began to suspect were the rich fantasies of a lonely man.

During the Second World War he'd worked as a clerk-secretary at a place called Ketcham Pump in Manhattan; when I met him he made his living copying music and giving composition and piano lessons to a handful of students on the old grand piano, on which he composed his own work, which he would sometimes play for me, along with pieces by his beloved Schoenberg. He knew everyone, from the very handsome, dashing artsong composer Ned Rorem to campily tart-tongued Virgil Thomson, who lived in a suite in the old Chelsea Hotel on West 23rd Street and who Ben gossiped with on the phone every day. (Whenever Thomson invited Ben to a concert or a party, he'd always say, "Get your ass in your black satin, honey.") Ben was famous for his cooking—he knew which market on West 4th Street had the endive flown in fresh daily from Paris via Air France—and his cozy kitchen, always redolent of herbs and spices and the scents of gourmet meals past, had a stout wood table with benches for four at a bank of windows that overlooked the huge interior courtyard garden of St. John's-in-the-Village church at the corner of Waverly Place, the church which owned the entire square block and was Ben's landlord. The first time he took me out in that most formal Christian church garden, he impishly showed me a stone head of pagan Medusa buried in the ground ivy just beyond his kitchen door. He also pointed out poet May Swenson's second floor apartment in another of the church's buildings across the way at the far corner of the garden, where at gatherings or parties there were mostly women guests present. Directly across from Ben's kitchen were the windows of a lively young priest of Episcopalian St. John's who held lavish parties without drawing the drapes, and whose guests, Ben would slyly point out over dinner, were mainly attractive young men, in and out of collar.

Ben was also famous—or infamous—for his operatic renditions in drag; gotten up in full make-up, impromptu headdress and drapery (such spontaneous costumes alleged to be the origin of the word, the drag of the long train of the costume). Standing on a chair as stage, the better to be seen, he'd lipsynch to 12-inch record arias of Wagner or Verdi, sometimes, depending on how much beer he'd had, through a whole opera. His other guests seemed thoroughly amused by it all; I found the first few minutes amusing but after that his "performances" in drag truly became a drag.

Anyway, Greenwich Village, even in the early 1950s, was quite a headily different atmosphere from the remote, near-wilderness enclave of Black Mountain College, for all its mental and artistic fervor.

1954

That I might not be able to afford to return to the college for the spring term since the faculty had voted to dispense with work scholarships as "undemocratic," was a real concern for me, since each student had to pay something of the $1,600 tuition and board. I was able to save only a little from my $48 a week salary at Prentice-Hall, and as I had no winter coat and it was an exceptionally cold winter, I had to fork out eighteen bucks for the cheapest overcoat I could find, a gray, alleged "French import" that I spotted in the windows of Orhbach's cut-price department store on West 14th Street. With its wide belt and broadly flared collar, it was at least "smart-looking," as Ben put it, when I hurried to his place to show him, even though it was flimsily made of the cheapest cloth and barely lasted out the winter.

Not only was I preoccupied with money worries, but I was also concerned about plans for graduating. The most important thing I wanted to be was a writer, but I knew I wasn't going to be able to make a living at that. Some kind of degree, though, might help me to get other jobs, so that I could do my writing at night. I voiced my concerns to Charles in a letter to him at Black Mountain and have decided to include the whole text of his reply, since it not only discusses plans for my graduation but Robert Creeley's imminent arrival at the college to teach and his plans to bring with him from Mallorca (where Charles and Robert's intense correspondence continued since it had first begun in April 1950, when Creeley was a poor chicken farmer in Littleton, New Hampshire) the first copies of the first issue of *The Black Mountain Review*. Olson also noted the proposed writing courses (rather ambitious!) that he had lined up for him and Robert to teach:

mike:

    it's been rather a forbidding month (cold etc) so excuse
me that i just now get an answer to you

                       (in fact wanted *more* fr you
than the letter gave - that is more openness, both as of what you
were getting, and toward myself:

                     you must seek that,
now as of grad/ see no reason at all why you shldn't stand in for
it...especially "in writing"...whevere [sic] it looks like yr time:

that is, what you wld do is declare that you wld now like to expect
to graduate as of such & such a date; then the comm. on grad. wld
give you intermediate, or something, judgments: what, fr their point
of view, are holes you'd have to fill by grad.; and what *amount* of
achievement in writing they will expect of you

                    (this latter is my
job, to say - or with March 29th [start of spring 1954 term] will be
Creeley's as well, i suppose. That is, by that date, there will be a "dept" in
writing! Two of us. So it will be both more valuable to you & more what
demanding (???

Anyhow: you declare when you think you'd like to grad.,
(2)kind of a degree you'd like (that is, a general AB, or one "in writing";
& then, if you give me this in a formal request, I'll convene sd intermediate comm., and they'll declare yr program, and what date they
think you can shoot at.

                  OK? does that answer yr questions?

                      In fact,
as things look, you & Goerge [sic; Jorge Fick] ought to be the first
graduates of the first time BMC had what more & more looks like
what is going to be
the strongest...

that is, by the time we open you will see the first
number of the Black Mt Quarterly [sic] (64 pages, 60c, editior [sic]
Creeley, contributing editors, rexroth, blackburn, layton, olson)etc:

Creeley carries

the first 50 copies with him when he leaves Mallorca March 13th.

So you shld get as much as anyone out of the new BMC!

In any case

hope you are steadily holding the gains of the first quarter. And I
figure you can get a jammed program fr C [Creeley] and myself:
on an announcement of courses which we are preparing i have him
and myself down for 9_____ courses:

        him, elementary & advanced prose
        me,   ditto verse
      him & me, a course in DHL [D. H. Lawrence]
        ditto,   ditto WCW [William Carlos Williams]
       "   "   EP [Ezra Pound]
     him, a course in EDITING & PUBLISHING
      me, ditto: THE REASONS CAUSES & CONSEQUENCES
            OF THE PRESENT ("History", say)

OK. See you soon. And write again. say hello to whoever,   O

Olson's letter was reassuring, and as for "the gains," most of
the writing I did then was in the form of letters back to the college, to Charles, of course, and especially to Mary Fiore and
Tom Field, who'd all stayed on (Tom had the GI Bill to support
him). Their own newsy letters kept me from feeling too homesick for the place I thought of now as my home. I also kept a
ledger, a Day book, which I wrote in every day, to keep the
writing pump primed.

During that winter of 1954 I discovered that William Carlos

Williams, despite several recent strokes, was to read at the 92nd Street YMHA. Olson, of course, spoke glowingly of Williams in his classes and pushed us, naturally, to read him, not only the poems, especially the early books of *Paterson*, but the prose, particularly *In the American Grain*. I'd read considerably more of his work—all I could find of his books in the Black Mountain library, plus a number of borrowed works from others, thanks to Charles' urging—since I'd first discovered Williams' stories in *Make Light of It* in the Prendergast Library in Jamestown the summer of 1952, when Williams "allowed" me to see how you could write a story in a fresh and vital way, using particularly *American* idiomatic speech. From Charles' February 18 letter, I was looking forward to Creeley's take on "WCW" in a classroom setting, since Williams the writer had been as big an influence on Creeley as he had been on Olson, indeed on all of us in Olson's writing workshops.

There was quite a turnout in the auditorium that evening; it appeared every seat was filled. Williams, though only in his sixties, appeared thin and fragile-looking in a brown suit, sitting alone on the big stage, reading his poems in a flat, slow, deliberate voice, once or twice apologizing for mispronunciations and word slips, due to the difficulties caused by his condition, which he patiently explained, telling us he'd been taking speech therapy to learn to speak clearly again, he who was a miracle of clarity in his written speech, now reduced to the struggle for it in his stammering. That he was there at all seemed another miracle to me, in more ways than one—just to be in his presence was an exhilaration beyond words. However, toward the end of his halting reading, he began to speak about poetry, about the composition of it, of measure most especially (besides "image," the other thorny problem Olson was always hammering on about in his classes). Williams addressed specifically his own use of the "variable foot," somewhat of a sorepoint with Charles, who wasn't convinced it was the way to go (just as he challenged Williams' sense of a "female spirit" or "energy" as the root of male endeavors, including poetry). Williams' voice became surprisingly strong, even passionate, fire leaped into those deep brown eyes and into his throat, and he didn't let the few stumblings in his slurred speech deter him at all as he gesticulated to emphasize his points.

Afterward, there was a great crowd around him as he sat at a table in the lobby, one of his sons, also now a doctor, standing protectively beside him, as his father signed books in a slow, careful hand, a hand as slowed by the strokes as his tongue, and graciously spoke a few words to each of his readers and admirers. I myself a grateful admirer, and excited to see him for the first, and I expected last, time in the flesh, wanted to get a closer look at him, at his face, and gradually pushed my way forward in the mob until I stood pressed up against the wall no more than a few feet from the table. I wanted to mention to him Charles Olson (who had traveled to meet him once at Williams' home in Rutherford, New Jersey, a while back), and Black Mountain, how Charles spoke glowingly of his work and often, and had us Black Mountain writing students read him, how he was held up as a model to us, as a way to go, a new direction. But, as after the Ben Shahn lecture in Philly a few years before, I was too shy, too tonguetied, really, to do more than gaze at him, at his lean brown face with those incredibly dark brown eyes that I could see now close up had, within their sharpness, a good-humored kindliness. In a pause between his painful, laborious and uncomplaining signings, I suddenly found him gazing back at me, as if reading my thoughts and sensing my timidity, gazing back at me with a faint, quizzical smile, before someone placed another of his books before him to sign.

Coming home from my mailroom job at Prentice-Hall late one afternoon, I was surprised to see Merrill Gillespie and Herb

Roco waiting for me outside the courtyard at Minetta Lane—shocked, really; the moment I spied them, I wanted to run in the opposite direction. I don't know how they found out where I lived; maybe Wes Huss, who'd taken all our temporary addresses over the winter break before we left Black Mountain (perhaps fearful of losing track of even one student in our increasingly diminishing student body) had passed it on to them.

They both looked in a bad way, scruffy and tired; both had colds. Merrill explained that, since arriving in New York from Black Mountain a few days before, and not able to find a place to stay, they'd been sleeping nights locked in Herb's old 1939 Ford on a deserted side street near the Hudson River, the car packed to the roof with all their belongings. I was wondering if they were broke—hadn't Herb been working for his father all those months? If broke, why hadn't Merrill asked his parents for money? Even with their modest means, they'd come through in the past. But I didn't ask any questions, most certainly not why and how Herb had left Houston to return to Merrill (I learned later Herb's father had died of cancer and Herb had closed the auto garage). I was more shocked they'd been sleeping in Herb's car, wrapped in their sleeping bags, those past few bitter cold nights, while trudging the streets by day looking for a cheap place to live. Merrill asked if they could put up at my place for a few nights till something showed up. I inwardly recoiled, still angry with him, and not pleased with the prospect of spending my next few nights in the same room with someone who'd thrown me over as soon as he'd heard Herb was leaving Houston. I was also uncomfortable in the presence of Herb himself, although a likeable enough guy. Still, he was someone I jealously perceived as my "rival," and the source of all my pain. If only *he* weren't in the picture, I mistakenly believed, failing to take a good squint at Merrill himself, not to mention at myself as well.

As usual, Merrill had some nerve.

Still, much as I disliked the idea, I couldn't be so heartless as to turn them away, they looked so pathetic, so ill, and I said they could stay, so long as it was only for a short time, the place was so small, as Mary Ann and I had found, even for two. Besides, I told them, Mary Ann might decide to come back any day, which was a bit of a white lie, but one I said to make my point, so that they shouldn't plan on too long a stay.

The very first night, glad of the first showers they'd been able to take in several days since arriving in Manhattan, they lay in their sleeping bags on the floor a few feet from my mattress, the cold wind as usual whistling in the rattling windows. After they no doubt thought I'd gone to sleep, which I hadn't, lying wide awake in the dark, fully aware of their presence, conflicted in myself not only over what I saw as Merrill's cold betrayal and now this additional exploitation, but the fact that I was really a sucker to let the two of them stay over, I heard stealthy rustling movements in the darkness, followed by the careful sound of zippers sliding open on the sleeping bags, then quickening breaths over the wind at the windows and then less stealthy movements, the mingled breathing becoming quicker and louder.

That was too much! Even though I'd taken them in off the freezing streets, the fact that he—for I blamed Merrill completely—had so little sensitivity, so little respect for my feelings, that he would dare to make love to Herb only a few feet from me, and after all I had only recently gone through with him.

I didn't know what to do—cry out in protest? Seething with rage under my blankets, my body stiff, my fists clenched at my sides, finally I did the only thing I thought I could do: I began to cough. I started to cough as loud as I could, coughed and coughed with false hacking, sure that my outrage could be heard in every cough, until the stealthy rustlings ceased, till the heavy breathing died away, the slither of zippers zipping up again. Then, I stopped my coughing and lay still, holding myself in rigid suspension, grinding my teeth for what seemed like hours, hating to be mean and yet felt in the right, too, coughing only now and again as fair warning till their heavy breathing faded and was replaced eventually with the quieter measured breathing of their sleep.

Knowing Merrill, I was secretly pleased in imagining how pissed he must have been not getting his pleasure (his *way*, really) that night, he who had in our final days together at Black Mountain spoiled so many of my days, not to mention so many of my own nights of pleasure. So there was at least a small—and mean-spirited, I admit—comfort in that. The thought of it helped me relax and finally drift into my own sleep.

The next day Merrill told me they'd found a huge dirt-cheap loft down on Rivington Street in the old Jewish quarter on the Lower East Side, a former factory space that needed fixing up but with lots of windows, many of them broken. But having all that space was the main thing, he insisted. They'd start staying there overnight in their sleeping bags and begin getting it in livable shape the next day.

How they'd afford it, I didn't know, and didn't want to know, or what either of them was going to do for jobs. I was just greatly relieved they wouldn't be spending another night on Minetta Lane.

In the meantime, Mary Ann decided to move in with Seymour at West 12th Street, and since I couldn't afford the $60 rent plus utilities at Minetta Lane on my $48 a week as a mail clerk at Prentice-Hall, I had to find a place, the cheaper the better, so I could save enough to live on when I returned to Black Mountain in March.

In the Prentice-Hall mailing room, when I wasn't at the teletype machine, I sat with the other clerks slitting open piles of envelopes with orders for books from the endless supply of big grimy mail bags. Some of the mail customers—from their handwriting, many appeared elderly and senile—were naïve enough to include actual cash with their orders, and once or twice I was tempted sorely, when absolutely broke (as well as thinking of lean times to come at Black Mountain, wanting to raise money to return), to slip a few bills in my pocket, but, fearful of the supervisor's sharp eye—and thinking of those older, probably misguided mail customers—never did. (I was also tempted by a handsome, dark-eyed clerk with brilliantined pompadour who had his own desk in the mail department office and whose name I drew at Christmas for a gift—I bought him a buck-fifty maroon necktie on 8th Street—who kept pressing me about what it was like to live in the Village; but he was so "straight appearing"—he lived in Queens, I believe— and I so afraid of losing my job if I guessed wrong, I stayed clear of him.)

Coincidentally enough, down near 8th Avenue at the far end of the block on West 12th from where Seymour and Mary Ann lived, I spotted a "Room for Rent" sign in the front window of one of the brownstones. The cautious woman who opened the door only a crack at my ring cringed timidly, peering at me with anxious eyes. When I told her I'd come about the room, she said, in a soft but deep, Southern-accented voice, "It's only a tiny room, do you want a *tiny* room?" When I said I'd like to see how tiny, she then asked, inexplicably, "Do you like opera?" Some instinctive sense said to say yes, even though opera was not a favorite of mine, despite Woody's efforts to enlighten me. At my affirmative response, the pale, thin face gave a small, tremulous smile and the heavy door swung open, revealing a truly fragile elderly woman with obvious henna-dyed hair and wearing a gauzy, curtain-frilly dress.

"I *know* I can always trust someone who likes opera," she breathed as she carefully locked the door behind us, leaving me to wonder how she'd feel about renting to the Phantom of the

Opera. "If you live here, you must always lock up," she drawled, and led me down the gloomy hallway and up the stairs to the second floor. "All the young men who live here *love* opera," she whispered (I immediately got the picture), and, stopping mid-stairs to turn and stare directly at me, "Except for *her*," she hissed, nodding to a shadowy upper floor, "*She* has a life on *another* street."

The room was indeed tiny, with barely room for the narrow bed and a small armchair in one corner. "There's no radiator," she sighed, "only that old heat pipe." She nodded, indicating a thick pipe from floor to ceiling behind the armchair. The window, overlooking the backyards and Trees of Heaven of West 12th Street, was open a crack to air out the mustiness. The whole dark house had an odor of shutup mustiness, as if no air, no beam of sun had ever penetrated anywhere, but through the window I could hear the horns of tugs and ships out on the nearby Hudson River.

"It's four dollars a week," she drawled softly. "Clean linen distributed once a week. Rent expected on time."

The price sealed it, that along with the river sounds. For the money it would save me, I knew I could put up with living in such cramped quarters for a month or two. Having grown up sleeping three in a bed, and after sharing the dorm in South Lodge at Black Mountain, not to mention the increasingly stifling space with Merrill, having a space of my own, no matter how cramped, was a luxury.

I hauled my meager belongings, all packed in my trunk that I'd had shipped up rail freight from the college, the several blocks to my new room, squandering $2 on a cab. It was an eerily quiet house to live in. I rarely saw any of the other tenants, who I assumed were all opera queens, in the halls or even at the shared bath on that floor. Once, I saw "*her*," who lived on an upper floor and had "another life" elsewhere, a woman of uncertain age with, one could see even in the gloom on the darkened stairs, once-pretty features heavily powdered and bright red lipstick gleaming. She appeared slightly drunk and smiled shyly at me as we passed wordlessly. The only sound I ever heard in that house was every Saturday afternoon when, without fail, the Southern-voiced landlady, who never went out it seemed, bolted herself in her apartment on the first floor and listened, along with, it appeared, most of the other male tenants, from the loud volume of radios in their rooms, for several hours to the Texaco Opera over WQXR radio. Neither forgotten keys nor, I suspected, bursted pipes could rouse her from her weekly ritual.

Squeezed in the corner in my tiny armchair, I spent my spare time away from Prentice-Hall reading everything I could get my hands on, including old paperback copies of *Discovery* magazine I'd picked up cheap in a second-hand bookstore in the neighborhood, so envious that James Leo Herlihy, my brief acting coach that past summer at Black Mountain, had a story in one issue, *Discovery* a popular and widely distributed literary magazine for new young talent that many more would read than *The Black Mountain Review* with its few hundred copies. I was still working hard to write something that editor Creeley might find worthy to print in the *Review*. In the meantime, I continued to write lengthy letters back to the college, to Charles and Wes and Mary and Tom, and went on every day writing in my ledger, selected entries from which it turned out I got to read aloud in Creeley's first writing class when I returned to school in the spring of 1954.

Before the semester began, by lucky chance, Joe Fiore and Tom Field had made a quick trip to New York City on some matter, and for the price of helping with the gas, I was able to get a ride from the city back to Black Mountain with them, in Joe's Jeep stationwagon.

Waking up at one point at dusk as we were driving through

the piney foothills of North Carolina, I glimpsed through the windshield an enormous dark bird with great wide flapping wings descend to the middle of the highway not far in front of us, its sharp beak disemboweling some small wild creature twitching on the asphalt. A shiver went through me, the vivid image of the great bird killing the beast staying with me the rest of the trip and for days after, an omen that became a delirious reality over a year later.

Early the next morning after we got back to Black Mountain, I walked all around the place, setting each foot down in careful gratitude. The end-of-February mountain air already had a raw hint of spring in it. Pushing up already through clumps of snow by the footpath at Lake Eden were clusters of bright daffodils. I bent to touch them, overjoyed to be home.

In that early spring of 1954, along with Terence and Tom Field, I'd moved into the downstairs of Meadows Inn, Natasha and Eric's old apartment. Tom, a slightly wall-eyed, round-shouldered painter who'd arrived that year from Fort Wayne, Indiana, had been a medic in the Korean War and was at Black Mountain on the GI Bill, the government subsidies for the few GI students on campus helping keep the place open. Tom talked often of his Korean experiences as a medic, not quite yet having left the army behind, funny surgery-tent stories and particularly of a nasal-voiced nurse whose response to everything from "Want a beer?" to "Stitch up that abdomen" was "*Why* not?" which for a time we took up as a comic reply to everything.

In the pinch, everybody by now had moved to the smaller cottages and barracks-like "Chances" on the land beyond the Studies Building, where we had to cook for ourselves and scrounge what food we could from the farm, after the lower half of the campus closed, including the kitchen and dining hall and North and South Lodges, in a shrinking of space and basic amenities as money and the student population shrank. No matter how hard Charles, now as Rector, and the few remaining faculty struggled to think of ways to raise both cash and students, including bulletins with exaggerated course claims and the leasing of college timberland to local loggers and Charles making the trip north to New York City in his old, ironically, Ford convertible to personally appeal for grant money to the allegedly liberal but actually stuffy board of the Ford Foundation, which turned a deaf ear to even Charles' considerable blandishments, nothing worked.

One morning, as I stepped out the door of Meadows Inn, the tall mountain grass in the front yard started billowing like a wind was in it, but there was no breeze, not the slightest, and I knew it had to be a rattlesnake, hearing the door and my steps and trying to get out of my way, slithering for the stand of pine trees across the yard.

I knew I was back where I belonged.

My first introduction to Robert Creeley was through Olson reading Creeley's early poems and stories in his writing classes at Black Mountain. Mostly they were read to us students in manuscript since little of Creeley's work was as yet published, even by his own Divers Press, the new work arriving regularly along with the almost daily letters from Mallorca, where Robert was then living with his wife, Ann, and children, in the voluminous correspondence exchanged between Creeley and Olson. Neither had as yet met in the flesh.

I first read Creeley early on in my Black Mountain stay in *Origin* II, the Summer 1951 issue of the magazine edited by Cid Corman out of Boston, which featured Robert's writing and included such stories as "In the Summer," "3 Fate Tales" and "Mr. Blue," and the poems "Love" and "Hart Crane (2)."

Here was a writer to ponder, and ponder I did, alternately moved and baffled. As with my first reading of Olson, Creeley was like no other writer I'd ever read before. He came at you out of nowhere, with no antecedents (as I thought then), with his perplexing sensibilities and acute but difficult perceptions. Whatever was he talking about? The incomprehension, of course, raw as I was, lay not in Creeley.

Olson's esteem for Creeley and his writing was obvious and strong, and my own feeling, as green and willing student, was that what Olson esteemed was worth paying attention to.

To an apprentice narrative writer nurtured (before but especially early on at Black Mountain) on Twain, Dreiser, Sherwood Anderson, Stein, William Carlos Williams, Joyce, Proust, and Virginia Woolf (the last-named as baffling to me in her writing as the newly-discovered Creeley was), this sparse, subtle and indirect writing, particularly the stories, was like signals from another planet. There were no familiar ear-sounds or sight boundaries of conventional and expected plot and character, no social conscience with a social message, no juicy adjectival orgies of description (weaknesses in my own written indulgences), no comfortable signposts pointing in any directions previously known to me.

It was only gradually that I began to perceive that its strangeness was grounded in particular experiences and methods of writing unarticulated and unperceived for so long a time they were coming back to us strange in their renewedness. Creeley was making the familiar unfamiliar with a cast of vision and intelligence that was making it all possible again; if not "see-able," to me, anyway, it was at least oddly hearable, tantalizingly intelligible: an experience of mind, of wit, the heart a muted drum, very taut, very dry-skinned. It was language dejuiced of expectant feeling; it was feelings and perceptions tuned to a newly received and more precise wavelength. If you didn't have a sharp ear, the highly acute sound of it was gone before you heard it, like resonances on the edge of meaning, like Anton Webern's music I had heard that past summer at the college, or earlier, the spare, muted horn of Miles Davis. I had to learn to pay attention, to empty my head of all preconceived receptions of what writing *ought* to be, of my own expectations. Creeley's compositions imposed the necessity of an almost total reordering of aural receptivity.

Holed up in the first study I had in the lower level of the Studies Building, I puzzled over those early published stories of Creeley's, trying to learn something. What I did discern immediately was Creeley's finely-tuned ear, his exactitude with words and the space of reverberating silences he carefully placed among them. Creeley's (later) "bouncing ball" avowal of composition to the contrary—"staggering behind the potential of saying things"—these openings were like interstices for activities of imagination and mind to participate in. When a bit of environmental detail, rarely, or a glancing thought, often, slipped into his narrative, I, overfed on naturalistic accumulations of some of those personally nurturant writers mentioned earlier, seized upon it like a famished dog on a splinter of bone, blowing it up to full-jointed proportions: You're energized by Creeley, I discovered, by being made to activate your own resources; he provides the place and space, like detonators that spark and explode (implode) your own engagement. Mindscape and mind-action being the main agilities, the untouched and unchanged territories inside your own skull become populous with possibilities of discovery. " 'You hear it as you play it.' "

As in actual one-to-one confrontation later with him, I didn't so much read Creeley as *listen*, not so much to what was going on outside and around him but to what was going on inside his skull. Creeley's writing is a cranial encasement of a very private world you either choose to enter or not. In his insistence on the validity of that world, he apparently doesn't care whether you do or you don't. You need to come to him, as with any writer at the spine of origins, on his own terms, or the speech of a highly sensitized intelligence is missed.

Creeley in those days once compared himself to "a radio," always flipped on, talking all day, in gravelly monotone, "even from the grave." That talk, earnest and serious and self-mocking, was and is extraordinarily informed, aware, talking on and on and on with an urgency both intense and quiet (it hadn't then as much of the mellow but pungent humor as now), with no station breaks, no commercials, for anyone who wanted to listen. It's terrific, and one of our wonders, to hear, after these many years, he's still on the air. And as he said in the 1970s, in a literal context, in a taped poetry workshop he gave at St. Mark's-in-the-Bowery, which was broadcast on WBAI in New York City, "I love to talk." And, assuming physical New England awkwardnesses and strictures, talk can also be love, and the next best thing.

What the writing was *about* was another matter, tuned as I was then in my early months at Black Mountain to a grosser babbly band where the long accumulated static and confusion of wavering and no less demanding voices and sounds were the daily condition in my own receiving headset. I, like most everyone, had brought my past intact down with me. I was trying hard to tune in, to hear Olson, others, like Wolpe, Morley, Fiore, Natasha Goldowski, Huss; and students, like Mary Fiore, Jonathan Williams, Joel Oppenheimer, even Fee Dawson, despite our differences, who had arrived there before me and picked up a thing or two. But my head was still jammed with a lot of pre-Black Mountain chatter-static which only over a slow period of time, in the slowing and quieting terrain of Swannanoa Valley, was I able to gradually fade out. And slowly, I was able to pick up those new, often bewildering but exciting and attractive signals sparking out of the inhabitants of the school, signals bouncing cupped in the 600-acre valley ringed by the Seven Sister Mountains that marked the boundaries of the enclave that was Black Mountain College.

Those surrounding hills appeared, over a time, to block out signals that earlier had still bombarded me from the strict time-clock, neurasthenically spastic and rigidly constipated conservative America I wanted desperately to drop out of (not that I ever felt a genuine part of it—only affected its tics and insanity drag, good at disguises, camouflage—but I was certainly infected by it; in many ways I came to Black Mountain, healthy remnants pointing me instinctively south, like a diseased and mal-fed victim seeking the only likely health and nutriment around). As was discussed in Olson's classes, the upper atmosphere in those times was so radioactive with the atomic dust of "clean" bombs and "dirty" bombs—Olson paused significantly to ask us what we made of that language—their poisonous clouds penetrating the sky, then raining down their radioactive rain, an analogous radiating all around of the fallout of attitudes and toxins even infiltrating the air of our long green valley. Olson was pissed off at the "boy scientists" in an Asheville *Citizen* photo whooping and dancing around, celebrating their latest nuclear weaponry successes, "like adolescents at a party," ignorant of the consequences of their actions. Those were the times, as we saw on Doyle's TV set in the farmhouse, "field trips" in Olson's newspaper class, of Joe McCarthy and his anti-communist and anti-queer hearings in Washington; of national paranoia and the Korean war; of the expansion of material glut through more extended and efficient production methods learned in World War 2—all that continuing without abatement into the 1950s along with the high-sell that smothered every other consideration, America one vast commercial from ocean to ocean. High on commodities addiction, the United States was well on its way to becoming a nation of spiritless, empty-eyed junkies ("Americans essentially without souls," as Olson once remarked in class). Black Mountain was a tiny bastion of alternatives, and, in spite of its poverty in money, it was vital and rich in excitement and energy resources, of mind and spirit and imagination in the wealth of variations and possibilities inherent in each of us. The Seven Sisters slept in the hills, the Seven Sister Mountains surrounding us, on which we walked and hiked, booted or barefoot, their chthonic energies ionizing up through the soles of our feet magnetic and charged implications of directions in as much strength and power as we were prepared to sense and follow, to fly up from.

Olson was the prime magician unlocking those potentials for the handful of young discontents, like myself, straggling in from all around the country, looking for a way out and for another way, for other paths to learning and practicing what was in us to do, who fled to Black Mountain as the only feeble wink of hopeful light in a very dark and morbid time.

And of course, the tallest and most powerfully vocal antenna on campus at that moment was Olson himself. I listened to him with all my might. And the news from Mallorca, those short-wave letters beamed from Creeley and picked up and transmitted by Olson in his writing classes, was pretty exciting news.

It took time, but gradually I began to be able to hear the rich profusion and variety of what was being broadcast around me.

Creeley's poems and stories, in their bareboned particularities, struck a realization in me, and a way to do it (although my own directions were eventually different), before I was able to comprehend, in even the skimpiest sense, what Olson himself was up to in his poems. Meaning and intent escaped me more often than not, but in the carefulness of language, true to his own ear, Creeley taught me—before he'd even become an instructor at the college—to begin to give a listen to my own, now that the wax was beginning to loosen. This was, of course, abetted by Olson, no mean ear-shaker himself.

As noted, there were those other aural-shockers going on around me: Lou Harrison's and Stefan Wolpe's music, Wes

Huss' concepts of theater, Natasha Goldowski's physics, plus the eye-opening paintings that were coming out of Joe Fiore's and visiting artists' classes. But it was Olson's presence, and my surrendering finally to his insights and intents with me (like some overwhelming natural force, you either surrendered to Olson or you didn't; if you didn't, you were as good as dead as far as he was concerned), and Creeley's strong presence via his writings to Olson through the mails, that gave me the focus to begin to perceive a way to put words down on paper in a process that was close to my own intents and capabilities: "Write what you know," from Olson, was starters to get to a point to write what you didn't know, to write what you didn't know was in you.

Despite Olson's own high-beamed and wide-ranging voice (at that time picked up only within the mountainous confines of Swannanoa Valley), a voice he never sought to impose on me, as apprentice, or on any other student for that matter, along with the intensity of Creeley's own highly-charged laser beam, I began to hear, amid all the persistent whip-crackings of my own past and accumulated authority-voices, the stirrings of a feeble, low-watted burbling voice that surprised me as mine, centering nearer the chords of my own throat, the experiences of my life, in Charles' insistence: "They're valid, go with them."

One of many prime things Olson (along with Creeley's early writings) helped me to do, in a catharsis of conflicting noise (paradoxically, since Olson's poems and much of his prose were still very much that to me—it was the personal magnetism and generous warmth, the talk of the man I responded to at first, rather than his writing), was to purge my ears and head of the clamorous voices not my own, the ones I carried around in the echo chamber of my cranium (for all it was filled with noise, still pretty empty of anything of substance—"You got to learn to thicken up," Olson told me, right off the bat). Those sounds had little actual relevance or importance to what I needed to attempt: to begin to become a questing and questioning instrument of a centered and singular voice, quiet *and* outspoken. (The outspokenness took a little more time; needing to listen, I still rarely opened my mouth in Olson's classes.)

Another increase of space for me at Black Mountain was the ability, in that permissive and tolerant atmosphere, to behave and be let be who I was (or to come out as much as that time and space permitted, which at Black Mountain, compared to outside homophobic USA, was considerable). That space was mostly sensual freedom, whenever the opportunity and without repercussion, plus the ability to live openly with another male, as I did with Merrill Gillespie, without censure or hassles.

In sum, back at Black Mountain in February 1954 for the spring term, settling in at Meadows Inn with Tom Field and Terence Burns, everyone looking forward to Creeley's arrival and the copies of the first issue of *The Black Mountain Review*, I was still a very green sprout (not very "bright," as Creeley later once put it, aptly, though meaning it in another, complimentary context as not surface "bright"), as yet totally ignorant and naïve as writer and student in protracted adolescence.

Little did I know that by summer all that would begin to change.

Creeley, having gotten out the first issue of *The Black Mountain Review* on the Spanish island of Mallorca, and leaving there for the USA "March 13" as Olson's letter noted, was expected to arrive at the college to start teaching late in that March of 1954. Excitement and anticipation generated by Charles became, as usual, contagious in the rest of us and had certainly built up in me. I was not only curious but eager to meet this writer whose poems and stories we'd been reading and discussing for many months now and whose presence, at least on paper, had played such an important part in my early student days.

Tom Field and I, both of us early risers, were up after dawn that morning in Meadows Inn, where we shared, each with our separate rooms, the whole first floor, along with Terence Burns, who only slept there, preferring, when he wasn't busy in his study, to spend most of his time working at the farm. Terence usually left before dawn to milk the cows, and the first thing Tom did when he got up was to shut the door to Terence's littered bedroom, where the long unchanged sheets on the bed had become the shade of a good strong brew of coffee, to "keep out the barn smell," as Tom put it, from the rest of the house. Burns, a very good collagist and aspiring poet, a widely read and acutely perceptive reader in both English and French, with a quirky, eccentric intelligence, agreed evidently, along with D. H. Lawrence, that too much cleanliness "impoverishes the blood."

Fixing breakfast together in our communal kitchen, Tom as usual pumped up the Coleman gas stove he'd installed after the college dining hall closed, then checked to see if the block of ice in the old wooden ice box would make it through the day. (Somebody with a car was always willing to haul a piece back for us from the ice house in Black Mountain.) As we puttered about, we wondered, since he was due that morning, if Creeley had arrived, knowing that if he had, we probably wouldn't be meeting him till later in the day, since we understood that Charles and he, after their enormous correspondence over the years, starting April 21, 1950 after William Carlos Williams suggested Olson contact the 23-year-old Creeley in Littleton, and meeting now for the first time, would undoubtedly spend the first hours together. At least we knew, from past experience, that Charles, in his excitement at finally having his "pen pal" (Tom's irreverent phrase) here at last, would determinedly see to that.

Checking the cupboard, I discovered we were out of sugar and running over the possibilities of who would be most likely able to spare some (no one's larder at Black Mountain was amply stocked at that time, the farm only marginally operating), decided on the Husses, Bea Huss' generosity ample, no matter the shortage of their own supplies. I volunteered to walk up to their house and see if I could borrow some.

The Huss' white clapboard house with green trim was just the next one up from the Olson's house, on the dirt road winding around to the farm. You could cut across the front yard of Meadows Inn and follow a path through some sparse woods running alongside a gully, cross the yard in front of Olson's house, with its small wooden park bench out front, and a little beyond come to the large communal vegetable garden laid out by Bea to supplement our meager diets, just this side of their house. This shortcut saved time without going by the longer way of the road.

I borrowed the sugar, a small brown bag of it, more than we needed, but Bea insisted, in her usual way. Coming back down toward Olson's place, I spotted Charles and a younger man in a dark blue beret, an eyepatch over one eye and what looked like rough, loose-fitting workclothes, sitting side by side on the park bench in Charles' front yard. The stranger of course had to be Creeley who, it turned out, had just arrived.

The two sat very close, almost of necessity, since Charles' girth and height were in themselves enough to fill the bench. They didn't see me approach at first, and I watched Charles talking earnest and close in Robert's ear, his huge body swung half around in relaxed and easy confidentiality. Robert, sitting stiff, listening with bowed head, stared down at the ground. My body tensed with anticipation, seeing for the first time the person whom I'd only known so far on typed and printed pages.

I planned only to nod and go on my way, mostly out of my own innate shyness but also respecting, as Charles had impressed on us, like a strong, tacit vibration (also conveyed to newcomers, verbally, by more seasoned students) his adamant insistence on his privacy in and around his own house. But Charles caught sight of me as I passed and, lifting his long arm from around Creeley's shoulder, waved to me and called out, with a radiant smile on his face, "Michael, come on over here and meet Robert Creeley."

There was something large and ungainly in Robert's hands dangling at his thighs, a worker's hands, thick-wristed as they poked out from the dark sleeves of his jacket. He snapped halfway up from the bench as I crossed over the yard, the first glimpse of him was of some awkward, sturdy peasant, like a Basque, his face pale and tense, his movements jerky, agitated. I wrote this off as fatigue (Creeley, I found out later, had driven through the night in his battered old pick-up truck nonstop from New York to North Carolina), but it turned out that Robert was pretty much like this all the time.

As I approached, he sprang from the bench as if poked from behind with an electric prod and plunged in my direction one of those large, work-roughened but very white hands. Caught off guard, carrying the sugar in my right hand, I tried to juggle the bag, not too successfully, to my left, hating the stupid brown bag I was stuck with at this important moment, but managed to grab the hand thrust out at me.

I liked him immediately because I discovered in that first instant he was as awkward and as easily embarrassed and uncomfortable as myself.

All that was exchanged then were some trivial pleasantries, and Charles, beaming, telling Robert, as if by way of "assurance," that I would be in his writing class, like Creeley had something to look forward to, which made me gawky and a bit panicky, fully aware of my own defects as student-apprentice.

My immediate sympathy with Creeley was enlarged by seeing in that one dark eye staring out at me—the one beneath the patch (lost in a childhood accident) began watering rapidly and he dabbed at it in quick self-conscious swipes with a wrinkled dirty handkerchief—an attractive vulnerability, a desperate desire to be liked. In his eye was a mute appeal of the painfully shy (magnified by his low, barely audible words) to overlook his clumsiness and shortcomings, to look beyond them (the paradox of the grace and deftness of his written words leapt into my mind).

Those first moments of meeting him were also like being dropped into the presence of a fierce, impatient bird, strapped down, restricted, in a too tight ribcage of flesh, an entrapment of spirit so visible I could instantly identify with it, the only difference being that mine was more "controlled" and being gay and out of necessity for survival being the better actor, more concealed. What stood before me was a person who seemed totally undefended and who, consciously and without apology, revealed to all his inner exposure and need. As we mouthed the customary inanities of greeting, Creeley's body and face spoke, in gestures and tics of awkward sign language, of someone quite another: here was a kind of man I'd never encountered before in the rawness and abrasiveness of his physical presence. Olson's own presence was mitigated in the large openness of his generosity and charm and, an accomplished player himself, in the swagger of his own unquestioned rightness. Creeley appeared like a man shrunken and gnawed by tremendous doubts and uncertainties, if not the same, at least on an equal pitch of intensity to my own.

Although I didn't know it then, or have words for it, it was my first glimpse of someone who stood revealed without subterfuge, in every gesture (and, later I was to find, in his words, in his classroom), in complete and unadorned honesty.

Olson convinced Creeley not to waste any time getting down to work, and so that same evening Creeley held his first writing class in the big classroom on the lower level near the front of the Studies Building, with about a half dozen students in attendance: Tom Field, as noted, painter and aspiring poet (we were encouraged to try everything at Black Mountain); Karen Karnes, former student now resident potter; Cynthia Homire, with long glossy black hair, barefoot early spring to late summer, in her perpetual worn faded levi jacket and jeans; Laurie Forest, short-cropped carrot hair, who loved Emily Dickinson and wanted to write but because of Charles' negative attitude on Dickinson took up potting instead, and who had a fine stash of wine in her apartment above us in Meadows Inn; Jerry Van de Wiele, painter and another aspiring writer, ex-regimental artist in the U. S. Marine Corps, of all things; perhaps one or two others, perhaps even Terence Burns was there, taking time off from the farm.

I've told pretty much what that first class was like to Martin Duberman in 1968, who quoted it in his 1972 *Black Mountain: An Exploration in Community.**

That part of the interview, as edited by him, is as follows:

. . .The first class was the worst. It met in the large conference room of the Studies Building, which had a huge table that took up most of the space. Six students bunched up at one end, and at the other sat Creeley, forlorn, alone, staring sideways at the wall, mopping at his eye with a handkerchief (the eye lost in that childhood accident Creeley usually kept covered with a patch but since the patch made him self-conscious, he'd left it off for the first class; only to have the eye—as always, when he got emotionally upset—run buckets). Creeley talked in a nonstop monotone so low and gravelly, that no one could understand what he was saying. After ten minutes or so, Karen Karnes asked him if he could speak up; he lifted his voice for a few minutes, but it soon sank back into a monotone . . .

*Martin Duberman, *Black Mountain: An Exploration in Community* (New York: E. P. Dutton, 1972), 393-394.

Creeley, casting a desperate eye, asked if anybody had ght any writing, perhaps desperately frightened that some-
e actually *might have*, I piped up, apprehensive but wanting to be of "help," said I did and read some excerpts from the Day ledger journal I had kept that past winter in New York. I was surprised when Creeley responded favorably to two of the entries: one about a middle-aged drunk I saw one night getting out of a taxi on Macdougal Street in Greenwich Village, a blond on each arm, hollering tipsily, "*Toujours l'amour!*" over and over; and another, a mood piece, about a woman, alone and late at night, staring out the upper windows of an office building downtown. It was a generous response considering the slightness of the material and its observations, and it warmed me to an encouraging start with Creeley.

Over the next few classes, Robert gradually improved, losing his shyness as he got to know us, becoming more and more an effective instructor as his own confidence increased. Moving the class to the smaller Reading Room (Olson's favorite "classroom" because of the close warmth and lack of drafts) on the upper level of the Studies Building, just inside the lobby, helped too, creating a space more amenable to Creeley's intimate and personal style. Also, given the snug size of the room, there were no more complaints about not being able to hear him, and Creeley seemed more comfortable, more relaxed, with the students gathered closely around. Creeley's classes never met for more than two hours, often less, again matching his style, contrasted with the endurance tests of Olson's marathon meets (or even Hilda Morley's three- and four-hour-long classes on metaphysical poetry and Henry James). In Creeley's class we read and discussed at length William Carlos Williams' earlier poems as points of departure towards our own possibilities in American speech, as well as the poetry of Hart Crane (a no-no in Olson's classes) and the jazz of Charlie Parker, Bud Powell and Miles Davis, whose records could be heard playing late the night from Creeley's apartment in the rear of the Stu Now and again a student would read a poem or piece of prose he or she had written (Creeley, unlike Olson, had no requirement that a student had to bring writing to class or else not be admitted), and we'd spend a little time talking about it, Creeley careful not to impose any absolutes or dogmas, respectful to leave space for openings. But mostly it was Creeley talking, and Creeley talking, on his best days, was plenty good enough, and I for one was an avid listener, respectful of the incisiveness of his intelligence, its liveliness, and the interpretation and range of his reading. He was more than just a fresh voice sounding within the Seven Sisters: he seemed to have his sights on and be in touch with every aspect of what was new and vital going on then. That included our first opportunity to clap eager eyes on the first issue of *The Black Mountain Review* (after editor M. C. Richards' earlier student-published yellow-covered one-time publication), which Creeley had carried with him on the boat across the Atlantic from Spain, where it had been printed cheaply. Vol. 1, No. 1, the Spring 1954 issue, a slim 64 pages, price 75 cents, featured Olson's "Against Wisdom as Such," Robert Hellman's story "The Quay," and modest Creeley himself as "Thomas White" ("White" his middle name) with the poem "Alba": "Your tits are rosy in the dawn . . ."

After a few classes, Creeley, perhaps out of a sense of obligation to be "useful," began to say the two of us ought to get together to talk about my writing, not that I had anything much to show. He was impressed by the number of hours I spent in my study writing, in longhand, since I still didn't have a typewriter, now that Merrill was gone and with him the portable machine he'd lent me, never having had enough money to actually buy even a used one. It was all pretty mechanical stuff, the short stories I was trying to write, awfully weak and spiritless, stenographic in detail. I had no way yet into the spirits of words, my own spirit being yet so muffled, like my voice, so unrevealed to me. Before coming to the college, I had spent so much time hiding from myself, and hiding that hidden self from others—although I'm sure I fooled no one—that I had had no time or energy left for discovery. At least at Black Mountain was breathing space to begin and learn. Taking to heart Wolpe's remark to Olson after my first reading with Fee, I was beginning to learn to lie a little.

And I did want to learn, in the worst way, was willing, and although I knew what I was doing wasn't of any account—not knowing yet how to achieve more fully that lie of the imagination which is the only reality, that creates the truth of that—I persisted with Creeley about our getting together to talk because I thought maybe he could hand over to me another part of the secret that might put me on the right track, to learn how, in particular, good liars make good writers.

Creeley preferred to work, like Olson, late at night, jazz blaring on his phonograph (the same as his beloved Hart Crane did in his time), and then only in erratic fits and starts, finding a consistency of rhythmic work difficult (it was around this time he wrote "A Wicker Basket," starring Liz, the ancient college cat with one pink and one green eye, who, even at her great age, was always pregnant, a poem on several levels on how Creeley was and was not "making it"). He would say to me, "I see you writing all day. That's good. I envy you. Keep at it," which, I guess, was about the only and best thing he could say. "*Write, write, write,*" Olson used to insist, and that was the main part of it then, a sort of grinding, plodding hope.

How I was ever let to stay on, or even survive, at Black Mountain those first two years, hard up as the college was for students, is a mystery to me. Well, even though I was a washout working on the farm, I could and did wash dishes and manage the dishwashing crews and take care of the kitchen, when it was still open.

Being a dependable and cheap source of labor was probably what saved my neck. Maybe I had such a skinny, pathetic look nobody had the heart to kick me out. Black Mountain, as I said earlier, was a real home for strays, not only for the endless pack of bone-sharp, homeless dogs that found their way there, but for the human kind as well. Of course it wasn't completely that. Olson, and I guess maybe Creeley, too, had sensed something, a long-shot hunch, I suppose, that I was unaware of. I often wondered what the hell I was doing there, but knew deep down there was no place else I wanted to be, or, at that time, could be.

After putting me off for a long while (I guess he'd gotten the drift pretty quick by then that with what I was writing there wasn't too much to talk about), Creeley said we'd get together one particular afternoon in his apartment in the back of the Studies. I encountered him at the time of our meeting hanging up his laundry, which I took at first to be old cleaning rags, on a droopy clothesline slung under the open back area of the Studies, directly beneath his apartment, Creeley evidently living as close to the edge of poverty in Mallorca as most of us at Black Mountain, right down to his ragged Jockey shorts. I was coming up from the library, taking the shortcut through the tall weeds and marsh grass (cut on rare occasions by student work crews with machetes and bolo knives).

Creeley was skittery and jumpy—perhaps he'd just had *his* first encounter with the second-hand (like everything at the college, it seemed) automatic washer in the old chemistry lab at the other end of the building, which certainly would've accounted for it, since the machine had an erratic will of its own, unpredictably skipping around the concrete floor so that on various cycles, particularly the spin, you had to sit on it to hold it down, all the while risking electrocution from the faulty wiring damp from the wet floor. (Even the commonplace at Black Mountain was not without risk.) Perhaps it was Creeley catching me observing his personal wash, for a look of embarrassed then angry rage came into that one eye of his, making it darker than ever. But it was really something a great deal more than that. His eye snapped from side to side, like it wanted to get around me, his body moved in quick sideways arm and shoulder jabs, like he wanted to escape, but couldn't, held trapped as he was, possibly, by his sense of obligation and responsibility, not only on this occasion of his talk with me but of his overall difficulties: his teaching classes for the first time, his adjusting to the place and getting down to a consistent rhythm in his writing, and, I guess, what it really was, concern and loneliness for his wife with whom he'd been having troubles he hoped to patch up, and missing his children, too; not to mention the work to be done with the Spanish printer on publishing and editing future issues of the *Review*. At this point his heart and mind seemed more in Mallorca than at Black Mountain, himself a thousand miles away and more.

It started to rain, one of those sudden afternoon mountain rainstorms, tropical in its intensity and abundance of downpour. (Mary Fitton Fiore was right: the immediate Black Mountain area had more inches of rain per year than any other in the region.) Water from the storm started blowing in under the exposed lower level and Creeley, abandoning his laundry, led the way up into the belly of the building on the open rickety wooden steps ("temporary" stairs, like some other features of the Studies when it was built back in the 1940s, and still so to that day) and down the narrow hallway lined with the shut doors of studies in the all but empty building to his apartment at the rear. When he opened the door, he stood dead in his tracks, seeing sheets of rain blowing in through the large pushout windows he'd left open and around the piece of cardboard over the broken pane in one. He rushed to the window ledge, simultaneously yanking the windows closed and snatching up small pieces of paper lined up on the edge. They turned out to be checks, new $2.50 per year subscriptions to the first four issues of the *Review*, most precious checks, given the necessarily slim financing for the project, which had been instigated by Olson in hopes of attracting monetary attention and students to the school. (The main purpose, of course, was to have an alternative to the deadness in print, as Olson saw it.)

It was an inauspicious time for our first one-on-one talk, to say the least. Having looked forward to it for some time now, I felt disappointed, and strained. Creeley was darting about the room, flapping the rain-splotched subscription checks in the air, trying to dry them as best he could, moving them to a safer place. He kept saying, "They'll be all right, I think," as if to reassure himself, glancing at me in agitated helplessness for some firmer reassurance. "They'll dry here, don't you think? I think they'll be okay, don't you?" He looked so pathetically vulnerable, like a boy caught slipshod at his chores. I only nodded agreement and made the best soothing noises I could as I helped him spread the checks on a dry surface away from the windows.

So our "talk," or rather Creeley's talk, chopped out in bits and pieces as he scurried about, didn't amount to very much, any more than some well-intentioned platitudes of encouragement, mixed with some sound advice: "Vary the length of your sentences," he told me, consistency and monotony of syntax being one of my many problems. "You'll be okay," and he gave a little nervous smile meant to comfort, the best he could manage under the circumstances.

I followed him around the room, incapable of articulating the questions that jammed my head, which all amounted at rockbottom to a basic question of and need for reassurance myself; not knowing then, wanting it all that day, that instant, the secret of time growth in apprenticeship requires; knowing, too, unconsciously, as Creeley himself did, seemed to sense anyway in regard to myself, that you can't rob anybody of his own expe-

learning, of finding his own rhythm to grow in. Or as ░░░░░ said some years later, "You ever try to tell a person ░░░░░░░░even years old and five foot tall that by the time they're sixteen they possibly will be six feet tall, you know? Unbelievable. Or try to tell someone who's never made 'love' to another human being what this will be for them . . ."

Live. Listen. Read. Open yourself. Take flights. Take risks. And write. It was no more than I was already attempting to do, the basic suggestions from Olson that Creeley himself, preoccupied with his immediate and across-the-Atlantic concerns, reiterated in that tight, nervous voice that was still tinged with kindness, that was hopeful.

Being young, I wanted more than that. I left him, walking back up to Meadows Inn, the rain now stopped, not having gotten the secret, not the one I wanted anyway, instantaneous, facile perhaps. But later on I realized, solidifying my own previous conviction, however unarticulated, that there was much I could do for myself, and learn, as a writer, given time, given that and a place at Black Mountain, which I had, precarious as that place was for each of us; if I would only be patient, give it my best shot, and keep my ears open and my mouth shut.

That was probably Creeley's last attempt at the tutorial process. As usual, much more was gained in casual talks over coffee with him in the kitchen in Meadows Inn or, more likely, over beers down the road at Ma Peak's tavern.

After that two months of teaching in March and April, Creeley left Black Mountain and returned to Mallorca to continue publishing the *Review* and also to attend to his seriously ailing marriage. The rest of that spring and summer I continued to write daily, spurred and renewed by my experience with Creeley, and the continued, solid presence of Olson in talks with him and in his writing classes.

I had been a student at Black Mountain for almost two years

now. On the top shelf of my study were three foot-high stacks of manuscripts, scribblings really, accumulations of apprenticeship measuring the bulk of what I had needed to write through, and out of, to get down to the direct application of my own experience and resources in a primary act of writing, to develop my own "sound system," as Creeley put it.

Little did I know then, that within a few months time I would do just that, writing for the first time a story of which Charles thoroughly approved and which Creeley would publish in *The Black Mountain Review.*

Betty Kaiser had large, deep-brown eyes and long silkily glossy hair the same shade as her eyes, which she sometimes let hang loose but often wore gathered at the back. Along with Bea Huss, she never donned slacks or dungarees, but always wore long, voluminous skirts, and even though her clothes were casual, there was something so poised in her bearing, she always seemed formally dressed up, even on work crews. Like Connie Olson, and perhaps even more so, she was so slight of figure, delicately boned, small-breasted and very, very thin, you felt if you clasped her too firmly she would snap. Just as with Connie and Charles, it was also curious to think of huge Charles and this delicate creature together, but that is what happened not long after Betty arrived as a student to study voice and music.

It's no surprise that Charles was attracted to Betty, since Betty and Connie were similar in so many ways: both incisively intelligent, with appealing sensitivity, each soft-spoken, and with a pleasing, quiet manner, a quiet grace in their movements, even holding their cigarettes in similar ways. One difference was in the eyes, and not just in the difference of color, but in that glimpse of occasional muted pain I saw darken Connie's blue eyes at times, but which Betty, fresh to Black Mountain, and eagerly curious about everything, never had in her wider open, deep brown ones, not then anyway. Another difference was in their smiles: Connie had a tiny, hesitant smile, painfully shy, vulnerable; I don't ever recall her smiling broadly or even laughing out loud; whereas Betty had the broadest, most engaging smile, which lit up her face, her eyes; it lit me up, too, and she had a quick sense of humor and an even quicker laugh. A few at the college called her "scheming" and "a flirt" with a will of iron behind her beatific smile, and questioned her motives for coming to Black Mountain, anywhere from trying to hook a man to finding ways to advance her career. I sensed none of that in her and thought, Well, if she is looking for a man, who isn't? and, If she wants to get on, more power to her. I liked her immediately, liked her graciousness, her insights, her empathy. I'm sure this is what Charles found attractive in her too.

She had the room directly above mine in Meadows Inn, and she would often invite me up for tea and a talk; or if Laurie Forest, who also roomed upstairs, was there, the three of us would share some of Laurie's wine. Besides studying piano with Wolpe, Betty joined Wes Huss' acting classes and the two of us did a lot of scenes together.

As with Connie, there was in Betty a wonderful spirit I resonated to; to be in the presence of either woman always stirred something in me, something I could never put my finger on, or name, but it was there strongly nonetheless—some bond, some subtle chord of sympathy and understanding, so subtle as to barely register, but ineffably powerful in its own way, something that nourished me in a different way than Charles did—a deep and secret identity beyond words, before words.

Perhaps it was that Olson saw too.

For one of our Sunday evening community entertainments in the Studies basement, we did a reading performance of Ibsen's *Peer Gynt* (Betty Kaiser as Solveig; me as the Buttonmaker), the cast so huge practically the whole college was in the play, only a handful for an audience, who were also part of the huge circle, audience and players as one. Wolpe wrote special piano music and songs for the production, "Solveig's Song," as I recall the title, sung by Betty in a touching and delicately shaded voice.

One morning, Act V, Scene II in *Othello*, Betty Kaiser as Desdemona, me as Othello; the suffocation scene: "Put out the light, and then put out the light . . ." Betty lying on a mattress on gray-painted concrete floor of Studies basement, Wes directing me to place the pillow lightly over Betty's face. In doing so, I became so seized with the sense of murder, of suffocation, so overcome with the role of murderer, I began to tremble and had to snatch the pillow away, and stop the scene. Betty sitting up smiling, puzzled—but I could see in Wes' eyes he got it, and got what he wanted.

Betty played the mother and I played her son Oswald in the final scenes of Ibsen's *Ghosts* in Wes' early morning class down in the Studies basement. At the end of the play, when Oswald stands silent while his mother tells him he has father-inherited syphilis, for which there was then no cure, and knows his fate— "Picture his brains turning to mush," Wes suggested helpfully .to Betty to get her into the scene—I stared out the window at the mountain stream while Betty, really getting into her role, continued to speak with dry and telling poignancy. I actually stood longer than I should have, I was so focused on the part, on her words, on what must be Oswald's thoughts and feelings, my mind wandering through all the permutations of his impending death. Then for a long time I stood thinking of absolutely nothing, of watching and listening to the rushing stream, it becoming an unconscious stream of life rushing away, much like Oswald's. Suddenly aware of the silence in the room, I realized the scene was finished, had in fact been long over, and when I turned (returned, really), saw Betty and Wes gazing at me, Wes' eyes tearing, the only time, ever, I saw him visibly moved. As actor, through Wes' guidance, I had achieved an effect without trying to make an effect, became zen empty in another serendipitous lesson stumbled upon at Black Mountain, where all such felicitous discoveries were also possible.

My room in Meadows Inn was austerely furnished: a mattress on bare springs in the corner; beside it, a simple wooden box painted blackboard-black on which was clamped the spot lamp for night-time reading that Merrill had left me; a straight-back, cane-bottom chair, salvaged from the long-closed dining hall, against one wall; and a plain maplewood chest-of-drawers in the other corner, tall enough so that I could write on it, and did often, standing up at it in my jockey shorts late into the night. There was a partition-like closet without a door where my meager store of clothes hung, mostly old dress shirts with frayed collars ripped off and well-worn pairs of workpants—all of it, though old in style and ragged in appearance, freshly laundered and neatly hung on hangers—revealing in my inner disorder my outer orderly need. Jorge Fick once stood marveling with a painter's eye at that symmetry of shirt sleeves hanging in careful alignment from the pole in my closet.

One of the conveniences of the room was a private door leading in from the outside, directly under the outside stairs leading to the second floor rooms of the women students, which I could use if I didn't want to go through the lobby if Tom had visitors there or in the kitchen. Its use was especially helpful later on for a certain midnight visitor to slip unobserved into my quarters.

Over the panes of that door leading to the outside was a tightly-drawn, ruffled curtain made of deep blue cotton, with looser hanging curtains of the same material over the window, all put up by a previous tenant. Located on the north side of the house and hidden under those outside wooden stairs, not a speck of sunlight ever entered the room, but the view was a satisfying one, looking out on the dense woods, beyond which lay the farm, the land then dipping down into the hollow where a mountain stream rushed, the same stream that flowed in the ravine beneath the footbridge and then dashed noisily—particularly in spring thaws when it became a torrent—past the north side of the Studies Building, before joining Lake Eden and, in spill-over piped under the county road, feeding the distant, swift-flowing rapids dashing over the boulders of Snake River, another mountain-fed stream across the road from the college. In summer Tom and I spent a good part of our afternoons there swimming among the newts and snakes—and occasionally having rocks winged at us by mischievous local farmboys hiding in the dense bushes.

One night in early spring, after I'd turned out the light, tired from reading, tucked under my blanket (blankets necessary even in summer in half-mile mountain-high night-time chill) and ready for a good snooze, drifting off, lulled by the rush of the nearby snow-cold stream out in the darkness, I was pulled back to wakefulness by a steady and persistent "tick tick tick" in the room. I clicked on the light and peered around, thinking one of those super-sized Black Mountain luna moths had somehow gotten in and was batting its wings against the pineboard walls to get out. But I saw nothing, turned out the light, made myself cozy, started drifting off again, only to hear the same light, dry tapping: *tick tick tick.*

Again, on with the light, a quick search of the walls. Nothing again. Then I scanned around down at the bare boards of the floor and there, over near the far wall, cocooned in a ball of dust (I wasn't always mindful to sweep the floor at laidback Black Mountain) was a tiny frog.

I got out of bed, went over, carefully took it in my hand, picked off the strands of dust sticking to its gelatinous skin, opened the door and set it down easy in the grass next to the steps. I came back in, slid into bed again, turned out the bedside light. Last thought before sliding into blissful sleep was a puzzling one: how could a frog, even such a little one, slide under the crack in the door?

Tick tick tick

My eyes popped open. I couldn't believe it! On with the light, bolt upright in bed, wide awake again, searching the floor and there, in almost the exact same spot, was the miniature frog encased once more like a mummified toad in a fresh ball of lint. Like the springiest of tennis balls, it was bouncing in the direction of my closet.

Sobeit, I sighed, clicking out the light and collapsing back on my pillow. At least it's a handy little dust mop, I consoled myself as I settled down to try to sleep once more.

Tick tick tick—now near my bed, now somewhere else across the room. *Tick tick tick*. It actually got to be a soothing sound, the clean dry tap of those tiny pads cushioned in dust, assuredly less noisy than the insistent, mechanized ticktock of an alarm clock (of which, in Black Mountain time, I was thankfully free). Living with the wildlife, the bats, birds, and snakes (poisonous and non-poisonous) which seemed not to differentiate at Black Mountain between indoors and outdoors, including wild plant-life, like the kudzu that swarmed and invaded everywhere, its tentacled and sturdy tendrils like rapidly-growing green octopi that yet managed to pinch through even the narrowest slits in the screens, and once inside, coiled around the walls of our living quarters—was a fact you just had to accept within the Seven Sister hills; so, too, this tiny frog, like the kudzu, managed to squeeze itself flat as a letter beneath my door.

So after that, I grew used to the nightly visits of the little frog; the flap of its splayed toes tocking on the floor became almost inaudible to my adaptable ears, in fact, became a regular and quieting sound, lulling me to sleep.

Eventually, I expect, it got too big to slip under my door, making a spotted green envelope of itself, a nightly night-letter I grew accustomed to, until finally, its visitations ceased altogether. I missed them.

It wasn't long, however, before I was being kept awake by another kind of tapping, this time in human form and much louder in volume. It came in the shape of Olson himself. Now, though, the noise came through the ceiling.

As I've said, Betty Kaiser's room was on the second floor directly above my own in Meadows Inn, and late one night as I lay reading in bed I heard the stealthy creak of a step heavier than the step of any of the women living up there, going up the outside stairs. Once at the top, there was a soft tap at the door, then the sound of light footsteps hurrying across the ceiling over me, the upstairs outer door scraping open, then Betty's voice quiet but bright in greeting, followed by Charles' more muffled tones, his heavier step as he entered. That I had seen Betty's bedroom—with its slope-ceilinged, brown-stained plywood walls, its bed, with its caramel-colored blanket, simply a mattress and spring, like my own—in one of my frequent visits upstairs for tea and a chat, only added to the vividness in my mind as the springs of the bed above, under Charles' gigantic weight, soon began crashing noisily with a persistent twanging through the ceiling directly over my head.

As I lay wide-eyed in the darkness, after nearly a half hour of loud, sledge hammer-like blows, I contemplated visions of a naked Charles and Betty, bed and all, crashing through the ceiling and landing on top of me in a splintery cloud of dust and plaster. (I *longed* for the little ticking of the frog and wondered how I could ever have thought it annoying in contrast to the thumping from above.) Saucer-eyed, to kill time, reading and certainly sleep out of the question, I lay there imagining head-

lines in the Asheville *Citizen* next day: STUDENT KILLED
BY AMOROUS TEACHER or VICTIM CRUSHED BY
FALLING LOVENEST. "In a freak accident . . ." the story
would begin.

I also envisioned, cringing a little in misplaced empathy, Betty,
skinnier even than myself, her slight body being flattened under
the venusian steamroller energy of Charles' girth: a single rose-
bud supporting the burden of the entire bush, so to speak.

Silly, fanciful concerns to while away the time, till the pounding stopped, usually as abruptly as it began, with no warning or
preliminaries.

That thumping, loud, insistent, long, would keep me
awake—I would look up at the darkened ceiling listening, my
mind a confusion—like it was my father fucking my sister (since
Betty was like a sister to me and Charles my spirit father), while
Connie, who I loved as a friend, I saw as "betrayed." The
almost nightly racket above was like listening to that father's
betrayal. I was slow in coming to the old, hard wisdom in realizing that the one living god in my life had the proverbial feet of
clay, Olson-Zeus thundering through the ceiling above me in
yet another awakening; not ready yet, as with my own father, to
recognize Charles as flesh and blood, something I hadn't quite
yet accepted even about myself, so buried still in Judeo-
Christian erotophobia.

Also wandering into my reveries, overhearing those nightly
upstairs trysts, was like hearing as a child my father and mother,
their furtive, whispered fumblings through the paper-thin walls
in the crowded, two-bedroom upstairs of our cramped, shabby
house in New Jersey, where there was no privacy except in the
dead hours of the night, nights when I lay awake listening for
hours, fearing to sleep, listening for the crackle of flame up the
stairs, sniffing for the smell of smoke that I was sure would
come, the self-appointed watcher in the night listening to my
father's beer-besotted snorings, occasionally hearing instead

those hurried creakings that enflamed my childish imagination, and fearing for my mother, knowing her own fear of having another baby when she could barely feed and care for the brood she already had.

The "god" Olson was not only betraying the "goddess-wife-mother" Connie, in my own shaky—and fanciful—mind he was endangering the structure of their life together, and by extension threatening the already threatened cohesion and continued existence of the college itself by his amorous and sexual shenanigans, he who, by the force of his own will and vision, had been up till then holding it all together. Although I hadn't stepped inside a church for years (no matter, I still carried my own around with me, like a shell—a hell, really), my Catholic head was still so fogged by the smoke of ritualistic incense and attitudes of purgatory, and, despite my youthful rebel's progressive belief in divorce, of a deeply embedded sense of marriage till death, no matter the death in it (no matter that then, like so many of us, I didn't know Connie and Charles weren't legally married), there was that deeper childish part of me that envisioned the household of Black Mountain imperiled by this marital rift between figurative mother and father.

In the spring of 1954, Betty abruptly left the college, returning to New York, ostensibly, she told some, to resume her music career, but in actuality, as it turned out, to have Charles' baby. Not long after, late one afternoon, I left Meadows Inn on some errand, or maybe it was just to take a walk up in the hills. As I approached Olson's house, Charles, whom we hadn't been seeing much of lately, suddenly strode out his front door in dress shirt and a frazzled bow tie I'd never known he'd owned, wearing his lone "dress" seersucker jacket and carrying a battered dark leather valise. He was heading for his convertible parked in front of the house.

I was surprised not only at seeing Charles unexpectedly for the first time in days, but also seeing him so dressed up, as if for a special occasion. Then, too, I'd never seen him carrying a suit-case before. My first thought was it must be some kind of emergency, Charles off on a quick trip to try to scrounge up more funds for the school. Otherwise, the entire college would have known in advance he'd actually planned a trip somewhere.

But this speculation evaporated in a feeling of vague unease. That Connie and Charles were having trouble since Charles had started seeing Betty Kaiser were persistent rumors among us, and Connie's own ever more tight-lipped, pained-eye silence gave credence to them. I myself was quietly troubled by such rumors, along with Charles' past stealthy night-time visits to upstairs Meadows Inn, the concerns of a still-egoistic child, really, whose mother and father may be on the point of break-ing up. Still, in that curiously symbolic but also very real way, the Olsons, mainly because of Charles' patrimonial hugeness, were very much like the unacknowledged "father" and "moth-er" of Black Mountain, the rest of us more or less siblings, or, as with Wes and Bea Huss, say, aunts and uncles, Joe and Mary Fiore, big brother and big sister, the familial structure of the col-lege unconsciously but inescapably patterned, in my own head anyhow, on the ancient extended tribal family. Charles was to many of us, particularly the young writers, the "father," a hier-archical denomination he would have resented and bitterly denied, but there was no escaping it. He became, whether he liked it or not, the spiritual and caring father so many of us had missed in our own lives, just as Melville and Pound had been writer "fathers" adopted by Olson in his own earlier years. Only Wes Huss fiercely resisted the appellation, saying once in his acting class: "I don't want to be *anybody's* surrogate father."

My uneasiness increased when I saw Connie now emerge rapidly through the front door and follow closely behind Charles down the path to the car. Both, not seeing me yet, were silent, except that pinched, strained look in Connie's eyes spoke worlds.

As Charles moved to the rear of the car to open the trunk to put the bag in, he noticed me coming along the road as I neared their yard. He looked momentarily startled, pulled himself erect to his full height, letting the bag hang loose at his side, and stared at me uncomprehending for a moment before his face broke into a sheepish grin. Connie, who seemed intent on speaking to Charles, spotted me too by now and stopped abruptly a pace or two behind him, peered at me a moment but didn't make any acknowledgement of my presence. In fact, none of us spoke, since I sensed, in that intuitive way a child does, that something peculiar was going on here and that I had blundered innocently onto a scene in which my presence was in no way welcome. I had paused several yards from them and now stood still, awkwardly hesitant, not knowing which way to go.

Charles now had a silly expression on his face, like a boy who's been caught in a particularly impish prank. And instead of putting the bag in the trunk as he had intended to do, turned around toward the house and, that same foolish grin on his face, looked pointedly at me and held a finger to his lips; dropped the finger, then held it to his lips again, pressing it firmly against his gray mustache for emphasis, making a "shhh-shhh" sound each time, as he started back up the walk, bag still in hand, to the house, Connie turning to scurry ahead of him.

I continued to stand there for a moment in the dusty road after they'd disappeared in the front door, my mind in a confusion about what I'd just witnessed. Apparently my unexpected appearance had abruptly changed Charles' mind to take off in his car, wherever it was he'd planned to go. As I turned to walk back to Meadows Inn, reluctant now to cross their front yard out of some kind of "respect" for their privacy—which was consistent with all other times but seemed more so now—in this obvious time of stress between them, I puzzled over what I'd just seen. The most obvious answer was that the long simmering unhappiness between them was now out in the open, that very afternoon perhaps, maybe just before that very moment I started up toward their house. And if Charles planned to leave Connie and Kate and the college, where would he have gone? To join Betty and his infant son in her West 72nd Street apartment in New York? If I hadn't come along at that very moment would he have left? Had he possibly been heading there? Was it that, having been accidentally discovered, his furtive escape detected, he changed his plans on the spot, decided to stay, rather than risk the gossip and possible censure of the rest of us? Or, torn between his duty both to Betty and to Connie (not to mention to the college), did he in that moment, after all their years together, decide to remain loyal to Connie?

He'd signaled me to keep silent, which I did, but it was very curious and puzzling. It brought into focus the intensity of the conflict Charles and Connie were going through, and the, to me, unthinkable possibility of their breaking up—unthinkable because, as the college itself was in the process of slow disintegration but was still tentatively being held together by the sheer force of Olson's will, his optimism and charisma, his still-infectious hopes and visions for the place—the possible fact that Charles and Connie, who had always seemed in their relationship a bulwark of deeply affectionate strength and unity and who so much, in my unconscious mind anyway, represented a strong "head" of the communal Black Mountain family, would split up, frightened me, not only for themselves but for the sign it would be of the lifted floodgate that might make the final washing away of the school an actuality.

Worrying it over, I was that child again when, one winter's night, my father, in one of his drunken rages at my mother, at his too-many children, stormed out of the house, shouting he'd never come back. Despite his unpredictable temper and his strap beatings, I was afraid he *would* never come back, worried about how we would live without him, without his pay from the shipyard where he'd finally found a job. I'd spent the next few days staring lost out at the distant swampland through the windows in Miss Newcomb's third grade in National Park Grammar School, not even roused from my preoccupation by her scolding me for inattention.

Even though Connie and Charles were both very circumspect concerning their intimate life together, it was becoming more and more obvious that something was amiss between them (the symbiotic and epistolary romance around that time—with previous occasional meetings in the flesh—between Olson and Frances Boldereff, which Connie also knew about, didn't come to light until years later).

One afternoon I was sitting alone at the kitchen table in Meadows Inn, meditating on my writing and my Shakespeare and Greeks tutorials with Olson, the direction they would take for my graduation, planned for the fall of 1955. Slumped over the table, I was filled with my usual gnawing doubts and apprehensions about the whole graduation business, when suddenly in the doorway Connie simply appeared noiselessly from nowhere, like an animal does in the wild.

"I hope I'm not bothering you."

I leapt from my chair, surprised, honored actually, since I couldn't ever recall her coming into our house.

She sat down at the stout oak table across from me and immediately brought out one of her cork-tipped, king-sized cigarettes and lit it, her thin sensitive fingers trembling slightly as she held the match, clamping the tip of the cigarette firmly between her teeth, a mannerism that had impressed me so much the first time I'd seen her do it, I'd imitated it ever since, it looked so classy.

She blew out a thin stream of smoke like a sigh. Her fine features appeared drawn, pulled back in subtle tension. In her dark eyes was an intensity of pain I'd never seen in them before. It said she had to get away for awhile—from the house, from Kate, from *him*—needed a sanctuary however brief, a sense of her being so smothered at that moment it left her no breath to speak.

We both sat silent. There wasn't any need to say anything. I was curious, though, waiting for her to say something, but she quietly smoked her cigarette, gazing now and again across at me with those troubled eyes, a look that spoke clearly of a struggle within she appeared hesitant to put into words.

She also seemed like someone taking a much-needed rest. I suddenly thought of Kate and how very much she was Charles' daughter, sturdy, willful, headstrong. Did Connie feel they were battering against her? Wearing her down? And Betty, too? Did she know about Betty? Surely she must.

"It's so quiet here," she breathed, almost enviously, peering about, then gazed across at me again.

She seemed to be trying to decide if she could trust me, and if she could, would I understand? Longstanding habits of privacy die hard, and I knew, from my own secret habits, born and enforced out of self-protection, the pride it cost to change them, not to mention the trust and courage. Maybe she sensed that.

But I could say nothing, said some trivial thing, to ease the tension, something innocuous. She appeared to relax, and also, with a quick swipe of her eyes across my face, to have made up her mind not to speak of whatever was so pressing it had driven her out of the house, away from Charles, from Kate, who, since it was mid-afternoon, was probably taking her nap, thus allowing Connie uncharacteristically to seek a moment of quiet, of refuge perhaps, in our kitchen.

I wish she had spoken, since, if she had, it would, in my own unspoken love for her, have been a privilege to listen, to ease, if only with my listening ears, the burden of pain she carried in her eyes that day. Looking back now, I feel honored that she trusted me even that much, to let me see the naked anguish, which was no small act of bravery for her, the smoke from her cigarette still curling up between her fingers with a faint trembling, as if there was a tiny breeze in the room, although there was none.

How little I spoke my own heart then, unable to bring it to my lips or bring its promptings into my hands. I couldn't then have lifted my arm across the short distance of that bare table-top to place my fingers on her hand, such a simple human gesture but all but impossible for me then—it might well have been the distance to the moon.

So that at night, thinking back to those times, as I lay in my bed around those midnights when I would hear the stealthy tread up the steps outside, steps trying to be light but still heavy enough to creak the boards, footsteps that I recognized with a certainty early on didn't belong to any of the women who lived upstairs—how I got to know the heft and pressure, the singular rhythm of each one's tread, so that it became a simple reflex to know instantly who was coming up or going down the stairs: "Oh, that's Laurie," or "Now that's Naomi coming down"— without ever having to see them. Knowing it could only mean that Charles, coming secretly at night, or so he thought, was once again visiting Betty in her room above. Now I felt Connie's betrayal even more, felt it as my own, seeing again the pain, the anguish in her eyes that afternoon in the kitchen of Meadows Inn.

Charles exclaiming angrily, irritated, when Kate had been sick and whiny for several days and needed a great deal of Connie's attention (which cut into Connie's attention for Charles), "When kids are sick they ought to be shipped off to *grand-mothers* to be taken care of till they get better!" Charles always had to be the center of care, his own needs gratified first, himself the central babe and at times a far bigger one than his daughter, himself living proof of Rimbaud's "great invalid babe"—and one perhaps with a guilty conscience.

Short of cash as always for food, Tom and I often went frog hunting at twilight early that spring in the marshy area back of the Stables, with me holding the flashlight, Tom's theory, perhaps lore from his native Indiana, being it was easier to catch hibernating frogs at dusk, when they were settling into a deeper sleep in the mud. Tom, squatting down, intensely looking, listening, himself become some wild animal on the scent, then abruptly plunging his hand deep into the muck and each time hauling out, despite their winter's fast, an enormous, plump-thighed bullfrog buried there, for frog legs for our supper. Then he stabbed each one in the brain with the sharp end of a thin-bladed butcher knife, one in a numerous set he owned and kept honed sharp as razors, a legacy from his dead father, who'd been a tugboat cook and had died a drunk (as did Tom's mother), the set of knives the only thing the father left his son, that and a taste for booze.

Back in the kitchen of Meadows Inn, Tom chopped off the frogs' legs, dipped them in an egg batter of flour and bread-crumbs and a sprinkling of herbs, then, pumping up the portable Coleman gas stove, fried them up in his biggest iron frying pan. I was a little leery, these being my first frog legs, but they turned out to be as tasty, I suspected, as in any high-class French restaurant, and nourishing, too, a delicacy that didn't cost us one red cent.

Given what remained of the farm, the few cows tended by Terence Burns, the wild berries and nuts we gathered in the woods, Bea Huss' communal vegetable garden, and frog hunting expeditions by Tom and me, we truly did live off if not the fat, at least what we could of the land—or what was left of it.

That was the time Charles had us all reading Homer, particularly *The Odyssey*. For weeks, Tom, like a delighted child, kept repeating the phrases "rosy-fingered dawn" and "wine-dark sea" at any opportunity, driving me coocoo.

That spring, just weeks before he had to finally, after so many years, leave the college, since he'd been drafted into the army in the Korean War, his 2-S student deferment status, that several of the rest of us had as well, ended, Fee Dawson, in his well-worn levi jacket and levis, was walking close beside me down the path to South Lodge. It was a bright summer afternoon, and he was saying confidentially, confidently, in a low voice in my ear, after a several weeks' flirtation, poling on the raft and rowing in the boat out on Lake Eden, and taking long walks in the hills, "You knew it had to come to this, you knew it would."

A crude, fumbling romance at best, I really liked him in those few weeks, the affectionate, friendly, flirty Fee, touchingly vulnerable now in his uncertainties about a new life—or possible death—my empathy strong because I, too, with a 2-S student deferment, had still to face my draft board in Gloucester County, New Jersey, once I left Black Mountain.

It was perhaps his anxiety about going in the army, that, coupled maybe with the usual scarcity of females on campus, not to mention the habits of male-male pleasure he'd learned at Black Mountain, is what probably steered him to me. Mainly, I suppose, more than anything, it was a diverting dalliance to relieve the tension of the fears he faced in the military and, perhaps more ominous, leaving the protection once and for all of that enclave that had been his home since he was a teenager.

But he didn't show up later that evening for our assignation in my room. After waiting a long time sitting on my bed, when I finally went and tapped on his door, there was no answer. Like Ellen Schasberger in the spring of 1953, I figured he'd just been toying with me, playing me for his own reasons.

Baffled, I avoided him after that (just as I had a year before when Olson had turned me over to Fee so Fee could "smarten" me up), and when at last he left for the army, I was relieved to see him go, not so much for the disappointment he gave me, but because Fee, like so many of us there, at that time or eventually, just seemed to have stayed too long in paradise.

One night in class Charles showing us a small-press book of poems he'd received in the mail for "review" in the fledgling *Black Mountain Review*, called *My Talon in Your Heart*, and all of us having a good laugh at the title.

An unspoken caution from Olson to watch our words, and our titles.

Charles scoffing in another class at T. S. Eliot's assertion: "Man cannot stand too much reality," intimating it was baloney.

Earlier he had scolded Fee Dawson for referring dismissively to Eliot as "that old queen," Olson enjoining not only Fee but all of us to read Eliot's prose for its clarity, Olson deciding T. S.'s prose more readable—and usable—than his poetry.

The night Charles read Douglas Woolf's "duffer" story, "The Kind of Life We've Planned," with its darkly twisted ironic use of "life" in the title, the manuscript sent to him by Creeley now back in Mallorca to get out the next issue of *The Black Mountain Review*, we all sneered at it, Ed Dorn and Jorge Fick being the most vocally dismissive of all. Charles, more insightful as to what Woolf was up to, was furious, chewing us out collectively for our obtuseness. We were taken aback—Charles praising a corny, melodramatic story about *golfers*?! How could anybody write an alleged "love" story about grown people— and boringly middle-class at that—smacking a little white ball around vast acres of neatly trimmed green? At poverty stricken, rough-around-the-edges Black Mountain, our prejudice at collegiate, snobbish "country club types" like Johnny Ryan, his

Atomic Driver and his "girl," "baby Margo," was evident. The subtleties of Woolf's rich and surprising ironies we missed at first hearing, the plot twists of dishonesty and false rape perhaps striking a raw nerve of fear, and, hence, maybe concomitant denial of the story, in some males in the room, a blinding to what was not wanted to be seen, admitted, even imaginatively.

Charles told us, in no uncertain terms, how ignorant we were to miss the point of the work. It was like he'd tricked us, keeping his opinion, as he often did, even a hint of it, to himself, but leading us on, letting us prattle on, till the very end, then pouncing, as he did that night.

Then, even more dramatically, for as must be clear by now, he certainly had a flair for the dramatic, he announced we should all read the story again, and *carefully*, when it appeared in the Summer '54 issue of *The Black Mountain Review*, news which still surprised some in the room—Had Creeley lost his critical and editorial senses along with Charles on this one?

Of course, when I did get a chance to read it, I saw what Olson (and certainly Woolf) was getting at, understood what all the shouting was about regarding this peculiar and wry-eyed new American writer whose first novel, *Hypocritic Days*, Creeley would soon publish through his Mallorcan-based Divers Press; and which, when the first chapters began to arrive at the college from Spain and were read aloud by Olson in our class, would open the field of fiction a bit more for a number of us, including myself, who became increasingly delighted with what Woolf was not only getting at but also getting away with.

As rector, Charles was even more desperately striving to contrive ways to get tuition-paying students to the college, a demanding, and in some ways a demeaning job, since energies that might have gone into his own work and his teaching were siphoned off by that preoccupation.

One target was the young man from Ohio named David

mentioned earlier, a quiet, parson-appearing, blond, blue-eyed youth with spectacles, who showed up, along with several other prospects, with his parents one weekend to look the place over. The only live applicant at that moment among the others, Olson pulled out all stops to persuade David, and his parents, that he should enroll as a student.

Charles was more persuasively gracious than ever, giving the family the grand tour and charming the pants off them, as only Olson, when he put his mind to it, could. He personally set up a Sunday evening program down in the bottom of the Studies, now called the "Weaving Room," since weaver Tony Landreau had moved his looms there from the Science Building on the mountain slope. Olson wanted to show David, and especially his mother and father, as well as the other visiting prospects, what we students were up to and could do, part of the evening consisting of readings by writing students carefully selected by Olson himself.

Charles strong-armed everyone to attend, about 20 or 25 of us in all then. I chose to read my episodic story about being a kid during the Depression when forced to wear too-small shoes with cardboard soles from Home Relief that gave me blisters, just so I could still go to school. But Charles, after I'd read it aloud, was rather, for show, I expect, since he'd initially praised it in class, good-naturedly dissatisfied with it, and insisted I go upstairs to my study and bring back a "better" work, a long and painful story called "The Brothers" about an older brother's wedding when I was about 12 or 13, which I'd recently read in Olson's and Creeley's classes, and which got a strong, favorable response, especially from Creeley, who had been so gripped by it, he couldn't speak, dismissed the class and headed down to Ma Peak's in his truck.

"That one, Mike," Olson beamed, insistent. "Read us that one."

I was embarrassed, thrown, too, by being put in the spotlight, expected to shine, to perform, really, the down side of being finally one of Olson's "fair-haired boys." But I also understood what was at stake, and did as I was told, would have, as always, for Charles, done anything, and read the story to Charles' approving grin. When I'd finished, he turned that considerably seductive grin on David's parents and on David himself, as if to say, See, an example of what we do here. I felt uncomfortable being forced to be the "star," being forced to be a part of Olson's commercial, actually, to sell Black Mountain, to prevent it from being sold.

It worked, though. Between Charles' blandishments and the readings and work exhibits of other students, David enrolled in the school. Reeled in, yes, but something of a fish out of water. In the few months he was there, I'm not sure how much he got out of it: a quiet-voiced, non-assertive, serious scholar-type, he didn't quite seem to fit in. A bit dull—I suspect he held back somewhat out of timorous uncertainty, just as I had in my early months—but he had a pleasant enough manner and opened up a bit once I got to know him. That was a little ticklish for me since David, who also had a room in Streamside, had been out in the lobby the night Merrill blew up at me in bed. I was somewhat embarrassed knowing David, in particular, had heard Merrill's shouting at me. Still, with Merrill so recently gone, I missed the habits of pleasure, such as they had been, and awkward as it was with Merrill, at the end, missed the habit of sleeping with someone, having that closeness. And there was always the scarcity of available males, so David seemed a godsend.

One night after a few beers, I tried to put the make on him. He confessed he was straight, almost apologetically, and since there were even fewer available females around, it couldn't have been easy for him either. Having learned a trick or two from Olson in seduction, I turned on the charm and pursued him as ardently as Charles had pursued him in trying to land him as a student. But David kept insisting he was straight—a baffling position to me regarding my proposition, I'd been so long now at pansexual Black Mountain I wondered what *that* had to do with it. This went on for several weeks and at times he seemed half willing, but he was so new to the open mores of the place he was very uncertain, frightened I guess. However, he was sympathetic, friendly enough, and even though he was still appealing in his soft voice and manner and his quiet sense of humor, I eased off, realizing he had to find his own way, just as I had.

But he couldn't seem to. He gave it a try, but I think the place finally bewildered him, was not what he wanted, and he left after awhile, perhaps needing a more structured academic setting.

Olson also strove to enroll black students at the college, but even though desegregation came legally in 1954, the racist mindset of centuries of white supremacist Southern tradition was still very much in place, and I suspected that made blacks cautious about coming to an all-white albeit private, and—probably a strong part of it too—controversial college. It was undoubtedly just still too risky (as it was too several years earlier for some nervous faculty members).

However, Olson did manage to enlist the aid of a black minister from Asheville, and invited him and his wife up to his house at the college, Olson awkwardly bustling about making tea for them, trying to find a few uncracked cups. They sat out front of the house on chairs Charles had carefully provided, while Charles made his pitch, extolling the virtues of a school where blacks and whites could work and study together, no doubt telling them of artist Jacob Lawrence teaching there in 1946, during Albers' watch, and the black students, though few in number, who had come to study, especially during the summer sessions over the years.

Everything seemed to be going quite well when suddenly

two-year-old Kate Olson, followed by baby David Huss, both—not unusual for children at edenic Black Mountain—appeared stark naked around the corner of the house, Kate dragging a dead bird by its wing.

"Oh!" exclaimed the minister. "What happened to the poor bird?"

Kate, big brown eyes round and solemn, lisped, "The fuckin' owl did it."

Olson, flustered, tried to smooth it over, but he could tell from the shocked expressions on the minister and wife's faces that they would not be recommending any students for Black Mountain College.

Feeling so down in the class one night in the Reading Room, Charles, somewhat annoyed, stopped what he was saying to ask, "Mike, is there something the matter?"—saying it in such a way as to suggest my long puss was bringing him down. I looked at him surprised, not knowing my moodiness was showing, since with long years of practice hiding my inner thoughts and feelings, I was convinced my face was always a perfect mask, and denied there was anything wrong. And it was true, I couldn't have put my finger on the reason for my blues.

It was another instance of learning, however, there was very little you could slip by sharp-eyed Charles.

I sat up in my chair and took pains to readjust my face again, to please him.

Maybe what I needed, after the fiasco with Fee and being over three months back now at the college and the ending of the spring term, was a little break. The incentive for that possibility came unexpectedly from Jonathan Williams, just back from Stuttgart and fresh out of the army.

Around that time, before Fee himself left for the army, Charles gave his class in Reading the Newspaper, a current events course Olson-style, a morning class, which was unusual for him, since he preferred the energies of the night. After the first few meetings downstairs in the Conference Room, we started meeting upstairs in the smallish Reading Room, appropriately enough, where you could read a variety of newspapers and magazines, many of them old and dog-eared, while lounging on beat-up old car seats. It was a bit cramped, with so many students and Charles himself, who took up space for several, but Olson, like Creeley, preferred this cozy-sized room.

The central text was the Asheville *Citizen*, which we had to read every day, extra copies of which Carroll stocked in his store. Charles, the acuity of his political experience in Washington during and after World World 2 momentarily revived, had us look at the ulterior motives of John Foster Dulles, Eisenhower's Secretary of State, in his Cold War global hysteria of phantom commie enemies lurking everywhere, and had us scrutinize closely the language of terms like "clean bombs" as opposed to "dirty bombs," in weighing the dangers of nuclear fallout. Earlier, as noted, in less strained times with the farmer, he had even arranged with Doyle and his wife to have us come to the farmhouse on several mornings to watch the McCarthy hearings on TV. He would watch us watching the spectacle, even more chilling on the grainy black-and-white screen, of more demonizing hysteria over "commie" and "fairy" enemy phantoms, this time in the State Department and the U. S. Army, watch us with a sly smile on his face, as if trying to gauge what it was we saw, to see if we were getting it. (So strange, and a jarring remembrance, in our remote enclave, to have Out There beamed in, like an invasion, over the airwaves over the high ridges of the Seven Sister Mountains, down farmer Doyle's skyhigh roof antenna into our eyes, a rude and abrupt reminder that we were still part of the world.)

We had to write a paper on some event of that time that had been written about in the *Citizen*, and I chose Truman's handling of the U. S. Steel strike, getting a lot of background material out of old issues of *Time* in the library, a magazine whose prose style Olson thought as much of as he did Senator Joe McCarthy's pernicious oratory. He told me he was very impressed with my take on Truman's actions and my ability to write a paper, despite my sources. It was not praise as ecstatic as his response to my "Bartleby the Scrivener" piece, but any praise from Olson opened me for further receptions, the erotic and fructifying taproot of teaching, which has, as Olson had flatly stated to me that day in the kitchen, as much to do with love as anything else, and just as with his first earlier praise, I basked in it for days.

I suppose it was Jonathan filling our heads with fabulous stories of the French Quarter in New Orleans, with its dixieland and jazz clubs and musicians like clarinetist George Lewis that, romantics to the hilt, particularly myself, fired up Tom Field and me to hitchhike the 500 or so miles there after the spring term in June 1954. That and most importantly, some friends of Jonathan's who lived in the French Quarter could put us up for the five or so days we planned to stay there, depending on how our money held out—a little vacation on a shoestring budget, for me, *very* shoestring as I scraped and saved for weeks in advance. (Tom, luckily, was scrimping along on the GI Bill after his service in Korea as an army medic, so was in a little better financial shape.)

Jonathan, who was returning to his parents' home in Highlands, North Carolina, offered to give Tom and me a lift there in his tiny imported English Hillman Minx on the first leg of our trip deeper into the South, and also generously invited us to stay overnight at the ancestral home (his parents were away) before we started our thumbing. Packing the new dark brown, fake crocodile suitcase my mother had shipped me by redeeming her Yellow Savings Stamps from the grocer, to replace the old battered one she'd lent me to go to Rider, early on a Friday morning Tom and I piled into the Hillman with Jonathan at the wheel in his Ivy League/Country Gentleman uniform of black corduroy jacket, expensive Abercrombie & Fitch hunter's red wool shirt, black suede cap and chino trousers. We set out for the even more mountainous far southwestern corner of the state, the Blue Ridge Mountains so precipitous as we approached Highlands that the tiny engine of the Hillman couldn't make it up the steeper, longer grades carrying all the weight of us plus our luggage. With Jonathan looking some-what embarrassed, Tom and I had to get out and push it over the crest of several peaks.

Jonathan's homestead was comfy pine-paneled ranch-style, furnished with beige tartan-upholstered pine furniture, his bed-room, which he proudly showed us like a small boy displaying his treasures, with neatly packed shelves holding tons of his books and record albums. He took us out to the deeply sloping front yard and just as proudly showed us the spectacular view of the deep-purple Great Smoky Mountains looming in the far distance, pointing out how you could see the three states of Georgia, Tennessee and South Carolina from that one spot. He stood tall and commanding, dispensing that information to us in his soft Southern voice with a calm, proprietary air as if he were the unacknowledged lord of the manor of it all, which I secretly suspected he was.

Early Saturday morning, Tom and I set out, maps stuffed in pockets and with preliminary directions from Jonathan, includ-ing a reminder to be sure to go hear George Lewis on Bourbon Street. Our first ride was with a scrawny trio of young drunks, evidently still out carousing from the night before, through the back roads of rural Georgia, who were so screechingly loud, whomping the sides of the beat-up old Chevy with the flats of their palms as they emitted earsplitting rebel yells at everyone we passed on the road. The driver, his red hair a match for the boozy redness of his face, tore at high speeds over the bumpy country roads with their sharp curves, while Tom and I glanced apprehensively at each other, holding on for dear life. At the next crossroads, we quickly cooked up an excuse to get out, saying we were heading in another direction. They were goofily genial about it, and I was gratified to plant my feet firmly on the safety of the shoulder, as the car with its drunken young bucks tore off in a lurching cloud of dust.

After a few more short hops, late Saturday afternoon we were dropped off by one of our rides in a poor section of Atlanta. Tired and famished, we found a greasy spoon called the Silver Moon Cafe on a back street and spent a bit of our carefully budgeted money on a good hot meal for the long night of hitchhiking ahead. Since I knew from experience it was always difficult to hitchhike in cities, and there was always the lookout for police, not to mention the fears of being nabbed as vagrants and put on the chain gang, we decided to spend a little more money on a city bus that would take us to the outskirts of Atlanta and the open highway heading south.

It was dusk by now but you could still see out the bus windows, Atlanta like a big old Southern town of old houses and neat lawns and tree-lined streets. While I had my nose pressed to the window, thinking of Peachtree Street and Vivian Leigh's Scarlett and of Butterfly McQueen's Missy, wouldn't you know, chatterbox Tom, as usual without a care or a thought to where he was, began piping on merrily in his loud, blabby voice, as flat as the earth of Indiana, about how wonderful it was to be in Atlanta in the heart of Dixie, and how "awful the Civil War must've been," and the cruelties of slavery and segregation (we were at that moment riding on a still-segregated bus), and how things might change now because of the recent Supreme Court school desegregation ruling, and on and on, till I just about wanted to slink down in my seat, pretending I didn't know who he was. Tom's voice *carried*, and it wasn't long before the other passengers, including the driver, squinting at Tom in his rearview mirror, were taking notice. I whispered to Tom he'd ought to cool it about the Civil War, but Tom, as he often was, was so full of himself, he just stared at me like *What was I talking about?* and went nattering on, unaware of the flinty looks around us. Till a skinny young man with a mousy burr cut sitting directly in front of us snapped his head around and with a murderous, flat viciousness in his eyes and a bitter, quietly menacing voice, snarled out in a deep Southern drawl, "*You damn yankees're all alike.*" I cringed in embarrassment, but Tom, undaunted, tried genially to engage the young man in a rational discussion, as if he were still in the safe confines of Black Mountain College, rattling on and on. But the young man swiveled his head forward, muttering through clenched teeth, "You damn yankees git ever'thin' *wrong*," and swinging around once more spat out at Tom, "An' it's the War *Betwain* the States, dummy!" then snapped around facing forward again and, to my relief, clammed up.

By now every white eye in the bus was on us, and they were not friendly eyes. I was so relieved when we reached the city limits and could pull the cord to get off, get off in one piece, the relief I felt similar to that I had earlier that day when we'd jumped out of the drunken trio's car in northern Georgia, sensing that on the bus we could've gotten killed just as well in a place where the murderous, and humiliating, War Between the States was still very much raging.

I myself could've killed Tom for his naïveté, as we stood on the shoulder of the highway waving our thumbs south.

Our next ride was with a tractor and trailer loaded with frozen fish heading for Laurel, Mississippi. It was both a lucky and unlucky hop because the driver, a wiry little guy with dark wavy hair and a sharp, Mediterranean face, was not only eager for company on his long haul—like Tom, he loved to gab, particularly about his mother, so they got along famously—but he also implied, in return for the lift, he expected us to be willing to help him unload the frozen fish once we arrived at his destination. Seeing the size of the tractor, I groaned inwardly at the prospect, but, like Tom, I was so glad to get such a long ride, and one that brought us pretty close to New Orleans, we both gladly hopped into the broad front seat of the big rig.

Whether he was hopped up on speed or not, as many truckers were then to stay awake on long hauls, I wasn't sure, but our driver sure could talk a blue streak, even a match for Tom, who certainly needed no speed to crank up *his* motormouth. I suspected the trucker, giving us endless variations on his "dear maw," in a Southern accent so sweet it was fairly dripping, even eventually wore out poor Tom, or at least Tom's chance to get a word in edgewise. Seeing him nod off, the trucker suggested Tom climb up into the narrow cramped bed space behind the cab for a snooze, which Tom promptly did, leaving the trucker's stream of gab for my ears alone. I bit my lower lip and forced myself to be polite and pretend to listen, out of gratitude for the ride, the price a hiker knew he had to pay.

At a truck stop near the Georgia-Alabama border, the driver decided he wanted to buy his mama a belated Mother's Day gift—"I always buy 'er a present ever' trip I make, she loves it so"—and in a gift shop filled with gaudy trash of all kinds next to the diner and gas station, he asked Tom and me what we thought he should get her. I, my stomach turning at the ugliness of so much glittery junk, said it was hard to choose, while Tom suggested the least obnoxious figurine of a shepherdess, but the trucker said he'd already "bought 'er one a' thim" on a past haul. Finally, he settled on a complete set of the flashiest dishware, all gilt curlicues and bright sentimental design, and tucked his treasure carefully for safekeeping behind our suitcases in the compartment under the seat, which he then locked.

"A boy don' love 'is mama is no man," he offered sweetly, for the umpteenth time.

After we started rolling again, I nodded off while the trucker jabbered on, and awoke to see in the smoky dawn of Alabama the first real palm trees I'd ever laid eyes on, stirring me to the roots of my overly-romantic soul, as we passed rundown cabins and shacks and split rail fences of poor sharecropper farms right out of the romanticized Old South of *Gone With the Wind*.

We arrived at the frozen food storage warehouse in Laurel, Mississippi, in Jasper County, by noontime Sunday, a most religious day in the Bible Belt, because there wasn't a soul around the place to unlock the huge refrigerator doors so we could begin to unload the enormous cargo of tons of frozen fish. The trucker made several calls from a nearby pay phone, but was unable to rouse anyone connected with the business. Tom and I sat in the shadow of the truck—it was blazing hot—hardly hearing anymore the incessant gab of the driver but hoping he'd reach somebody soon. As a diversion, I amused myself by watching on the sly a comely lad in dark glasses, his lean, bikini-clad body draped on a deck chair as he sunbathed on the spacious lawn of a house across the road. As the hours ticked away, I saw our chance of reaching New Orleans that night quickly evaporating. A problem was our suitcases were locked in the storage area beneath the cab, along with the flashy Mother's Day dish set, the trucker holding the key. I was afraid if we said we wanted to push on to New Orleans, he'd refuse to give us our belongings, holding them and us hostage until somebody came to open up the place and we could unload.

Finally, when he returned once more from the pay phone and said somebody would be there but not for another few hours, I'd had it, and got up the nerve to tell him we were sorry but we had to move on, we'd lost too much time already, and would he please give us our suitcases. You could see he was pissed that we weren't going to help him and spat out his cigarette butt muttering something about "all I done fer you, givin' yawl a lift and ever'thin'." But when I insisted, thinking by this time we'd be there all night unloading that truck, he relented and stormed over and unlocked the compartment and stood aside frowning to let us get our cases. "Mind the dishes," he warned darkly.

I felt really bad, like we'd betrayed him, and thanked him for the long ride, and Tom thanked him, apologizing effusively. But the trucker wasn't having it and for once didn't say a word; you could see in his dark, tight-lipped face how mad he was. So I figured we'd better just get out of there quick as we could, and we did, heading down the two-lane tar-top road in the direction of Biloxi, Tom just as glad as me we were on our way again.

We got several lifts through to Biloxi, Mississippi, with its magnificent long beach and large fine old verandaed homes along the Gulf of Mexico, stretching west to Gulfport. Hot and sweaty as we were, we couldn't resist it and found a fairly secluded spot to change into our swim trunks and batted about in the tropically warm surf with its mild waves. Then, both of us sun-worshippers to the core, we lay for a short time on the sandy, sparsely-populated beach in the broiling sun for a much-needed snooze before reluctantly getting ourselves together to push on, having told Jonathan's friends, whom we planned to stay with in the French Quarter, that we hoped to arrive Sunday evening.

My first sight of the Mississippi River as we approached New Orleans in the final hike of our three-day trip was in total darkness, since by the time we got there night had fallen. But it did-n't matter, I was so bleary-eyed anyway I couldn't have appreciated it properly. The driver left us out on Market Street where he told us we could catch a trolley car to the French Quarter. I was wondering if it would be the streetcar named Desire, but when we hailed it it just said "Canal Street" on the front. You entered at the rear doors, and as soon as Tom and I got on, weary from so many hours on the road, we just dropped our bags and collapsed into the first seat we came to, long seats along the walls at the back of the car. The other passengers were looking at us funny, which puzzled me, but I figured it was because we looked such a sight from our long travels. It only dawned on me gradually that the conductor was yelling something over and over again in a flat, insistent, deep Southern voice: "*White* folks to the *front* of the car, please, gentlemen!" till Tom and I finally heard it and figured out he meant us. So, reluctantly, more from the effort of having to haul ourselves up again than anything else, we moved on up to the front seats, where I noticed there were wooden signs on pegs on the backs of the seats either side the aisle, reading "FOR COLORED ONLY." This was an ingenious device of segregation, meaning, we came to learn, that if the car was crowded with black passengers and a white got on, the white, to sit down, only had to move the easily movable "FOR COLORED ONLY" sign back a row to make it a "WHITES ONLY" section, and the blacks in that seat would have to get up and stand in the rear.

Having lived in the South now for over two years, albeit in the protected enclave of Black Mountain College, this was first-hand experience, for me, at least, and I suspect for Tom, too. For certain, though, it was the first welcome to New Orleans for both of us, where, it was plain to see, the power and privilege of white supremacy through segregation was as deeply entrenched here as it was in North Carolina.

As it turned out, when we finally found Jonathan's friends' place in the Quarter, they weren't able to put us up after all, throwing Tom and me into a momentary panic, since it would mean we'd have to spend precious bucks on a hotel room and might have to cut our stay short. Trudging back to Bourbon Street, which was alive with lights and crowds and the sound of dixieland blaring it seemed from every doorway, we spotted a little hotel with a sign that announced cheap rates for tourists. It looked clean and tidy enough and the woman at the desk, though somewhat nervous and harried looking, seemed obliging, but said we would have to be "approved" by her husband. It soon became apparent why she was so nervous, since when her husband appeared from the back room, an older man with frizzes of gray over his ears and the most bilious face I'd ever seen, he took one look at us and started shrieking like a mad man, "*Get out! Get out! I don't want you here! Get out!*" shouting with a terrible psychotic energy. His wife, standing a little behind him, an expression of permanent misery in her eyes, lifted her brows and shrugged her shoulders ever so slightly as if to say, You see how it is, you better move on.

And move we did because he really scared the hell out of us, Tom and I totally baffled by the man's behavior, in this continuation of mishaps in our initial "welcome" to New Orleans. We were both so thrown by it, and so numb with fatigue, that once out on the street, we got suddenly goofy and began to laugh giddily, Tom aping the old man's crazed, "*Get out! Get out!*" We couldn't imagine how they stayed in business.

Fortunately, we found an old gray hotel on Dauphine Street, the entrance up a dimly lit alley. In sharp contrast to the first place we'd stopped in, the middle-aged woman who ran the hotel was plumply congenial, telling us her place wasn't for everybody but the rooms, "though old-fashioned, are cheap and clean." She led us up wide gloomy stairs to the third floor to an enormous room crowded with bulky ancient furniture and with old bathing crockery pitchers and basins on a stand between two of the hugest beds with, it turned out, the deepest, softest mattresses, piled high with antique featherbeds. The nondescript wallpaper had a stained, yellowed, 19th century air. There was, appropriately enough, the faintest odor of mildew everywhere. We loved it, of course, the second we stepped in the door. There was a bath down a wide hall, and also in the hall, "fer shavin' and brushin' yer teeth and such," a sink in front of tall broad windows, a bit grimy but they overlooked, so you could see plain enough while you shaved, a good portion of the Quarter and the Mississippi River in the distance.

"If you wanna' wash clothes there's a tub down in the courtyard, no extra charge."

After she gave us the key and left, Tom and I looked at each other and grinned, feeling better now our first evening in the Big Easy.

Our first days in the city meant learning, first and foremost, to move *slow*, like New Orleans natives, in the oppressive, semitropical heat; learning, while reading the *Times-Picayune* over breakfast, to order coffee "with or without," that is, with or without chicory; learning where the really cheap but good restaurants were, like The Court of the 2 Sisters Jonathan mentioned, with its lone tall palm in the patio and excellent bouillabaisse; and learning to like po' boy sandwiches, sold everywhere; learning, especially for me since Tom was still in a sexually indeterminate state (he was professing to like women but never acting on it), where the gay bars were, which didn't take me long, quickly finding the Dixie Jazz Cafe with its legendary Miss Pepper, and Jean Lafitte's Old Absinthe House, one of the oldest bars in the Quarter, although it seemed most every bar had a sprinkling of lively queers; learning how to get out to the extraordinary New Orleans cemeteries, particularly the Lafayette Cemetery which Jonathan recommended we see at night; and finally, and most important for Tom, learning how to get to the fabulous beaches of Lake Ponchartrain to swim and sunbathe.

Black/White was everywhere: black/white drinking fountains; black/white seating on all transportation and in the movies; even the same restaurant in the Quarter would have a black and a white restaurant in the same building with black back and white front entrances. Segregation struck us as extraordinarily costly in more ways than one.

The beach at Lake Ponchartrain, a vast inland sea of magnificent blue-green water just north of New Orleans, so wide you couldn't see to the other shore, was, however, strictly white, except for the busboys and cleanup people in the awninged cafes along the boardwalks. Tom and I quickly learned that it was now the *bus* named Desire that would take us to Lake Ponchartrain. To my disappointment, the famous streetcar of the same name had been taken out of service some time before, summoning up yet another Vivian Leigh reverie, this time of her as Blanche Dubois.

Everyday at noon we set forth from our antiquated, mildew-smelling gray hotel on Dauphine Street, with beach towels, swim trunks and suntan lotion, to catch the Desire bus to spend our afternoons at the lake, learning, as one more final thing to learn, that promptly around two each afternoon, to follow the exodus walking casually off the beach for shelter in the cafes along the boardwalks—a good time for Tom and me to have a quick lunch of a po' boy and a beer—because without fail, the sky suddenly blackened, a torrential tropical storm hit, blotting out beach and lake in its density for several minutes. Then, as suddenly as it came, it stopped, the merciless sun shone down once more, quickly drying the vast stretches of sand in its intensity, and everyone made their way back to the beach for an uninterrupted afternoon of sunshine.

Innocent of this ritual our first day on the beach, we and our belongings got a thorough soaking before we blindly in the blinding rain found our way up to shelter.

There was a slow sense of regularity over everything—including a slow sense of decay: I could feel the powerful pull of an old city at the bottom of the land at the bottom of the Mississippi, engulfed by bayous, an air of murky decay everywhere, rank in the heat, the brutal sun, a city, with moldering roots still sunk in

Europe, that you could really go to hell in. There was even the appearance, on the beach at around the same time each day as Tom and I arrived, of two well-built young men with a blond and very attractive young woman, who Tom and I at first thought were both maybe vying for but who turned out to belong to one of the males, the blandly good-looking sandy-haired one. The other male, handsome, with black wavy hair, must have spent a lot of time in the sun, a beach bum maybe, his tightly muscled body was the color of teak. Finally, though, you could tell by the way the black-haired one glanced and smiled at the other guy that he was nuts about him. The woman didn't seem to pay any attention to this or, if she did, didn't seem to mind. Tom and I got to watching them out of the corner of our eye each afternoon, like a beach soap opera. They were all so friendly and sat or lay side by side in the sun, the woman in the middle, laughing and talking intimately, although the teak-colored guy always appeared to lay a little apart from the woman and would often talk or crack jokes over her to his pal on the other side. I got the feeling the two guys might have been sharing the woman as a way of sharing each other, especially the teak-dark guy, without admitting that's what it was, a not uncommon phenomenon, then and now.

Late one evening, close to midnight, we took the Canal Street trolley to the end of the line at the outskirts of the city where the cemeteries were. By chance, there was a full moon, just perfect for a romantic wandering among the graves. The graves, though, were all aboveground in little mausoleum-like houses, a necropolis, really, because the water level in this swampy country was so high, a grave dug in the ground would soon quickly get flooded. We were surprised to see the number of people shadowily walking among the tombs, the white-washed brightness of many of the mausoleums even more brilliant in the moonlight, so that you could clearly read the chiseled inscriptions. Some couples were sitting on a few of the little houses of the dead, holding hands or with arms about each other, kissing. Even more surprising were the number of semi-wild bobtail domestic cats lying placidly on or slinking around the bases of the tombs, the little stone houses were their homes, too, as well the final resting places of the departed within.

Except for making the mistake of seeing a dog of a movie, *Indiscretion of an American Housewife*, with heartthrob Montgomery Clift (rumored to have been seen with pretty young boys in the gay bars of midtown Manhattan) on Market Street one evening, most of our nights were spent in the dark, smoky dixieland clubs (blacks allowed only on the bandstand), especially the one where George Lewis played, before we went off to the Jean Lafitte or the Dixie Jazz to finish the evening, Tom willing to go anywhere so long as there was a beer at the end of it. Between seeing so many beautiful guys on the beach all afternoon and so many beautiful ones in the bars at night (and after the recent sexual drought at Black Mountain), I was determined not to leave New Orleans without a carnal souvenir. So, our last evening there, a Friday, I went off prowling alone, kiddingly telling Tom not to wait up, and he, tired from our day and all our crowded past days, went obligingly back to Dauphine Street for an early sleep.

The huge, square-shaped bar of the brightly lighted Dixie Jazz, perfect for eye-cruising in all directions, was packed night after night, mostly with gay men eyeing each other, most of them regulars, I noticed, a boisterously loud and genial crowd, with brassy music blaring in the background at all times. And my last night in the French Quarter was no exception. I was unaware at first of the young man slipping in beside me, but when he spoke in a silken voice loaded with innuendo, breathing close to my ear, "Ah see yo' frien' is gone," I knew my final souvenir of New Orleans had appeared. I turned to a face I'd spotted several times during the week at the bar, but now close up was even more handsome: heavily-lashed, almost ebony eyes, delicately fine feline features, with full black hair slicked back European-style; an exotic look about him, not only in his facial features but in the long, deeply tanned body that leaned easily against the bar, he still smiling down at me on my barstool, revealing the most perfect teeth, all the whiter in contrast to his darkly bronzed face.

I sat staring, unable to believe my fairy-tale good fortune.

Still smiling, he slipped his hand into mine and in a slightly tipsy voice purred, "Ahm a proud Cajun from the bayous and don' give a dame who knows it." Then he ordered me a drink, and then another, regaling me with stories of "that ho, Miz Peppah," and just before closing time whispered in my ear, "Ya wanna come see ma pretty l'il place?"

His apartment was in an old white building in the heart of the Quarter, which he shared with a roommate, another Cajun, who "fo'tunate fo' us is visitin' kinfolk back home in the bayou fo' the weekend." We climbed an outside staircase up to a third-floor wrought-iron balcony overlooking a huge courtyard with palms and exotic tropical flowers awash in moonlight. My Cajun youth, despite his ease in the bar, seemed especially nervous about his neighbors knowing his business, and had an air of cat-like stealth about him. He expected the same from me, as we crept along the outer balcony like burglars. The shuttered door to his apartment was just off the balcony and, inside, the windows also had partially opened old shutters, a large roomy place with ceiling fans turning slowly. There were lime-green sheets on the bed, which he showed me quite proudly and which he fussily insisted on covering, saying, "They're new and I don' want 'em to git stained."

He mixed me a nightcap and told me, "Make ya'self comfortable, honey," and winked at me in a way that suggested I should start stripping down while he went into the bathroom, "Fo' some necessary ablutions ta' make mahself fresh," his faint

Cajun speech mixed with a distinct New Orleans accent.

Since he spent an inordinate amount of time in the john, with great flushings and runnings of water, I suspected, as I lay naked now on the bed and sipped at my bourbon while breathing in the commingled aromatic scents of the tropical flowers blooming riotously below, that he was giving himself a careful enema, since he had already whispered in my ear on the way to his place, "Ah want ya ta' fuck me like Ah've never bin fucked befo'."

I had grinned and nodded, in my heart shouting, *Hallelujah*!

When he finally returned to the bedroom, in the light of the still near-full moon through the slats of the shutters, I could see that his boyishly hairless body was tanned *all* over and wondered if there was a beach at Lake Pontchartrain Tom and I had missed. The bush at his groin was as black as the hair on his head, his long, lean, uncut cock swinging as he approached the bed and lay down and curled himself around me. With the odor of exotic blossoms still sweet in my nostrils, our arms went about each other. I discovered what a good kisser he was.

He sighed murmurously as he rolled over on his belly. "Ahm all greased and ready, baby," and spread his legs wide on the coverlet, his slender back, arching in anticipation, brindled with moonlight through the shutters, the pencil-stroke cleft of the target as dark as the shadows in the corners.

When it was over, he kissed me, thanked me, and once again closed himself off in the bathroom with more great runnings of water, flushing himself out again, I assumed, a wise precaution and habit, I also assumed, in a city that reeked sensuality, and its concomitant diseases, in every nook and cranny.

When he returned, he knitted his brows, annoyed that, in our eager thrashings, a bit of the protective coverlet had ridden up and K-Y had smeared the edge of one of his new lime-green sheets. He immediately wet a sponge with soap and tried to scour it out, clucking his tongue irritably the whole time.

I began to have the feeling it was time for sleep.

But he announced he wanted to get off too, and though I was willing, bringing to bear my most subtle ministrations of lip and hand, he failed to get aroused, that long, lank member refused to lift, its dark eye remaining firmly shut behind the lid of its foreskin.

At first he was frustrated, insisting if I did this or did that he could get it up, but nothing worked, no matter how hard I tried. Then he became embarrassed, admitting it happened sometimes. "Maybe Ahm just an assman like Miz Peppah and not a cocksman," he sighed ruefully.

You could see it bothered him a lot, and I began to wonder if he had stayed too long in this sensory paradise—and what a powerful seduction that must be—but my eyes by then were beginning to droop and with the scent of bougainvillaea blowing in at the slatted windows, I drifted off to sleep.

Early next morning, a Saturday, the day Tom and I planned to start hitchhiking back to Black Mountain, my Cajun took me to "breakfast" at the fluorescent-garish drug store he clerked in (*very* unromantic) on Bourbon Street, chicory coffee for me, "Co'-Cola," for him. He introduced me to a couple of his co-workers who eyed me archly, a defiance in him as if to say, Yeah, Ah slept with 'im. But there was a nervousness in his eyes too, that old 1950s fear even in New Orleans, the same climate of fear I would discover a few years later in even, for its times, so similarly open a city as San Francisco.

I hurried back to Dauphine Street and a worried Tom, who feared the worst when I hadn't returned to our room that night. I apologized profusely, but I could see he was still annoyed with me, his mood not changing till, after I'd packed hurriedly and we settled the bill with the landlady, we were once more out on the road. On the return trip, we chose to hitchhike back on the more westerly route north, through Baton Rouge, so we could see the bayou country, then on back through

Mississippi and Natchez, once again through Alabama, this time to Tuscaloosa and Birmingham, then finally up to Chattanooga, Tennessee, where we'd swing directly east to North Carolina and home to Black Mountain.

It was in Chattanooga we met our first real trouble, and it came in the guise of a gangly, good-looking boy with choir-boy face and straw-colored hair and a Tennessee mountain accent so sweet it fairly dripped like syrup from his lips. He really took us.

He picked us up somewhere outside Chattanooga early Sunday afternoon, well into our second day on the road, and said he was going "jist t'other side a' the city limits," which we were glad to hear, to get through the city. He was chatty and smiled a lot—which should've been a tip off—and Tom and he got along like a house afire, since Tom, as always, was happy to hold up his end of the jawing. So, as we neared Chattanooga, we weren't at all suspicious when the driver asked if we were hungry, that he certainly was—"Ahm so famished ma' belly's kissin' ma' backbone"—and he knew "a cheap but good li'l cafe down a back street in Chat'nooga fries the best li'l ole burgers in the world."

Tom and I hadn't eaten since early that morning, so of course we agreed, Tom generously offering to treat him to a burger and coffee and slice of pie as a show of our appreciation for the ride.

"That's mighty white a' ya," he purred sweetly, his lips stretching in their most ingratiating grin.

The hamburger joint was squeezed between old buildings down an alley-like street in a slummy part of the city. The young driver waved a skinny white arm and with another of those ingratiating grins told us to go on in ahead and order him a hamburger, he'd be in in a minute after he checked out a tire on the car. Dumb lambs that we were, Tom and I swung open the screendoor to the cafe and went in and used the restrooms, then ordered the burgers and that, of course, was the last we saw of the tow-headed boy with the innocent smiles. As the latter's hamburger sat getting cold on the counter, Tom decided to take a look to see what was the hold up and returned with a stricken face, muttering to me in a low voice that the kid was gone and our suitcases along with him. "Maybe he'll be back," he added feebly. But after a decent wait and there was no sign of him, we knew it was us had been held up.

I had so few belongings, that the week's worth of clothes I had packed in my suitcase, even the razor and toothbrush, would be costly to replace, given the money I'd spent in New Orleans, careful though we both were, and I was sorry to lose that new suitcase from my mother, the only new thing I owned. Tom at least had his GI Bill coming in and had a few spare bucks besides; I was coming back with less than nothing.

Tom, as so often with him, was more philosophical and got over the initial shock of the robbery almost immediately, shrugging his shoulders, saying what could we do, it'd be a waste of time reporting it to the police, best we get back to Black Mountain, and he was right, of course. Whereas I held onto being bitterly resentful we'd been taken in by such smooth-talking white trash with one of the oldest tricks in the book, that we'd been made fools of, my pride hurt more than the loss of my belongings.

Despite our good fortune to hitch a ride outside Chattanooga (a city I never wanted to see again) with a portly ornithologist through the rest of Tennessee into North Carolina, in a car only slightly larger than Jonathan's Hillman, I was still so furious I sat silently in the back seat with my arms folded tightly across my chest, while Tom, up front, gabbed merrily about our recent "adventure." The calm, genial ornithologist offered sympathetic interjections, which only exasperated me all the more. Soon Tom was babbling away cheerfully as if nothing had happened which was even more annoying. To top it off, the ornithologist had one of his birds with him, "a goshawk," he offered genially over his shoulder, a fierce creature in a not too securely closed cardboard box jammed against my feet in the cramped floor space. It kept flapping with its broad powerful blue-gray wings against the loose top of the box the whole trip, almost escaping each time, its furious yellow eyes burning in on me with each leap, as if I were its captor and tormentor and not the lump of placidity filling up the front seat *and* my ears with a detailed history of the bird.

I suspect my own eyes looked just as fierce as the goshawk's, since the ornithologist soon gave up trying to draw me out and turned all his attention on Tom, who was as amiable and chatty as himself.

When we got back to Black Mountain late that Sunday afternoon, hungry and exhausted, there was nothing to eat in our kitchen at Meadows Inn except a box of Mother's Quaker Oats, which Tom quickly cooked up on the Coleman. Charles passed by, picking his way carefully over the pine tree roots in the rutted path outside—I had the sense he'd been watching for us—came over with a big grin to talk to us through the screened window and to welcome us back, emphasizing how glad he was to see us back. I myself, despite my vile mood, was glad to see him too, having ever more powerfully that overwhelming feeling of being *safe* again once I was back on the land of Black Mountain. Tom, now with some hot food in his belly and a second wind, chattered on happily yet once more about the trip and the robbery, Charles, who always loved a good story, listening avidly; I, childishly, still so pissed and embarrassed to have Charles hear what fools we'd been made of in Chattanooga, kept my mouth shut, longing only for a long hot bath.

To top it off, a few days after Tom and I got back, I discovered I had a dose of crabs, my first, a souvenir I hadn't counted on from my darkly handsome Cajun. Yet it seemed somehow a fitting conclusion to my first visit to the city of pleasure, and to the entire trip, all part, as I was able to see in time when I was able to laugh at it, of my education—Tom's too—on and off campus at Black Mountain College.

Maybe it was the hitchhiking or maybe it was for the sheer convenience, because after our New Orleans trip, Tom became the newly proud owner, bought with his GI mustering-out pay, of a gray, chrome-shiny 1950 Buick in good condition, and with three small decorative chrome "portholes" on either side the hood (what sold the model to Tom, and to millions of others as well), that now sat parked out on the grass in front of Meadows Inn. Besides getting ice for the ice box, especially important now in summer, we could make runs into the town of Black Mountain now whenever we needed supplies and, equally important, make beer trips to Ma Peak's, or even ride into Asheville for an occasional movie.

The rest of that summer, in the long, lazy afternoons, Tom and I swam in the whirlpool of Snake River across the road from the college and sunned on the rocks, occasionally, those hostile farm boys winging rocks at us from nearby bushes: not exactly Lake Ponchartrain, but in its own smaller way, much wilder—in some ways a metaphor for Black Mountain itself. Swimming around us were lots of what Tom called "newts"— so as not to scare me, I think—but what looked like snakes to me. Since they didn't bother us in the fast-foaming waters, I soon lost my skittishness at their presence. Tom and I were soon dark as earth from the sun.

Charles was annoyed that we spent so much time at the river instead of working at our writing and painting. Tom figured maybe he was jealous.

Teeth were always a problem, not only because of the cavities caused by my sugar addiction (penny candy the comfit of poor kids), but I could only ever afford, like so many others at the college, to see a dentist in extreme emergencies, a handy excuse given my dread of them. But at poverty-stricken and, more to the point, reasonably healthy Black Mountain, doctors and dentists were for most of us the least of our concerns.

However, one day after lunch, a large filling, among the many in my mouth, fell out, and the tooth began immediately to hurt like hell. Having had so many of them from childhood on, I knew the prolonged agonizing pain a toothache can be, and panicked. That panic gave me the nerve—as urgent as the throbbing nerve in my tooth—to hurry to Charles' back door, since he was the only one around at that moment with a car, since Tom buzzed off at every opportunity in his new toy. Through the screen door, I could see him reclining on his bed down the hall (clothed this time), perhaps resting after his own lunch, or, for him, at that hour, his breakfast, and felt a moment of the old timidity at breaking in on his privacy. But the insistent pain emboldened me and I knocked. When he appeared and I told him my problem, he looked annoyed and let me know it was a real nuisance, an imposition, one of the many he felt perhaps forced on him at that time, depleting his energies.

I had to ask him twice, pleading even more earnestly the second time, and hating myself for it, to convince him that it was a real emergency. Reluctantly, he agreed to take me, and we piled into his old Ford convertible, Charles surlily and unusually quiet on the ride into town; I, keeping my mouth shut to lessen the pain, feeling awful about putting him out (wondering what meditations I had dragged him away from), somewhat ashamed, too, of being such a coward over pain.

As we walked on a back street in the town of Black Mountain on our way in search of the dentist, we passed black women laundry workers, drenched in sweat, toiling in the steaming heat, not only from inside the place but from outside as well, behind the rusty screen door of the local laundry.

The dentist's office was on a side street up narrow stairs, on the second floor of a brick building in the business block, a no-nonsense, old-fashioned kind of office, the dentist himself a small, plump, gray-balding man in a white coat who was direct and efficient in getting the job done.

It was just a couple of bucks, but how ever did I pay him?

Charles was just as quiet on the ride back, and I kept quiet too, grateful the pain in my tooth had stopped, grateful to Charles in spite of his silence.

After the college farm closed and we no longer had access to fresh—and free—vegetables—and before Bea Huss began her community vegetable patch—one afternoon Tom and I went food shopping with Connie in Tom's new Buick to the A&P in Black Mountain. Standing before the usual rather meager produce selection, Connie, who pronounced, New England-style, I presumed, "potatoes" as "badadoes," sighed dejectedly and murmured, "I *wish* God had invented more vegetables."

With so much of the farm closed and our need to shop in town increasing, we interacted more frequently now with townspeople. Charles came back to campus furious after another trip to the town of Black Mountain one afternoon with two-year-old Kate, about the treatment one of the women shopkeepers gave Kate—and him. Kate, as a kid will, evidently was rummaging in the candy or whatever, and the shopkeeper was overly sharp about it, Kate not in the least understanding her anger.

Charles was really pissed and let everybody at the college know about it.

There was a dark-haired, nondescript playwright in his early 30s who stopped in for a visit that summer, and, it being an opportunity to hear a fresh voice, Charles suggested he read a new play the playwright had written and brought along as one of our Sunday evening programs in the Studies basement. The

guy, as he began to read, sounded pretty sure of himsel
with a pacifist theme. However, that soon change
Charles, chuckling, began to sneer at it, first in whispers, u..
loud enough for the playwright to hear, egging the rest of us
on. Although I felt for the guy, having been there myself, still I
joined in as part of the chorus, laughing along with the others,
by now having become a regular Black Mountain thug. The
playwright, now casting alarmed and baffled glances at us over
his pages, hurried through his script at a gallop.

Charles had no truck with pacifism or pacifists, often openly
criticizing the occasional visitors expressing such philosophies,
who mistakenly believed Black Mountain was still strongly
allied with its Quaker, passive-resistant past. But Wes Huss was
the only one on board who held such beliefs, and mainly kept
mum about them, as he did that evening, keeping his usual
controlled face throughout.

The pacifist playwright sneaked off into the night after his
flop of a reading, and was never seen again.

Charles once more loudly expressed his opinions on the matter in his next class, he who was also intimately acquainted with
the dark, twisted root in all of us, he who then once more asked
the class how "one prepared for the marauders over the hill," as
well as the marauders in oneself.

After spending what little I had in New Orleans, and losing a
good bit of my belongings to boot, I was so broke, with no
prospects of money to feed myself, even in our cheap communal Meadows Inn kitchen, I once more confided my worry to
Charles who, though sympathetic, again insisted we all had to
tighten our belts even more, make do somehow. He recommended one more time, since my staying at Black Mountain
was so important to me, that, as he said he had suggested also
to several others in the same financial scrape, I apply for a job
down at the woolen mills in Swannanoa, where they made

blankets. He'd heard rumors they might be hiring for the night shift; that way I could still get to my day classes, including his on Reading the Newspaper.

I didn't like that idea at all. When I asked him how would I get to and from the job, especially at night, he said that the bus running down on the county road by the VA hospital went that way, but I was doubtful it ran at night.

The thought of leaving Black Mountain forever was depressing enough, but equally depressing, not to mention alarming, was the thought of leaving the sanctuary of the place for an eight or ten hour night-shift at a tedious job with probably hostile co-workers, once they found out I was a student at the college. Worst of all was maybe sleeping through, and missing Olson's morning class, his presence the main reason for my staying.

Having worked at a number of factory jobs in the past couple of years, including the shipyard with my father, I had had my fill of such work, and decided no matter what, I wouldn't go back to it. Besides, the idea of such work sapping me of the energy to write and study—and I knew from first-hand experience what a drain such labor was—seemed pointless and even more unappealing to me.

I thanked Charles for his suggestion and said I'd think it over, even though my mind was already made up not to follow his advice; I'd work something out. He must've read that in my face, sharp as he was at that, because as I was turning away, he said, come to think of it, he and Connie had been wanting to get their windows washed and the books on their bookshelves in the living room dusted, and seeing I needed the money, would I be willing to do it for five bucks?

Would I? Five bucks sounded like a small fortune and would enable me to eat for at least another few weeks, thanks to Tom's parsimonious menus and his money-saving shopping tips at the A&P in Black Mountain, plus what we would scrounge off the land.

I suspect Charles hired me more out of the kindness of his heart, given his and Connie's meager college allowance, they more often than not just as dead broke as most of the rest of us.

The windows I had to clean were the narrow slotted ones, filmy with years of fireplace and cigarette smoke, up near the ceiling above the book shelves, and I also had to dust the hundreds of books packing the wall-to-ceiling shelves themselves. That afternoon, while I perched precariously up on top of a tall, rickety stepladder wiping away, there was a knock at the door. When Charles opened it, there stood a guest from the outside world, rare these days, a rather formally dressed man to see Charles on some business. Olson offhandedly introduced me, and I, grinning impishly, a measure of my confidence now with Charles, called down cheekily to the visitor, "I'm the houseboy!" and Charles grinned back up at me, pleased, and only a teensy miffed at my corny joke.

After a drunken party one night that summer, just after he'd returned from the army in West Germany bearing additional copies of Olson's *Maximus Poems* 1-10 printed in Stuttgart (the party perhaps in celebration of that), Jonathan Williams, losing his Southern Gentleman reserve under the influence of a little bourbon bonded reserve and Ma Peak's ale, came to me, said he knew of a little nearby lake with a beach, deserted at that hour of the night. We could skinnydip. Did I want to?

I was beyond saying yes or no, having not quite the hollow leg of Jonathan, and before I knew it, we were in his little black Hillman Minx flying over twisting country back roads, then we were lying naked side by side on a sandy beach. There seemed to be a moon, the sand glowing whitely ashen. The darkness was all around, I was aware of the trees pressing in and, just as at Snake River, drunkenly imagining the eyes of farmboys hidden behind the bushes and boulders there, was abruptly seized with a sudden sober fear that there were hill people hidden in those trees, eyes watching us, two men lying naked together. I jumped up, and despite feeling foolish, told Jonathan it was too dangerous, we had to go, back to Black Mountain, back where it was safe. Jonathan, exasperated, tried to quiet me down, but I was insistent, and seeing he wasn't getting anywhere was finally obliging. We dressed hurriedly and drove back to his visitor's room in Streamside.

Flola Shepard, the brilliant language teacher with whom I studied French after Madame, invited the field mice into her quarters to live with her at the rear of Black Dwarf, leaving dozens of sardine tins of food scraps around for them on the floors and up on the bookshelves. Perhaps they were her familiars, her animal helpers and spirits, there was often in her own epicanthic eyes a subtle but wild playfulness, just as there was a mouse-like, twitchy play around her thin mouth and a wriggling of her tiny sharp nose when she grinned, which was often. Hundreds of the little rodents evidently took advantage of her hospitality (mousepitality?), because after Flola left in 1954 and newly-appointed writer Robert Hellman moved in (I helped him get the place in shape before his wife arrived, to earn a few extra still badly-needed bucks), the cleanup of mouse droppings was tremendous.

Robert was even more appalled by the toilet seat in the bathroom, insisting, exaggeratedly I thought, he'd get "a brown ring" around his bottom if he sat on it in the condition it was left, and insisted I scour it for all I was worth. Hellman wasn't the easiest person to work for, so I really earned those few measly bucks.

Hellman took over the teaching of languages from Flola and, while Creeley was temporarily back in Mallorca and since Olson, I suspect, wanted a rest from it for a time, was also induced by Charles to teach a writing course. This in spite of the fact that after Hellman's first public reading at the college down in the Weaving Room of the Studies one Sunday night, Olson firmly cautioned him to "Stop trying to be Tolstoy." Hellman also read that night, though, a curious story from his army days while stationed in Australia during World War 2, about a voyeur queer hiding in the bushes watching while soldiers bathed nude in a stream, with the usual homophobic overtones of the times but which I found fascinating for its homoerotic implications.

I grudgingly took his writing class, telling Charles ahead of time I didn't think I'd get much from Hellman. And I was right, since Hellman cavalierly pooh-poohed just about every-thing I wrote. I only attended because Charles, sensing a prob-lem, wanted Hellman to have at least a few students. But his blunt Bronx manner, coupled with his flat-faced arrogance, put a lot of us off, and that he lost the only copy of a short story of mine about the summer I worked with my father in the ship-yard didn't endear him to me either. I was relieved when the class ended. Despite problems with Creeley's teaching, I missed his class, and certainly would have wished for Olson to teach. But as 1955 approached, I began to sense I'd already gotten the best of what I needed from both men and, given the sense of imminent collapse of the college, knew, though I wouldn't yet admit it, that it was getting time to move on.

In August 1954, Betty Baker, ex-editor at the *North Carolina Historical Review* and recent ex-WAC (I believe the Women's Army Corps was the service she served in) arrived in her gray Cranbrook Plymouth to take on the job of "adminis-trative secretary" of the college.

She lasted till December.

Tough and outspoken, with close-cropped, prematurely gray hair and a smooth, creamy-skinned face with no make-up (unusual for a woman from the outside at that time), she always had, like a lot of those fresh out of the service who ended up at

Black Mountain, a trim, freshly-bathed appearance (in contrast to the usually unwashed-appearing, straggle-haired, ragtag rest of us) and a plain, severely-cut, close-fitting greenish dress that always, given the severity of her bearing, made me think she was still in uniform.

Underneath the no-nonsense drill sergeant aspect, though, was a warm and outgoing woman with an offbeat sense of humor, very Southern, often bitchily biting, that Tom and I, strays that we were and always looking for a big mama at hard-edged Black Mountain, or at least a big sister (like Mary Fiore), roles Betty Baker seemed willing to play, found irresistible. Tom and she, of course, enjoyed swapping service stories like old army buddies.

As a result, we used to visit her quite a lot in her apartment at the rear of the Studies, for tea or for simple meals, which Charles, I suspect, although he said nothing, took note of. Betty pumped us for information and, as usual, was quite out-spoken in her views, in and outside of faculty meetings, on what was wrong with the college and what should be done. She was often critical of Olson, which made us both, perhaps I more than Tom, uncomfortable. She came on like a brash outsider, new on the scene, putting down Our Father. But, starved for a fresh face—and ears—we enjoyed the laughy, gossipy times at Betty's place, feeling at moments, at least in my own conflictions toward Olson, a delicious irreverence.

She so fit one of the crisply militaristic, button-down, I-don't-need-a-man stereotypes of the day, Tom and I used to wonder if she were lesbian, which of course would've been an even bigger plus in our eyes. If anything, she was certainly in the tradition of strong Southern women. I suspect Charles, because of her assertiveness and, like Natasha, not taking any guff from him, thought so too, picked up on that and resented her even more because, again like Natasha, Betty Baker would stand up to him.

Particularly in Charles' writing class in the Reading Room, which she sat in on a few times. One night Betty was arguing with Charles over a piece of my writing, saying he shouldn't lead students to believe "they're great," accusing him of misleading Tom and me and the others in the class, and saying it in no uncertain terms. Charles, pulling himself up in his chair and looking her square in the eye, responded by saying the purpose of the class, of indeed Black Mountain College (as he'd firmly stated earlier about his fair-haired boy Duck Daley) was "to create Dostoevskys." And when Betty went on, calling his bluff in an unflinching, assertive voice, insisting he was mistaken, Olson shot back with, his own voice hoarse with rage and high-mightiness, "*I'm tough, don't mess with me—I'm dynamite!*"

As usual, I sat wriggling with embarrassment, feeling caught in the middle again, feeling again, too, how Charles really "fought" for his students, the ones he liked, and grew to love, like they were his, his possessions (what he once accused Natasha of with her students, "a squirrel taking the nuts home"). He probably had felt threatened that Betty was stealing Tom and me away, which in part she had because we both liked her, our big protective sister at big old macho Black Mountain. Yet I also liked—loved, really—and, as I've said so often here, *needed* Charles, for clues, directions, for validation in my writing, for personal approval. So, there I wriggled on the creaky slats of my cane-bottom chair in the Reading Room that particular night, torn in two again.

Betty always parked her car in front of the Studies and one day not long after the above blowup, Charles and Tom and I were standing outside the main entrance and Charles was going on about Betty. He glanced over at her squat gray car and said sneeringly, "Well, what can you expect from somebody who drives a *Plymouth*—and a Cranbrook model at that!"

It's no wonder she packed up and was gone by December.

In doing scenes from Eugene O'Neill's *Anna Christie* in Wes' class, I played Chris, the cantankerous old scow captain, while new student Lorraine from New York City (she later married Harvey Harmon in San Francisco in 1957) played Anna, a role I really should have been playing, I could identify with her more, as downtrodden queer, also increasingly dependent on booze, also growing sick of men (after my contretemps with Merrill).

Lorraine and I also did scenes from Molière, practicing them at length in Wes' class and then giving a performance to the community as part of one of our Sunday night entertainments in the basement of the Studies. Playing an old man to Lorraine's perfect, innocent-faced, round-eyed ingenue, thanks to Wes' careful patience and insight, for the first time I really got what Molière was up to, and the pleasurable sense of what acting could be about: the pacing, the just-right pauses and intonations to convey the full wit, were all there in the playing that night, the sure sense, being so much inside the role, that I couldn't put a foot wrong. And Wes, no easy critic, afterwards told me so, while Charles, for once, hadn't anything to say except to give both Lorraine and me a satisfied wink.

One night, as the evenings were growing chillier with fall, a group of us wanted to go to the movies at the Roxy in Swannanoa, that cramped 1930s-style fleabag of a place with its shaky rows of hard seats that Charles always had difficulty folding himself into. Olson, however, inexplicably, with no previous warnings to us, perhaps wanting to throw his weight around, rounded us up for an unusual emergency night work-crew to help replace broken windows in the Studies Building to save on coal with winter approaching. When he was grumblingly told about our plans for the movies, he insisted rather angrily, rather as if we were traitors, that we stay and help him fix the windows. A few, whining and complaining, said to hell with it and defiantly went off to the movies, while several others grudgingly stayed to help, including myself, who felt not only guilty but, as usual, loyal to Charles and his commands, ever eager to please him. We were like unruly sons, and he the father reining us in, some of us at least.

It all ended prematurely, however, when Charles, still agitated over the defections—perhaps as an old sailor he saw it as mutiny—and not always so handy with his hands, cut his thumb badly on a pane of glass while trying to cut it to size, down in the lower stairwell.

"Look at that! Look at that!" he cried in an amazed voice as he stared at the blood pouring from the gash. "See, see, where Christ's blood streams in the firmament!" flashed in my mind, Charles having quoted Marlowe's lines in class some weeks earlier—a not unlikely cosmic and mythical connection, since Olson loomed in my childish mind as large as that. I felt for him, the same as I did years earlier, when my father in his sagging, old chair in the parlor after a hard day's work at the shipyard was lighting up a cigarette and the pack of matches exploded in flames in his hands, burning him badly. My mother, who was not, as usual, speaking to him, sat silent, continuing her crocheting on the couch, pretending she hadn't seen anything. I wanted to run to my father (as I had wanted to run to Olson at that moment) to comfort him, get butter from the ice box to put on his charred fingers, but dared not, so deeply fearful of him (just as I was, still, so deeply fearful of Olson), even more deeply fearful of betraying my mother.

Once Charles had left for home to have Connie bandage his wound (one hoped she would! given his past night-time sneakings up the Meadows Inn stairs to see Betty Kaiser), and since Olson, the self-acknowledged master glazier and gang boss was now gone, like truly unruly school boys, we all immediately defected, piled into Tom's Buick and made it just in time for the first show at the Roxy after all.

It was in the autumn, in the midst of all the uncertainties about the future of the college, after two years of confused false starts and superficial scratchings, that I wrote my first real short story, although, in what was to become usual for me, I didn't know it till after the fact. Heeding Charles' advice, what I did to get it was reach back into my adolescence in the mid-1940s to a street gang I got to know through a childhood pal, a former next-door neighbor, who had moved with his family from our sleepy little South Jersey town to the northern section of Camden, in a tough, working-class neighborhood.

The gang members, the scene of the abandoned truck on the vacant lot where they all hung out, all came back to me as I lay in bed in Meadows Inn one cold night in late September. It pestered me so much, I had to get up out of bed, get a pencil and some paper, then stood shivering in my underwear as I started writing the early draft on top of the tall pine bureau in the corner. Every time I thought I was through scribbling for the night and put out the light and got back under the covers, more ideas came to me and I had to get up in the chill, go lean over the bureau top again and write some more, then jump back in bed, only to have another idea or bit of dialog come that I just had to jot down right away for fear I'd forget it by morning. The rough draft of that story was mostly written—up and down, up and down—that first night, the excitement of it giving me no rest. The faces of the gang, their voices, were so intensely clear in my eyes and ears; I could even *smell* again the musty, gasoline odors of the inside of that old abandoned truck in the city lot.

Now that I had some respect in Charles' eyes, I was allowed to read my work aloud. When I read "The Truck" in class one night soon after, timid as always and not daring to look up from the pages to see the faces of the others as I read, they were all so silent, I thought I'd flopped again. But as I read on, I heard now a laugh from Tom Field or a chuckle from Jerry Van de Wiele—in the right places, too—that was encouraging. At the end of reading it, to say I was bowled over by Charles' enthusiastic response would be putting it mildly. "It's a breakthrough for you, Mike," he said, adding he liked the characters and the way I had them talk, particularly Muskrat, and especially Rosemary, the double outsider (black *and* queer), whose lingo really flipped him, and who Olson felt was "the most decent one in the whole bunch" in his "concern" for getting the drunk Gyp home safely when the others in the gang couldn't have cared less. He went on to say, "I like the way you got the pair of them out of the story in a clean way," meaning, I supposed, there was no suggestion of cheap and leering sexuality. (Language new to Charles often hit him right between the eyes, it was so visceral: in "The Truck" the boys' use of the reform-school slang "brown eye" to denote butt-fucking between two guys—in an opening passage cut from the original, since Olson thought the whole of the passage "extraneous," something I later regretted doing—the jolt of his eyebrow-lifting surprise, and his asking me about the term, commenting on the vividness of it during the discussion.)

The others in the class were especially pleased with the story and said so, Tom's cheeks grinning red with pleasure as he glanced over at me. But an additional wonder to me was the agog look on Jorge Fick's face, like he'd seen a miracle (which I expect to everyone else, after so long a time, including me, it truly was).

Looking back on it, writing "The Truck" had been my first totally pleasurable writing experience, something Charles told us "writing should be," a terrific sense of enjoyment in the first-time experience of words as *living* things, of letting go and letting form grow out of content, as Olson, via Creeley, suggested. With the response of Olson and the others to back me, I felt the possibilities of really becoming a writer at last. In their eyes, and starting in my own, I was beginning to smarten up, learning to "lie."

"And it's the first thing you've written with no social messages," Charles concluded, approvingly.

He suggested I send the story to Creeley in Mallorca to consider for *The Black Mountain Review*, the use of scarce college resources for that project another of Charles' schemes to attract students, this time through a literary magazine; the main reason, however, to provide an alternative to what Olson saw as the limited criticism in Cid Corman's *Origin*.

"It's good enough for the *Review*," Charles ended. "Let's try it out on Bob."

I was over the moon.

I had begun to correspond with Creeley several months after his return to Mallorca beginning in August 1954. Now, in October, I airmailed "The Truck" to him and waited impatiently for his letter on it. But before I heard from Creeley, news of his feelings about the story was delivered by Olson himself at an afternoon tea at his house in honor of a distinguished visitor to Black Mountain.

Caresse Crosby, a wealthy Washington socialite, who with her husband, Harry, ran the Black Sun Press in Paris in the 1920s, was an old friend of Olson's. He'd met her through Ezra Pound's efforts while Pound was incarcerated in St. Elizabeth's Hospital after World War 2 (where Olson frequently visited him) for his naïve pro-fascist radio speeches in Italy during Mussolini's dictatorship. That fall, Olson invited her down to the college to visit and give a talk to us students.

Caresse had been in Greece working with an organization called World Community that had to do with a "One World" concept, and that seemed to encourage individual secession from the pitfalls of tribal nationalism, an idea that was floating around in some liberal and progressive circles in the States and the world in the 1950s, with the horrors of the Second World War still fresh. During her visit, Charles invited her to speak, aptly enough, to his Reading the Newspaper class on her work with this group, and to give us its ideas.

I would rather have heard her speak about her husband, Harry, blowing his and his mistress' brains out in that seedy New York City hotel room in 1929, but I knew there was fat chance of that.

It was a crisp sunny day, with the apples from the nearby trees thumping to the grass (apples Tom Field and Mary Fiore gathered, not only for eating but for baking pies and making apple sauce), so we all took chairs and sat out on the wide concrete terrace entrance to the Studies Building. The class listened politely but not too enthusiastically to this petite woman in, incongruously for ragged-jeans Black Mountain, an expensively tailored navy-blue dress, and still wearing the bobbed hair of the 1920s flapper. In another incongruity at makeup-free Black Mountain, there was bright red lipstick on the remnants of what was once a very pretty face. She had a sweet smile and an easy charm as she spoke, but when Charles asked if there were any questions after she finished, there was an uncomfortable and embarrassed silence from us. The talk had sounded very abstract and idealistic, even to me, who was no slouch at meringuey idealism; however, the idea of One World was as far removed from my reality as Greece was. Charles didn't appear too thrilled with it, either, perhaps more deeply aware, and suspicious, of human contradictions and paradoxes, not to mention sheer human orneriness. As Caresse spoke, you could see him watching us, as he had at the farmhouse during the televised McCarthy hearings, to gauge what we were thinking. I couldn't imagine the practicality of it, let alone the dream, still caught as I was in the mind-set of boundaries and differences of peoples and, on the less meringuey side, "the tyranny of culture," as I heard Charles quote in class one night (culture, and society, the obverse tyrannical face of nature), a hopeless sense of the ongoing, deeply-entrenched power of things, universal queer-hate, for starters, which made any idea like World Community not matter one way or the other. I was grappling more with "the tyranny of nature," my own, and the one up in the mountains, and also had more immediate concerns, like learning to write and reading as many books as I could in the library, including, at Olson's suggestion, D. H. Lawrence's *Kangaroo*, a political and ideological novel that threw ice water on some of my own ill-conceived idealisms, including the seductions and dangers of a charismatic leader (squeamish thoughts of Olson not far from my thoughts as I read). Then there was the constant worrying where the next few bucks were coming from to keep me eating for a week in our Meadows Inn communal kitchen, painter Tom Field chief cook.

Crosby appeared so perky and cheerful, so obviously sincere and, given the sullen, unresponsive stares of the class, nervously vulnerable. But the day was beautiful and with her bobbed hair and her plumpish short figure and those bright remnants of youthful loveliness still clear in a face beginning to loosen and crevice with age, I was touched by her being game enough to share with us some of her own enthusiasm for global oneness. There was a kind of optimistic innocence about her that didn't go down well with that bunch of hardened and often cynical realists that formed the core of Charles' classes. It was hard for me to grasp or accept her overly optimistic vision: all I could see was one vast planetary bowl of Cream of Wheat, bland and pallid and unappetizing. But her eyes were lovely and filled with a pretty light, much more real to me than One World. The world I wanted to hear of was her world of the 1920s, and the husband who blew his brains out after putting a bullet in the head of a young woman while they lay side by side in bed in that New York hotel room.

Charles, aware of the resistance, was all courtly smiles, fluttering about Caresse with little fussy attentions to soften the apathy of the class, his actions telling us all too clearly what we already knew: that the talk had been a dud. He was trying to make up for it a bit, but I suspected Caresse knew.

Besides her husband and Paris in the 1920s, I would also have much rather heard her talk about D. H. Lawrence and especially Hart Crane, since she and her husband were the first to publish *The Bridge*, that "failed attempt," in Olson's eyes, Crane "stuck with pentameter." Luckily, it wasn't long after her talk, however, at Charles' urging, that she did get a chance to tell us anecdotes about both writers, at a tea Charles and Connie gave for her one damp, chilly afternoon in their living room near the end of her October visit.

Teas at Black Mountain were really very pleasant occasions (in contrast to the occasional ugliness and abrasiveness of the Saturday night moonshine parties), often gotten together spontaneously on such dark cold afternoons (Mary Fiore giving some of the best teas). It was, however, unusual for any of us, especially students, to be invited to the Olsons', and even more unusual to be invited as a group, since Charles was so zealous in guarding his privacy. (The most time, up until Caresse's tea, I'd ever spent in the Olson house was that time Charles hired me to dust and clean the hundreds of books on his living room shelves and to wash the windows.) But on special occasions, such as Crosby's visit, he would lay out the welcome mat and do it in style, even donning his old wrinkled seersucker as "dress coat" and scrounging up his old rope of a tie to hang around the collar of his ripped and faded blue workshirt.

A fire was humming in the grate, and there were little cakes, and the tea served in real cups and saucers. The sloping, high-ceilinged living room, with its by now well-dusted floor-to-ceiling bookshelves and bank of shiny windows up near the ceiling, exuded, with its maple-tinted walls, a toasty and cozy air against the raw wetness outside the lower bank of large windows, with a view of the rain-soaked woods and the farm beyond. Such a special occasion with a special guest, made us awkward and strained—most Black Mountain people, women as well as men, easy with each other in a rough and tumble way, were more constrained and uneasy in a "politely" formal situation such as this. I found myself sitting next to Caresse, near the large windows, and couldn't find a thing to say to her, awed as I was by someone who had actually talked with and seen in the flesh such giant mythical figures as D. H. Lawrence and Hart Crane and F. Scott Fitzgerald, and was much too shy and tongue-tied to ask her anything about them. What made me feel a little less uncomfortable about this was the sense of herself as a gracious and unobtrusive person, with a smile in those beautiful eyes of hers even when she wasn't particularly smiling. She undoubtedly sized us up, saw the situation, seemed not to want to intrude on anybody, and appeared more at home there in Olson's house than any of the rest of us. Except perhaps for Connie who, as always, quiet and unobtrusive herself, poured tea and passed around the plates of cakes, while two-year-old daughter Kate napped in another room.

Charles, the gracious host when he needed to be, loomed over everything and everyone, smiling, cheerful, large arms going from one shoulder to another, a kind and sociable word for everyone, himself sizing up the situation. And soon, as only he could do, he got Caresse to tell us some stories out of her past.

The first one was about the time in 1928 when she and Harry eagerly wanted to publish, through their Black Sun Press, a piece titled, appropriately enough, "Sun," a story by D. H. Lawrence. Lawrence, who was leaving for Italy by train within the hour, said, on a whim apparently, he'd let them publish the story, but only if they paid him in gold. So, the Crosbys scurried around Paris and with difficulty managed finally to find a bank that would exchange francs for gold pieces. They rushed off to the station just as Lawrence's train was pulling out and, racing alongside the moving cars, at last spotted his slim, bearded face and thrust the bag of gold up to the startled Lawrence through the coach window.

He was surprised at their taking his whimsy seriously but pleased (money always in short supply with D. H. and Frieda), although Caresse speculated that her and Harry's shenanigans must have provided additional grim grist for the sardonic mills of the Nottingham Crank on the antic behavior of two more crazy, and rich, Americans.

Next, as the cold, rainy afternoon darkened the windows with dusk and Charles poked up the crackling fire, she told the story of how much trouble they'd had in 1930 with the visiting Hart Crane to get him to sit down in his little room on an upper floor of their converted mill outside Paris and finish *The Bridge*, which they were as eager to publish as they were Lawrence's story. But even though, after years of work on it, he had only a bit more to do, Crane was resistant about finishing his epic, not wanting to let go of it perhaps, and was just as eager to duck out night after night to the village bistro and tie one on with the boys. It got so that the Crosbys—after an evening of drinking, when such a thing seems a good idea at the time—finally locked Crane in his room and ordered him to finish the poem, warning him that he wouldn't get out until he did. Meekly, Crane agreed, and, smugly, the Crosbys went off to bed, thinking they'd solved the problem and that they'd have their poem ready for the printing press by morning.

When they unlocked the door next day, Crane was there all right, sleeping soundly in his bed, but the Crosbys were baffled to see the floors and even the thick whitewashed walls and the sheets on the bed itself black with foot- and hand-prints. And the still incomplete manuscript of *The Bridge* lying untouched on the writing table. Hours later, when he awoke, Crane, severely hungover, sheepishly confessed he'd squeezed out his tiny bedroom window not long after the Crosbys had locked him in, climbed down the rainspout, gone to the village bar as usual and, after a night of carousing there, also as usual, picked up a guy, a small and nimble chimney sweep. Given his profession, the sweep had no trouble shimmying up the rainspout with the athletic Crane, who liked to box, and once in Crane's room, the poet immediately, being something of a sexual athlete as well, chased the sweep about in amorous pursuit, the latter leaving the tell-tale prints of his job, and the chase, all over the place—thus betraying Crane to the irritated but amused Crosbys.

Crane, of course, did eventually finish *The Bridge*, a handsome, out-sized Black Sun first-printing copy of which we would soon see in the exhibit Caresse would lend to the college, after her visit.

After her stories, Olson, ever with a keen sense of drama, put his hand on my shoulder and drew me over to the fireplace. With a big smile, waving the letter in his hand, he announced he'd heard from Creeley just that day, and that Creeley liked my story "The Truck" enough to want to print it in a future issue of *The Black Mountain Review*. That the news made my day would be a definite understatement. I was overjoyed to know I was to have my first real story published in the then to me, to all of us, in fact, one and only most important magazine going. ("It was our Bible," as I told Martin Duberman in 1968, when he interviewed me for his book on Black Mountain.) I couldn't say a word. I just kept grinning and grinning up into Charles' own firelit grinning face.

Shortly after, I received the following letter from Creeley:

Casa Martina
Bononova Palma etc
October 25, 1954

Dear Mike,

We've just moved to this new house—hence somewhat of a chaos. But I wanted to tell you how very damn much I like this new story—I think it's the real break-through, or certainly look how the detail now moves, put into mouths & so forth. Well, by god.

Anyhow, if agreeable, I'd like to use it in this albatross I have hung from my neck, etc—I can't tell you just when, but I think it wd probably be #5—the spring issue. (We have a long story by Larry Eigner in #4, or else it could go there—anyhow bear with me, please, and I'll use it as soon as possible.)

Also—tho at the moment I'm damn well in no state to make it—I'd like to ask you about a few minor things, in it. i.e., places where for me (for literally a word or two) I think the thread slacks a little. But that would not involve anything, either way—i.e., do what you think of course, and don't feel it constitutes any actual objection. Or worry about it, or whatever. I'm sorry not to be able to make it this letter, but I'm too damn fuzzy and rushed etc to make any sense. But I'll write again, very soon, and note these things for you,—and again, no matter. Ok.

Well, very great. People in it come thru—however dull that sounds—very well, very widely—a real business. I also like very much the kind of shrink that is effected, in them—or, as it begins, these more or less substantial types in the truck, to the final whimpering. It is very damn sad—and your study of it all, very acute. I think Rosemary, too, is as sharp a 'character' business as I've seen in some time.

Too, it was wonderful to hear you speak of the pleasure of writing it—it ought to be, god knows it should *have been*. All that feeling comes so much into questions of rhythm, of tone, and all of it—even to the 'chances' one can't of course take, feeling 'willed' or niggardly or 'with a purpose,' etc. Please let me see anything else you write—it is very kind of you to bother. Well, you know. I'm very damn happy to get this one.

All love,
Bob

Have you read Ford Maddox Ford, i.e., I just was—particularly the first of the Tietjens series, *Some Do Not*. His handling of sequence, also of a lot of people in a room, etc., very damn good, at times. I am also very damn moved by the way he handles the relation between this Miss Wannop & Tietjens. If they have copies there (and if you haven't read it), might be interesting?

I don't think I touched ground for at least a couple days after reading his letter. I read it over and over, just to be sure. I had finally begun, I had finally written a story. After that, I went on to work with abandon and increased energy and wrote a half dozen or so additional stories in rapid succession, working consistently up to the end of the 1954 winter term and into a winter break spent in New York City. And of course, given Creeley's suggestion, I read not only Ford's *Some Do Not* but all of Ford's books in the college library.

But before the winter break, there was the matter of the Crosby exhibit. During her visit, Caresse had offered to put on at the school an exhibit of a batch of correspondence she and her late husband had received back in the 1920s and 1930s from writers such as Ezra Pound, D. H. Lawrence, Hart Crane, and Crane's and Lawrence's friend, poet Slater Brown, as well as Black Sun-published books of theirs and other writers, including that first printing of Crane's *The Bridge* in 1930. (Caresse, continuing the press on her own, later published Olson's first book of poems, *y & x*, in 1948, pamphlet copies of which were available in Carroll's store, one of which I eagerly purchased and read and reread.) It was perhaps her contribution to help bring some attention to the college—and maybe, as a result, a few much-needed students.

Hart Crane was not a particular favorite of Olson's. His poetry was simply not discussed at length or in depth by Charles in any of his classes, and if it was mentioned at all it was with an air of impatient dismissal. On one occasion, when a student mentioned *The Bridge*, Charles replied with a sympathetic grimace and wave of his hand, with words to the effect that "it didn't go far enough," that it was "a failed attempt," "trapped in description, like poor Keats," "trapped" in the old metrics. But he did, grudgingly, give Crane respect for at least trying as hard as he did, particularly in the more free-form segments of *The Bridge*. In a viciously merry attack on Slater Brown, Olson did a little impromptu performance in class one night, mockingly imitating bathetic and self-pitying tears Crane was supposed to have sopped over some of his letters to Brown, trying to win him back from another man. (In light of Crane's gargantuan drinking bouts, they might well have been the tears of a sick alcoholic.) "O please come back, Slater—*Puh*-lease come back!" Charles, ever the ham, moaned melodramatically, getting us all laughing, he was such a good comedic performer.

When the several letters from Crane to Brown in the Crosby collection were put up in the exhibit on the walls down in the now-Weaving Room in the Studies basement (where weaver Tony Landreau plied his craft), by painting teacher Joe Fiore, who, as in everything he did, was fussily nervous that they be placed just so, I checked for tell-tale tear stains on the letters. Finding none, I decided Charles' little spontaneous mimicry, with its suggestion of scornful homophobia, was just another of his erroneous tangents that concealed rather than revealed his true feelings about Crane's and Brown's relationship—and perhaps a few uneasy fears of his own, given his powerful androgynous nature.

Because of Olson's low opinion of him, as with many other

writers Olson consigned to oblivion, Crane was a kind of underground secret guide for some of us, ironically, in that underground of undergrounds, Black Mountain. Later, during the winter break of 1954-1955 while staying at composer Ben Weber's basement apartment on West 11th Street in New York City, I read Crane's selected letters and Philip Horton's biography that had just come out (bringing Crane more publicly out of the closet with it). Immediately empathetic with Crane, marveling at his openness, in his life at least, given his time in the 1920s, and starved as I was for any queer information and experience, I avidly devoured both books with a need to feed my own hungry and ignorant queer self, however indirectly and with the necessity of reading between the lines—the opacity of which, in Crane's poems, hid more than they revealed. (Talk about using language tortuously, to conceal and, with hope perhaps, stealthily to reveal; a mark of most terrorized homosexual writers into the 1960s.)

Once, during that winter break from Black Mountain, when I was walking down First Avenue on the Lower East Side trying to find the tenement where poet Maxwell Bodenheim and his third wife had been recently murdered, surprisingly, by chance, both also in the city on the break, I spotted Jorge Fick standing in the doorway of a tenement not far from the Bodenheim apartment, reading aloud poems by Crane to Pat Nelson. They did not see me, and I stood at a distance and listened to Jorge reading the lines in that emphatic way of his and with boyish enthusiasm and gesticulations to the faintly amused Pat, her seductively cool and intelligent eyes gazing into his.

What encouraged this secret admiration for Crane, in spite of Olson, and besides my own mystical wonder let loose and reverberating in Crane's lines, was the moving poem by Creeley, "Hart Crane (2)," in editor Cid Corman's *Origin* II, as reaffirmation of my own, and I expect others', feelings about Crane and his work. (It was probably Creeley's poem that set off the discussion on Crane in Olson's class that night.)

So when Joe Fiore got Caresse Crosby's loan exhibition mounted down in the bottom of the Studies Building, I stood in awe before the few samples of actual letters of Hart Crane, disappointed they were typed and not in his own hand. But even in scrutinizing the typeface, and the boldly inked signature "Hart" on each letter, I had that sense of youthful amazement of closeness, if only in the artifacts, to a writer very close to my own identity, if not my own direction, who had the power, in shamanic words I rarely comprehended, yet was stirred by in some preconscious primal place at the origin of words, to shake language up from the deeps of the unconscious. I searched in vain for overt mention of men-loving-men in those words, in those opaque poems that were yet luminous with intoxicating language holding a darkness—"He had a kind and northern face"—and though often disappointed, I was still excited and deeply moved by them, by their shimmering suggestiveness, and had to settle for that.

With Olson there was of course no sense mentioning any of this, fearful as I was of his disfavor, and, inarticulate as I was then for the most part, I kept mum. When Olson's vastly discursive mind closed, it closed with a snap, and better forget it. There were no half measures with Charles, he had his own visions to pursue. Best to pursue one's own course and inclinations thereafter, even if in secret, as Jorge did, as I and others did, with Crane and other banished writers, much to Olson's displeasure if he got wind of it.

At Olson's suggestion, hoping yet again to drum up some publicity for the college, and maybe a few prospective students, Mary Fiore wrote up an announcement of the Crosby display, and invited me to drive with her in the Jeep stationwagon into Asheville one afternoon to the *Citizen* offices to put the announcement in the paper. We were surprised when people from all over the state showed up as a result, people who were just as surprised that there would be such a display of letters and books at such a small, out-of-the-way college in the far western hills of North Carolina. And they seemed surprised at the place itself, that, just like my own initial reaction, it didn't look like a "real" college, its rundownness aside, which probably explained why Olson's hopes of attracting some new students via the exhibit didn't pan out.

When the exhibit was over, there was some indecision and much palaver about who would return Caresse's archives, and how. I'm not sure exactly why, but the indecision dragged on for weeks (*nothing* was ever easy at Black Mountain College), and finally Olson delegated Joe Fiore to do it. Joe, who like several others, had become increasingly nervous about having this treasure as the responsibility of the school, in case of fire (memories of the 1952 forest fire and the burning of Roadside evidently still fresh in his mind), or flood—the latter not an impossibility at rainy Black Mountain—was relieved to get it all into the stout trunk it had arrived in and shipped back, heavily insured, to Caresse in Washington.

Tom Field, Terence Burns and I hosted Thanksgiving dinner at Meadows Inn in 1954, inviting everyone in the community, which had shrunk so much by that time we all fit fairly comfortably in the lobby, where the dinner, much of it prepared by good cook Tom, with others contributing pre-arranged dishes, was served at tables and chairs borrowed from everywhere. While Terence was up at the farm tending to what remained of the cattle, Tom and I had cleaned and scrubbed and polished our first floor rooms. We even washed the windows and had tactfully left the door to Terence's room firmly shut because of its barnyard odor. I'd gathered plenty of wood for the great fieldstone fireplace which I kept roaring with logs, and there was plenty of food, from several turkeys (the gut-gurgling aromas of the ones Tom was roasting had been permeating the house for hours since dawn), to creamed onions and home-baked pies and, of course, plenty of red wine.

The talk before dinner was typically outspoken and wide-ranging Black Mountain talk: The usually blunt-spoken Wolpe was even more so after a glass or two, as I overheard him snorting heavily in an even looser German accent to a group by the hors d'oeuvres table in the corner, while I stoked up the fire: "I very much *like* hot chili peppers, yes? But in the *mawn*ing they burn my asshole," and vigorously fanned aside the plate of chilis Tom, a favorite spicy delicacy of his own, was holding out to him, while Hilda, always indulgingly amused by Stefan's frank talk, grinned hummingly.

So hidden in myself, I always admired Wolpe's openness, especially his ability to tell unflattering stories about himself, all with relishing good humor. One story he told another group of us, including wife Hilda, at our Thanksgiving, was about how he, as a young, impoverished but dandified student in 1920s Berlin, had been sleeping with a number of women—some of them smitten and sympathetic prostitutes at no charge—all at the same time without any one of them knowing it. When by chance several of the women who knew each other got together and discovered this, they each took turns shitting in a shoebox, wrapped and tied it up nicely with ribbon to look like a gift, and placed it outside the door of his shabby room in a poor quarter of the city.

Wolpe of course, seeing such a pretty package, was surprised, and pleased, even more surprised and not so pleased when he tore off the wrappings and saw, and smelled, what was inside, including a note signed by all the women. He laughed heartily as he told us this story on himself, of how instantly he got the message, the deep folds of his hangdog face spreading in the creasiest of grins, the fleshy, apple-red cheeks of Hilda, who once more seemed amused at just about everything her Stefan said, again grinning good-naturedly along with him.

Not long after I joined them in the corner, somehow the curious combination, or perhaps not so curious, at radically juxtaposing Black Mountain, of Marlene Dietrich and Jean Cocteau came up, and Stefan exclaimed vehemently, "They are *bugs* that should be *stepped* on!" Tom and I were aghast, since we loved listening over and over again to Dietrich's smoky, husky voice on scratchy 78s campily singing "Falling in Love Again" and "See What the Boys in the Backroom Will Have."

I wasn't quite sure what Wolpe meant by that; I didn't care too much about Cocteau being "stepped on"—he never "fed" me, to again use Charles' word, who, as far as I recall, he never fed either. But I, like a lot of queers of the day, had a camp affection for Marlene—hadn't she been a gender-bender wearing that tuxedo in the cabaret scene in *Morocco* (which I'd only read about since the film was made in the year of my birth, 1932), and then coolly, smilingly kissing the lovely woman at a table full on the mouth, slyly admitting for all to see that rumors of her lesbianism, at least over the gayvine, were not just rumors? Didn't we also have a camp affection for her total fabrication— like a totally artificial work of art—perhaps maybe more Josef Von Sternberg's, her director's, creation in ultimate control, but a work of art, still? Come to think of it, perhaps the same could be said of Cocteau, except he was his own total fabrication. (Perhaps we all are.) Maybe it was their complete artificiality Wolpe detested, and perhaps his perceived "decadence" of that *and* the queer in each.

I moved out to the kitchen to see if Tom needed help, and came upon Charles, staying close to the food, no doubt, talking to Wes and a few others, and to Tom, who was busy basting the turkeys in the Dutch ovens sitting atop the Coleman stove. When Charles spotted me coming in the door, he called out, "I was just talking about your new stories, Mike, and how each word is sharp, is like cutting words out of metal with shears," and he held up a hand, made scissor-snipping motions with his fingers.

I blushed redder than the goblet of wine in my hand (goblets loaned to us for the occasion by Mary) and, as always with praise from Olson, felt a rush of intoxication higher than any alcohol could give.

After dinner, one side of the room was cleared, and several of us from Wes' theater class performed segments of plays we'd been working on in class, scenes from Pirandello's *Six Characters in Search of an Author*, for one. Then, to end on a lighter note, a number of us did the Pyramus and Thisbe playlet from Act V, i, in *A Midsummer Night's Dream*, in which I played Moonshine in barefeet and an abbreviated toga-like sheet—"This man, with lanthorn, dog, and bush of thorn"— said dog a stuffed toy borrowed from a grudging two-year-old Kate Olson, who along with same-aged David Huss, stood wide-eyed at the very front of the audience, taking in everything, Kate, I was certain, mainly to keep an eye on her scruffy stuffed pet. The room was so crowded, with people jammed together on chairs or sitting on the floor, and with little Kate and David standing so close, there was hardly room for me to lift and swing my lantern—an old rusty barn lantern from the farm—so I incorporated the two children into the humor of the piece. When I declaimed in a loud, corny voice (I must confess when I first read it in class, Wes had to point out the humor to me):

"This lanthorn doth the horned moon present;
Myself the man i' the moon do seem to be . . ."

as I swung high the lantern, I lifted my eyes with scathing, hammy disdain at the round-eyed ragamuffins practically standing on my bare toes. Everyone laughed, except the two children, Kate's eyes fast on her stuffed dog clutched in my arm.

After the play scenes, which everyone enjoyed immensely, especially Charles (nothing like a little wine to pump up the laughs and applause), several of us moved back to the kitchen.

I had just the day before reread "Maximus to himself" in the copy I'd bought from Jonathan Williams, and had been so moved by it again, because it spoke to me most powerfully, particularly, "I stood estranged/from that which was most familiar . . .," I wanted to tell Charles. I rarely if ever had the confidence to tell him what his work meant to me as my deepening appreciation and understanding of it increased. But that Thanksgiving day, late in the afternoon and myself by now wine-brave, I found him leaning against the refrigerator (Tom, using some of his GI money, had replaced the old ice box with a used fridge) and went up to him and putting my hand lightly on his chest told him how much the poem meant to me, how "open" about himself he was in it.

He reared back, stiffened against the refrigerator door and, looking offended, drew himself up to his full height, glared down at me with a hard, haughty and uncomprehending look. I pulled back, withdrawing my hand, puzzled, realizing I'd made a mistake, had perhaps been too familiar. (Charles would touch you lightly, deftly, affectionately, but you got the feeling he was uncomfortable being touched.) He then loudly insisted, annoyed, more to Wes Huss who'd just come up, than to me, "Maximus is *not* me—is not about *me*—Why would people take that to be me?"—put out, probably both by my remark and the forwardness of my light caress.

And I backed off, slunk away, feeling foolish, confused, stupid, really—and that after his earlier praises!—the only sour note in an otherwise wonderful day, the last carefree, festive gathering at the college that I remember, where everyone felt high-spirited and congenial. There were other get-togethers, but as the situation at Black Mountain got grimmer, there was a forced, increasingly harsh and ugly edge to each of them. Thanksgiving 1954 was the last gathering with the sense of the old convivial, self-sustaining Black Mountain spirit, where we made magic out of next to nothing.

So, one more time, in December 1954, the faculty decided to close the college for the winter to save on coal and utilities. Again, Olson's notion, borrowed from the program at Antioch College, that we Black Mountain students were "at work in the field," a euphemism actually, since the finances of the school were now so depleted and hopes for replenishing them so dim, it was imperative the school close for several of the harshest months to save what little money was left, and with hopes, too, the students who could would return with a little cash, Olson's idea to attract new students to the college via the new *Black Mountain Review*, including a few other desperate cash-raising schemes, simply not working.

Also, Huss and Olson informed us, returning students would be expected to pay at least a few hundred dollars for tuition in the next term, and now that the work scholarships were gone, that continued to present another real hardship for me. When I voiced my concerns to Wes, he said there was such a thing as the Bovingdon Fund I might be able to borrow from at low interest, which I wouldn't have to pay back until a year or so after I graduated. He'd give details later. I felt somewhat relieved hearing that, but wondered what kind of job I could get once I left Black Mountain that would enable me to pay all that money back.

I'd kept in touch with Ben Weber through correspondence, and when I told him I'd be coming to the city again that December and mentioned I didn't have a place to stay (Mary Ann and Seymour were now married and had moved uptown to a brownstone apartment on 122nd Street), Ben generously offered to let me share his bed until I found a job and could get a place of my own. I was a bit reluctant, knowing Ben's feelings for me, and was concerned that that might cause complications, but since I was desperate to have temporary shelter of any kind, I wrote back thanking him and told him the approximate date he could expect me.

So once again, in a less darker mood than last time, with thoughts of Merrill receding from my consciousness, but, as with my last trip to New York City, with barely a few bucks in my pockets, I packed my battered suitcase (the very old one from my mother, which I had fortunately kept, since the new one she sent me was stolen in Chattanooga), bid Tom and everyone goodbye the day before, and at dawn next day walked once more past the Gatehouse, feeling a slight rush of fear at leaving our sanctuary, fear mingled with excitement of the unknown possibilities of being on the road again and wondering what lay ahead for me this time in Manhattan. I marched down the mountain along the county road in the direction of the main highway east to Raleigh, where I'd hook up with U. S. 1 to hitchhike again the long trip north.

One night over dinner shortly after I arrived at 230 West 11th Street, Ben, grinning with flushed shy pride, told me he'd won a Prix de Rome for one of his compositions and would be flying to Italy for a week or two. He hadn't wanted to tell me in his letter, wanting the pleasure of telling me when he saw me, but said the timing of my trip north worked out fine: He felt better having someone stay in his apartment while he was gone (there'd been a recent rash of break-ins on the block), and in the meantime I could look for a job and a place of my own.

Ben was very kind to me and, as I've noted, taught me a lot about music, especially contemporary music, beyond what I'd learned at Black Mountain from Wolpe and Harrison. He also introduced me to a lot of his friends in music, including Ned Rorem. Drinking beer with him was fine, and I certainly enjoyed his cooking, mostly European dishes I'd never eaten before. But I wasn't attracted to him physically, and never gave him any encouragement or opportunity along those lines. Certainly he must have sensed this, because usually after a few of his tall glasses of beer (he'd stopped showing me his porn), a nasty, critical edge would come into his voice, and sometimes, often before his friends, he would say some cutting thing, especially about Black Mountain, including about Olson, since I talked a lot about the college and Charles. Ben seemed to be reacting in a kind of blind jealousy, since the only things he knew about the place, or indeed about Olson at that time, were what he heard me or Mary Ann or Seymour say. Mary Ann, who was now studying mime and taking a film course at Columbia, and who took me, for old time's sake, to see Bunuel and Dali's *Un Chien Andalou* and Eisenstein's *The Battleship Potemkin* at a tiny art movie house near Times Square that also showed "commie" flicks, perhaps was another cause for Ben's jealousy, since his beloved Seymour had not only met her at Black Mountain but had now gone on and married her.

What I needed, as a green, queer unemployed 22-year-old in Manhattan, was looking after, and Ben filled a part of that need, for which I was grateful. But I was lonely too, and his friendship and apartment, his feeding and fussing over me, at least in the beginning, was a safe haven as opposed to the gay bars I had haunted on weekends my last trip to the Village.

With Ben gone, flying off to Rome to receive his prize in music, more nervous over his first flight to Europe than over the ceremony itself, I felt a drop in tension and loved having his apartment completely to myself. Since it was close to Christmas, and with letters from my mother asking if I were going to visit for the holidays, I decided to try to mend a few fences and hitchhike down to Gloucester County, New Jersey, to see my family, who I hadn't seen for a long time. I rode the A train up to the George Washington Bridge early on a freezing Christmas Eve morning and, as I started walking across the bridge, I spotted in a steel-riveted alcove at the base of the south cable an old drunk apparently frozen to death, he was so purple and stiff when I touched him, empty pint wine bottles scattered around him. "Nothing can be done now," I thought, "They'll find him soon enough," and, with a long hike ahead of me, I hurried on my way, heading for the entrance to the New Jersey Turnpike on the other side of the bridge. Shaken by the sight of the dead man, I still stored away in my mind, for future jotting down in the notebook I always carried in my hip pocket, when my fingers were less numb, all the vivid details, the cold, dispassionate eye of the writer beginning to sharpen.

It took me most of the day, getting short hops from exit to exit, to finally arrive at Exit 3, where I got off to head for my hometown of National Park a few miles distant. As I was hurrying along in the now-darkness along the winding exit ramp of the Turnpike, I encountered a car full of drunken servicemen traveling up from their base in the South, on leave to spend the holidays home. One of them was a marine with a bandaged hand who was more drunk than the others and who lived, as it turned out, in my hometown, and who the driver of the car, a young soldier, sick of him, was trying to dump on me. As earlier, with the dead wino on the bridge, I took notes in my head of all the vivid details of that experience for future use, including, as I tried to call the marine's father from a drugstore, the violent fight his son got into out front with three soldiers who happened along.

With the help of a few holiday shots of Carstair's and a few quarts of Schmidt's of Philadelphia, my father and I were superficially amiable enough—after his limp handshake, his only comment being, "Whyn't you get a haircut?" I could see through the warm alcoholic haze that the seductions of familiarity and "safety" of home, however spurious, topped with that most cloyingly sentimental holiday of the year, including midnight mass in the little white church I'd served in as an altar boy, had a strong pull on me yet, no matter how, like Maximus, I was becoming "estranged/from that which was most familiar. . ." Still, the pull of Black Mountain, and now

New York, was even stronger, the ruthless pull of what I had to be about, so it was with some relief, using as my excuse the urgent need to find a job immediately, I got back on the highway and hitchhiked north to Manhattan early in the morning after Christmas.

When I got back to 230 West 11th, I sat that night on one of the wooden benches at the stout table in Ben's kitchen overlooking St. John's-in-the-Village garden. Experimenting with a glass or two of the fine wine in Ben's wine closet (aping Faulkner's suggested writing ritual of "a finger or two of Bourbon" to stimulate the imagination, which I never repeated, finding alcohol dulled rather than enhanced it), I began writing about my chance meeting with the marine, continuing to heed, after the success of "The Truck," Charles' advice to "write what you know," and worked on the first draft of the short story titled, aptly enough, "Exit 3," making use of Ben's portable typewriter which he said I could use in his absence.

With Ben away and the apartment to myself, I worked on the story steadily through New Year's eve, during the days making the rounds of the employment agencies in midtown. As it turned out, Merrill Gillespie, still at his loft down on Rivington Street, was at loose ends with his Herb again in Houston, attending to family business. I tried to keep my distance but when Merrill found out I was staying at Ben's, I'd give in and we'd occasionally have supper at the Fedora on West 4th Street, a speakeasy in the 1920s, or see an "art" movie like the comedy *Jour de Fête d'Henriette* ("art" perhaps because it was in French). To my surprise, he showed up the night of December 31st at Ben's with a pint of whiskey and invited me to see 1955 in at Times Square with him. I stood frozen in the doorway, dubious of starting up again something I'd been hoping was pretty much dead. But it wasn't. My brief visit home had charged me not only with the need to reassert myself as a writer and Black Mountaineer rebel, but as Merrill stood smiling before me in all his sharply remembered erotic appeal, to reassert myself as a queer as well.

Neither of us had ever spent New Year's Eve in Times Square before, and in those days the crowds were enormous, hundreds of thousands, mostly paper-hatted, horn-blowing drunks, less controlled by the police and crowd barriers than they are today. Even after we'd finished most of the whiskey, the pressure and manic energy of the crowd was so frightening that we decided to try to escape to a side street, away from the main crush, but I had never before had the terrifying sensation of being swept up in a human riptide, of being carried powerfully along, will-lessly, uncontrollably, by a drunken, howling mob. Merrill and I clung to each other frantically, I was afraid if we fell we'd be trampled underfoot and, with both of us feeling tipsy after swigging at our pint, there was a real possibility of that. Somehow, we managed to fight our way into one of the less crowded streets off Times Square and retreated down to Bryant Park behind the Fifth Avenue Library (a big cruising area in those days), where we finished off the whiskey on a park bench and heard the horns and sirens and occasional shotgun blasts all around us in the distance welcoming in the new year.

Back in Ben's apartment in the early morning hours of that new year came another new experience for me. In Ben's big bed, with enough whiskey in me, and enough in Merrill, I suspect, to embolden him, Merrill calmed me enough to convince me to relax and for the first time, did what he'd always wanted to do at Black Mountain, a pleasure, after the first sharp pain, occurring on Ben's own bed, a pleasure with a twinge of guilt, along with the ingrained Catholic one, a pleasure Ben himself would have wanted with me, and one which, good at secrets, I would make sure he never knew about.

The other best gift I received that holiday was Creeley's *A Snarling Garden of Verses*, a wickedly funny and bitterly satirical booklet of poems, with appropriate pitch-black cover,

Creeley had had printed himself in Mallorca for the season and sent to friends, a salutary charge amidst all the sickly sentimentality of Christmas.

1955

So 1955 was truly a new year, an old fear, the last virginity, vanquished; a new story begun; and Creeley's chapbook; not to mention a possibility of a new job and a place of my own to live.

On Ben's return from Rome, he was quietly jubilant at the recognition he'd received. However, the tension between us soon made it impossible for me to continue living with him. Because he had been so kind to me, one night in bed I gave into him, but, after Merrill, I realized too late I'd oughtn't to have given Ben the chance in the first place, offering myself as some kind of payment (different from my arrangement with Woody, where no reciprocation on my part was expected), and when he reached for me thereafter in bed, I turned away, not without a twinge of empathy, remembering Merrill's cold shoulders at Black Mountain. Finally, one morning when I innocently surprised him masturbating in the bathroom, he was so furious, he shouted, "I want you out of here!" I could hardly blame him.

To his credit, he tried to get me various jobs so I could afford to move out on my own, one a part-time position reading to a wealthy old woman on Waverly Place who was losing her eyesight and who was a friend of Carson McCullers: "Poor thing, she was here visiting only last week, so young and so lame all down her left side from her stroke," the old woman sighed. I made a sympathetic murmur, amazed that I was sitting, however anxiously, for my reading job interview, in the same room McCullers had been in only a short time before, her meaning and presence as a writer was so strong in me, despite Olson's displeasure. To add to my uncertainties, the old woman had invited as well a young buttoned-down youth, a protégé it appeared, obviously, crisply gay, to look me over that afternoon of my "tryout." I could see in his cold, sharply appraising eyes that I wouldn't be getting the job I so desperately needed.

Finally, after making the rounds of the uptown agencies, where I was warned by an interviewer at one not to reveal I lived in Greenwich Village, it had such a "sinful" reputation for artistic and, more damningly, sexual wildness, mainly of the queer variety, I finally landed a job, amazingly, for a scruffy-haired writer from radical "commie-homo" Black Mountain of all things, at the *most* ultra conservative button-down outfit going at that time, IBM World Trade Corporation (part of *the* IBM), on First Avenue across from the United Nations. As a clerk-typist I'd be making the then-magnificent sum of $60 a week, $12 a week more than I had made at Prentice-Hall the winter before. I figured I'd be able to save even more than on my old job in the mailroom, so felt a little easier about my being able to return to Black Mountain. (At IBM World Trade, in the event my temporary job turned into a permanent one, I lied and told personnel what they wanted to hear: that I planned a life-long career with IBM, even though I knew I'd be high-tailing it back to Swannanoa Valley in early March.) The man who hired me, John Connolly, was a former editor at the old Brooklyn *Daily Eagle*, where Walt Whitman had also worked over a century before. Connolly was the kindest, most patient boss who, I later learned from the office gossip, was a recovering alcoholic. He was pretty much on a quiet-voiced, even keel, no matter what the problem, no matter what the mistakes I made learning the job—many of which were on the hair-trigger keys of the then still-new, just-recently marketed outsized IBM electric typewriter I had to work on for the first time. I was also the main fact checker and often called the Fifth Avenue Library for information, the most interesting part of the job. Connolly was always good-humored and calmingly serene in dealing with me, perhaps sensing in my nervous fear the future fellow drunk I eventually became. Drinking was forbidden during working hours at IBM and at its corporate "family" functions, and Connolly it appears, as part of company policy, had been given a second chance when he'd made up his mind to throw in the towel and get sober. (In those days, nobody was fired at IBM;

an employee in trouble was simply demoted and demoted again until he or she got the message.)

I worked in the news/public relations department which put out slick promotional in-house magazines and brochures (on expensive glossy pebbled paper) for IBM's burgeoning overseas operations, especially in post-war Europe, and so was surrounded by writers and artists (most of them frustrated novelists and painters), most of them, for such an international outfit, bi- and even tri-lingual, a bright, wittily glib and sophisticated bunch for the most part, so that my oddities of dress and manner were more likely to be overlooked. So, there I was, thrust into the rudely contrasting world, compared to Black Mountain, of business and the punching of time clocks, and the necessity of quickly scrounging up a suit and tie. Fortunately, Henry L. Wood, or Woody, who I contacted early on when I'd recently arrived in New York again, invited me over to his Lafayette Street apartment in Brooklyn and, learning of my clothing dilemma, gave me two of his old expensive tweed suits, one blue and one brown, both still in good shape despite the fact they'd been in mothballs since the 1930s. And, to add to the stylistic incongruity, he threw in two tab collar shirts with collar buttons, also from the 30s, that were still, inexplicably, in their original Macy's wrappings, for some reason never having been worn by Woody, who, I was learning, despite his small apartment, apparently never threw anything out. Amidst the IBM male uniform of dark conservative suit and tie and white dress shirt (women employees were expected to wear modest up-to-the-neck, below-the-knee dresses), not to mention my long ragged hair in contrast to the preferred IBM butch cut, curiously no one commented on my anachronistically outmoded style of dress or asked where I'd managed to dig up such sartorial relics. I expect the rest of the department, working as writers and artists for hire, and not held to quite the same dress standards as other departments (although most dressed within the IBM guidelines) felt themselves too sophisticated to mention my curious, mothball-smelling garb. Of course John Connolly would never have commented on it, apparently accepting everyone for who they were as they were.

One morning, though, I sensed someone peering over the wall of filing cabinets blocking off our little department at the rear from the rest of the huge floor, with its precise rows of desks at which sat men mostly in their precise IBM uniforms. It turned out to be Alan Watson, the founder's youngest son, who I recognized from his photos in the department's overseas magazines and who had been put in charge of IBM World Trade Corporation (and who, despite the strict teetotaling policies of his father, IBM founder Thomas Watson, Sr., would, like boss John Connolly, indeed as I did some years later, have trouble with booze). He often appeared on the floor unannounced, darting about as if always on some perilous errand and, no doubt seeing me for the first time as he peered over the cabinets, eyeing my curious dress and unshorn locks (I was waiting for my first paycheck so I could afford to get a haircut), asked John Connolly, *sotto voce*, who I was. My heart started to race, thinking the game was up, that I'd be fired on the spot for being out of uniform, *and* exposed as a student from commie/homo Black Mountain College, and not IBM material at all; discovered to be lying in my teeth that I wanted to become a lifelong part of the great IBM empire, exposed for secretly mocking their drab, gray, floor-model computers, sneering to co-worker Marisa Traina from San Francisco, another secret sneerer, over forbidden Dubonnet cocktails at lunch at Ferdi's a few doors down First Avenue, that IBM computers (shrunk considerably from the room-sized UNIVAC model Glenn Lewis had shown me at Princeton a few years earlier and now shrunk even more to the desk-top size I'm at this moment typing on, year 2000) looked "exactly like the grimmest caskets of the dead." (A prophecy?)

But whatever Connolly replied in his modest, serene manner, Alan Watson nodded curtly, gave me one last piercing glance and hurried on his way, appearing not altogether certain but evidently his doubts quieted, as indeed were mine, my pulse gradually slowing.

A letter I wrote to Charles back at Black Mountain at the time, pretty much gives the flavor of what was going on:

[230 West 11th Street] Jan. 13, '55

Dear Charles,

I've been waiting to get settled enough so I can start working on Shakespeare again [my tutorial with Olson for my graduation project]. Things have been pretty hectic, getting a job and a room, etc., but now that I've got both [the latter in the same house as Ben's apartment] (tentative as it all is—the job's a temporary one with IBM, six weeks, with a possibility of its becoming "permanent" if there's an opening when the time's up, which I hope there is, at least, anything to keep me going til the end of March). I'll probably start working again, picking up with Richard II, as you suggested, and, if I can get through that, going on to Hamlet. I'm anxious to start work on Chaucer, but that'll have to wait til the spring when I get back to BMC and I'll be able to work directly with you. I don't know how it'll all shape up, but, as I've told you before, I'd like to graduate sometime in June and will try to work it in within that time. Started one story since I came here, but have somehow lost the grip and can't get into it as much as those stories I wrote this fall. All the discipline of those months went falooie as soon as I got here and began a big splurge of self-indulgence, which was pretty wonderful, except that I find it hard now to dig in again. It's so damned easy here to say to hell with it and go off to a movie or some bar, or maybe call up a friend, but the first month's novelty of that is wearing off, and I'm glad of it because I'm anxious to get back to work.

This job at IBM pays 60 a week. It's at their World Trade branch, across from the UN, and from where I sit there's a marvelous view of the East River and the UN Building itself. That's about the most wonderful thing about it. I feel like I'm in training for a junior exec. job what with a big desk and telephone and electric typewriter all to myself. Fortunately I don't have a THINK sign on my desk, like everybody else. It's very peculiar, I don't understand it. One wise guy has a sign REFLEXIONE propped in front of him and it's a wonder somebody hasn't 'spoken' to him yet. They take all that stuff so dread serious.

The department I'm in . . . is their news dep't., which also handles a little of their advertising. The manager and I get along pretty well and I think he's grooming me for a writing spot on the paper, The IBM World Trade News (which is a very neatly printed and unimaginative affair) because word's in the air he's about ready to can one of two certain writers, because one, a very young, pretty italian girl, who "dabbles in poetry," comes in late too much, while the other young man from Holland, who's been here 3 years and bummed his way from coast to coast, working several months here and there on several newspapers, isn't very enthusiastic about the IBM school, in which all employees can take numerous and various courses FREE, and on which enrollment rests *all* employees chances for raises and promotion. I don't know which one of those two it'll be; neither one much cares because their [sic] both bored to death with the dull routine of the respectable stuff they have to write; most often the same story over and over with different names added each time, and from what I've heard them say of the screening they went thru to get the job, it sounds like you'd have to be Dostoevsky himself to come up to IBM's standards. This dutch guy is terrific—life just pops out of his eyes, and he's so quick in his movements, his face is so mobile and alive, there's something of the sea about him. I don't know what, but in a crazy way he makes me think of the ocean. He is very restless and in everything he does there's a wonderful explosion of energy, and to see him sitting at a typewriter, hunched over it like he was ready to eat it up and his eyes bulging that way, and punching the keys with such force (two finger method, and a pencil clenched in one hand, to boot) well, it's hard to believe that he's merely smacking out dry stories on how many typewriters were sold, say, in Paris, and what color, and who sold them—or any of the dull stuff that goes into that paper. I've gotten to know him very well, and he tells me that he wrote stories when in Holland, wrote them in Dutch, but since he's been here he hasn't been able to do much. This gal, the pretty italian one, she lived in Mallorjca

[sic] once, was crazy about it, and is fascinated with the idea of BMC, of which I've been telling her plenty. Maybe the three of us'll come back together. It would certainly be our gain, and I don't think IBM would be too unhappy. Already they're feeling me out to see if I'm regimentable. Up to a point, yes, but they better watch out.

I've been hearing several nasty cracks about you from writers who're "in the know." I forget their names, but most of them (Well, there're maybe three) put you down as a "stutterer," with "infantile talent," and never quite capable of expressing anything "coherently." One guy said you have "no logic in your imagination," like Skeats and Kelly had, he said; stuff like that. It's really awful and I hate to be put in a spot like that, since I tell them BMC, when they ask and up pops your name and then follows the above quotes—and I really don't think I should be put in a position [in] which I have to defend someone who is close to me, because it doesn't feel right. I have a hard time handling these situations, I usually try to get at what the guy means, but he just goes on and on, the same way, and I get pretty mad and say something sharp, then there's a deadly silence and everybody looks at me askance as tho I said 'nigger' or 'kike' or something—I guess really I'm supposed to agree with these guys, as the gentlemanly thing or something, know what "camp" they are beforehand, or just what the tastes are this season, I don't know. I just know they make me very angry. Everything is dismissed so quickly, and rudely, too. I don't want to get onto harangue. It's just that I don't see how they enjoy anything, they all go around disapproving so much.

My hand's getting cramped. Forgive this pencil, I know you hate by hand stuff, but I'm fresh out of a typewriter since I parted company with Ben, and this is the best I can do since I left my ballpoint at the office.

Write to me, and say hello to Connie and Kate – Love, Mike

Fortunately, as noted in my letter to Charles, just after I got the IBM job, one of the rooms became available at the top of the wide, long stairs on the second floor at 230 West 11th, and Ben quickly arranged with the super and his wife, a grizzled old pair Ben told me were addicted to cheap, homemade booze they fermented in their basement apartment, for me to move into it at $7 a week. It wasn't much wider than a telephone booth and not much longer than a telephone booth on end; hence, it had only room for a narrow cot-like bed jammed beside a small, butt-scarred table that I could use for writing while sitting on the bed, my long legs scrunched beneath the table. There was also a tiny closet alcove hidden by a dreary curtain, and that was about it, except, since the once-spacious rooms of the upper floors of the one-time private house had been long ago carved up into these smaller, similar-sized cubicles—I expect, to maximize profits for the landlord, i.e., St. John's-in-the-Village Church—the ceiling of my miniscule room was quite high and there was even one large six-over-six pane window crammed between the narrow walls that overlooked the huge magnificence of St. John's formal gardens, the same gardens that could be seen from Ben's kitchen windows directly below. The bath was across the hall (I never did find out how many of the other tenants on that floor shared it). As soon as I moved in, I sat on the bed, savoring the privacy, free of Ben's sharp and angry tongue, his dark moods, his hurt, sullen frowns, because I couldn't find it in my heart to sleep with him, to love him as he wanted me to, in his deeply possessive, romantic way, a hunger so deep it frightened me.

Romance, however, came from another more unlikely but no less equally frightening direction. Jack, the journalist and would-be novelist from Holland that I wrote Charles about, had glossy, lush, wavy brown hair, a fierce handsomeness, a fierce hand grip too, as I discovered when I enticed him to attend a revival of *Camille* starring Greta Garbo at the 57th Street Playhouse near Carnegie Hall. We sat in the near-empty last row, Jack's heavy winter coat over our knees, and fumbling beneath it for my hand, he gripped it so tightly throughout the movie, my finger bones began to ache well before poor Greta, not a curl out of place, coughed her last.

A handsome figure indeed who, with his attentions and flatteries, his articulated intelligence and charm, quite turned my head. And frightened me too, that power in him, the steel-grip of his hand, in that fine body and those fierce, penetrating eyes, which bespoke an even fiercer desire and appetite that unsettled me even more. Attractive as he was, in the fire-blue intensity of those laser-like eyes, in those palpable energies, I felt choked, had such a fear of being smothered, that, much as I was flattered by his gaze, by his attentions, skittish as a highstrung horse, my impulse was to bolt.

One Saturday afternoon as I was coming out of West 11th Street from my room and entering Sheridan Square, bent on some errand, I was surprised to bump into Jack, who said he "just happened" to be in the neighborhood (afterwards, since he knew where I lived, having pumped me to find out, I wondered if the meeting had really been such an "accident"). As he talked on in his usual energetic and forceful yet silkenly charming way in his perfect, only slightly Dutch-accented English, his eyes were on me. I could read in them quite clearly the unspoken words that were really on his mind—that we could possibly, no, *should*, go back to my room, since Jack shared his uptown apartment with two other men from the Netherlands, who apparently didn't know of his private life. But I stood there staring at him, barely listening to his words, reading that other message with great clarity, baffled, conflicted, really, that a man so desirous and desirable could, in the intensity of that desire, be so intimidating as to kill my own passion for him. Again, I wanted to take off, and did, mumbling some excuse that I had to be somewhere important, although I really had nowhere that pressing to go, and could have invited him back to my place, nervous as I was at having sex there at any time, the space so cramped and the walls so thin (the only person I'd chanced it with was Merrill, soon after I moved in, after a night of barhopping when, both tipsy, we threw the mattress on the floor for a little more room).

I could see an edge of disappointment in those magnificent eyes, but only barely perceptible: Jack was a man too proud, too sure of himself, too certain to admit uncertainty, to own up to a turndown.

Hurrying away down Christopher Street, I felt relief that I had once again escaped.

"Escaped" from or to what was uncertain, except an unconscious urging that I had to avoid ensnarements, dispersions of energy, to focus on where I sensed I was heading. At that time I wrote another letter to Charles, a somewhat listless letter about earlier stories I'd been working on, but my main purpose was to probe him on "Exit 3," which I'd mailed to him earlier, this period a brief lull before I was hit with the full force of a fierce and unexpected storm.

February 2, 1955

Dear Charles,

Here is a rewrite of the "boredom" story, written in a slump of my own particular boredom so that, as it stands now, the thing leaves me with a feeling of having been slapped together. I lost the drift almost entirely and that made it hard to get back into the thing. If you'll recall, this is the story that has to do with Irvington and the roomful of students. I wanted very much to try to finish this story because it was one of those incompleted things that keep annoying the back of my head.

I'm not quite sure what I've done, it strikes me as being such a hodge-podge and I'm still pretty much close to it, so I would like to know what you have to say about it.

I've decided to call this story The Jest, not for any particular reason, except that the title struck me while rewriting the story, and since it appealed to me, I decided to use it. It seems to fit.

There is a new character, Finchley, who appears to be a counterpart or brother to Irvington. I tried to bring out the others as clearly as I could, but for some strange reason they were never as vividly defined, say, as those guys in The Truck. I couldn't *feel* these others as strongly as I did Wally and Muskrat, etc. Steve fascinates me more and more and I would like to do another story on the same kind of theme but with fresher characters and a different atmosphere and setting. In Steve there is a kind of aimlessness and ennui whose face is a frenzied perversity which haunts me. Not so much that I have revealed that here, except I think in a few spurts in the story, but that he is a character that I have grasped solidly in my mind and one that I would like to do more with.

I don't know exactly where I'm going or what I'm doing with this stuff, but right now I feel more comfortable to continue on as I have and that is, letting the characters talk and act for themselves as it comes along, without any preconceived notion on my part about the conversation and action. It's better for me that way - it sets a boundary, and yet, crazily enough, is fantastically limitless. I rarely ever know in writing a story what's coming up, what's going to happen next, and this is very pleasurable and exciting for me. It makes me feel wide-open.

Anyway, getting to do the thing this way has been a terrific opening for me and the only lament I have is that I should've dared to do it sooner.

Forgive this wretched carbon copy. The typewriter I've borrowed is pretty poor. I wish I could have done it on this electric one that I'm using at work while the big majah is off to visit the greek consulate and a few prominent turks at the embassy, la-de-dah. Anyway, I think the carbon copy [of "The Jest"] is readable and I hope you don't have too much trouble with it. Please let me hear from you as soon as you have time to write. I'd also like to hear what you have to say about Exit Three [sic]. I've read Richard II and will read it again, hope to have a paper to you soon.

Love, Mike

The "different atmosphere and setting" of "another story" was soon to be realized, a story that so seized me all else paled beside it.

I received the following reply from Olson to my February 2 letter:

February 10, 1955

BLACK MOUNTAIN COLLEGE   BLACK MOUNTAIN, N. C.

Mike: This is not an answer to your two, and mss. You will excuse me, but I am selling cattle, plows, property, etc., and it will soon be in hand, and I can get back to you, and porper [sic] work.

But this is to tell you officially that the turn has come, and that it is forward, again: that we will operate spring and summer quarters, and I wanted you to know, simply that you, Tom, Jerry, and Ed are our solids - solid core, and all that - around which we are buidling [sic], taking only students who are sharp and directed themselves, and expecting a strong summer group, if the spring thing shows no surprising additions yet.

OK.

How we are doing it, I damn well don't know. But we are, and it feels wonderful. The Appeal* was peanuts. And we haven't sold the down piece**. But somehow we are making it, and can clear forward.

Now I did specifically want to come to grips with your own financial picture. As you know there are no further scholarships. But we feel that you are both of yourself and technically able to have one of those Derek Bovington [sic]*** loans, for either or both quarters ahead, until you graduate. And so, whatever you don't have from your winter earnings (?) you and Wes should

* A letter from the College sent out to friends and relatives of students and faculty appealing for desperately needed funds. ** The lower half of the campus. *** The Derek Bovingdon Memorial Fund was named for an exceptional Black Mountain College student killed in WW 2.

arrange to make up from the Bovington Fund. (I assume you know something of it, yes?)

And keep at me on your things, and add new things. And I miss you, and
look forward to your return.

And if those two sidekicks at
IBM do want to come for the sring [sic], tell em for crhistsake [sic] to apply.
For I am stiff, this year: I will only admit (1) those who know what they want,
and fit what we can give *as we are*; and (2) they have to have 1/3 of $850 per
quarter. And we'd like em, for only with additional students beyond you piv-
ots will us guys have anything to eat! So spread the word. And spit in anybody's eye - especially those literary friends of yrn, who have now added Keats
and Shelley to Swindle and how many others I should rsemble! [sic]

Love, and quick,

[signed] Charles Olson,
for the lot of us

A damn nice letter
by the way
on the Appeal
from your Ma [Scrawled in Olson's hand at bottom]

As a footnote, as it turned out, my "two sidekicks at IBM"
showed no interest in actually attending Black Mountain, and
that was that. And as for Charles mentioning my mother, it was
a surprise to learn she'd been brought into a part of my life that
I kept so far from her.

It was in January in that claustrophobic closet of a room on
the second floor at 230 West 11th that I was soon so powerfully possessed by the energy of a story, that it consumed just
about all of my waking hours (and even my dreams) for weeks
to come, including my hours at IBM, where every spare
moment, including moments stolen from my work, I spent jotting down ideas and dialog and description for the narrative

growing in my pocket notebook. Then, since I've never been able to compose on a typewriter, I surreptitiously typed the notes up, between my job-related duties, on my IBM electric typewriter, the story so filled me with energy. I stayed locked in my room in the evenings after work and on weekends, scribbling away until late at night, spent the next few weeks working away on draft after draft by hand, since I had no typewriter of my own at 230, and couldn't get away with that much typing of it at work, as the story grew into recognizable shape.

When it was finally all written down, it only *seemed* finished, the possession by that narrative seized me for several years to come, its story running through me, the electricity of it a constantly circling cycle of energy. I may have brought the story to an *arbitrary* close—perhaps there are no endings, only pauses, rests, a beat maybe—but it was never "finished," never finished with me, at any rate—that luminescent energy of it running through me for a long time after.

So, when I saw the beginning coming round again, I knew it had come full circle, and also knew that what I finally needed now was a typewriter in my room to type it up in readable shape, since I couldn't risk and wouldn't have time anyway to type the full draft at work.

Still unable to afford to buy one or even rent one (I was saving all my extra money, as mentioned, so I could return to Black Mountain), and realizing it would be a bad idea to ask to borrow Ben's downstairs, I remembered Merrill had his old portable Remington down in his loft on Rivington Street, and, putting my pride in my pocket, I borrowed his machine to type up the first typescript drafts of what I finally decided to call "The Pipe" (which won out over my original title, "Mud").

When I finished typing it up in February 1955, I mailed it immediately to Olson, and waited impatiently for a response, still high on the writing of the piece. First thing in the door for days each evening after work, I eagerly checked the tenants' mail laid out every day on the big table in the lower hall by the super's wife, a rotund, clay-colored woman, almost always tipsy and always draped in a stained, loose bathrobe. On Saturday mornings, my day off, when the mail arrived, she'd holler your name up the stairs if you had anything, rarely climbing stairs if she didn't have to—or even "doing the things she had to" as a super's wife, according to Ben, who I still saw on occasion but avoided as much as possible.

As days went by, and then weeks, Charles, who was often so prompt in his responses, particularly to manuscripts, which he continued to ask for in his letters and to criticize like he was running a correspondence course whenever any of his writing students were away from Black Mountain (to keep in touch, to not "lose the gains"), remained silent, not a peep out of him, no letters from him appearing on the hall table. I put it off to his being more busy than I imagined, "selling cattle, plows, property, etc." But my exhilarated spirits were gradually dampened as time passed and no word came, finding it hard to accept that his silence meant the story wasn't even worth criticizing negatively. I rationalized that he was also undoubtedly squeezing in work of his own, always a fact, as he was seeing to the dismantling of the college's property (giving me the blues just to think about that alone), but it didn't help. He'd always found time for my work in the past. Then, too, could I have been misled by all that excitement in writing the story, had it been another false start, another false dawn? It was hard for me to accept that.

Meanwhile, I needed to get some questions answered regarding my future at the college and at that time wrote the following letter to Wes Huss:

Dear Wes,

If I were to return, say, for the spring term alone (or even perhaps including the summer) what would the deal be with this Bovington fund that

Charles has mentioned and suggested I write to you about? Since there are no longer any [work] scholarships I assume that I'll be expected to pay tuition. As things are shaping up with me here, that would be impossible. An encouraging note from Charles was that paying the 6% interest a year would be the minimum on the loan (tho I would, of course, try to pay back more than that each year) and I decided to write to you for details.

Now, about tuition, how much will I be expected to pay? And as for the amount of this, how could I borrow from the Bovington fund? I won't be able to save much from what I earn here, and what I do save will have to go toward food, etc., with no allowance of tuition. Thus, the necessity of this loan, if possible and agreeable.

Another obstacle to returning to Black Mt'n is saving enough for food & general keep alone. As it is I haven't been able to save anything. It means that I would have to save enough in the next 3-4 weeks to tide me thru a term or two.

A hundred bucks I found lasts four months (maybe a little less) ((at BMC,)) if you're careful and not too lush) Maybe I'll be able to swing it. I don't know—

In spite of my financial concerns, I still found time to tell Wes in the same letter:

I've been dying to see some Ibsen—just missed (thru lack of funds) A Doll's House which was playing here in Dec.—and am going to make it a point to see The Master Builder which is on at the Phoenix Theatre over on 2nd Ave. Mar. 11th a friend is taking me to the Cherry Lane to see Anouilh's Thieves Carnival which is supposed to be good. I don't really much care about seeing anything, except the Ibsen, and possibly some Shakespeare; if there's going to be anything around. I'm mad to see Lear! But I'm not holding my breath—mostly only the "Comedies" are presented—Merchant of V., etc.—and they somehow don't arouse me enough to want to go see them, although I suppose I should. Mostly I've been gorging myself on movies, but I'm getting kind of sick of that—

And coming down from my high of writing "The Pipe" and dejected from not hearing a word on it as yet from Charles, I added the following:

Other than that I haven't been doing anything except read and write and put [in] the abysmal 8 per at IBM, the latter of which puts me in a zombie state hard to shake off. The depression & weariness of the job makes the desire to read and write come in spurts, altho I've done plenty of both—3 stories and've read plenty of books—But there are plenty of miserable hours.

On and off, I've been trying to think of possible sketches for the theatre class but somehow my imagination won't work in that way and the few fragmenting ideas I've had have gotten bogged down in a kind of uninspired stiffness—mostly I guess because it's removed from story to the stage (acting it, etc.) and if I could only keep that out of mind I might be able to accomplish something—Just write straight dialogue like I would for a story and forgetting about the stage and actors—In short, Drama. If that's possible.

Since I'd now have to begin paying tuition, at least a few hundred dollars (despite my savings from my IBM job, still more than I could afford), and Wes' suggestion of a loan from the Bovingdon Fund was a way out, I was still concerned: How would I ever pay it back? That, plus not hearing anything from Charles on my story, I felt ready to chuck it all in, and wrote Olson telling him so. He responded:

The Black Mountain Review
Black Mountain, North Carolina

February 25/55

Mike: Yrs in, and me upset back that, you end para with "And besides that, the way things are going, I don't know whether I'll be getting back to the college or not".

What is this? Or at least, do let us

know when whatever it is is definite, if it should be, simply that,
like you'd know, or I may have sd, it's you Tom Ed and Jerry whom
we look to to form the hard center or something. And if you knocked
out, well… at least it wld not be so hard!

Not at all to press you. You know I figure men find their own
way, and I wldn't educate the way I do if I thought education was anything to die for! So this is only for information: that you let us
know anything definite, if you shldn't be returning, yes?

And I might add that you oughtn't, I think, to let the Bovington [sic] scare you. That is, after two years, interest at 6% is one way to
keep acknowledging it, so that for $36 a year, you cld, I shld think,
well

Ok. Just, that yr letter bowled me over. And I'd miss you. But
you do just what you damn well think is best for yrself
And keep the mss piling in. The 1st thing I get rid of trucks,
cows, inquiries, plumbing, tables, chairs, iceboxes, what what, I'll
get back to you   All yrs,
        [No signature]

Charles' letter was heartening on the Bovingdon loan, but
disheartening about keeping "the mss piling in," regarding his
inability to get to "The Pipe" because of the necessity for him
to be junk dealer of the goods remaining at Black Mountain,
just in order to keep him and the others—and the school—
coughing along a little longer. In the meantime, backtracking a
bit, shortly after I mailed the manuscript of "The Pipe" to
Olson, still exuberantly confident, heart still high, one bitter
cold night after work, story in hand, I took the subway down to
the Lower East Side to Merrill's loft (his lover, Herb, was still
back in Houston). In that huge space, the grimy bricks of which
Merrill and Herb had painted white, where the freezing wind

through the numerous broken windows (it had once been a factory loft) ballooned out the plastic sheeting Merrill had tacked over them (so that inside the loft was just about as cold as outside in the streets), sitting beside the cold glow of a Japanese lantern lamp with its bulbous white rice-paper shade, lamps which were popular then, particularly among Black Mountain expatriates "into Zen," and habitués, such as Merrill and Herb, of the Orientalia Bookstore a few blocks north, an Eastern-style lamp Merrill had squandered precious bucks on to smarten up the place a little, unrolling my story from my pocket and with steam coming out of my mouth in heated excitement, I started reading, stumbling and stuttering over the words, Merrill, with an attentive, quietly amused smile in his eyes (he still liked to be read to, to hear a story, just as during our evenings together at Black Mountain), was the first to hear the story read aloud.

I was so full of beans over it, at work I even babbled about it to Marisa Traina, the darkly pretty, carefully spoken, transplanted San Franciscan, who also yearned to be a writer, like several others in that department of hired hacks, and with whom I rebelliously continued to drink those Dubonnet cocktails she'd introduced me to at lunch at Ferdi's up the street, our time cards often showing red ink for lateness when we punched in after such forbidden lunches, boss John Connolly noting, I observed, but as always keeping his own counsel. Marisa insisted I let her read it, and when she finished, she handed me back the manuscript, saying, "Well, it's not exactly *Pas comme un étranger*," using the French for Morton Thompson's popular American novel of the day.

One of the secretaries, whose desk abutted our department, overheard me going on about "The Pipe" and asked if she could read it too. She was a woman who displayed a sisterly warmth and concern for me, in sophistication the complete opposite of Marisa. I was hesitant at first because she was a devout Catholic, had just married, and planned a large family. In some way, she reminded me of my own only sister, Mary, in her looks and her aspirations, and although I felt an easy friendliness and affection for her because of that, I was still hesitant to show the story to her. But she pleaded so much, still high in my exuberance, I gave in. (Jack, frustrated at our not getting together perhaps, feigned no interest in the story whatsoever.)

From my desk, I could see her reading the manuscript with great absorption, between typing her departmental letters. When she finished, she called me over to her desk. She appeared somewhat baffled and surprised by what she'd read, as if she were trying to fit me to the story, her cheeks noticeably flushed, saying, "I've never read anything like this before," that warmly pleasant smile still there, but in her pale blue eyes (just like my sister's) there was an edge of confusion and concern, even though she said she was "very impressed," perhaps out of politeness.

I suspect now having let her read it was a litmus test for deciding, if the story were ever published, whether to show it to my own sister and mother. And later, my mother did see it, when I screwed up the courage and sent her a copy of *The Black Mountain Review* with "The Pipe" in it, to show her what I planned to do, a test, perhaps, an assertion. She wrote back and said she knew I could write a "clean story" if only I really tried, not that "dirty" one. Why didn't I write a story the *Saturday Evening Post* (where my brother Bill worked in the press gang) would publish? (I learned years later from my cousin Kay Hoffman, to whom my mother gave the magazine to get it out of the house, that my mother had carefully sliced out all the "dirty" words in the story with a razor blade, in case my youngest brother, David, discovered the magazine hidden away in a bottom drawer of her bureau.)

When I returned to the college in late February 1955 for the spring term, a number of wild flowers were already up, the first grass up, the early daffodils again by Lake Eden, spring as usual coming early to that region. Even so, the place looked, especially after the winter, shabbier, even more rundown than when the majority of us had left a few months before. Creeley was still in Mallorca, but Charles was cheerful, optimistic as always, and I had brought back with me in my suitcase a batch of new writing, especially the two short stories, "Exit 3," which, even though Olson hadn't passed judgment on it yet, I felt less uneasy about than "The Pipe," which I considered a flop since up to the day I left New York to hitchhike south I hadn't heard a word from Olson on it. So I forgot about it, was just enormously grateful to be back, safe, *home*, and to begin to adjust again to the longer, slower rhythms of Black Mountain life. But I was finding it hard, unable to write as I had been doing at that fairly intense pitch up in my Greenwich Village rooming house. Back in Swannanoa Valley, it wasn't long before the same old uneasiness and insecurity set in, about myself, and particularly about the shaky future of the college. I felt disloyal, but in the privacy of my own thoughts, it was hard sometimes to share the same unshakeable faith as Charles had.

"I've been dreaming a lot about you," he said to me with a shy smile soon after I arrived. I was of course pleased, wondering what it meant, what I could be in his dreams. He told me of that one dream several years later in a letter from Fort Square, Gloucester, in February 1958, regarding our approaching together the Temple of Black Isis. But that day in early 1955 that was all that he said. It was enough for me.

Wasting no time, and probably missing us over the winter break, Charles, always needing an audience to field his ideas, to be heard, how they sounded, if they worked, and obviously relieved not to have to think for awhile of being rag-and-bone man to what was left of the college chattel, began his writing class almost immediately, meeting again in the small Reading

Room in the Studies. After I'd read "Exit 3" one night to the class, Olson and the others responded favorably, Charles only suggesting I drop all mention of Christmas: "We all bring emotional freight along with Christmas," he said. "Just leave it winter." After that, I had nothing more I wanted to bring to read and several sessions later when Charles asked me if I had anything, I said I hadn't. He said, "Well, Mike, you know my policy." I said I did and was about to get up to leave when I remembered the story I'd sent him and hadn't gotten any response on. I told him about "The Pipe," reminding him, but said I didn't think it was worth reading in class since he'd never bothered to write me about it. Olson looked blank, gaping at me round-eyed through his glasses, thoroughly perplexed.

"When'd you mail it?"

"When I was in New York."

He scratched his head. Still a blank. He asked me where the story was, and I said in my study. "Go get it."

As I went down the hall, my step was light: my weeks of doubt about the story began to lighten a little, only "a little" because since Charles hadn't read it, then there was still hope he might like it, and I was hesitant also because I'd be exposing myself to criticism on it for the first time where it really mattered, not only from Charles but from all the sharp-eared others in the class as well.

As I read it, it seemed too long, too impossible, there was too much of a deadly silence, no one was laughing in the places I thought were pretty funny when I wrote them. I glimpsed Charles listening, as he often listened to our readings, hunched over in his chair, great balding head down, all listening concentration, a Camel smoking forked in his big hand. My apprehension was similar to that first time I'd read "The Truck" out loud back in the fall before the winter break, and despite the positive—and surprising—response to that story, my "breakthrough," as Charles and later Creeley termed it, that same nervousness and uncertainty, the same rapid heartbeat was with me, except heightened this time, that night I read "The Pipe."

When I finished the final page, the room was silent for what seemed like a long time. Charles didn't stir, still sat hunched, head down. Then he slowly lifted his head—his face, as often in the intensity of his listening it seemed, was flushed, a full-blooded red—and he stared at me with utter seriousness, then his stare went from face to face about the room. He stood up abruptly, said he had to take a leak, and cigarette in mouth, hurried stooping out the door. We could hear his workshoes clattering down the metal stairs to the men's room on the lower level. Was the story that bad? I was thinking to myself, in an agony of suspense. Nobody said much of anything while he was gone; I could feel them watching me but, as before, I didn't dare look back at them, afraid what I might see in their eyes. The only thing I could gauge was I'd sensed they'd been listening.

When Charles returned, he plunked himself down in his chair, spread his legs, clapped a hand on either knee, and with a broad grin creasing his face said, "Shall we begin?"

Seeing his smile, I felt myself relax for the first time that night, for the first time in weeks, really, that part of me that worried constantly what Charles would think of my work, the only one whose opinion still really mattered to me. In that grin of his, I knew there was something to the story.

We spent, or rather the others spent, the rest of the class, which lasted for several hours, discussing nothing but "The Pipe," Charles in particular, who was especially animated in his excitement over the work, swinging over his large discursive counters of association of myth and folktale, of fantasy and the real, the particular. "The opening's about as professional as you can get," he said, for starters. "Can't get it any better." He was especially struck by the use of the birds, the chickenhawks, and Billy's acting out the story at the pipe before the blow: "It borders on vision," he said, specifically Billy's hallucination, albeit "a second-rate vision. Make it more of a *real* fairy tale, less literal. Billy *should* fly up and *talk* to those chickenhawks. Make it go all the way, make it a *real* vision."

I wasn't quite sure what more I could do, but I tucked that one away for future mulling over.

The energetic response the story aroused that night really knocked me out, the surprise of it. It scared the hell out of me too, the enthusiasm was so much more than I could handle, already having decided, because of Charles' earlier silence, the story was a failure. I sat stiff, gripping my cane-bottomed chair, tense with hushed gratitude bordering on amazement at the extravagant comments—and praise—that not only Charles but also the others in the class heaped on it.

As the hour passed midnight, everyone, even the usually indefatiguable Charles, appeared worn out. He called a halt, saying we'd devote the next class to nothing but "The Pipe," an unheard-of precedent.

I was of course out of my mind with happiness.

In the next class, Charles, apologizing profusely, said he had hunted through a stack of papers on his work table and had, inexplicably, found my manila envelope with "The Pipe" in it, that I'd mailed from New York City several weeks before, it mysteriously turning up "at the bottom of the pile," buried under a bunch of letters and manuscripts from other correspondents he'd been meaning to get to but had been too preoccupied with the business of trying to keep the college afloat (which, sadly, *was* cutting drastically into his own work).

After the reception of the story in the class a few nights before, I was ready to forgive him for anything. In that second workshop discussion of "The Pipe," I was much less agitated, much less nervous, so that I was able to hear more of what was said about the story—and there was, to my surprise, still plenty. Small bits of criticism emerged now, Olson remarking he didn't like the phrase "in a death grip," rightly calling it a cliché, and also didn't care for the phrase "to boot," which was archaic in his ears; he also insisted I should delete the phrase "it was stunning," he didn't think Carp would say something like that. As with all his criticisms, I agonized for days over whether to delete or revise those parts, but, not a total robot, left some as they were.

There were demurrers who read the story: Joe Fiore was bothered by its violence; he wondered out loud why there had to be a murder—it didn't make sense to him, it wasn't logical.

Mary only said, "This is it. I guess Olson's glad he's got a writer."

I only hoped it was true.

When it was over, Charles recommended I immediately send the story to Creeley in Spain. I was a little uncertain since Creeley's earlier response to "Exit 3," in a letter dated February 25, 1955, hadn't been enthusiastic:

Many thanks for sending those two stories [the other was "The Jest"], I like the EXIT one best, or think it's got the most potential (dull word). Myself, I would tighten it up—just how god knows is not so simple to say. I like, for example, detail of woman washing the window (drugstore), also of the four soldiers—but at other points, it seems slow to me. Also, I think you might take the one helping and make him either more in or else more out, mobile lamp-post, etc. Like that. This way, he's a little obtrusive at points, because he is 'on-looker' & perhaps too simply? . . .

He also noted:

The magazine at present is a little shaky, mainly a question of $$$—which they are finding very simple. Too, it will probably be changed to a biannual— longer (circa 150/175 pp/ in a smaller page dimension)—and I think more simple to manage generally. Distribution (and also the time to print it here) is now not at all very gt/. But in any case—please don't worry about it for the time-being, i.e., re THE TRUCK. I will write you as soon as things become more definite, and/or as soon as Charles writes me. I am goddamn sorry there is any question at all . . . .

After so many years it's difficult to convey an exact sense of the kind of teacher and editor Creeley was at that time (his writing, naturally, is its own most exact sense). The best way to give more precisely an idea of those two qualities would be pertinent quotations from the letters I received from him during this period. I quote the following letter from Mallorca to convey those qualities in Creeley's response to "The Pipe":

March 12, 1955

Dear Mike,

Many thanks for the new story, and also for your letter (and another that came a few days earlier). I *like* the invention in this one very much, i.e., your sense of it, viz what you say in the letter, is again I think the very damn necessary break-over into that 'world' where things finally derive their own logic, and/or make you follow them, by virtue of a presence that can only be held (actually relieved) by the writing. (I can remember very vividly my own sense of this, the first time, and I was longer reaching it than you, i.e., for a long time the best I could do was to work variations, in a sense 'tests,' upon a 'world' which was for the most part altogether autobiographical—and I think that limit (at least in this character) is too much of a one.)

Anyhow, very damn good. I have a few kicks, mainly against the *time* it takes you to reach the first of the 'tales'—perhaps that could be condensed, i.e., the lead-in parts? First para/ for one is very vivid, however—that pipe is very damn clear. The two 'tales,' for me, are the wild parts of it all, and, in that, the center—or I think they lift very wildly, and carry reader along willy-nilly. Conversation thru-out, very good. At the end—could the play (viz, the further detail etc.) after the fight be cut some? Again I tend myself to be impatient. I don't think this is a story that resolves finally in terms of the literal actions in it—or, not that precisely, but I think again that those two 'tales' implicate much, that the literal action then settles, or provides a reference for. And that's why, over-all like they say, I think it makes it so much . . . .

. . . Actually, at these points (again not to bug you with thumbs & all): 1) lead-in to Carp's tale of forks, just a little quicker, i.e., a question of going thru cutting out any too repetitive detail, or bunch of adjectives, etc., in short even a little terseness here might be useful; 2) between Carp's and Billy's tale of the baby, where they are coaxing him to tell it, i.e., this now I think carries on too long (however reluctant he is, etc., and/or you can make that clear, and actually do—without quite such a length of persuading, etc., and 3) perhaps at the end, i.e., subsequent details following fight, maybe hinge all that on the car going off, simply, or else, like the detail of what'shisname poking his finger in the wound, etc. Just a short sharp thing, to close it up, etc. A bit laconic, certainly, but not too much at length . . . .

As to BMR—Charles sent a telegram that the mag was 'safe,' and I'm now waiting to hear just what it all comes to. And will write directly I do. Ok. At least it looks a hell of a lot better.

All love,
Bob

That pipe is a beautifully handled 'image'—I think you managed all that completely. Very goddamn much there. As is the whole place . . . .

After "The Pipe," Charles, in his exaggerated way, would kiddingly refer to me as "a master of American speech." I took it all with a grain of salt, but what I really heard was that I had done something, in his eyes, and that was enough for me, all I wanted to hear, and was secretly pleased, again, to have his approving eye on me.

In the meantime, focusing on more practical matters, Wes

had me sign the following agreement:

> Two years after final date of attendance at Black Mountain College,
> I promise to pay to the Derek Bovingdon Memorial Loan Fund:
> Two hundred eighty-seven dollars and fifty cents,
> payable at a rate of interest of 2% a year payable annually,
> and if unpaid at the date due at a rate of 6% a year payable
> annually thereafter.
> $287.50   Michael Rumaker
>   March 29, 1955

I signed it in both relief and trembling, relief that this loan took care of my tuition, so I could graduate; trembling at the thought of how would I ever repay it all, $287.50 no inconsiderable sum in my eyes in those days; worried, too, if I'd be able to eke out my stay on the little I'd been able to save from my IBM job. (As it turned out, I was forced to borrow another $50, this time from the college itself, on June 13, 1955, at the same terms, which helped me to stay till early September.)

In that spring of 1955, Charles got wind of a short story competition for college students throughout North Carolina, in conjunction with a spring arts festival sponsored by the then all-women Greensboro College, located in a town I'd hitchhiked through several times on my way to and from the North. The serenity and sense of comfortable wealth was so seductive, I envied each trip through that sleepy, placid Southern college town, as green as its name, those wide, tree-lined streets and lawns evenly spaced with well-kept, traditional, ivy-covered college halls and dorms and crowded with well-dressed, fresh-faced female students who appeared never to have known a day of want, a sharp contrast to the shabby poverty and shaggy dress of Black Mountain. (Comfortable in its knowledge too, since during a lecture on modern music at a past festival, Carroll

Williams reported that while a musicologist was lecturing on the 12-Tone System, Lou Harrison, then our composer-in-residence at Black Mountain, screeched out exasperatedly from the audience at one point, "Well, *that* isn't the way *Schoenberg* explained it to *me!*")

Charles got all het up about the writing contest, eager to show off what us apprentice Black Mountain writers could do, certain a couple of us at least would win hands down (and hence bring a little desperately needed positive publicity to the place, that would maybe attract some students, given that most Tarheels who'd heard of Black Mountain thought of it, as Mary Reed had first reported to me, as a cesspool of commies and queers). And certainly for all of us, the possibility of winning a little money was not only attractive but, given our empty pockets, a downright necessity. Charles' enthusiasm, as always, was infectious, and when he suggested I submit "The Pipe" for consideration, I did so without a qualm, thinking, given the response in his class, it might stand a chance.

We all waited with eager curiosity for the results and a few weeks later were sorely disappointed when all our manuscripts were returned, without even so much as one honorary mention.

My story had a single word penciled in at the top of the first page: "Ugh." That was it, "Ugh."

Although I didn't say anything, I took it hard, my first authorial experience beyond the relatively safe confines of the Seven Sister Mountains, unable to comprehend the rejection after all the glowing words in Olson's class, especially from Charles. But Charles was amused, grinning at me broadly when I showed him that one word on my manuscript, grinning at my loss of innocence perhaps, not in a mean way, though; grinning as much as to say, not only for me, but for all of us who'd sent in stories, *We know better*. If he was disappointed or annoyed by the judges' decisions, he kept it to himself and appeared to take a humorous philosophical view of it, experienced in rejections and misreadings of his own work (as that earlier letter of mine quoting a few of the literati in Manhattan suggested), a shrug-of-the-shoulders view which I, and the other Black Mountainear competitors, came, in time, to share.

In the meantime, he said to me, "Send it to the *New Mexico Quarterly*," which he suggested might be adventurous enough to publish it—*and*, most important, pay a little money for it. They, too, rejected it, and I was beginning to wonder if all the hullabaloo over the story in class had been maybe unrealistically exaggerated, when Creeley, over in Mallorca, decided, certainly on his own but also I suspect with a nudge from Charles, to publish "The Pipe" in the No. 6 spring 1956 issue of *The Black Mountain Review*, no payment, of course, but worth to me all the gold in the world.

Charles was heading up a work crew one Saturday afternoon to clean out a stopped-up sewer line along the lake side of the road between the dining hall and Studies Building. I was supposed to be on it but was in some kind of down mood and declined to help, even though I felt guilty and nervous saying no to Charles. Instead, I went walking in the hills and along the road by the neighboring farms. John Wieners, who'd arrived shortly before from Boston just to study with Olson, and who was on the crew, I suspect, because he was beginning to follow in my footsteps of trying to please Charles in every way, later told me Charles had said scoffingly, standing amidst the stench and muck as they tried to clear the line, "Rumaker can only *write* about this kind of stuff, eh?" referring to "The Pipe." "Doesn't want to get his *hands* in it."

Charles, post-"Pipe," as if trying to "explain," "account for," me to himself, announced rather forcefully in writing class, not long after the marathon discussion of that story: "You are undoubtedly a throwback."

My first response to myself was: What the hell does that mean? My second was: So *that* explains it all!

John Wieners' first contact with Charles Olson was when he heard him talk over a Boston radio station ("radio," as Charles once said scornfully, "that disembodied voice") about a reading he was to give at the Charles Street Meeting House. Curious, John went to hear Olson read his poems, during Hurricane Hazel, appropriately enough, and was instantly hooked, just as I had been a few years earlier in Philly, hearing Ben Shahn talk about Olson and Black Mountain. And similarly, it eventually led John, with his volunteer fireman lover, Dana, from Swampscott, Massachusetts, to drive from Boston to Black Mountain College in the spring of 1955, another, like myself, touched by Olson and thus, I suspect, impelled south by a sense of destiny.

John was a pale slender youth of about 21, with a warm, ever-ready smile, his Boston accent couched in a soft, appealing voice. He had a courteous manner that drew you in immediately. In his eyes, in his movement, was the quick alertness of a bird; there was even something bird-like in his face, his features honed to a sharpness, I fancifully imagined, not only by the swift suppleness of his expressions, but also by his extraordinary flights of wit and imagination. John had a terrific sense of humor, and even in his early poems you could clearly hear a most attractively singular voice and could easily understand why Olson was so captivated by what he caught in John's early work.

Dana, on the other hand, was a big blond bear of a guy, a little older than John, amiable, a simple heart, really—somewhat jittery, I suspected, at finding himself, a young man from a conventional enough background—besides being a volunteer fireman he had also played football in high school—thanks to

John's persuasions, in deeply conformist, rabidly homophobic mid-1950s America, the lover of a somewhat femme, quicksilver, ultra out-queer poet. I also fancied John as pipe-playing faun prancily piping his blond bear out of deep forest hibernation into sunny springy glades. Now, that same faun had seductively piped Dana a thousand miles south to the near-wilderness of the western North Carolina hills to study with a giant of a poet his faun lover had only heard once on the radio and at a reading.

The first test Charles set John, who was fresh from the rigors of a Catholic education in acquiring a B. A. degree at Boston College and who had arrived in Olson's class after the two-day marathon on "The Pipe," was for him to read the story and write a critique of it. As I handed John the manuscript, I felt a twinge of empathy, remembering my own initiation trials with Olson.

In the very next class, Charles had John read his paper, which turned out to be rather snidely academic in tone. Among other accusations, John said "The Pipe" was a trashy ripoff of other Southern writers, obviously I was too influenced by Faulkner, that I wrote too much like him, and since John was suffering under the misapprehension that I was Southern, and that "The Pipe" was set in the South (not too far wrong given the "Southern" nature of Gloucester County, New Jersey, where the story is set, not too far south of which the Mason-Dixon Line slices). When John finished, I squirmed in my seat for him, knowing his own baptism of fire with Olson was on the way, and it came, bluntly and swiftly, and far much sooner than mine had.

Charles really laced into him, chastising him roundly for his "misreadings," telling him he had got the story all wrong and that he needed to learn to read. Although John was quite caught off guard by the vehemence of the attack, I could see in his confused but still-admiring eyes a glint of surrender, that he was "seeing the light." He, too, had found his master.

Our queerness aside, our sharing a master eventually brought us close, overriding Charles' ploy of using my story in order to snare John into the charmed circle. (In 1956 John would find a second master at Black Mountain in Robert Duncan.) Not long after, John began to shape up, to listen avidly and become fast with Olson, becoming willing to learn, to serve as apprentice. Olson then, as he had with me, opened his mind and heart to him as only a teacher can to such a hungry and eagerly willing student. Part of Olson's method of teaching (as he had done with me and others, and now most recently with John): Shock treatment, as in "O my soul, slip / the cog . . ." in "As the Dead Prey Upon Us."

But "The Pipe" aside, John had a more major problem in his first days at Black Mountain: he confided to me that he was still very upset that Dana who, since John didn't drive, had done all the driving from Boston to Black Mountain, hadn't spoken a word to John the last hundred miles or so of their trip, had sat behind the wheel with teeth clenched, eyes fixed on the road. To John, in his inflamed poetic mind, theirs was a marriage already throughout all eternity; but to Dana, in his more pedestrian brain, it was a tentative, somewhat more scary attachment. Given the rigid norms of malehood at the time and the deeply entrenched homophobia against such male-male attachments, Dana was caught between fiercely wanting both The Norm *and* John. John was obsessed with losing Dana and, like Creeley and his uncertainties with his own wife, compulsively talked about nothing else, especially to me, choosing to bend the ear of his specially chosen fellow-queer confidant, worried that his hard-won romance was over. I tried to comfort him as best I could, mainly (as I did with Creeley) by just listening, but John would not be comforted. Like the lyrics, and life, of the jazz singer he later idolized when he discovered her on the jukeboxes of North Beach San Francisco, I could already see John's lovelife (which it seemed *was* his life) as a perpetual torchsong à la Billie Holiday, a sweet misery that richly fed his language and his poems, his troubles with Dana the main subject.

John's dream was that Dana would stay on with him at Black Mountain, but Dana, after only a very few days, returned to Boston to finish school. He certainly didn't appear to fit amidst all the rest of us misfits, having more conventional ambitions in mind: a suit-and-tie job with a respectable corporation for one. Dana, with blond crewcut, built like the stereotypical fullback, blue, blond-lashed eyes in a round, open face with pleasant, broad features, a kind of All-American white-boy-next-door look, five years older than and somewhat embarrassed and baffled by his attraction for John, that small, agitated, bird-like, unpredictable creature who was already the poet in embryonic form who would, in 1958, just three years away, in a cheap hotel in North Beach San Francisco write "A poem for cocksuckers"—both seemed to most at Black Mountain, including myself, the oddest of couples. John may have brought Boston down with him, but Dana, it seemed, had never left the comforting confines of Swampscott, and couldn't wait to get back there. (In fact, years later he did get married and had several children, according to John in an on-and-off-again interview that spanned four years, "1973/7," with fellow Boston poet Charley Shively.)

After Dana left, John was beside himself, talked to me incessantly of nothing else, in his room (Madame's old room in Streamside where I'd had my curious French tutorial); or on walks, or after acting classes with Wes, he expressed his fears that, back in Massachusetts, Dana would forget him, that they would break up, that someone would steal him away and he'd lose him forever. (As indeed did happen later, in San Francisco, and is recorded in "A poem for the old man," written the same day, "6.20.58," as the previously mentioned poem.) I knew there was nothing I could say to quiet his fear, so continued to do what I did best, listen.

But hanging onto Dana was maybe a way of John's hanging onto Boston, which, as I said, he carried down with him, intact. Just as I had to learn to do, indeed as most of us had to, he slowly worked his way into the life of Black Mountain, mainly through his contact with Charles and his evergrowing esteem and adoration for him, not to mention Olson's pushing him to consider new ideas, new sources of writing. Dana's departure, I suspected, was the proverbial blessing in disguise. The pain of the separation certainly made John miserable, but it provided him with lively grist for enumerable poems.

Tom, John and I were returning from Asheville from seeing a movie one night, and, Tom taking a shortcut on a winding back country stretch, we suddenly came upon an over-turned red convertible, the young driver thrown out on the narrow road. He was lying moaning on his back, his face and arms, his t-shirt and levis, totally drenched in blood. Tom, the former medic in the army, leapt out of the Buick and dashed over to see what he could do, crouching over the unconscious youth and shouting at him, slapping his bloody cheeks, trying to raise some life in him until help arrived. At that moment another motorist stopped, and at Tom's command, raced off to find a phone, no easy job in that isolated rural area.

In the meantime, John and I stood by, able to do little more than stare in horror, John whispering to me how much the victim, with his blood-streaked blond stubble of hair, resembled Dana; he shuddered, imagining if it had been Dana sprawled there in the road.

All the while the radio in the young man's overturned car, a flashy new model, was still softly playing country music, the headlights, also still working, slashed into the ragged red clay ditch. Wisps of smoke and steam seeped up from the exposed dark underbelly of the convertible. Maybe he'd been drinking, maybe he'd been speeding on this little-traveled back road that twisted dangerously through the hills.

After what seemed forever, we were relieved to hear in the distance the sounds of sirens coming from the direction of Asheville, and soon saw approaching headlights and flashing red lights illuminating in jagged flashes the far-off black hills thrusting up either side of the winding road. Not long after, several squad cars of North Carolina state troopers roared up, followed swiftly by an ambulance. After Tom gave them what information he could, the injured youth, who, silent now, his face a ghastly white beneath the streaks of blood, and at this point appearing close to death, was shoved into the ambulance, which then sped off, siren screaming, back in the direction of Asheville.

John and I sat silent on the drive back to Black Mountain, while Tom at the wheel, more used to such horrors, animatedly chattered on about the accident. In the kitchen at Meadows Inn, unable to sleep we were still so shaken, John and I sat at the table while Tom, who insisted he had seen "worse" in Korea, busily boiled us coffee on the Coleman stove and, in contrast to ourselves, curiously enlivened, continued to chat on about the accident till I wanted to bop him. Back in his room, John later that night wrote a poem about the incident, naturally threading Dana into it, which he showed me next day and gave me a copy of.

As for me, I lay in bed that same night unable to sleep, unable to erase the bloodied face of the young man from my mind, filled with uneasiness. Months later, when I recalled that night, I saw it as an omen leading up to terrible events that summer that ended finally with an equally horrific car crash right at the very front doors of our Meadows Inn—the beginning sign of worse things to come, the beginning of the end of Black Mountain, really.

Soon after Dana departed, John, perhaps not quite yet ready

to face the wilds of Black Mountain alone, urged two other close Boston friends of his to come down to look the place over. Put up in Mountain Stream along with John, Joe and Carol Dunn, recently married, and about the same age as John, evidently liked what they saw and, to John's great relief, decided to stay on.

Joe Dunn, who would later spend time in prison because of heroin, was even smaller and sparer in build than John, with skin so pale it seemed never to have known sunlight. He had boyish Irish features topped off by a great shock of heavily oiled brown hair—a "pompadour," as it was called among Irish-Catholic working-class teenaged boys in those days, hair perhaps slicked up to make him appear taller. (It always seemed the shorter the guy, the taller the pompadour.) Like John, he had a soft, appealing voice, and an engaging manner that made me, for one, feel immediately comfortable with him, much of that manner being his ability to take you into his confidence. (He also reminded me of certain South Philly Irish-Catholic cousins of mine.) In his eyes was a sharpness, like a small wild creature's, shrewd and watchful, perhaps made blade-keen on the streets of South Boston, where he also undoubtedly honed his sly intelligence and humor. Also like John, Joe was *eager*: eager to talk (a cigarette always forked in his small, slender, nicotine-stained fingers), eager to listen, to learn—eager, especially, to be liked. He also immediately fell under the spell of Olson and began to write short, oblique poems on occasion, "on occasion" because much of his time was spent with John and Carol and increasingly with a few others, including myself, talking and listening and soaking up all he could as fast as he could of all there was to be learned at Black Mountain.

Although Carol often insisted, hugging him playfully, that in bed "Joe is *all* man!" still, Joe, with his almost angelically boyish face and because he was so slightly built and soft-spoken, plus his unself-conscious mannerisms—his hand gestures, the way he walked, the way he held a cigarette, perhaps in imitation of his friend John—could be seen as "effeminate" in that rough rural valley where guys our age, many reared on neighboring farms, or descendants of hill farmers now living in the town of Black Mountain, had height and a heavy muscularity, like their fathers, as slow and deliberate in movement as they were in speech. Such young men, too, gathered at Ma Peak's for Ballantine ales or beers, sitting most of the time, all males together, in the booths that lined two opposite walls of the tavern. On the surface they were courteous enough to those of us from the college, but distant. We never really mingled except for the occasional Sunday softball game when a local team from the town or the valley would come up to play, or when, in better financial times, one or two of the nearby farm boys did odd jobs on campus with T. J., the former hired handyman. (At past harvest or corn-shocking times, it was usually their fathers from the neighboring farms that had lent us, lent college farmer Doyle, really, one of their own, a hand.)

A trip to Ma Peak's was a rare occasion for most of us at the college, chronically broke as we were, since we needed most of what little money we had for food that we couldn't grow on our own in Bea Huss' community garden, basics such as coffee, sugar, flour, lard, etc., purchased (or, by the bolder of us, shoplifted) mainly at the A&P in Black Mountain. (When it came to food shopping, Tom, as I've suggested, was a master at stretching five bucks into twenty.) So, for some reason, one night when John and Carol were busy elsewhere on campus and Joe and I had a rare buck or two between us for a few bottles of ale, the pair of us hiked down the mountain to Peak's, Joe, his hands flying before his pallid face in the darkness, babbling away about the latest revelatory book Olson had recommended, or the newest observation Olson had made in class that Joe was still puzzling over; quick, funny verbal energy bursting from him all the way down the dark winding county road past the Veterans Hospital. It continued in a booth at Ma Peak's where after a second ale, I listened in boozy contentment (the 2,400 foot altitude seemed to double the 3.2 alcohol content, or so we liked to think), listened to the excited child-like enthusiasms of this recently transplanted Bostonian who was well on his way to becoming a Black Mountaineer—one more Black Mountain-ear, really, he took in everything he heard, it seemed.

Across the room in another booth were five or six young ballplayers on one of those local hardball teams I mentioned, still in their dust-smeared uniforms, evidently having a few beers after their game. A few I'd noted in the tavern before, or up on the softball field across from the Gatehouse at the college, when they played our pickup teams, all looking very much like the local lads I described earlier, whom I watched with furtive—and hungry—eyes at a distance, at increasingly partner-scarce Black Mountain College. There was one in particular, his lean handsome face deeply tanned, his wavy blond hair bleached even more golden it seemed in the sunny ball fields of the valley. Outside the protective confines of the college, I was a careful watcher trying not to get caught. That evening, while appearing to listen to Joe, his lively speech, heightened with the ale, punctuated by his even livelier hand gestures, his perpetual "like-me" smile, I was actually observing on the sly the young ballplayers guzzling their ale direct from the bottles as they slouched in the booth directly across the floor, particularly slyly glimpsing the wavy-haired blond youth who, to my surprise, and sudden apprehension, was glancing across at Joe and me in our booth. Occasionally, he would turn with a grin and whisper something to his teammates, who also now stared across at us, especially at Joe's flying fingers. I quickly averted my sidewise gaze and tried to focus on what Joe was saying, instantly on guard. As students from Black Mountain College, which had a longstanding reputation among the neighboring hillfolk as an asylum—in the other, lunatic sense—for radical artist freaks and mad scientists (one local fucklore myth went that under a full moon we mated our most perfect specimens of male and female students, trying to propagate the perfect infant), Joe and I might be in for some harassment. And not only for that but also, as a queer, observing Joe's animated features as he spoke and his equally animated hands, a sure sign of "strange" in this neck of the woods, wife Carol's insistence on Joe's being "*all man*" aside, we could be in for some dangerous Bible Belt sodomite-hatred as well.

Still nervous, at one point I surreptitiously glanced sidewise again across the room and now saw the young men with their heads together over the table, whispering and laughing, one or two, including the wavy-haired blond I found so attractive, staring across at us again. They appeared to be cooking up something. I was about to suggest to Joe, who was oblivious to all that was going on, he was so caught up in what he was saying, that we finish our ales and head on back up to the college, when at that moment, the wavy-haired blond, with a shove out of the booth by his pals, got up and started across the floor in a stiff, uncertain gait, shuffling directly toward our booth, an unlit cigarette clenched in one corner of his mouth. (Those were the days when even professional ballplayers advertised cigarettes on TV.) The others were watching him intently with big grins and eyes glistening with expectation. As he drew nearer, I turned, facing him fully for the first time, could see that close up he was even more handsome, fine eyes and fine, carefully sculpted features in that deeply tanned face, a crease left in his brilliant, damp hair by the sweat band of his baseball cap, the shirt flaps of his dust-streaked uniform hanging out loose, could even smell the sweat of him from the game as he leaned on the table, his fingers clenching the edge, his lean body shifting uncomfortably, a crooked, sheepish grin twisting his parched lips. I could only stare at him, my own mouth agape, wondering whatever in the world he wanted, my heart trip-hammering. Joe, finally noticing him, dropped his hands, quit talking, and with his usual boyishly friendly grin, glanced up at him expectantly.

"Uh—y'all got a light?" the blond asked, his voice strained, staring directly at me.

I fumbled for my matches on top of my pack of Homeruns, struck one and held it up to him. He cupped his hands around my hands and drew them up to the cigarette hanging between his lips. I was surprised to feel his hands shaking so badly they shook my own trembling hands even more. Once his cigarette was lit, he mumbled a barely audible "'Bliged," nodded his head curtly and moved, with a quicker step this time, back to his cronies in the booth across the floor. As Joe, once the young man had left, took a swig from his ale bottle and commenced energetically to babble on again, oblivious still to anything, I caught, out of my slit-eyed sideways glance, that the blond ball player's teammates were all slapping him on the back and butt, like he'd just hit a homer, as he slid, with a look of relief it seemed, into his seat, that sheepish but now pleased grin on his face. Evidently he'd won what appeared to be a dare, or a bet, to approach the two odd Black Mountain Asylum types to ask for a light, when matches could've easily been gotten at the bar from Ma Peak herself. Perhaps they had sniffed out my own secret from seeing me in the place before (or heard from their daddies some of the college homosex rumors and scandals of the past, particularly the June 1945 arrest of BMC faculty member Robert Wunsch caught being sexually intimate with a U. S. marine in Wunsch's parked car near Asheville, a possible police setup to get "nigger-lover" Wunsch. With no support from his colleagues within the college community—again, deeply entrenched American homophobia no stranger at otherwise forward-looking Black Mountain College—Wunsch was, after local influential friends managed to get him a suspended sentence, forced to leave the school in disgrace). Perhaps these baseball player sons assumed it was Joe's secret, too. At that moment, one of the ball players threw up his arm and called out to Ma Peak behind her bar to bring them beers all around. Short, stout Ma Peak with her pinched, pasty face and dark beady eyes, her black hair worn in her perpetual tight narrow braids wound around her small head, who kept her own tight-lipped counsel, readily obliged.

When Joe finished his ale but not his need to talk, really wound up now with a few brews down him, and wanted to split another with our few remaining coins, I said there was some writing I wanted to get back to in my study, which probably was true, and suggested we leave, relieved we'd gotten off so lightly, uneasy, though, that if we stayed longer, and the bottles of beer continued to pour down the gullets of the ballplayers across the way, there might be trouble.

After our hike back up the mountain (on the way, I kept looking nervously over my shoulder everytime headlights flashed behind us), and as we stepped off the county road onto the college grounds and passed the Gatehouse, I was no longer listening to Joe, preoccupied with my own thoughts. I felt once again, as I had so often felt in the past, a rush of relief to be back on college soil, feeling safe once more in our 600-acre enclave, reasonably safe anyhow against the potentially hostile and dangerous world beyond the Gatehouse, that fear never far from my consciousness, as had been proved to me in Ma Peak's that night. In spite of that, it was a danger now mixed in my mind with powerful erotic sensory images of the wavy-haired blond ball player, his sharply handsome features vivid in my eyes, the scent of his sweat in my nostrils still. As Joe and I walked up the road toward Streamside, I realized how lonely I was, a loneliness, however, that was about to change, and sooner than I could ever have imagined.

John was just as poor as I, and his Boston pals, Joe and Carol Dunn, not much better off. Olive-skinned Carol, loud, assertive, a good, hearty laugh and manner, just the opposite of her mild-mannered, soft-spoken husband (Wieners teased her about being a possible dyke), who'd been a hairdresser back in Boston, could've, strapped as she and Joe were, earned a couple of spare bucks if she'd charged for the haircuts she gave us in her and Joe's room at Streamside, but as far as I remember she insisted upon giving them for free, although some of us tipped her what we could, a half a buck or so a cut.

The three of them had a thin and pallid malnourished look. I was in a somewhat better situation, having Tom Field in the kitchen of Meadows Inn, with whom I pooled my meager resources and who cooked up sturdily nourishing stews and soups on next to nothing. One simple soup he taught me to make that even a culinary moron such as myself could handle, was a milk and butter-based vegetable soup with herbs that cooked up in a matter of minutes and was delicious and warming on cold nights in the mountains.

I knew John was scraping along and not eating well, living on black coffee and cigarettes, and having just acquired some baloney (still very cheap then) at the A&P in Black Mountain, and a loaf of whole wheat bread, I invited him over one evening for sandwiches. Little did I know, Joe and Carol, undoubtedly just as hungry, would tag along with him. I actually only had enough baloney for John and me, but figured since I'd only invited John, to hell with it and, embarrassing as it was, I'd make the sandwiches for just the two of us since there wasn't any extra to spare, which I did. It was even more embarrassing as we all sat around the square oak kitchen table, John and I chomping on our sandwiches, while Joe and Carol, puffing on their cigarettes (spending money on tobacco, for those of us addicted, was more important than spending it on food), eyed our every mouthful.

It was hard to swallow, given the situation, and I was never so relieved as when our poor repast was over, quickly enough, thank goodness, given the sharpness of our appetites, sharpened ever more keenly in that high mountain air.

I vowed never to try sharing my meager larder again with John, knowing now I'd be inviting not one but three guests.

With Dana gone (he and John would hitch up temporarily again later in San Francisco) and myself at loose ends, and with our emotional affection and growing closeness because of our powerful connection to Olson, John and I, after a couple of ales at Ma Peak's one night tried to get it on back in his room at the rear of Streamside, fumbling half-heartedly on his bed for a few minutes. But we both knew in our hearts our attractions for each other bypassed the carnal, his heart still in Swampscott, Massachusetts, with Dana, "the old man" of the later poem; mine, still in waiting. John would continue to pursue his burly blond volunteer firefighter, while I, infested with my own misconceptions, sought out only those men alien to me, all I couldn't stomach in myself, my father, the first man I ever wanted to love and to love me, still stuck in my craw.

John Wieners, Naomi and Mona Stea, sisters from the Bronx who shared rooms upstairs in Meadows Inn, a new guy named Jake from Philly, and I had no understanding of the scene we were performing in Ibsen's *Hedda Gabler* in Wes' early morning theater class in the basement of the Studies. Huss promptly canceled the class until we did.

John Wieners, who was nuts about Edna St. Vincent Millay, entreated Wes to let us do a performance of her play *Aria da Capo* in the acting class, which Wes agreed to, although I don't think the project excited him even a shade as much as it did John. We worked long and hard at it, Wes at the helm guiding us with his directorial exactitude. One night, after a few ales at Ma Peak's, the cast, including John, of course, me, Jake, the Stea sisters, and Joe and Carol Dunn, tipsily wended our way back up the mountain and decided, late as it was and drunk as we were, to have an impromptu rehearsal around the Steinway grand (moved up from the now-closed dining hall) downstairs in the Studies in our usual acting class space, to be ready for Wes the next morning.

"Rehearsal" quickly degenerated into a merry mockery of the lines, our voices, instigated by John and me, taking on the camp Southern drawl of Blanche Dubois in *A Streetcar Named Desire*, so that any resemblance to Millay's play was lost in our satirical exaggerations. I, however, in spite of feeling no pain, grew increasingly nervous, unaccountably fearing Wes might somehow overhear our mockery, or hear of it, hear us being camp, being gay; might indeed be spying on us at that very moment outside the night-blackened windows of the room, Wes, in his Protestant severity and bearing, as actual descendant of Jan Hus, with his piercing, northern-blue eyes, I childishly believed, had such extraordinary powers, Wes replacing the all-seeing—and all-punishing—eyes of the priests of my blue-collar Catholic childhood.

On the other hand: The early spring afternoon when Wieners, the Dunns, the Stea sisters, Terence Burns (who had taken a shine to Mona Stea, and hence now got out of the barn once in awhile; he later married her and they moved to his hometown, Providence), Tom Field, a few others and myself hiked north into the mountains for a picnic. On the way back to the college, we got caught along the trail in the deep woods in a terrific rainstorm. We were all soaked to the skin immediately and, giddily defiant, began to dance around in the muddy path under the tall trees, despite ear-shaking claps of thunder and numerous bolts of lightning crackling all around us. We laughed and danced, none of us seemed afraid of the storm or the lightning, one more of the fears we seemed to lose in that wilderness of Black Mountain, where in some queer way we began to feel genuinely charmed.

John had a gentleness and humor, a concern and openness, and though he was still shy about it in his poems, was beginning, if just barely, to speak of his gayness there, a less messy and troubled acceptance of who he was than my own. One Sunday evening down in the Weaving Room in the Studies, after he'd heard me read "Exit 3" aloud to the community, he was surprised that I was so bold as to have the drunken marine at one point kiss the hitchhiker Jim directly on the mouth.

"You dare to have the two men kiss like that?" he asked, "*And* read it out loud?" standing up close to me, speaking in a bit of a shocked whisper so others around us wouldn't hear, speaking with a smile of admiration, too, tinged with hesitancy, which revealed his own uncertainty about putting to use in his own work that vital aspect of his existence.

I nodded, smiling goofily in turn, surprised at his surprise. Despite everything, it hadn't occurred to me that I should be *afraid* to put in that clumsy kiss of drunken comradely affection, restrained at that time as any lesbian or gay writer had to be about being even partially open, honest, and celebratory in one's written words, such truths assuring publishing censorship.

I've often wondered if it wasn't at that moment, among many other moments, that a seed of an even more expanded possibility was sprung forth in John, since it wasn't long after that question of his to me that night that he began to openly introduce queer-related experience and imagery directly into his poems, more solidly accepting but essentially a torchsong victimized-woman identity and awareness, approaching finally the verse John dated "6.20.58" "A poem for cocksuckers" (which, speaking of censorship, at that time was printed as "A poem for [blank space] suckers" in the 1958 edition of *The Hotel Wentley Poems*).

Black Mountain, like a bold lover, opened John, as it opened so many of us, our eyes, our minds, our hearts, gave each other permission to extend the ground, to see how to get on the ways ahead, the ways that led to our own directions, our own freeing discoveries.

So it turned out that not long after, there was Olson's quick and delightedly amazed reaction in class to that squib of John's (which appeared later in 1964 in Wieners' *Ace of Pentacles*) that went:

> Strange with women when
> They find out you love men
> More than they
> Never let you kiss them
> On the mouth again.

Once Joe and Carol Dunn had left the college, unable to economically stick it out, John took quite a shine to Ed and Helene Dorn, and the Dorns to him, particularly Helene, who had a bony thinness bordering on malnutrition but who radiated an air of fine-boned, unkempt loveliness. There was a paradoxical open energy in her manner and smile—a most sweetly engaging smile—coupled with a suggestion of dazed and smoky hiddenness in her eyes, a signal of unease and confusion betraying the radiant, ready laughter always playing nervously about her lips.

I was gaga over her, too, probably for the same reasons as John, who, as noted, had a penchant for blues and torch-song singing women: Libby Holman, Billie Holiday, Kim Novak starring later in 1957 in "Jeanne Eagles," etc., etc., particularly such women who were drug addicts or who had died of drugs, as Eagles did, as John, later, almost did. Such women outwardly dramatized his own inwardly private queer soap opera (Dana, the big blond volunteer fireman, star of the moment), the dross of which even then, still in rudimentary alchemical voice, he was beginning to transform into poems of pure gold, which culminated in the 1958 *Hotel Wentley Poems*. But Helene Dorn, with her silkenly low voice, her looks and manner, had a glamorous coolness, seemed, in my young and overheated, sensory-deprived Black Mountain imagination, to be a movie star trapped contradictorily in the most abject poverty. She often did appear, so handmedown and threadbare was her wardrobe, to be a lost princess in rags, with several kids from her first marriage and baby Chanson from Dorn, who were, as well, not much better dressed.

Dorn, of course, like Wes Huss, had his own elegance, tall and leanly muscular, blond, taken to wearing black vests, worn, run-over black boots, and wire-rimmed spectacles, presenting the illusion of a foxy preacher from the Old West. Cagier than Helene, with a slyer wit, but a seductively quiet, thoughtful, equally silken-voiced manner no less engaging than Helene's, he, too, was appealing, if somewhat distant, watchful. His guarded but intense gaze seemed unnervingly to penetrate to the core of everything. Careful in his pronouncements, and classy in his own way, he was a "star," too, in my over-erotically heated movie fantasies at seasonally eros-lean Black Mountain. But about Helene and Ed there was that most attractive air of threadbare elegance (not unlike the Olsons, the Husses, in their own distinct ways), a peculiar combination of heartland America and Camelot nobility fallen on hard times, of serious intents leavened with witty good humor, despite their being dirt-poor. And of course Ed was miles ahead of most of us in the breadth of his understanding of the poems then evolving in Olson's masterwork (as clearly revealed later in his 1960 *What I See in the Maximus Poems*), and a smilingly skillful dissector of our own lesser works in Charles' writing classes.

At times Ed, too, given a profile as chiseled as John Barrymore's, had a mannered stance, a close-up way of speaking, of holding his hand-rolled Bull Durham, that was subtly, quietly, Big Screen dramatic. No wonder Wieners and I, as youngsters, he in South Boston, I in South Philly, steeped in the queer tradition of darkened movie houses, seeking traces, clues, of our own validation in gigantic celluloid creatures of either gender—which accounts in part for the rich fantasy life of gay guys, "anything to do with the imagination," as writer Richard Hall put it to me years later—were both quite taken with the Dorns.

So taken, that one night over ales around a table with the Dorns at Ma Peak's, John and I haltingly shared some aspects of our own lives, of what it was like to be gay, sharing, in a most risky time, even at Black Mountain, that inmost aspect of self with the two people we so very much admired and trusted. But to my dismay—I can't speak for John, but I sensed the incomprehension in his eyes—Ed said, and Helene, though with a hint of empathy in her own eyes, backed him up on it, saying it in the most charming, the most reasonable manner, however, "That's something we don't understand anything about," the tone in his voice, for all its surface friendliness, implying that it was something they didn't want to understand either, that it didn't touch their lives in any way, and there were no questions asked. Yet there sat John and I directly across from them, plain to see, ready to give witness. Dorn's wasn't, of course, an uncommon attitude at the time (he later expressed his underlying hostility in the 1959 poem "When the Fairies" which editor Don Allen included in his *New American Poetry 1945-1960*), the lost habits of such pleasures and enticements, if only occasionally behavioral, atrophying in many over time after generations of Judeo-Christian repression and neglect, even the imagination for it stunted. So, to my regret, because I liked them both so much, I had thought, naïvely, perhaps as John did, too, that I could trust them to see, but after an awkward moment of the silence that murders, the conversation moved on to other things.

And this from a man who had told the draft board back in his hometown in Mattoon, Illinois, during the Korean War he was "a homosexual" and was so convincing he was given 4-F exempt status. I can only assume it was that fine acting instinct and his "peculiar" poetic look that to less sophisticated Midwestern eyes on the draft board turned the trick. As for myself, later at the Newark Induction Center in New Jersey, after graduating from Black Mountain and no longer "2-S"-student protected, being the real McCoy, I had no need for acting.

Helene, her delicate features pinched and harrowed, her eyes, her face, clayey with exhaustion from caring for several kids on meager diet, in a rare moment of honesty confessed to John and me one night in the back room of their place in Streamside while the kids slept in the other room and Ed was off in his study, that Ed was "constantly after" her, "night after night after night." She wanted "a rest" but was afraid to protest, to complain.

Having sweated a few times myself on the body of a woman, the "salvation" being to be a "man," the potency of orgasm proof of it, I began to feel at Black Mountain like a double-agent. Perhaps like those male Provençal poets, so admired by Creeley and poet Paul Blackburn (there were at least *twenty* female Provençal poets as well that are rarely heard from), in their courtly love sighing for their own salvation of communion (completion?) through their etherealized visions of women, their later, more American counterparts appeared to be sweating for that redemption on the actual bodies of women, seeing that push as the whole matter.

But from Helene's description (I heard again in my ears

Charles powerfully pounding away through the ceiling over my bed in deep-night Meadows Inn), there seemed so little joy in it, if any joy there was, only a grim and sweating declaration, sullen and spiteful, the woman's body the recipient again and again of an insistence that seemed to have nothing and yet everything to do with her. A grinding against darkness, against death perhaps, a desperate pounding to enter again the portal to the matrix of creation, to be again in her, the woman, safe again in her, bucking in the warm amniotic sea, the sweet, and harrowing, death, drowning momentarily in the intensest moment of being, then escaping, then pulled back, again and again, a man a wave to the real and eternal power of the female.

Charles could, in a touch of the Provençal himself, express a courtliness toward women that no red-blooded feminist would abide today. He was also able to remark in class one night in a slightly disparaging tone on the "androgyny of Mao, like the American Indians, too." And as for those such as John and me, "the marginal creatures," perhaps we were what the Sioux called "two-spirit people," those with double-sexed souls, that are empowered to constantly cross and recross the bridges between worlds, two-way spirits in a one-way world. (And what of Olson's own shamanistic androgyny, most marked in such poems as the 1955 "A Newly Discovered 'Homeric' Hymn," where he decries the dionysian—and perhaps his mistrust (fear?) of it, the descent and ascent into the nondifferentiated— as he intones on the side of the measured hierophantic apollonian, which poet Allen Ginsberg later characterized as "too Catholic"?)

Maleness, however hidden the homoeroticism, walked the hills of Black Mountain ("Bill Williams is wrong about the female principle being the thrust of the universe," Olson once said emphatically), just as it dominated in the society beyond the gates. Except that within our rapidly shrinking 600-acre protectorate, the difference was a flexibility, if not to accept then at least to make an allowable tolerance, not for the full strength and recognition of female power in art (that male subterfuge) and community, but at least a space for it to exist, however limited that space. At Black Mountain, unlike elsewhere in the USA of that time, the androgynous spirit of the male artist, touched as it was with the masculinist assumptions we all grew up inculcated with, was at least open to the possibility of that experience, as it rarely was anywhere else. Jung's influence, via Olson, had a lot to do with it, including the vital presence of several strong women on campus, such as Natasha Goldowski, M. C. Richards, Karen Karnes, and Hazel Frieda Larsen, to name a few.

In my own dreams, I was discovering, through Jung, through Maria Von Franz, the women to love, and obey, come from within, come in many guises.

Still, Olson could in a writing class mutter threateningly to Betty Baker, the administrative secretary hired that past August, and a gadfly to Charles, "*I'm tough, don't mess with me.*"

Hence, I was loyal to the world Charles personified, yet also loyal, in secret, to the "female" world of Connie, and later of Betty Kaiser; and to such other women as Helene and Bea and Mary and Natasha; worlds of overt and hidden powers, one hurly-burly, the other fine-tuned, which Charles, I suspected, on a grander scale, wrestled with too.

Further still, the intense competition of two or more male friends for the same woman, sharing that woman, seemed at a deeper, unacknowledged level, like the two guys on the beach at Lake Pontchartrain, the only "acceptable" way they could share, could touch each other in buried, unspoken intimacies, Dan Rice and Bob Creeley a later prime example. (Another was Jerry Van de Wiele one night punching out Creeley on the asphalt on the road back from Ma Peak's in a fight over student Martha Davis—Creeley's almost pathological obsession, and insistence, to have a woman, at all costs, almost murderous, and it nearly came to that.)

But at Black Mountain, women were allowed a certain space, so long as they didn't step beyond it into the larger space where the assertive male spirit (no little of it generated by Olson's strong presence) predominated. The few assertive lesbians on campus had an even rougher time of it, with less visibility and vocality. The open, self-acknowledging gay males, being male, had a better, freer time of it, more participatory and active, so long as we also knew our place. A few lesbians, such as Ellen Schasberger's admirer, left Black Mountain in defeat, or rage, being mainly ignored, misunderstood or unwanted.

Late spring 1955, walking with Charles on the path by the lake below the library, Charles delighted to hear that John Wieners, now back in Boston, was rumored "to have a girl-friend," probably one of the sex-worker friends John so romanticized. "That's just what John needs," exclaimed Olson, slapping me on the back with a big, good-natured laugh, "a little poontang, eh?"

I had been for some time now in Merrill's old study on the upper level, Merrill rarely having made use of it while he was at Black Mountain. He had allowed me to use it, letting me know that he wouldn't turn it over to just *anyone*, that after long consideration, I had become, in his eyes, "worthy" of it. It was a north-side study, overlooking the mountain stream that rushed along that side of the building, the windows looking out toward Mount Mitchell twenty-five miles distant. The walls of the room had been painted by Merrill an austere Franz Kline black and white, like so many of the other studies. In all, it was a neat, tidy room, quiet and Eastern in its spareness, like Merrill himself, and suited to my own similar inclinations, with one of the ubiquitous pallets in a corner on the floor, covered with the black and white striped throw, hand-woven on the college looms, that I'd "borrowed" from the top of one of the Steinway grands in the dining hall.

Creeley was impressed, as had been Fee Dawson, by the number of hours I spent in my study pounding away on the big old upright Merrill had also lent me, but didn't take with him when he left the college. That was a godsend to me, since I never had enough money to actually buy a typewriter, even a second-hand one. Most of the typing I did that spring and early mid-summer of 1955 was part of my graduation project that Charles, as my faculty graduation adviser, had set up for me: to write at least a half dozen essays on plays of my own choosing by Shakespeare. I focused, largely through Olson's influence, on *King Lear, Macbeth, Coriolanus, Timon of Athens, Pericles, Hamlet, Othello, Richard II, The Tempest,* and *The Winter's Tale,* using my Cambridge Complete Shakespeare, with its illustrations by Rockwell Kent, that Stephen, a scholarly factory worker who worked at the lathe machine next to me at Fischer Machine Works in Philly had given me back in 1951, while I was struggling to save money to get back to Rider College. Less specifically, to me, at least, Charles said to read something about the Greeks, particularly Pausanias (fl. AD 143-176) and Herodotus (b. 484 BC?-d. 430/420), the first Greek first-hand historians who had done, in Olson's estimation, what he wanted his students to do: to trust the evidence of our own eyes and ears, to see and hear for ourselves, to find out on our own, as useful primary sources, and to write it down. He also strongly recommended Jane Harrison's *Prolegomena to the Study of Greek Religion,* a copy of which was in the college library. I told Charles right off at our first graduation conference that I had an easier time reading Pausanias, Herodotus and Harrison than reading Shakespeare, of understanding it. He said, "Just read it as story," and left it at that, and left me pretty much on my own. I found a red-covered copy of Onion's *Shakespeare Glossary* (suggested by Mary Fiore) in the library and really dogeared the pages checking out Shakepeare's archaic words and usages as I read through the plays and began to write "essays" for each one I read. I put essays in quotes because out of the whole batch the only thing I recall that impressed Charles was my word "meringuey" in reference to Othello.

I was so disturbed and confused—scared, really—about the tasks Charles had set for me, plus the formal requirements of the graduation process, one afternoon in my study I banged out the following letter to Charles on my typewriter:

June 5, 1955

Dear Charles,

I certainly feel as though I've frittered away this whole quarter as far as the graduation project is concerned. I've thought and worried a great deal about it, but because of feeling in a kind of fix about retackling it, I've avoided discussing the subject with you. As I told you earlier I feel at odds with myself and still don't know what to lay my hands on next which would be of any use or be meaningful to me, in the sense that I can go at it as hard, say, as the Shakespeare tutorial last fall. Well, I can't seem to get into Shakespeare this time. I've read Richard II a number of times, and Hamlet, (as you suggested) but it's like a funny kind of plateglass window stands between me and them that I can see through well enough, but can't penetrate. It leaves me feeling that I'm not 'in' it, much as I try and want to be. Attempts at papers on these two plays have been futile - nothing comes out but the kind of ugly and lazy unattachment that spoiled Macbeth for me - and perhaps it was that break away from the drive of trying to get *into* Shakespeare which has kept me out of him ever since. At least *one* consolation arising out of the work last fall is that even though now Shakespeare has gone a little stale for me, there is still a strong desire to go on reading him, and I'm confident that once I'm through this 'repulsion' that I'll go on reading him at some future date - a year, two years, how can I say when? But the urge to read him is there, like always, and it's only that now the urge doesn't amount to enough to deal with him as totally as I feel I should.

It isn't that I *haven't* been doing anything this term. I've certainly been reading steadily and have written as much as I could. I certainly would have liked to have written more, in fact, *wanted* to - but that long drive that propelled me through those stories last fall (like the Shakespeare) has disappeared for this time, and has been replaced by a kind of vacuity broken only by bits, singular instances, of activity - so that in between I squat like a toad - very vacant, yet troubled. But this doesn't necessarily mean an end. I've had this before, only in shorter and less troublesome spells, and I feel I'll work my [way] out of it as I've done in the past. But when?

You see, what bothers me is that I feel the time creeping up and I have no direction or sense of what I must accomplish before graduation. As the time set for this is the end of the summer I would like to know what must be done between now and that time. The idea of graduation was in a state of change last fall - nothing was definite as to what kind of degree was to be given or what exactly would be the procedure of graduation. Have any of these problems been discussed or settled? If so, I want to know just exactly what the graduation procedure will be and what I must do regarding it.

Everything is very unsettled now, but at the moment, I think, in some future time, to perhaps go on to graduate school with the object of teaching later on. I think, also, that I would like to *experience* a university (in the graduate school sense) for my own education.

What troubles me, concerning the graduation, is the probable prospect of an oral examination (if it is as it has been in the past) before all members of the faculty. I have often wished to God that I could talk spontaneously off the top of my head. I have always admired people who can do this. When I am confronted by a group, am directly questioned, my mind panics, and whatever meaning I possess to answer the question is erased in utter blankness. I have fought against this without much success. I cannot maintain sensibility in a direct questioning within a group - rather, for me, sensibility is controlled obliquely, away from, in another room, say, by myself with my own thoughts and pen and paper. It is, I think, the intensity that arises in a one-to-one questioning relationship, the mind fighting for such balance and control that it overshoots its mark, meaning scatters and the mouth makes gibberish-like, halting noises, void of sense.

Now, if the oral examination counts for much, I am lost. I would prefer an examination consisting of written things. It is not that, say, even in a written examination I would know all the answers, but that there, in writing, my ability to answer would not be as greatly hampered as it would if I had to answer orally before a group. If my very life depended upon answering certain questions before a judge, I swear I should be hanged for silence. It's not that I'm afraid of making a fool of myself, of falling flat on my face, goodness knows I've done that often enough, in writing as well, but my brain simply refuses to function properly under the eyes of others. Imagine them away, I cannot - try as hard as I will. Speak the gibberish that comes in the vacuous wake of a mind out of which all thought vanishes is frighteningly unsatisfying. Why this is I do not know. The very fact that I am incapable of making answers in a group, or even simply to another person, has discouraged me a great deal about graduation. Why I must feel that my very life depends upon each word that I utter I do not understand. I have always been deeply concerned about this - and since it has arisen here, I go on talking about it - because I've never been quite able before to put down what this thing is. Perhaps it sounds ridiculous to you? Perhaps it is. I've often felt it to be a ridiculous situation, one that I should beat down, and, yet, so far I haven't been able to. The problem concerns me more and more. So it is I most often speak better on paper than through the mouth. Orally I speak well only in brief, fugitive flashes.

But the thing seems to go deeper than this. And here perhaps I flounder: You remarked how pleased you were with my definition of "incantation" and "supplication" that night in class. "A dozen roses," etc. Yet, I had never thought of those words before, had never before considered their meanings. And yet, regardless of this, I had defined them to your and my satisfaction. Without previous reference or knowledge, the meaning and differentiation between the two words appeared instantaneously, and, strangely enough, very silently, in my mind, so that I can think of it only as intuition - stemming from what, I don't know. The same with the word 'sensibility' - I had never before thought of it, it had never been meaningful before. It was *not* an important word to me as I said it was in answer to your question. That answer "yes" was a sudden blurting out of a word (it could have been any word, I swear) because of that sudden unbalance in my mind, again that scattering of thought, which followed the swift, silent precision of defining a word, again, I think, intuitively - a word which was not at all meaningful to me before that instant. Another thing I want to mention is the critique I gave of Ed's [Dorn] story, <u>Dust and Oats</u> - how it weighed upon me like a stone, without relief of any kind. You said this critique was generated by *feeling*, was "post-esthetic" as opposed to Jerry's [Van de Wiele] critique which you termed "esthetic." You said that in the post-esthetic is a way to form. *Feeling*, then, was the mark of what I said that evening. Now what troubles me is *thought*. I feel it is conspicuously absent in me. The intuitive is something I think of as occurring at brief and rare intervals. Feeling, with me, is always there, more or less, but not always. But I think of thought as being constant. Perhaps I am in error, but it is this conception of constancy which fascinates me, because it is the very thing I think I lack, because it represents to me a tool to have on hand at all times, unfailing and ready for use. Feelingly, intuitively, I have *seen*. Thoughtwise, it is another matter. In thought I am blind. I miss a great deal in class because of this. I cannot think. I do not *see* the thoughts of others, do not grasp or understand them. Yet, often, I *feel* the sense of what is meant - but it is vague. I have noticed that when the thought verges on feeling that I comprehend the most.

The thing is, I feel that feeling is uninteresting to you. I feel that I must always meet you on your own ground - i.e., what I conceive of as *thought*. And I can't - always. Now, have I veered off completely? Am I wrong? If you could help me on this, I'd certainly be grateful. And it does all, somehow, have to do, not only with my work aside from the graduation, but the graduation as well. Well, if you have any ideas - ?

Mike

After he'd read the letter, a few days later he came to see me in my study. He said not to worry about Shakespeare, repeating that I should "read him as story." He also insisted, regarding my writing, "You need to be modest where you are immodest and immodest where you are modest." And about my work in general said I needed to focus "on vectors of force in your writing," a statement I chewed over for days.

But his talk with me quieted me a little, reassured me. When he left, I went back to work on the Shakespeare essays with a will.

Except for my stories, which were my strong suit, the essays were all pretty mechanical stuff, although Robert Duncan, chosen by Olson and Creeley as my outside examiner for my graduation ("We don't want any academic types," Olson had said)—*very* outside, since Duncan was then living with his lover, Jess Collins, in Mallorca, where Creeley's family still was while Creeley hopped back and forth to teach at Black Mountain—had a somewhat different take on those essays, as Duncan expanded on in a letter to Creeley dated October 7, 1955, a month after I'd graduated:

From the three critical pieces provided for my consideration, it is clear that Rumaker's work in this type of essay is better than average, certainly as good as average graduate work. The papers are casual, not academic—but it is a difference of task set, not of difference of competence in organization and craft that would distinguish here. And the insights, the constant interplay of experience and new materials which is of the essence of a critical intelligence— these are here, as they are not often to be found in graduating students at the "A" level . . . .

Since Dorn and I were both studying the Greeks with Olson as part of our graduation projects, Charles—I suppose to give it a passing scholarly flavor—had us do some research on

Pausanias and Herodotus et al., including Euripides, his *Medea* and *The Trojan Women*, the "only" Greek dramatist, to Olson. So, the two of us in Dorn's dusty little black Morris Minor drove into Asheville to the Pack Library to do "research." I, of course, ever the dutiful son (to the commands of Olson, the father), was ready to spend all afternoon at the library, returning to the campus only in time for supper. I had gotten several reference works from the stacks (*dusty* volumes, the ancient Greeks evidently not all that big in that neck of the woods) and began to take notes, with great effort since the books were so old and the antique academic language so dry, it was hard to focus. So, feeling like we shouldn't, still, it didn't take much to convince me when Dorn, restless, more ornery, more bored than I, no doubt looking on getting away from the campus and family for an afternoon as a bit of a holiday, hustled me away after an hour or so. He drove us to a dimly-lit blue-collar-hill-folk bar he'd earlier discovered with Dan Rice in the poorer section of Asheville, to drink beers at a table surrounded by affable, tall, stringy people from the hills with sharp-featured faces and big eyes and ears, who all seemed to have wide-brimmed soft felt hats pushed back on their damp brows. With our own lean looks, long stringy hair and rough worker's wear, we seemed, until we opened our mouths, to fit right in. After our first beer, Ed intimated he knew I would like the place, that being there was more of an education than being holed up in dead old Pack Library. I still felt a little guilty, not spending the time we promised Charles we would doing research. But after a couple of more bottles of Ballantine ale and listening to the honeyed lyrical hill music of the stories in the voices around me, I soon lost my scruples worrying about the dead old Greeks who, through the sweet haze of cheap cigarette smoke and alcohol, and the soft *live* chatter in the dark, yeasty air, had, in the midst of all that conviviality, indeed become living remnants in the very mouths of those hillfolk, *and* a hell of a lot livelier than the dead musty tomes at Pack. I rationalized that the two of us were actually doing what Pausanias and Herodotus had done— actually doing what Olson kept stressing we do, to be and act like them in our own pursuits, not reading about it but out looking and listening on our own.

Down in the Weaving Room in the Studies one evening early in 1955, where a group of us gathered after Charles had driven us to a movie in Asheville, we fell to discussing John Huston's upcoming movie version of *Moby-Dick*. I was eager to hear the great Melville scholar's opinion on the then-being-shot flick, which was succinct: he jeered at the prospect of seeing Gregory Peck's "mad coffee-bean eyes" as Ahab and, even though he admired Huston, because of the mechanical whale problems in the stormy Irish Sea and his casting of Peck, all noted in the press, Charles, sight unseen, was negative about Huston's prospects as well.

John Chamberlain, ex-sailor in the U. S. Navy, was a sculptor working in metal who came to Black Mountain via Chicago and the Art Institute of Chicago in 1955, persuaded by Jerry Van de Wiele, himself a former battle artist in the U. S. Marine Corps, who also later convinced artist Richard Bogart to make the trip, and who all knew each other as students at the Art Institute.

Chamberlain was a sturdily built man, big arms and shoulders with a generously rounded stomach I teasingly referred to as a "buddha-belly," with a navel, visible because the fronts of his shirts were always riding up, large enough to comfortably insert a half-dollar coin. He had thick black wavy hair and broad sensuous features, suggestively Slavic and Mediterranean, a puggish, somewhat bulbous nose; attractive eyes that were quietly observant and tinged with an appealing warmth, eyes that made you feel the person behind them was understanding, accepting, non-judgmental. He exuded a very quick power of trust and gentle, bear-like strength. I liked him right off, as did most everyone, particularly women: you could see they just wanted to eat him right up. I felt from the start I could tell him my most inward secrets and thoughts, my silliest ideas and fears, and he would understand, without saying a word, as so often happened: he would just look out at me with those unjudging eyes that had such a look of kindness in them—a seeming paradox in a man of such burly build and rough and shaggy exterior. Another paradox was that, besides contorting metal out of shape to fit the shapes of his visions of it with burning torch and welding torch, or with the sheer strength of his own sizable muscles, John, to scratch up the money to go to school and do his sculpting, worked now and again as a hair-dresser. It was a job he admitted he was very good at, and, as he explained to us without in any way being defensive (remember this was the 1950s), it was the most sensible way to make quick and easy money in a profession that, although dominated by women and gay male workers, given their paucity of economic options then, was always looking for help and paid handsomely, especially in tips. For a guy like John, who said he had "the touch" and knew how to listen to women, he did all right. In those days, John could always, when he needed to, walk into a beauty parlor and get a job anytime, anywhere, for as long as he needed it. The fact that he was a man who genuinely loved women—loved the woman in himself, as I intuited it—helped considerably.

Elaine, the young woman artist and devout Catholic he was engaged to, was still back in Chicago spending a good deal of time trying to arrange a papal dispensation from the Vatican so she could marry the divorced John. John's Chicago and Detroit pals at Black Mountain razzed her for being such a churchy Catholic, especially for not wanting to sleep with John till they were married in the Church. John was more exasperated, not to mention frustrated, by it all, but he seemed willing to wait. However, John without a woman at Black Mountain was like the metal sculptor he was without a blowtorch. You could occasionally see him eyeing the few available, and non-available, females on campus, using his most subtly seductive beauty-parlor techniques, taking an especial shine to Connie Olson, his eye occasionally and unobtrusively on her.

Although he thought much of what was going on at Black Mountain was pretty mickey-mouse, especially the "community" aspects of it, he was powerfully attracted to the writings and presence of both Olson and Creeley. Although I can't remember him ever being in any of their classes, he was still very much a student of their work and a shrewd and perceptive listener in their one-to-one conversations with him.

Chamberlain was a real original, kinky and individualistic as an artist, as were most at Black Mountain. But John was always a little more so with his own often more peculiar—read "fresher"—way of seeing and saying things, which were given a quite different twist (like the torsions of increasingly new forms in his sculptures) from the way the rest of us saw and heard things. In a place where to be off-center was the norm, John appeared eccentric in spades, even more so sometimes than Olson himself (who now, it becomes clearer and clearer, was more centered than all that was considered the center, then or now).

Not that Chamberlain, lone wolf that he was, was off in left-field somewhere (to outside eyes, we *all* seemed that); he just needed to go the way he had to in his work. He was the only serious sculptor on campus at that time, the only sculptor, in fact, in my stay there, so he had to depend a lot on himself and on his own growing ideas, fed into by Olson and Creeley, particularly the latter. Again, what Black Mountain provided for him, as it did for so many of us, was the space and time, a congenial climate to put his sculptural ideas, his visions, into material shape. It began to show in his work, which started to change almost as soon as he arrived at the place.

Speaking of leftfield, softball at Black Mountain was played on the crudely laid out diamond in the broad field across the road from the Gatehouse and along Lake Eden. Sunday afternoons, I, as pitcher, wearing jaunty handkerchief cravat for the occasion, stared down batters, psyching them out, especially my prime tormentor, Jorge Fick of Detroit, who was so rattled he kept stepping out of the batter's box, loudly but laughingly protesting.

John Chamberlain, as ump, called somebody safe at first, which Olson was covering, and Fee Dawson, who thought they were dead out, shouted at Chamberlain, "You *motherfucker*!" And, apparently hearing that word for the first time in his life, Charles' eyes bugged wide, like somebody had punched him in the stomach, as he expelled a thin, high breath of shock and delight.

In the beginning, though, they stuck me out in leftfield, figuring, I guess, from the looks of me, I could do the least damage there. One Sunday, the game was close, a long fly was hit to me, and Richard Bogart, recently arrived painter student from Detroit and pal of Fick, playing rightfield, was furious, hollering, as the ball arched up and up, "*He'll* never catch it, damn it! There goes the game!" But miraculously I did catch it, with cool aplomb, which surprised the hell out of Bogart, not to mention the others on both teams, even surprised myself, although maybe not as much as the others.

I could play tolerably well (after all, I grew up in a family of jocks and in a town where all the boys—and many of the girls—played baseball), could hit, pitch, etc., fair enough. But I got bored with the way Charles and Fee and Jorge, et al., were so dead *serious* about The Game (one reason why I never joined their smoke-filled poker marathons down in one of the empty studies in the Studies Building). So, as pitcher, I made a playful sport of it, campy, wearing those improvised cravats, using some of what I learned from Wes in acting class—a fairy on the field, trying his best to defuse the testosterone grimness.

That year the Bishop of Raleigh expressed interest in a possible purchase of the college as both a retreat for his diocese and, most curious, some sort of Black Mountain-style Notre Dame, and arranged a visit with Olson to look the place over. Although in my heart I resisted any thought of a sale of the place, I realized the end of the school was impossible to avoid, and so went along with it when Charles, increasingly desperate to sell, had us make the place as presentable as possible. With his help, we swept and cleaned the Studies, washed windows, and replaced broken panes. He then persuaded a few of us remaining students to be in our studies working the Saturday morning of the bishop's visit, "with your door open," he pointedly advised, for display purposes, to make the place look a little alive when Olson gave the bishop the grand tour of the property.

I was dutifully pounding away at my old upright typewriter when Charles and the bishop, a pudgy, pasty, bland-faced man in clerical black and traditional white collar, came down the hall. Charles, at his most affable and charming, wearing a broad, genial grin (knowing what he thought of the Church, what an effort it must have cost him, he who in class one night stated, "Christianity became irrelevant when it went after sex in the 1500s"), stopped at my door to introduce us. I stumbled up, a bit tonguetied at being in the presence of the embodiment of an old struggle, a religion I was still as conflicted about as was Charles himself, and fighting mightily to free myself from, the first contact I'd had with a priest, and a bishop no less, since I'd been on campus. While Charles described me in elaborately glowing terms as a student, I bobbed my head and grinned foolishly while the bishop's small eyes peered at me blandly.

I was relieved when they left, moving down the hall in the

direction of the sun deck, and was glad my part in the pretense was over, as I listened to Charles' enthusiastic voice, somewhat theatrical and forced in his unaccustomed role of real estate agent, extolling the benefits of the building. I was still resenting that the place had to be sold at all and bitterly resenting it might fall into the hands of a tax-exempt institution that could afford it, particularly one whose doctrinal and dogmatic tyranny I resisted with a passion.

As I was thinking this, I could hear the public phone ringing down the long corridor in the entry (the only phone now on campus). I went to answer it, pleased to be doing something truly useful and meaningful. It was a call for Charles, and since I knew he and the bishop had been heading for the sun deck, I hurried back along the hall, hearing Charles' voice outside now on the deck, pointing out to the bishop the farm in the distance and the magnificence of the view, all prime selling points of course. As I shoved open the door to the deck, to my horror I almost knocked the bishop, who'd been leaning against it, flat on his face. Charles' grin stretched even more—I suspect he was as secretly delighted as I was abashed—as he clutched the arm of the tottering and disconcerted bishop, solicitously asking if he were all right while dusting off the chalky white paint smudge from the door from the shoulders of the bishop's black coat. As for me, I stuttered out an apology and managed to tell Charles he was wanted on the phone, then beat a retreat back to the sanctuary of my study.

The deal never did go through. I liked to think my practically knocking the Bishop of Raleigh on his ass might've jinxed it. I was as relieved as other students were when we found out the diocese had dropped its interest in the property, knowing it gave us a little more time yet to live in what was, for many of us, our first and only real home.

After the bishop had left, Charles bragged to us with great glee that when His Excellency asked how the college and its staff and students managed to get along on so little, Charles told him in all seriousness, not without cutting irony given who he was speaking to, that he and the rest of us had long ago decided "to take the vow of poverty, chastity and obedience."

He got the poverty right.

Jake was a tall, jug-eared youth with the whey-colored skin of a redhead whose hair was literally bright as a carrot and lay close to his round skull in flat, fine curls. The skin of his large-featured face had a coarse, grainy texture, like someone who eats poorly, a chalky translucence that revealed the slightest blemish. His milky-blue eyes could be filled, all at once, with an intense desire to please so you would like him, as well as a sly and guarded suspiciousness that you probably never would. Some people mistook this dichotomy in his eyes for sneakiness—it did give him a certain shifty look—and as a result they kept shy of him. He was a year or two younger than I, 20 or 21, a nervous, high-strung guy who I could identify with because of his own transparent confusions, the ones closest to the surface anyway, that caused his blue eyes to snap from one uncertainty to the next in the split second of a blink.

He had a quick nervous laugh and could be "sincere" when it suited him. He was very much the actor, which was what he'd come to Black Mountain to study, and yet underneath I sensed in him that genuine, almost desperate need to be liked, to be allowed to fit in.

He was also from Philadelphia and that was another cause for identification. But at first I had trouble with him, as everyone else did. I always felt, when I first met him, those quick eyes of his were working me over, were probing for chinks, for flaws, looking for a way into me that would expose to him any weaknesses he might be able to make use of. And of course the most immediate vulnerability—I wouldn't, even in those bleak, uncertain days, call it a "weakness"—he spotted was my queerness. And just as I was always on guard for homophobia, I suspect Jake, as a Jew, was always sniffing for anti-Semitism. So, in those eyes that darted to mine, then as swiftly, as if caught (or in fear of getting caught), darted away, there was not so much a question as a look that he *knew* and that he was working in some way to make use of that knowledge. I felt uncomfortable about it only because his knowing—and I could see right off that he did know—carried with it a heavy dose of contempt and, perhaps for both of us, an even heavier dose of self-doubt and guilt, more for him, perhaps, because he was always mentioning a "girlfriend" back in Philly. But desire was there, too, that part of him that wanted to be liked, that wanted to be desired, that burned, as I burned, as only the hungriest can, as only outcasts can, Jew or queer.

So often people seemed to come to Black Mountain actually looking for something other than their stated, conscious purpose. They would come down saying, I want to paint, or, I want to write; when in reality the urge was to escape from a tyrannical or abusive household or an equally tyrannical and boring school situation (such as my own Rider experience), or a town or city neighborhood they felt alien in (like my own queer self); or, maybe strongest of all, unnamable hungers drove us all, in some measure, south, urged on by vague rumors that at Black Mountain we would find a place to be free and be as we needed to be, to find what we needed. I came, essentially, because I wanted to learn to write, but I think beneath was also an urgent prompting from my unconscious to go seek the release it needed, to find a place where my unruly erotic impulses could be set free in an atmosphere of relative unrestrictedness and, most important, safety. Mary Reed's observation back in Philly of Black Mountain as "a hotbed of communists and homosexuals" was certainly true regarding the latter, and no doubt an unconscious boost to my own motivations. (As for "subversives," language instructor Flola Shepard had been the only communist around and, given it was the height of the McCarthy era, she'd been pretty closeted about it, on campus anyway.)

Jake, like most of us, studied acting and theater with Wes Huss. He bunked in the apartment in the rear of the Studies (Creeley's old apartment) with Jerry Van de Wiele and John Wieners, John living there temporarily after he first arrived, till he moved up to Streamside with the Dunns when they showed up, Wieners more comfortable with his fellow Bostonians, and possibly to get away from Jake. Jerry told me, in high gossipy amusement, that shortly after Jake had arrived Jake'd taken to parading around stark naked when John was in the apartment, in a way, Jerry conveyed in vivid imitation—strutting, chest out, neck rippled in muscles (Jerry was a weight-lifter), his head strained back, mimicking a cocky rooster—that was apparently designed to get John all hot and bothered and want to make it with Jake. Black Mountain wasn't equipped to deal with our various neuroses, personality quirks, or even the psychoses of some of the students who were beginning to show up, so many of us damaged refugees from families, homes, and, later, mental hospitals and the growing drug world out there. What it offered was a space to work in the field you chose and a faculty with considerable experience in that field; to learn our craft in a dynamic and interdependent relatedness to all other fields. Anything outside that was possible, even tolerated, permitted. The sense I got from Jake was that he'd come to Black Mountain primarily for the "outside" things, the acting also a driving but perhaps secondary impulsion; had come to find, if not solutions, at least an accepting and comfortable place to test and perhaps put to rest those troubles that had such obvious snap and preoccupation in his eyes; that offered him the slim possibility at least of his own release.

Jake pranced around and posed bareass all he wanted, hoping to lure John into the sack, but Wieners, carrying the torch for

Dana, wasn't buying. Jake did have his physical attractions, having the wide shoulders and slim waist of a swimmer. (In the scarcity of possible male partners at Black Mountain, not to mention female partners as well, snobbish or picky attitudes on "defects" of physique or personality diminished considerably.) But hungry as I was, I was again, as perhaps John was too, wary. That something in Jake's eyes, that being pulled two ways, and a strong sense of his uncertainty in either direction, turned me off. Where Jake was coming from was a place I had once been and no longer was nor wanted to be again. One of the fringe benefits of the openness and acceptance at Black Mountain that had allowed me to heal that previously unhealable "infection," was that I could begin at least to act on my desires in an environment where there was neither danger nor threat of being beaten up, raped, imprisoned in jail or in a mental institution, blackmailed or murdered, all of which possibilities were realities (a few of which, including threats of murder, I'd personally experienced) in that homophobic world beyond the gate. Perhaps, as with any number of us, Jake too had made the journey to Black Mountain sensing this possible freedom, more perhaps than even his need to learn acting from Huss.

Having failed with Wieners, however, Jake soon turned his attentions on me. I liked him well enough, even though his watchful manner kept me on edge. Perhaps to put me at my ease, and also maybe send me a signal, he asked me, since I was also from that area, did I know of a new gay bar that'd opened in North Camden, New Jersey, "out by one of the traffic circles." He even told me how to get there by bus, next time I was up there. Besides Philly, we also shared an interest in acting and drama, both of us studying with Wes. Jake would often drop in to talk with me in my study, or sometimes, by "accident" I sometimes thought, catch me alone in the kitchen of Meadows Inn, and we'd sit at the table and have coffee. I knew what was bearing down and tried to skirt it as much as I could. A lot of my uneasiness with him centered around that, the unspoken erotic energy that crackled in the air, not so much between us as around us.

What also held me back, despite his tall swimmer's body, was no doubt some deeply ingrained prejudice from childhood when I picked up the myth that redheads were different, peculiar; to be a redhead was funny and odd and in no way attractive, often an object of ridicule. Like the blue-collar Catholic anti-Semitism of my father, a stupid and contorted prejudice surely, but there it was. Even Olson later on played on this myth in his 1956 poem "The Lordly and Isolate Satyrs":

> . . . The red-headed people have the hardest time
> to possess themselves. Is it because they were over-
> fired? Or why—even to their beautiful women—do the red ones
> have only that half of the weight? . . . .

In my weakest moments, in my own enflamed eyes, Jake's hair burned with a mythical satyr's fire, himself as "isolate" as I myself felt to be, another attraction and connection.

Jake evidently picked up on this pretty quick. If he had come to Black Mountain trying to find out something about himself, he was also maybe genuinely sincere and, picking up on my probably not too carefully concealed need, was offering himself to "help" me out. Not totally unselfishly, of course, but it was an opportunity that more and more, as our accidental meetings (or so they seemed) and our increasingly open and frank talks continued, was becoming a decided temptation.

If sap can be said to sizzle in the blood it was doing just that, with a hot spit to it that left me no rest and preoccupied and diverted a great deal of my energy. I had been particularly impressed on reading a passage in the original Patchen manuscript of *The Journal of Albion Moonlight*, published in 1941, that Jonathan Williams had showed me some months back, where Patchen wrote, "My sex is still tonight." He went on to say he felt glad about it, having rest from it, surcease. That was an incredible statement to me since my sex was rarely ever still, gnawing at me with persistence, even though I hadn't the opportunity lately to put it into action, except by my own hand, which is only half the satisfaction. It made me think again of Charles, his own admissions regarding women, his hand on my knee in his darkened convertible that night: "There is no end to desire . . ." he had written.

So it wasn't long before Jake and I shared more in common than just coming from the city of our birth, and finally did obey William Penn's sweet injunction in regards to "brotherly love," transported south and celebrated Black Mountain-style. I decided that a study would be more private than my room in Meadows Inn; since we were so few on campus and good, juicy gossip always at a premium, you had to take special pains to cover your tracks in any endeavor you didn't want all over the community by 8 a.m. the next morning. Even though great care was taken by myself and my partners, I was certain that what I was doing and with whom was no real secret. The old saying "the walls have ears" was never truer, especially in Meadows Inn, since Tom Field—alert as a bird to the remotest shiver of sound—bunked in the room directly next to mine.

So one night after supper, Jake and I for the first time made use of a study that had, most important, a mattress in it, one of those bare, mildewy, pillow-ticking mattresses scattered everywhere at Black Mountain. This one was in the study next to my old now-vacant one on the lower level which, with its wall of frosted glass windows, was too risky to use, with the ceiling lights of the hall shining in, I was concerned our shadows could be seen through the glass. My face was flushed and hot with excitement, and some nervousness too, not only because it was the first time with Jake, but because the study we were in was almost directly across from the apartment Jake shared with Van de Wiele and Wieners, within earshot anyway. I could hear Jerry talking and laughing through the walls and was worried he would hear us. Even at Black Mountain, old habits of secrecy and shame persisted. Perhaps, too, it was in my own silly pride, my not wanting anyone to know I was fucking a person no one liked.

There was a bluish light in the room coming from the moonlight and low-hanging Southern stars of the night sky glimmering in at the windows. But there was also a feeling of dense blackness, and a sense of hurry on my part, both out of the genuine urgency of need and also out of a fear of getting caught, or that someone might hear us or try the knob to come into the room and find out we were there—Black Mountain people were always wandering about at all hours looking for this or that necessity in the studies, a lightbulb, an extra chair, etc.— even though I knew it was an unused study, had even picked it out ahead of time.

In those first few moments, my prejudice against redheads dissolved in the darkness. In the starlight through the windows, I could faintly perceive Jake indeed had a smooth and hairless body, except for a sparse tuft of red at his groin that seemed a light of its own in the shadows. Lying full length beside each other on the bare mattress, we embraced, then kissed, his skin beneath my fingers surprisingly cool in contrast to my own heat-flushed eagerness. And yet I sensed a part of him holding back, a part that said, Now I'll let you take over, let you be responsible for whatever happens.

Afterward, I would barely admit into my consciousness a troubling remembrance of that certain coldness in him, that holding back, a rigidity of him, keeping himself at bay; a silence beyond the tacit and instinctively agreed-on silence, as my body grappled over his on the dark mattress.

And barely admitting to myself, too, away from him, alone in my study or on walks in the hills, in moments of retrospect, that it wasn't Jake alone using me, I was equally, if not more so, a part of it. We used each other, and if giving was in it, gave only what we knew how to give.

Unlike Patchen, my sex was never still.

At one point not long after we first got together, Jake abruptly returned to Philadelphia to visit his much-mentioned girlfriend. We were all surprised, myself perhaps more than the others, when he brought her back with him and announced that they were married. She was a plain, fussy young woman with glasses and bobbed, mousy-blond hair, seemed very practical, very distant. She and Jake were put up in the now-vacant lower apartment in the Studies, since Jerry had moved up to Black Dwarf and Wieners to Streamside. You could see that Jake was eager for her to be liked, in what appeared a mixture of shame and affection, as if she were now an appendage of his own need in that direction. But she was quiet and colorless and, like Jake, never seemed quite to fit in, even among those of us at Black Mountain who took it as a virtue not to fit in.

I wondered if Jake had married her for safety (using her, too), or because he desperately hoped, a not uncommon notion given the traditional ignorance of the times, that marriage would effect a "cure," if he was indeed gay. If his times with me were only the result of raging hormones and he'd only turned to another male for relief, in another time-honored tradition, such male behavior occurring when there is a scarcity of females, even sometimes when there is not (as I've emphasized, there definitely was that tradition at Black Mountain), then that conjecture only gave me another example of having been used by him, of allowing myself to be so used.

But bickerings between them began almost immediately; there were rumors of loud arguments that could sometimes be heard through their apartment walls or through their open windows in the Studies. Jake, fitting the myth of the fiery redhead, had a temper, and his wife, for all her colorlessness, could match him on her own terms. She continued to make no effort to be a part of the place—she may have taken an acting class or two with Wes—but she also seemed too reluctant or shy to make friends with others. As a result, given the friction between them, it wasn't long before she returned to Philadelphia.

It wasn't long, either, after her departure, that Jake came tapping on my bedroom door after midnight.

Before the night of the party in Streamside, we had been together several times, in my room after midnight and once at night in my study after a little beer party at Peak's, the Ballentine's ale adding insouciance, so that I left the overhead light on—the only eyes able to see in the big double windows from that height being the eyes of owls and luna moths and the whippoorwills endlessly chugging in the nearby trees. I had to guide him in, his hands seemingly wanting nothing to do with it, wanting it and not wanting it, as if in participating as little as possible, he couldn't be held accountable, had been taken over, led to it, and that didn't make him guilty of that, or guilty at all. *I* was the true "queer"; the biblical "sodomite" of his ancient desert fathers, who were terrified of diminishment, of squandering seed.

I began to resist Jake after that night, then began to avoid him, finally not liking to use, not liking to be used. One afternoon, shortly before the party John Wieners and I planned at Streamside, as I was sitting alone reading in the kitchen in Meadows Inn, Jake appeared in the doorway. I could see what was in his eyes, but looked away. He had come to offer himself again, seduction in those eyes, sacrifice himself more accurately perhaps, in the loose cant of his swimmer's body, in the way he slouched across the table from me. But I resisted, silently, coldly, talked desultorily of other things, of nothing at all, really, and when his looks persisted, I grew silent and stared directly at him.

He glanced away, his sly smile faltering—and from the icy look now in his own eyes, a look tinged with fury, I knew he'd gotten the message.

After a moment, he got up and left without a word.

As in the old days of teas, Mary Fiore may have suggested it, but it was John Wieners and I who were the prime movers in throwing that Saturday night party in the lobby of Streamside, the house where Wieners now lived, that late spring of 1955. It was one of those impromptu affairs gotten up to break the monotony of routine and the tendency among us toward isolation in living and working habits, holed up for long stretches of time, each of us hiding in our separate lives, social life having shrunk to almost nothing at the college. Then suddenly, in a spirit of boredom and desperation, somebody would suggest a tea or a party to liven things up, to shake off the blues. This time, Wieners and I took the bait, and there we were, a fair-sized number of the community gathered (we must have been no more than a dozen in all by then), a bring-your-own booze and snacks affair, to bravely try to have a good time, "bravely" because even at this point the college was beginning to change, to deteriorate and break up, inescapedly so. More likely we threw the party in a last attempt to give a sense of cohesion and solidarity among the remaining people holding on steadfastly at the place, a last-gasp try at community.

Although we were reduced in numbers (and reduced in space since the closing up of the lower half of the campus, the huge space of the dining hall no longer available—or needed, given our size—for the parties which had a long and imaginative tradition at Black Mountain—perhaps in Mary's and my mind the party was another feverish grasp at the past), the lobby at Streamside was reminiscent of one of those Saturday night get-togethers in my first years at the school, where practically everybody showed up. That night, music such as was played at those earlier moonshine dances—Miles Davis, Charlie Parker, Stan Getz—was playing quietly on a portable phonograph off in a corner. To my relief, perhaps to the relief of us all, Connie, who had returned by now from New England with Kate, maybe to try one last time to patch things up with Charles, showed up with Olson. I was surprised that they did, since they rarely attended parties, even in the old dining hall days, especially Connie. Another reason I was surprised to see the Olsons together was because of the apparent rupture in their "marriage," rooted, no doubt, in Charles' carryings-on with Betty Kaiser. Surely Connie must have known of that, along with Charles' heated correspondence with Frances Boldereff.

But that night there was a certain vivacity about Connie. She was dressed in something light, a cream-colored dress I'd never seen before, very attractive, a "dressy" garment, unlike her more usual denim skirts and Mexican blouses and trousers. She had done something with her hair, let it hang loose about her shoulders, rather than her more usual bun or rubberband-held ponytail; the style gave her a freer, more youthful look. She placed herself, drink in hand, by the stairs in the north corner of the lobby (Streamside, unlike Meadows Inn, had an interior stairway to the second floor with a solid-board "banister"), standing at a decided distance from Charles, which was unlike her. Charles himself stood off at the far south end of the room, holding forth as usual. She invited John Wieners and me and several other students to come talk with her. Another surprise was that I'd never seen Connie drink before, or at least drinking as much as I saw that night, and she was not only making a point of drinking, as if determined to get drunk, but appeared to have had a few before she'd arrived. She wasn't tipsy, not yet anyway, but there seemed a reckless, and appealing, energy about her that evening. She was very complimentary to me, and to Wieners, telling us how much she liked us, quite outspoken about it, which was very unlike her. Her usual New

England reserve dissolving in the warmth of alcohol, she was relaxed, charming and intelligently perceptive as always, as she touched on other subjects, only more so, more determinedly so that night. Appealingly open, chatty, flirty, even, something I'd *never* seen in her before, also almost determinedly so, as if she had made up her mind beforehand that, come what may, she was going to have a good time—and obviously was going to have it apart from Charles. She didn't cling to him at other gatherings so much as always to be near him, very much in his presence, mainly because you got the feeling they genuinely enjoyed each other's company and exchange of talk. Perhaps too there was a tacit understanding on Charles' part, given the occasional slip of his jealousy, to have her close; and for her part, perhaps there was a protective need of her own to be close to him, never far out of his sight. And they were certainly a fine pair together when it came to conversation in company, with Charles taking the edge, but Connie's fine-honed intelligence and spare insightful remarks often clarifying or outdistancing his own.

Tonight, however, it appeared she had decided to shine on her own. And shine she did, attracting a growing cluster of us around her, including now John Chamberlain, who was still awaiting fiancée Elaine's arrival from Chicago and the papal dispensation that would permit her, in Elaine's then very Catholic eyes, to marry the once-divorced Chamberlain. Connie continued to be very complimentary to Wieners and me, in asides, telling us things she liked about us that she had never told us before. As the evening, and the drinks, wore on, her vivacity and charming talk continued, an almost forced gaiety, it seemed, with, I began to detect, a decided edge of defiance aimed at Charles, perhaps a desperate declaration of independence, a quiet but scintillating rebelliousness to prove that she could talk to and attract others, be appreciated quite apart from himself, that she was capable of doing this on her own. And, maybe even more to the point, to show him that other males, even the two queer partygivers, found her attractive. Perhaps she was trying to teach him the age-old lesson, born out of bitter envy and the pain of prospective loss, that two could play the cheating game as well as one.

I loved Connie even more that night. I had the feeling that I wished she would let herself go like that more often (as I wished my own mother would have).

And then John Chamberlain, hovering stocky and bear-like close by, black mustachioed with long, shaggy hair, who had always been partial to her in a distant, respectful way, especially with his being separated from Elaine, letting words drop to a few of us on occasion to reveal his admiration and affection for Connie, now moved in closer. He began to talk quietly and earnestly in that seemingly confused but always magnetic way of his, quietly, immediately intimate. He gave you the feeling that he was talking only to *you*, with a direct warmth and humor that always won you over, just as he began talking now only to Connie that night, leaning one big arm thrust up against the wall above her shoulder, talking intently to her alone, as if they were alone, as if he was, although his words spoke of other things, verbally making love to her, his strong arm thrust above her shoulder like a wall blocking out the rest of us.

Connie listened, attentive, she too giving the sense that the rest of us were no longer present. Occasionally, when she interjected a response, I saw an even more subtle flirtation in her eyes, a look I had never seen before in those private and carefully concealed eyes, a look which alcohol, and perhaps a desperate anger borne of jealousy, had helped bring to their dark surface.

I couldn't see Charles, my back was to him, but I was aware of his voice still sounding, now in a rumble, now in excited exclamation, not unusual for him, as he continued to hold forth to whatever small gathering of listeners of his own across the room. But I suspect he was fully attuned to what was occurring over in our corner, especially now as John Chamberlain drew in even closer from the outer ring of our little group and began talking even more directly and earnestly to Connie alone. There was nothing unusual in that under any other circumstances, but tonight, with the look in Connie's eyes, and the rumors of a rift between Charles and her because of the now-departed Betty, and my strong underlying sense of Charles' strong possessiveness, especially regarding Connie, I had the suspicion trouble lay ahead and began to be filled with uneasiness.

Of course I myself by this time was beginning to feel no pain on the cheap whiskey—County Fair Bourbon, that particular, and inexpensive, favorite of mine, purchased on rare occasions because of lack of funds at the State Liquor store on our weekly and bi-weekly trips to Asheville in Tom's new Buick.

So, in part, because of my uncertainties with the future of the college (and my own future once I graduated), with my writing, with the constant day-to-day scraping along and preoccupations with the nickels and dimes—my own and the school's—in the bare necessities of survival, I was determined, although for different reasons than Connie, to tie one on, opportunities to do so were so infrequent, and because of my years, because of the lack of the chance and of money to go to Peak's or into Asheville all that often, drink was not yet playing a central need in my life. That came later.

So when John Chamberlain moved in on Connie, and after our merry little group broke up, sparked by Connie's need to, if not outshine, at least draw some of the customary magnetic spotlight away from Charles, in anger, it seemed, because of her own increasingly shadowy existence in his life, I circulated around the room in a growing and pleasant blur of convivial booziness, feeling the edges of anxiety and tension on all counts lessen with each swig of bourbon.

As a result, I wasn't aware of Connie's disappearance from the party, or noticed that John Chamberlain had also disappeared.

Charles was still there, getting a little high himself, it seemed, more voluble than ever, but relaxed. If, in that time, he knew Connie had left with Chamberlain, he made no sign of it. He seemed at ease and garrulous, and I listened to him now with the old, glad-hearted fascination and expectation, as pleased as always to be close and listening to him, as pleased as I had been to be with Connie earlier in the evening.

After the party had been going on for several hours or so, I found myself sitting at the square oak table in the center of the lobby, drinking now with Mary and Joe Fiore. That part of the room was dimmer, the other half of the lobby in brighter light. I no longer sensed Charles' presence in the room. Now that he was unaccountably gone, and Connie, too, along, presumably, with Chamberlain, our talk was intermittent, had a forced tone to it. The atmosphere in the lobby now was a combination of a grudging determination to have, if not a good time, at least a passable one, mixed with a kind of ragged, high-charged energy, the few of us left at the college having lived off each other for so long we had begun to anticipate each other, and were frankly bored. Still, the energy in the air was of an impatient waiting for something to happen. Right from the start there seemed a tense exhaustion in the atmosphere, no matter how much Wieners, with his chattering laugh and gaiety, or my own smaller attempts at conviviality, tried to diffuse it. Soft jazz was still playing on the phonograph, but it failed to lighten those heavy, charged surroundings. Mary did her best, struggling to make conversation, get something going, and then grew silent. We looked about the room, looked carefully away from each other. It was simply that we had been through too much, had had too much of one another. Everything seemed past tense now.

Then I saw Jake standing outside the door, the bottom half of the Dutch door closed so that only his upper torso in a grimy t-shirt was visible through the outer screen door in the open portion, the redness of his hair glowing in the dense shadows of the mountain laurel growing thickly around the door, making the black night beyond even blacker. In the wan light of the lobby through the screening his face had an even whiter look, a flat, drained face that peered in on us with an expressionless hard mask. Seeing his face, the blunt shove of his chest against the screen door, I felt myself stiffen, grow reptilian still. The room felt suddenly cold.

He stood outside only for an instant—I seemed to be the only one to notice his arrival—then he yanked at the screen door, kicked the lower half of the Dutch door open and stalked a few paces into the room standing, in chinos and scruffy sneakers, with legs spread wide, fists clenched at his thighs. His face now was a stiff snarl. His eyes scanned the room in a slow icy circle alighting on everyone with a look of contempt, everyone except myself. His accusing eyes avoided me as if I wasn't there.

It's me he's come for, I thought, instantly sobering, and although I felt a sudden inward shaking, I remained still, a reptile watching.

For sheer dramatic impact and intensity, his timing, his concentration, was perfect. I kept watching to see if this wasn't only acting, some acting out of anger, a psychodrama, some extracurricular acting exercise left over from Wes' drama class that we would be taken in by and laugh at afterwards when Jake dropped his role. And in part I think it was that, all that he wanted to be or fancied himself to be, but wasn't, didn't permit himself to be: the tough, coldly fearless male. But the set of his face and eyes was real enough with anger. If he was acting—and what courage the performance must have cost him, a better performance than any I had seen him do in Wes' classes— beneath it was the substance and weight of an actual neediness, of a total and genuine pain.

Then he began to speak in a loud, harsh voice, haranguing us, his mouth twisted and ugly with hate, like his face, a face unrecognizable to me it was so pulled out of shape by his hatred. What he was shouting no longer stays with me, only the sound, the pitch of it, which was like a shrill barking against my eardrums, a stabbing resonance of sonant pain, trip-hammering in vibration to his own.

The face I had seen under me alive with pleasure in our dark and lovely moments, slipped into my consciousness, seemed, in that moment, the face of another, a stranger.

His angry words had to do with his sense of not being liked, his feeling he had been excluded. With Jake it was a game that went: I won't give you a chance to like me, I'll make you dislike me, do everything in my power, test you over and over, till you really do dislike me. "Kike," "nigger," "queer," it was all the same self-imposed, self-perpetuating hatred, an internalization I knew well on the queer side; for Jake, too, perhaps not only from that side but as a Jew as well. There was something else too, that he hadn't been *personally* invited to the party, perhaps imagined, preferred to believe, that he wasn't wanted—although the open invitation had been for all. Out of his strangulated throat, he was spewing forth all the pent-up resentments, slights and hurts, real and imagined, of hostile attitudes of others, out of a heritage of being outside, beyond the pale, constantly shoved there and now shoving himself beyond the center where he so desperately yearned to be, as I, too, so desperately yearned to be; was constantly seeking a way in, a way back in, at any cost. This was the essence of Jake's "performance" that night, an essence that I could certainly identify with, the psychic mechanism of his own self-hatred and oppression as a Jew in no way dissimilar to my own as a faggot. And Jake seemed to be caught in that double bind: Jew *and* possibly queer. Perhaps, underneath everything, we were attracted to each other, beyond all else, in recognition of that kinship and that, despite the contempt and hate in it, unverbalized, unconscious, we gave to each other, outcasts under the skin, the only pleasure we could, the only thing not taken from us, the nerve-ends of ourselves, giving some small measure of that at least as comfort and momentary affection to each other.

Spewing out all the slights and hurts that had been damming up since his arrival at the college, since his arrival on earth, no doubt—all except one, it seemed, in those moments, to my sharply attuned ears. I waited breathlessly for him to say it, to accuse me, too, to tell everyone, right there, out loud, in public, that I had abandoned him as well, like everyone else, that I had let him down. At that moment, paralyzed with guilt, with fear, I wished I hadn't.

And all the time he harangued, his eyes riveted on one and then another. His accusations, founded and unfounded, were lashed out at most everyone there. But his eyes never once lit on mine, even for the flicker of an instant, and no accusation spat through his lips into my face as into the faces of the others.

Feeling left out (and mercifully, secretly, relieved that I was) convinced me more than ever that a large part of his anger was directed at me, perhaps at that side of me he found so rawly enticing and yet so intolerable in himself, shadow identifying with shadow. And, despite that confliction, contradictorily, sparing me because we had shared those stealthy moments of dark kindness.

And I had withdrawn that intimacy, pulled it out from under him, perhaps the only measure of warmth and acceptance he'd had since he arrived.

Jerry Van de Wiele called out, half cajoling, half exasperated, "Aw, come on, Jake. Come off it. Quit acting. Come on and have a good time. Sit down and have a drink."

And Mary piped up with, "Yeah, come on and join us, Jake."

This goaded him even further. He was even more insistent, his mood becoming uglier, his accusations wilder. He would not be mollified. There was no turning back.

He was really attacking someone verbally now—was it Jorge

Fick? Or was it Jorge made a move toward him, as if to silence him. One of the men did, and it was at that moment, as I watched frozen in my chair, Jake snatched an empty beer bottle off the table Joe and Mary and I were sitting at, and cracking it against the edge, held it menacingly out in front of him, a sharp jagged weapon of green glass.

Incongruously, or perhaps not so, the scene from the 1954 movie *The Wild One*, the rebel motorcycle gang movie starring Marlon Brando, that'd had a powerful impact on a number of the young males at the college, no doubt including Jake, leapt into my mind, where one of the characters in motorcycle gear, threatened or is threatened by an attacker in the exact same way, except that if Jake had been acting up until then, it was plain he no longer was now.

The room grew very still. All eyes fastened on him. (The pinnacle of performance he had always wanted, in power, in control?) The person who had approached Jake froze for a moment staring at the splintered glass, then started backing off, as Jake, his legs still spread wide, slightly bent at the knees, his head jutting forward, craned low, shoulders hunched, bare arms swung out, one fist gripping the neck of the bottle tight as he moved it in a slow threatening arc in front of him, his body leaning forward, every muscle tense, alert, as he wielded his weapon from side to side, his eyes no longer a milky blue but slate hard, his lips curled back baring his teeth.

"If any you bastards come near me . . ."

My impulse was to do something, anything, and yet, feeling, rightly or wrongly, the full weight of his unspoken malice, knew if I made a move I, or anybody, might be cut or slashed or, from the maniacal hatred in his eyes, murdered without a qualm.

Again, incongruously, but the unexpected seems always a characteristic in such dangerous moments, the small comfort we'd had with each other strangely leapt to mind, and I was seized with an irrational impulse to offer my body, to soothe him, to quiet him, to make him less dangerous, eros as healing—To offer myself in an erotic gesture to turn around his violence, much as when I was a child and my father was beating me with his belt or kicking me, the same impulse, to offer myself, a primordial impulse of survival.

But before I could act on this wild thought (even if I would have, even had I had the courage only to interpose my body), Joe Fiore leapt up from the table, spun Jake around, grabbed him by the neck of his t-shirt and the seat of his chinos, pointed him at the door, and hollering, "Get the hell out of here!" aimed a powerful boot at his ass (the kick actually hit smack at the small of Jake's back) with so much force behind it, it lifted Jake clear off his feet, the jagged beer bottle flying from his fist, and propelled him swiftly out the door into the darkness. Joe ran to the door making sure he didn't try to rush back in.

There was a scuffling sound around the side of the house, footsteps pounding in the gravel, a sound of stumbling and a cracking noise of branches from the mountain laurel there, then the footsteps continuing, running off into the night.

I had never seen Joe take such immediate and violent action before. On the surface, he had a patient, easygoing nature, a stolid, thoroughgoing approach to things, his speech slow and considered, a striking contrast to his huge abstract paintings at that time which were bursts of lyrical, sun-drenched colors— They made you elated just to look at them. And he also had dreams that were the envy of us all, "seven moons in a row across the horizon . . . ." Coming from a stable, loving Mid-Western Italian-American family and often annoyedly baffled by the kooky insecure behavior of any number of the college's inhabitants, he had a temper, I knew, that burned low and slow and which would finally erupt in a dark and austere anger that made his handsome Italian face even darker, but it had always been verbal. Now I saw another, surprising side of him, experiencing two shocks when he kicked Jake out of the party: the empathetic physical one as his foot planted itself in Jake's back, and the one of surprise, that Joe was revealing a side of himself I'd never seen before, the army vet from World War 2 perhaps, that few of us at the college had seen.

Beyond that actual moment of danger, perhaps behind it, was Joe's own long-smouldering detestation of Jake, the phony actor always slyly sucking up to you, brought to a head that night when Jake threatened the room with his broken beer bottle.

Perhaps, in his desperately enacted psychodrama, Jake had found what he had come looking for: a vindication that he wasn't worthy of anything or anybody, wasn't worthy to be loved after all.

After Jake had been kicked out of the gathering, there was low talk about the incident, about Jake, his problems; I sat silent, hardly listening. Despite the murmurs around me, there was a quieting down, almost a sense of tranquility: we had had our sacrifice, it seemed. Sensing that, I had a sudden desperation to *really* get drunk that night, a recklessness, perhaps not unlike Connie's, in the realization that all that I needed, that all that I had had in the last few years at Black Mountain was slipping out of my hands; that what I needed to grasp I couldn't lay hold of.

Wieners and I ended up together, arms wrapped around each other, under a blanket or two on bare mattresses we'd evidently shoved together in the middle of the lobby floor. Obviously I had succeeded very well in my determination to get swacked. We slept fully clothed, without, I blearily recalled, ever a hint of erotic arousal, two friends sharing a makeshift bed, taking warmth and comfort from each other in drunken, animal sleep.

I say this, not remembering when I lay down with John, or how we decided on it, or even how or when the party ended. Clearly both of us were too drunk to make it back to our rooms, me, the short hike up to Meadows Inn; Wieners, the even shorter distance around the side of Streamside and in the back entrance of the house. I know only that we slept together, and then at some time in the early hours of the morning—it may have been later, there was an ashy light in the room, a chilly gray light in the windows, so it was close to dawn—I was abruptly awakened out of my booze-soddened stupor to hear the Dutch door of the house slam open, followed by loud foot-steps pounding across the floorboards of the lobby. Their vibrations woke me further. My bleary eyes opened just in time to see the long legs and big soles of Charles' work shoes stretch in a wide arc of a step directly over my face as he strode in one quick huge bound across the double mattress and over our prone bodies. It was then I glimpsed John, breathing softly beside me, his breath of sleep in my ear, undisturbed by this sudden intrusion. I could also hear Charles' breath, he was breathing so heavily, almost panting, like someone enraged. My sleepy, still-drunk mind was incapable of even wondering what he was doing there at that hour, striding through the place with such purpose and energy. He continued on through the lobby, followed closely behind by someone else who was with him. I glimpsed the blur of another male, someone more quiet-foot-ed, but since I snapped my eyes shut on immediately recogniz-ing Charles I'm not sure who it was. Charles was now banging open the first door in the narrow hallway leading to the back of the house, then his heavy footsteps were pounding along the hall, stopping, another door being thrust open, some sharp muttered curses, then the door slammed shut, then another door yanked open, even the bathroom door too, it sounded like, as he continued his march to the rear of the cottage.

I was more awake now but no more able to think, wonder-ing, in a feeble way, what it was he was up to. It certainly sound-ed like some emergency, and yet I was in no condition to puzzle it out. Wieners went on sleeping quietly next to me, his arms still flung about me. Apparently he hadn't heard a thing.

Then a moment of clarity as the evening came back: He's looking for Connie, I thought, he's looking for Connie and Chamberlain.

My only other thought before starting to drift off to sleep again was that Charles had seen Wieners and me lying together in an embrace in sleep, and I was strangely, and foolishly, worried about that, what he would think, in spite of my wondering that night in his darkened blue convertible, his hand on my knee as he spoke of women, if he himself were queer, because what Charles thought of me was always uppermost in my mind, I still needing his acceptance, his mighty approval.

I was falling back into a troubled sleep, thinking of Connie and Charles and Chamberlain, and worried if there would be trouble, falling back into being a child again, as when my father drunkenly, in their bed through the thin wall, accused my mother of cheating on him, my childish fears of losing them as I lay awake listening between my sleeping brothers, all that rushing back to me in that moment.

The last thing I heard before sleep overtook me was the crash of the back door slamming shut, the outside door to Wieners' room, Madame's old quarters, and heavy footsteps clattering down the backsteps, then the diminishing sound of them echoing woodenly in the distance as they crossed the footbridge over the ravine in the direction of the Studies Building. I thought of all those hundred or so study doors being forcefully yanked open and slammed shut as Charles continued his search; the thought of it took on the quality of a dream, and I wasn't sure then that I wasn't dreaming. And what would he do if he found them? The thought caused such a turmoil in my already addled brain, all I could see was the sharp, jagged end of the beer bottle clutched in Jake's fist.

The house was silent again. Birds began to rustle and chirp in the dense leaves of the mountain laurel pressed against the windows, where light like ashes matched, in early hangover, the color of dust in my own head, the taste in my mouth. I snuggled closer to John and dropped off again, this time into heavy, undreaming sleep.

Of course, next day everyone on campus knew that Charles, goaded to it after patiently waiting for her to return to their house and, when she didn't, went out in a rage near dawn, hunting for Connie and Chamberlain, searching everywhere, the Studies, The Eye, the Stables, and of course through Streamside, but didn't find them anywhere. Tom Field said he figured Charles would've wanted to kill Chamberlain if he'd found them together, because of Chamberlain's taking what Olson considered to be his own and no one else's, certainly no other man's.

Also next day, early, without saying a word or a goodbye to anyone, Jake packed up and left the college.

Not long after, Ed Dorn drove Olson, Tom Field, Jorge Fick, John Wieners and me, with one or two others squeezed in, all of us packed in his tiny Morris Minor, to Ma Peak's where we all got pretty beered up celebrating, rather prematurely, the forthcoming graduations of Dorn, Fick and myself, in a boys' night out. It was another one of the rare times I saw Olson feeling no pain, and on the way back, all of us were in a pretty jolly mood. Especially Ed, although to look at him when he drank you'd never know he'd had a few, his lean face always a perfect mask I envied. Playful, he drove right past the Gatehouse and ignored our confused protests of what the hell was he doing, was he that drunk? Ed only grinned slyly and without a word, kept on going and turned in at the back road to the farm where he began driving all around the edge of the cornfield, then steered into the cornfield itself, while we all laughingly bounced and bumped around in the back seat over the furrows. Olson, filling the front seat beside Ed, was enjoying himself immensely.

"We should have Wolpe along!" he shouted. "He'd enjoy this!" Tipsily uncaring, I went into an imitation of Wolpe's heavy German accent and his improvisatory soprano of screeches and chirpings and burblings. Olson snapped his head around, shouting, "Who is that? Who is that?" and when he saw it was me, looked surprised and even more delighted, as I let slip, under a few brews, my usual guardedness.

Not long after, on another drunken outing to Peak's, the results were quite different.

Tom and Charles and I (I don't think anyone else was with us) had driven to Ma Peak's for beer and coming back, Charles was in a more expansive mood than usual, a loose and reckless good humor and high spirits. On the way back up the mountain road Charles, driving, leaned over to playfully slap me on the back, grinningly teasing at some erotic innuendo he'd made. Connie, after the fiasco party in Streamside, had left again for Massachusetts with Kate, so we were all taking turns, in a way, taking care of Charles, inviting him over, feeding him. Tom in fact had invited Charles to supper that night at our place in Meadows Inn, just the three of us, the first time Charles was to eat with us, and Tom had prepared something special.

When we drove up to the entrance of the college, Charles spotted a couple of men, maybe four or five, fishing off the dam of Lake Eden. There'd been some trespassing and illegal use of the lake since that lower part of the property was no longer in use. Charles was incensed and said something like, "Let's get these guys out of here—They have no right to be using our property." Something like that. He sped up and slammed on the brakes, and jumped out. Tom and I got out, too. A couple of the men were big men, farmers probably, or mill workers. I guess they'd also been drinking. One, in a plaid shirt, was big-muscled and his face was red and stiff, and when he saw huge Charles coming up to him his small eyes got a hard set look, a surly, mean look. Charles started telling them in a loud voice they had no right to fish our lake, that they were trespassing and for them to clear out. But the men made no move and the man in the plaid shirt said they had a right and that they'd stay and if he wanted them to get out he'd have to make them. Charles was overdoing it and I was embarrassed that he was making a big issue over so little a thing—these men were, after all, in a way, our neighbors, people from the valley. But Charles was bull-headed and loud and insistent. I kept pulling at his arm telling him to come away, pleading with him not to start any trouble or make such a big thing out of it, because I could see the faces of the men were getting a really ugly look and I was scared to death. But it was like Charles had to prove something, something to do with more than just those guys taking a couple fish out of the lake. It's like he was storming for a fight, or to prove something, to prove his authority over the place, that they were in the wrong to be on it. Then one of the men said, "You look like a Jew. We know what you are. You shut your Jew mouth or we shut it for you." I don't know for sure what happened next, or who started it, whether Charles shoved at them (and I think that's what he did) or one of the men took a swing at him but I think it was Charles deliberately provoked it. Anyway, one of the men took a swing at Charles and caught him square in the nose and knocked his glasses off.

"Look what you did! You broke my glasses! You broke my glasses! What am I going to do? You gotta pay to get them fixed. You see what you did? They're broken," Charles staring down vaguely and pointing his finger at the shattered glass in the frames lying on the asphalt of the road, saying it awestruck, as if they'd broken his eyes, which, seeing him without his glasses, a rare thing, his eyes weak and vulnerable and unfocused, taking the strength out of his face, they had, in fact, done.

I was torn between staying (I wasn't a fighter, had lost every fight I'd ever been in, except once in 5th grade when I knocked

Joey Haley's tooth out for tormenting me) and was scared sick of violence, of the particular hard violence in these men, not unlike that I'd known as a child in my father, and I ran for help. Natural coward that I was, I ran for help, down the path that ran along Lake Eden toward the dining hall. For some reason there weren't many people around the college at that time. Somehow the thought of getting Ed Dorn to help was in my head, though why I don't know, unless I thought he might be in the immediate area, or maybe I was running back to Streamside where he lived with Helene and the kids to get him and come back and help. My mind was racing with fear and panic. Then I stopped dead in my tracks in the middle of the path, in a wooded area almost equidistant from the dining hall and where Charles and Tom and those guys were (Tom had also been trying to persuade Charles to let the men alone) and stood stock still, debating whether to go back or go on to get help, and not able to do either.

The next thing I remember is suppertime, with Charles and Tom and I eating in the big front room with the huge fireplace. The food was good, Tom was an excellent cook after all, but I had no appetite. I was sick at heart. Charles said little except to say, "In America you never get the chance to know what kind of man you are," implying maybe he had found that out that afternoon, that he had done it. He himself didn't have his usual gargantuan appetite. I could feel his eyes on me, a look that said, You betrayed me. I drank heavily but didn't get drunk. Tom served the meal and chattered merrily, like he always did when he was entertaining, as if he'd already erased the events of the afternoon. But they sat as heavy on me as the look in Charles' eyes, that I'd run away and left him, that I hadn't stayed with him.

When Creeley returned to Black Mountain from Mallorca in June 1955, the situation at the college had deteriorated and grown even more bleak financially and in morale than on his first trip. The scene matched his own personal crisis regarding an impending break with his wife.

To say that he was in an extremely agitated state would be putting it mildly. He had been unsuccessful in mending his marriage and this failure became an obsession with him, dominating his talk as he poured into any and every ear, in compulsive necessity, the most intimate details of the breakup. He would look at you, his one eye glaring and watering, a bit mad, but coaxing the sympathy out of you, as he shook his head in disgust, his brow wrinkling in bewilderment. "Can you imagine a woman saying *that* to her husband?" and he would pause to shake his head again before launching into another passionate monologue about how wronged he'd been.

In an atmosphere where sanity was often pushed to its limits, including my own later excesses, Creeley appeared at times in the weeks ahead to be not quite sane. Olson told me how Creeley had come to him one afternoon in August drunk and high on pot, crying "crocodile-tears" and complaining, "If this is the way the world is, I don't want it—If this is the way it is, you can have it." And Olson, who had been a paragon of patience and tolerance and support was getting pretty fed up by this time with Creeley's boozing and pot-smoking, letting his attention to his classes go slack, bellyaching constantly about the bust up of his marriage. Charles, all but abstemious in those days, a few beers now and again, afraid of it, I think, and with good reason, having seen him high on the two occasions already cited; Charles, the private person, silent on his own impending breakup with Connie, sat down, after he'd gotten rid of Creeley, and wrote, out of anger and affirmation, in what sounded to be a white-heat of energy, the first draft of "A Newly Discovered 'Homeric' Hymn," with its dedication: "(for Jane Harrison, if she were alive)," that cautionary apollonian avowal in the face of disorder, perhaps not only Creeley's but the college's as well.

Ahab's obsession with the white whale was as nothing compared to Creeley's obsession with the woman he felt had betrayed him and whom he was about to lose. It got so that people started ducking him when they saw him coming, not wanting to endure listening to yet another hour or so harangue of accusation and self-pity. Tom Field, who was docile and understanding up to a point, finally exploded to me once after a particularly long and earbending one-way talk from Creeley on his marital woes, ringing in a change on one of Robert's own poems, suggesting the blindness obsessions are, exclaiming, "The night has a thousand eyes and *thou* but *one*!" Yet Tom said it not without sympathetic humor, despite his chagrin.

Naturally, Creeley's teaching suffered, not to mention his students' suffering, since he often had to be dragged out of Ma Peak's bodily by one of them, usually Cynthia Homire, to get him back to the college in time to teach his evening class in the Reading Room.

And Creeley, even without the beer in him, wouldn't have been much good to give his best attentions and abilities to teaching (which were, when he left the first time, gaining steadily and which I hope I've made clear were considerable), possessed as he was by his marital demons. One night—I think it was Cynthia who once again got him out of Peak's this time—when he seemed to have had a few more than usual, sitting in his chair under the windows in the Reading Room, stiffly, acidly drunk, his "teaching" consisted of going around the class, student by student, with a quietly vicious and menacing appraisal of each one of our shortcomings as human beings and hopeless lack of abilities as writers. When he got to me he said, sneering, "What's the matter, Rumaker, taking too many baths?"

That crack from Creeley, ill-intentioned as it was, was not without a particle of truth. If there was a shortage of women at

Black Mountain at that time—I look back and shudder not only at the sexual but the emotional burden as well placed on the few females available—there was even a greater scarcity of openly active gay males. (There was the pretty, underage girl who came as a prospective student and who was promptly propositioned by several of the hungry males, one of whom was alleged to have succeeded with her. When the girl's father found out, he created a row over it and threatened to prosecute with charges of statutory rape, but was persuaded by Charles and Wes not to, and the incident, much to the relief of everyone involved, except of course the father and daughter, was hushed up.) Sexual tension was just one more too finely strung string on my own instrument of doubt and deprivation. Like they say in the Boy Scout Manual, cold baths and showers are not only a healthy cleansing ritual but, up to a point, a sexually calming one as well. Masturbation is great, given an inventive imagination, but, as I intimated earlier, it's only half the fun. I bathed regularly once a day, which for some at Black Mountain was considered extreme.

I probably wouldn't have had to take so many baths to relax if some of the emotionally and sexually uptight males at Black Mountain had let their homophobic hair down once in awhile (or let me reawaken the boy-boy habits of pleasure of their childhood). I think, too, a larger part of the ritual of daily and compulsive bathing was that, bombarded daily, first externally and then internally, by the traditional beliefs in the "dirtiness," "criminality" and general all-around "worthlessness" and "subhumanness" of queerness, my daily baths were also perhaps a ritualistic attempt to scrub away culturally inculcated misconceptions of "uncleanness"—no less, or more, than Creeley's own incisive realization, in spite of all his blind talk (seeing, at last, in his poems, making us see, too), making sense of it in one poem in particular:

Nothing for a dirty man
but soap in his bathtub, a

greasy hand, lover's
nuts

perhaps. Or else

something like sand
with which to scour him

for all
that is lovely in women

and in extension, to expand from the title, for "all that is lovely in men," too; for all that we discover lovely in each other.

Creeley, no longer able to stand the isolation of his drafty apartment off in the all but deserted Studies Building, spent most of his time in Dan Rice's quarters in the rear first floor apartment in Black Dwarf, behind where Hilda Morley and Stefan Wolpe lived in the front apartment. There, Robert and Dan would hole up, drinking and talking—knowing Dan to be a good listener, I can imagine who did most of the talking— nobody laying eyes on them sometimes for days on end. Creeley had said about Dan in the afterword to the 1955 Jargon edition of *All That Is Lovely in Men*, "I have an immense hunger for such space as he knows . . . ." They shared two main things in common: jazz (Dan had done stints as trumpeter in the Stan Kenton and Woody Herman bands) and a love for the same woman, Cynthia.

Dan, an extraordinarily forceful and sensitive painter, whose status at that time at the college, neither student nor instructor, was more like hanging around because there was no other more likely place to go (he'd first arrived as a student in the late 1940s; several months earlier, with Fee Dawson, he had built the tobacco barn with its leaf-drying racks for our small tobacco cash crop, whose planting he also oversaw, maybe to justify his being there and to help out the college, and earn his keep); yet his presence exerted a quiet, invisible force: it helped maintain a stoic, unspoken attitude, especially among the men.

Dan and Robert were like twins, inseparable; non-identical though, since Creeley was dark-haired, the taller of the two, with the look of a Spaniard, while Dan had a smooth boyish face, epicanthic folds of dawn-blue eyes, a tight face that rarely smiled and when it did, a small smile, very tight. Small, baby-like teeth, perpetually stained with nicotine; short in stature but muscular in arms and chest and legs—Dan, stripped to the waist in levis on a hot summer afternoon, carrying on his back several of his large abstract canvases, almost as tall as himself, on his way to his studio in The Eye; blond, close-cropped hair, blonder in summer, tanned like a brief god in summer sun, boy-angel sailor (he had actually served in the U. S. Navy in World War 2), Billy Budd incarnate, in a way as innocent, only with brains and artistry, seeing his beauty as an affliction because of the many certain men (including a young and infatuated Merrill Gillespie when Merrill first arrived) inside and outside Black Mountain, who turned on to him; Dan puzzled and disturbed: Was he one of *them*? But his ex-marine brother, Jack, as noted, Black Mountain maintenance manager for a brief time till he quit in a frustrated rage against broken-down, irreparable Black Mountain facilities and what he perceived as faculty non-support, had always been around to keep his younger brother strictly assured.

Dan was like a composite, in one, of the various beauties of his preceding generations. A heavy drinker, perhaps alcohol helped dim that unwished-for light of himself, cutting the glow.

But beauty, if given, is to serve its uses, and must serve, deferring to dreams of the unawakened; not kept to itself, to spoil in vanity or narcissistically among its own reflections, for the hoarding and self-indulgent waste of it. It's to be exploded in the air like pollen, to smart and enliven the eyes and throats of all who are brushed by it, germinating seeds of the eyes to see sharper wonders and to tickle the throat to sing new songs of praise in generative and spatial creation. Closed to it, we dissolve back into the earth, unpollinated, blind.

Beauty is to be free as pollen in the wind, it's got to get around, is meant to, in visitations of awareness, extensions of sight. In its presence, rooms become too small for the reach of our arms, even the beat of our hearts. It enlarges us to seek other spaces; it discovers undiscovered spaces in ourselves.

Perhaps it was something of this, the attractive and mysterious "space" in Dan that Creeley responded to, obverse twin to his own, and sharer of affections for one woman, who had by this time departed the college; empathetic sharers and bolsterers, too, in the ruptures of their individual marriages, Dan's occurring before Creeley's.

Dan had this emanation to touch people, of whatever identity, the aura to move, himself unmoved, unknowingly the idol of his own beauty enshrined in a heart held fast and secret and unattainable, like the glint of mystery frozen deep within that only his ice-blue eyes kept steadfast watch on in protective uncertainty.

The spell of Dan's complex and unconscious emanations commanded loyalty, including Olson's, who had a high regard for him, like an esteemed and favorite son (perhaps the one single compelling reason why Dan was able to stay so long at Black Mountain in his "non-status" position); as well as other male students; some of the women, too, responding to Dan, quietly fretting over him, especially Connie Olson, Mary Fiore, fretting over him, by turns, in solicitude and exasperation. He had that power, without lifting a finger, to affect the lives of those around him, to have those close to him want to do things for him, like a beautiful and helpless vulnerable male babe, strong in its ability to capture and maintain the attention and ministrations of others, the permission to do so as the allowance of a great favor, like Rimbaud's "fabulous invalid," like Olson, on a grander scale, himself.

I kept shy of Dan, timorous but also instinctively put off by that certain rigidity that I sensed had in it an element that was too narrowly judging, that kept out more than it allowed in. Perhaps I was picking up intuitively what Bert Morgan told me years later Dan had said to him, that I was "a poor bastard" because of my queerness. I admired from a distance this fair-haired lad who could do no wrong, and if ever he did, was quickly forgiven.

Tom was too amusedly skeptical to take Dan, or Creeley, or even Olson for that matter, very seriously. Tom had a sharp eye for clay feet and, with an equally wicked tongue on occasion to match, was a healthy presence, helping to keep things in proportion at least in himself, and for my sense of balance, too.

There was something unshakably solid at Tom's core, but he seemed also to have a wonderfully soft and luxuriant divan somewhere inside himself where he reclined comfortably and at ease, eyeing with amusement the various foibles being committed around him on an almost daily basis. This slattern's sinuous detachment and tart tongue (that was rarely ever still) was a red flag that enraged many a bullish eye locked in the fixed stare of the exclusively male world that made up much of that side of Black Mountain and flourished like a hardy infection carried in from the world outside. Yet, as proved later, Tom could be needled and prodded off his luxuriously androgynous sofa.

After I wrote "The Pipe" I seemed more readily "accepted"—perhaps because, if nothing else, I had at least proven that I could write. I felt then I was allowed to hang around, at the college and later at the Cedar Bar in New York, rub shoulders on occasion with the privileged inhabitants of this exclusive male circle so long as I played the game by its very strict rules (and kept my place). No one was allowed to step out of bounds. That was seen to in subtle and nondirect ways, the signals always tacit but understood. The Black Mountain hipster, for all his savvy, pulled up short just this side of emotional and sensual boundaries beyond a cool poker face and a narrow stiffness of bodily movement. But back of the eyes, that hysteria always deep down in every American male, at one time or another, the sneaking suspicion he may not be measuring up as a "Man," Jake's illness, perhaps; the illness of all of us, perhaps.

It's easier now, and in hindsight, finding words for what then were shapeless and half-realized and half-understood feelings of anger and isolation, an undefined and insistent yearning, the discomfort in sensing that things weren't quite right in me or around me and this in spite of the activity and energy, in the midst of a real and tiring struggle for survival of the school, of the genuinely exciting work that was being done, despite that daily struggle. Still, the feedback of negativity was there, as it was everywhere outside, even infiltrating Black Mountain College.

It's difficult, too, and easier, to speak of attitudes extant over forty years ago, my own, and others, reflecting the society at large. I doubt very much if Creeley holds to what he once wrote in "A Note to Franz Kline," published in the Winter 1954 *Black Mountain Review*, to the effect that "There is nothing quite so abrupt and even pleasant as rape—ask any woman," although at that time it was never thought necessary any woman should be asked.

Those early forceful attitudinal imprints are later like rubbery hard cortices on the mind, fiercely held and resistant to change, but they change, like peelings, in actionable time and the space love through understanding creates.

We change. We grow. We are what we come out of as well as

what we dream to become and act on to make a reality. There is a paradise of the heart in the ever-changing. You can't write about the light unless you've also seen the darkness. Creeley knows this too.

Perhaps that summer spent close to Dan was for Robert an actualization of a past fiction. The poignancy of forgetting, in all our upbringings of rigidly enforced heterosexist determinations, what might also have been an extended affectionate reality—or one that holds as true as the decided one, or the one decided for us, of ourselves or by others—seems very much to have to do with Creeley's story "In the Summer" in that same Winter 1954 issue of *The Black Mountain Review*. The narrator's adolescent love for the other boy is kept embryonic, undeveloped, aborted finally, the genuine pathos of the story (there is an air of lingering remorse throughout), because nothing is grown into, not allowed to grow, as if we ever "grow out of that phase" rather than, later, recognizing it as one more little death or undone thing tucked away for the future facing or, more often, the running away from. Another example of the peculiar onesidedness of male-male friendships, that they often go no further. "One more step and we'll blow your brains out," as novelist Mitchell Goodman noted in a letter pseudonymously signed "M.F." in that same issue of the *Review*.

Accepting all closenesses offered, receptive of all opennesses, we would have relief from each other, from imposed behaviors, women and men, as well as women and women and men and men, from the way we hurt each other. "That you can hurt both of us," the woman in "In the Summer" says, who also echoes official realities. To stop the dying into one another, boxed in, egoistically, selfishly—"it's yourself you care about," she also says; to move out of self to the nonperceived and generous possibilities, within and without, that keeps love lively, that keeps us lively to ourselves and to the world.

I can't leave it at this, since the uglinesses and violences, even the sillinesses of that time were in no way equal to or ever over-shadowed the accomplishments in the work done at Black Mountain in those years, in the ideas and enthusiasms and camaraderie that were exchanged on a daily basis. In trying to sum up (impossible task!) what it was like knowing Creeley and what Creeley's writing has meant to me, the impact of him in my own life, I'll try to say it this way, realizing there isn't any end to the saying it:

His is a scrupulous and highly exact examination of conscious processes. His own clearances, then as now, are in areas of excruciating wakefulness. If his demons are "conscious" ones, they are, paradoxically, no less real and terrifying than those lurking in the dark under-roots of the unconscious. Yet much of his writing has the quality of dreams, in definitions of con-sciousness so newly realized they have a netherworldly aura, so foreign are they, seen from the prospect of his unique and stripped-down acute angle of vision.

In the darkness of bedrooms, in the darkness of his own mind and heart, trapped in a head of the night that can't sleep, a head insomniac through the day, grinding in flinty obstinacy to strike a few precise sounds of conscious meaning in the opaque densi-ty of incomprehension that surrounds us all our waking and sleeping hours:

My mind to me a mangle is

To press and press, on, to squeeze from the skin of one's own reality refractions of it that might possibly conflagrate—and in Creeley's writing often does—a larger illumination.

From the narrow base of his concerns, tight in its strictures, in its methods, whole formerly darkened and inaccessible areas erupt in veined light across the eyes, they are so physical and penetrating. Having read Creeley, who is, like all who are given the gift of a loan of the secrets and who challenge and claim a particular space as their own, none of us will ever see the same again.

What is sometimes taken away is given back a double-strength in another place—With Creeley, half-sighted has been more than enough to focus and deliver the power of vision behind it. Through it, we have all been given additional sight.

I was sitting on the front steps of Meadows Inn one evening after supper. Earlier, Tom had taken his Buick and driven down to Ma Peak's with Creeley, Dan Rice, Robert Hellman and Jorge Fick. I don't know if I'd been invited to go along or not, or if I had, if I'd refused (refused maybe for lack of the buck or so for a couple of bottles of Ballantine Ale—ale, we believed, got you high faster in the altitude—scarcity of money continuing to be a constant fact each of us lived with daily).

I know for certain I was moony and lonely, feeling dissatisfied with myself, and wanted only to be alone that night, remember a feeling of relief that I was. Living so close and intensely among so few people, having to depend so much and for so long solely on each other's company, could get wearing. "You're so *intense!*" was a kidding accusation passed around among us, but there was some truth in it, for all of us. We often got on each other's nerves because of it. Either way, I chose to be by myself that evening, and was secretly glad Tom and the others had gone off to the tavern, not wanting to sit in on another beer-bust that would probably end up with the others needling Tom who, befogged with booze, always lost his tartness and edge of resistance.

The large open grassy area in front of the house had darkened in the later summer dusk, but beyond the road the thick-standing trees up the nearby slopes of the Seven Sisters to the south gleamed with a purple light in the last rays of the sun. I kept looking at that purple light near the tops of the hills, watching the shadows thicken as they crept up the trees at the foot of the mountains and slowly climbed toward the crests as night came on. The twilit sky was clear, not a cloud, and over the ragged tops of that part of the hills, a few stars were beginning to show in the still-light sky.

Indefinable yearning and the uncertainty of what will be, and what you will be in it, are terrible things, and I guess are always a particular affliction and preoccupation of the young. I felt pulled apart in so many ways, it was hard to get a sense of the way I should be going, pulled backwards as I was by the still-strong fastnesses of what I had come out of and what had been implanted in me, with all its negative seduction of deep and unborn sleep, nightmare-troubled as it was; and pulled equally strongly forward in other directions of wakefulness by all the attractions and possibilities Black Mountain had to offer. So often my energies turned in upon themselves, even at Black Mountain. "Sucking the cock of your own experience," as Olson had crudely but accurately termed it that day outside the back door of the dining hall kitchen.

Something of all that, I suppose, contributed to the blue mood I was in, the blue on the mountain tops holding an allurement of identity because it matched my own coloration of feeling. Projecting my loneliness, the trees looked isolated and silent as they slowly disappeared in the darkness creeping up the hillsides. It was a simple fact for me, too.

Behind me, the dark house felt deserted (I didn't know till later that Laurie and Naomi had been upstairs in their apartment). It was a perfect moment for youthful self-pity and a luxuriant wallowing in amorphous feelings, envious of the vast starlit skies above the hills, my earthbound and problematic self wanting to fly up and be lost and free in them forever.

I don't know how long I mooned along in this state as I sat clutching my knees on the dusty wooden front steps of

Meadows Inn, but when I heard the motor of Tom's Buick as it echoed to a roar against the hills as the car wound up the twisting dirt road in the distance, complete darkness had fallen. I guess I'd been sitting there for several hours.

That snapped me out of my self-indulgent reverie: Tom was returning, with Creeley and Dan and Hellman and Jorge in tow, and if they all decided to end the night in the kitchen of Meadows Inn, that meant endless exhilarated talk at increased volume from Ma Peak's beer into the small hours of the morning, additionally fueled by the six-bottle cartons they'd be sure to bring back with them.

Reluctant to move, unwilling to leave my sad, delicious mood quite so abruptly, I sat where I was, determined to savor my solitude right down to the last few moments.

The car's engine grew louder, amplified as the sound of it pitched back and forth among the close hills. Presently, to the left, over the stream and through the trees now black with night, I saw its headlights slashing and cutting through the gaps in the branches and brush as it sped up the road, clouds of dust kicked up in its headlights.

Tom was driving faster than usual (and he was a pretty fast driver), so I expected he must have gotten a snootful at Peak's. I could hear voices over the distance coming through the open car windows, hollering, but what they were shouting I couldn't make out. They sounded like they were arguing.

The car braked abruptly at Black Dwarf, the house up on the other side of the road where Jorge had an apartment upstairs above Dan's and Hellman's, so Tom must have stopped to drop Jorge and Hellman off, and probably Dan and Creeley, too. I felt relieved at that thought. There was more shouting and hollering and slamming and unslamming of car doors, then I heard the car start up with a sudden lurch and watched its headlights through the trees as it swerved away from Black Dwarf and barreled into the dirt lane which turned down towards Meadows Inn by Olson's house.

The Buick gathered speed as it came fully into view now in the open grassy area, its headlights, blurred in swirls of dust, glaring directly into my eyes and lighting up the front of Meadows Inn. Someone inside the car, either Creeley or Dan, was shouting, "Tom! Tom!" and then Jorge was saying in a loud voice, "Aw, Tom come *on*" (so he, too, was still in the car). All the doors except the driver's were swinging open and shut as if the occupants were trying to jump out (perhaps the three of them had tried to back at Black Dwarf) as the car came on in a loose zigzag, a fat low mushroom shape of chrome and gray metal, moving fast over the wide field and heading directly for the steps on which I sat.

Another voice was shouting, sharper now, aware, "Whatta ya doing, man? Hey, *Tom!*"

I sat there paralyzed, the way a wild animal must feel, frozen in the middle of a road at night, its eyes hypnotized by the beams of an onrushing auto. I kept thinking, "Sure he's going to stop. He's just drunk and kidding, give them all a scare. Sure he's going to stop."

But Tom didn't stop, and he must have had the gas pedal shoved to the floor, the car was moving at such a fast clip. Although veering erratically left and right, he kept it steered pretty directly for the front of the building, so large a target no matter how he went he couldn't have missed some part of it. I realized now in the hairsbreadth of an instant he was so close he couldn't stop even if he wanted to.

"*Tom!*" The car was so near I could see through the windshield and make out arms scrabbling over Tom's shoulders, trying to get at the wheel, and Tom's voice above the loud racing roar of the motor shouting, "If this is what you want, you're getting it! If this is what you want!"

With the car no more than a few feet from the steps and heading directly at the spot I was sitting in, at the last possible moment I clicked out of my hypnotic trance and suddenly leapt up, shoved open one of the French doors and bounded into what I decided in a split second would be the relative safety of the lobby, unsure as I'd been just which way the car was going to hit on the outside, deciding there might be more safety behind the thick and heavy stones of the fireplace where I now stood, a little way out from the front of the wide mouth of the hearth, facing away from it, stiff with apprehension.

All this happened only an instant before the front end of the Buick crashed into the fieldstone chimney directly beside the steps with a sickening punch of metal tangling against stone, a crunching impact that shook the entire house from the cellar up. The building shuddered around me, was still.

I stood a moment immobilized in the middle of the lobby floor, then slowly turned around. The crash had been so forceful I was surprised the chimney was still standing, even the front of the house. Staring out through the glass panes (curiously unbroken) of the French doors with the taut gauzy curtains Tom had put up, I watched the steam and smoke swirling up in the fractured beams of the headlights of the car which were, equally curious in my dazed mind, still on.

As often happens in such moments of shock, I became suddenly very calm. I hurried out the door to see Jorge wandering around in little circles on the grass at the rear of the car. I heard some moaning from the backseat, and in the driver's seat, his face illuminated by the still-lit greenish blue gleam of the dashboard, sat Tom, slumped forward, his glazed eyes staring out the windshield, his face red and glistening, muttering to himself, "I told them to stop—I told them I'd do it—I told them—"

I was amazed that any of them were still alive, let alone conscious. In the glow of the broken headlights that still lit up the rough stones of the chimney and the weathered green shingles in a stark eerie light, Jorge's pallid face was whiter than usual as he stumbled about in his heavy black boots, clasping and unclasping his hands to his head, stopping now and again to bend slightly at the knees and peer through the open rear door of the car. When I ran up, Creeley was hunched near the floor in the rear seat, trying clumsily to pull out Dan who sat flung back, his head thrown against the far corner of the backseat, eyes closed, his mouth, pulled down at the corners, slightly open. Then I ran around behind the car and to the driver's side and leaning in the window asked Tom if he was all right. He said he wasn't sure, his knees were caught under the dashboard. His eyes were dull, unseeing. I managed to pry the door open and looking down at Tom and not seeing any blood, felt reassured, relieved at least they were all breathing, surprised, from the violence of the crash, not to see any blood at all.

As I jerked my head to the backseat, Creeley was still fumbling awkwardly around Dan, who seemed unconscious, his head twitching from side to side, his face ashen and deathlike.

Turning to Tom, I asked him, "Did you break anything?" He said he didn't think so, just his legs were stuck. I said I'd help him get out and after maneuvering his body and carefully easing his legs out from under the dash, he was able to move. I took his arm and gradually helped him out of the wreck but his one leg buckled under him, painfully. He couldn't stand on it and leaned on me heavily.

By this time Laurie and Naomi had come down from their upstairs apartment and were standing staring wide-eyed, uncomprehending at the scene. Several others began to appear: Olson and Wes Huss, John Chamberlain with newly-arrived Elaine, Joe Fiore. I think Mary too, but she might have arrived later.

There was so much confusion at this point I'm not certain of all that occurred, except that up till that time I was still keeping a pretty steady calm, helping as best I could, mechanically mostly. We got Tom and Robert into the lobby, Jorge being able to walk himself, and Dan was carried in and laid on a couch that was pulled up in front of the fireplace. Creeley sat there beside him.

Strange how, after all this time, a few details remain vivid in the aftermath of the accident: the bed Dan lay on, with Creeley next to him, with its pink and rose coverlet with white and yellow stripes, in need of a washing, that Tom had picked up somewhere when we first moved in and had thrown over the old sour mattress on box springs to make a "daybed" out of it to help smarten up the lobby.

As I leaned over to see how Dan was, Creeley suddenly seized my hand and pulled me down on the bed to sit close beside him, squeezing my hand in a tight grip, a strength that surprised me after what he'd just gone through. Staring directly, intently, into my eyes, his own eye riveted on me in insistence, as if fearful my attention would leave him, he began to talk in a harsh quick voice, not about Dan, not about Tom or Jorge, not even about the accident, but about his wife and himself, in a nonstoppable rush of words, his hands squeezing mine tighter and tighter.

I felt uncomfortable, and annoyed, too, still stunned myself from the aftereffects of the wreck. Why was Creeley babbling on about this, now, all over again, what we'd all been hearing for months on end? I wanted to punch him. Instead, I tried to look away, to the side or down at the floor but his voice always pulled me back. Listen, listen! was the demanding tone of it. Tears began to run down his cheeks and wouldn't stop running, like his words, which ran faster and faster, and for the first time Creeley didn't reach for a handkerchief to sop at them as he did in other times of agitation, but let them run freely.

I grew even more uneasy, like a fraudulent priest hearing the confession of an utterly desperate man. What perplexed me even more was that this man, whose writing and perceptions I respected so highly, that I had struggled to comprehend, with whom I felt (although he was only six years older than myself) very much in the position of novice writer and student in the face of all his own steady and solid achievements, whose uniqueness and whose personal life, in spite of its "unconvention," was in the main "acceptable," who could speak aloud and at length of it, and most certainly did, of its happinesses and unhappinesses, contrasted to my own buried dreads and forcibly stopped-up heart and silenced mouth, in the low rasping torrent of words that came from a throat sounding as if it were choking with rage and fear and hurt, was asking me for forgiveness. And interspersed in his rapid talk now were phrases of "You're a lovely man, Mike," and "Tom is a lovely man," and beneath it all, in the tone of all he was saying, I could only hear, Forgive me, forgive me.

Forgive him for what I didn't know—that, as later came out, his, along with Dan and Jorge, digging at Tom was the main cause of the car wreck? Not knowing, all I did was sit and listen, not having any words, not having the space to speak them even if I did; or the ability to grant it, whatever absolution he so desperately needed, for whatever unspeakable crimes of the heart.

The brunt need of that low, fast-talking voice in its gravelly naked openness was like a tormented child baring itself in a breathless stumble of words. It had such an impulsion of necessity behind it, the need to speak and speak, as if words themselves could fill a particular harrowing void made more numbingly empty in the aftermath of the suddenness and shock of the "accident," the jolt of bewildering recognition that, in its raw feeling, had nothing to do with words but only with the comforting resonance of their pure sound, the sound of the self like a falsely brave and stuttering noise in a fearful vacuum.

I kept silent. I listened. It was the only kindness I could do for him.

There was some reluctance to call the police, but when it was seen how badly Dan was hurt (it appeared maybe his back was broken), and that there might be unrecognized injuries to Creeley and Tom (Jorge appeared to have escaped relatively unharmed), someone was dispatched to the pay phone in the Studies to call for help.

After that, everything was a blur in my mind. The lobby was crowded with people, doing what they could, which wasn't much. Tom was talking endlessly and Charles was moving about from one to the other of the injured, trying to ascertain how badly hurt each one was, and also trying to get information as to what had happened, which was almost impossible from the somewhat hysterical and contradictory talk of the three who were able to speak.

Whether the story was made up then, before the state police arrived or after, I don't know, but Tom decided, or others decided, in order to avoid any legal complications (and any further tangles with the local authorities), he would tell the police the gas pedal had stuck as he was driving into the front yard of Meadows Inn, that he couldn't get it unstuck and the car had plowed into the chimney before he knew what was happening. Since the wreck occurred on private property there was no real danger of police involvement, but I guess the decision was to play it as safe as possible, Black Mountain College's image not being the best in Swannanoa Valley nor throughout the length and breadth of the State of North Carolina either.

Then there were several big state troopers arriving, Smokey the Bear hats on their heads, in a powerful car with red lights and siren. They poked around in the harsh light of the naked front-door lightbulb, checking out the wreckage of the Buick slammed up against the chimney like a crushed accordian, taking flashbulb photos of it and filling out some kind of accident report, while the rest of us stood in a glum circle looking on behind them, their gray-blue uniforms with shiny buttons and leather belts with gun holsters and bullets a jarring, incongruous sight on the place (we were accustomed more to button-down, insurance salesmen-type F.B.I. agents paying visits), adding to the harsh and surreal quality of the entire bizarre scene.

After Creeley and Dan and Tom were taken off to the hospital and the state troopers had gone, several of us remained talking in the lobby till the small hours of the morning—Olson and Huss, and Mary and Joe Fiore, some others, Elaine and Chamberlain, I don't remember who or how many. Then everybody left eventually, except Mary and Joe, and I was glad there weren't so many people around now because my nerves were really beginning to go. I was very tired but still so keyed up from the events of the night I knew sleep was out of the question for the time being. The three of us sat in the kitchen drinking tea for awhile—Mary and Joe were really the most comforting people to be around at such times (I had great need of them *that* summer), without them saying anything, that something quietly solid and assuring about them both.

After awhile I said I wanted to get away from the house and go for a walk down near the lake. They said they would come along, they wouldn't be able to sleep anyway. I was glad they came along.

Dropping back now for the sense of it, not necessarily the facts of the events but the feelings, letting my mind and hearing flow backwards as I've done writing this book, to touch and hear again the buried cells and sensors of memory, I remember it was dawn when we started back from the lake, Mary and I walking side by side across the wooden footbridge over the ravine to Streamside, recent scene of the party where Jake had threatened us, Mary talking about nothing in particular, then her mind going back in that way she always worried a thing she didn't understand, talking about what had happened, just as upset about it as everybody else was, yet solid and steady, baffled but noncondemning, trying to understand it in her slow, careful way. Mary, a great unrecognized strength of the place.

Joe, following behind, his presence, too, real and strong.

The leaves of the trees over the footbridge were beginning to lighten and grow visible, the early morning light filtering down. I told them I could sleep now and thanked them for walking with me.

We walked along the path at Streamside and up to Meadows Inn, glad to see the wrecked Buick gone now—hauled away I guessed by Percy Justus and his brother, the garage mechanics Tom used to get his car serviced by at their place on the way to the town of Black Mountain.

The three of us parted, Mary and Joe heading up the road to Minimum House.

Before going in to sleep, I looked down to inspect the damage to the chimney and was surprised to see in the growing light only a chip or two clipped out bumper-high from the sturdy fieldstone where the Buick had hit.

Mary and I went down to visit Tom and Dan in the Veterans Hospital, just off the narrow county road leading up to the college, a huge sprawling place that looked like a military camp with rows of barracks-like wards, or a factory, with its large heating and generating plant with its tall smokestacks. I had passed it innumerable times, drunk and sober, hiking or riding back and forth between the college and Ma Peak's, but this was the first time I had ever been inside; I guess it was for Mary, too.

Tom, it turned out, had broken a leg and Creeley came out of it with a severely wrenched shoulder, but didn't require hospitalization. Dan, the unluckiest, had his back badly dislocated and would be in the hospital for a longer period of time, and in a back brace even longer after that.

As Mary and I sat by Tom's bedside, he was chirping away like a cricket, a distinct change from the night before, in mood anyway, as if the car crash had never happened, his old, merry, gabby self again. As an old army medic, he seemed right at home in the VA hospital ward. His humor helped erase some of the leaden horror of the previous night, which still sat heavy on me, his high spirits lifting my own. He pooh-poohed the seriousness of his broken leg and our concern that he might not be able to take care of himself back at the college. He said he'd be up and around in no time and could manage on crutches.

It was as if the accident, with himself as chief instrument of it, had released enormous energies in him, had freed him in some way—into what, I wasn't sure. Perhaps he felt he had "proven" something, that in a rage he could risk death and live to laugh about it, that he could be a "man" after all, as foolhardy and self-lethal as any male suffering the severe macho malaise of the 1950s, his deep, gnawing suspicions of uncertainty allayed.

I felt an uneasy certainty that it was all very much the end of it, for our time up there in the Seven Sister Mountains, the end of it for me, anyway. It wasn't many months after that, for many reasons, the college finally did close for good, Olson finishing out the business of closing the place, holding on till the last, and in 1957 the last to leave.

As I look back now, what happened couldn't have been otherwise, this horrendous culmination of so many small and growing disasters of that summer. So many underlying and hidden malevolences seem to have been set loose in each of us in those last dying months of Black Mountain, as if the spirits inhabiting the space of the land itself had also finally turned against us and wanted us out of there, to rid the place of a certain destructive sickness which would only grow worse with our continued presence, the seeds of which were in, or touched on, everyone of us who had somehow survived and remained clinging in blind hope and stubborn belief right down to the desperate end.

Perhaps after so many negativities of experience, we no longer loved the place enough, secretly harbored hatred for it in our hearts, and the wild and green spirits of the mountainous forests picked up on those unvoiced emanations of hatred and turned their own malevolence against us to preserve the spirit of forested spaces that, literally, we were helping to destroy, forced as the faculty had been to lease out large tracts of the hilly woodland to timber cutters for meagerly extended survival.

Perhaps, too, and the most likely, it was that the hour had finally come, unaware to us, that the varied and multiple shapes and ideas and perceptions spawned at Black Mountain over its last years were ready to be scattered out into the world, after a painfully protracted and overdue birth.

He was a painting student, from Detroit, where he had worked, being an artist of course, having studied in Chicago at the Art Institute, shaping full-sized clay models of prospective automobiles at Chrysler, before coming to Black Mountain. There was already a small "colony" of former Art Institute and Cass Tech (Detroit) High School students who had migrated to Black Mountain College before him—John Chamberlain, Jorge Fick, Basil King, and Jerry Van de Wiele, the latter having lured several of them down. They all knew each other and had encouraged him to join them, telling him, in the hip lingo of the day, what a cool and far-out place Black Mountain was.

Richard had dark brown hair cropped close, in the style of the 1950s, almost a crewcut. He was high-shouldered and slenderly built and often wore a dark blue V-neck sweater which set off the fine curly hair of his chest. He was somewhat hard of hearing, from mastoiditis as a child, the same illness as Merrill and my older brother Bill had had when young, so I was immediately sympathetic to him. Behind his horn-rimmed glasses were those attentive, listening eyes of the partially deaf. It may have only been due to habit from his deafness, the necessity to catch every word, but he appeared to be a good listener, as was my brother (as was Merrill, perhaps this pull to deafness rooted in the simple, affectionate heart of my brother, one of my first loves), and this was part of his attraction for me, that Richard seemed to have such an empathetic ear. In spite of his heavy masculinist attitudes, which were so thick in the air, even in the relative freedom of Black Mountain—this was, after all, the 1950s—where you breathed them in unthinkingly, and which even then, in some deep, as yet inarticulate place in me, were repulsive, there still was a side to him that was appealingly gentle, and added to it was the fact that he spoke with the often soft-spokenness of the deaf.

When we got to know each other better, he told me that he'd also had a lot of trouble with his stomach as a child and that part of it had had to be surgically removed. His face, his skin, had the curious pallor of the invalid, and that also I think helped raise my fraternal instinct, finding another brother, like Bill, who I understood, who was familiar, and who perhaps needed me. That, I believe now, was the primary impulse, and the attraction was secondary, at least during the initial stages of our friendship.

He arrived at the college in the spring of 1955, the year in which I had been preparing to graduate, a time when the student body was smaller than it had ever been before, almost nonexistent, the school itself in ever deeper financial trouble, and everyone, faculty and students, suffering an even worsening morale.

All this affected me too in my last months there. I felt the decline of the school like a decline in myself. At that point I only wanted to graduate and get away. I knew that what the best of Black Mountain had been for me was now behind me. And yet I was frightened of leaving. Only Olson, continuing as rector, the last rector, still had an incurable optimism, struggling mightily, and ingeniously, to keep the place afloat. But the school was as doomed, in the increasingly cynical and uneasy eyes of most of us, as the *Pequod* of Olson's spiritual brother, Melville.

I grew increasingly uneasy, too, because, come September,

I'd be leaving a place which had been my home for the past three years, the most meaningful and exciting one I had ever known and will probably ever know, where I'd learned a great deal, especially about writing from instructors like Olson and Creeley, and had lost some of my raw greenness, though by no means all of it; where I'd been able to live my first year in an open relationship with another gay student without any particular harassment from anyone (it's hard to convey today how rare and extraordinary an occurrence this was in the rabidly homophobic atmosphere of the 1950s, especially in the Bible Belt South). Black Mountain, although it didn't exactly welcome lesbian and gay students and faculty with open arms, was at least tolerant in its respect for individual privacy, which at that time was pretty much unheard of elsewhere in the land; in the good old American tradition of moralistic nosiness, everybody was minding everyone else's business, starting with Senator Joe McCarthy, terminal homophobe and fag-baiter supreme.

In short, I had a case of the shakes at the prospect of what I would have to face again in that world beyond the Gatehouse of the college, a terrifying world in which I had to develop once more, since my life was illegal, the rat-like cunning of a genuine criminal to survive. This meant, after three years of relative free breathing up in the clean air of the Seven Sister Mountains, a return to that dungeon of the closet. No matter how much imaginative gay men, then as now, may try to pretty them up, with flocked paper and *objets d'art*, or black walls and leather and chains, a closet is a closet, one which I would have to, again, clumsily carry around with me each and every day, furtive and secret and extra careful, once more speaking double-speak, thinking double-thought, watching my every word and move, to not let my identity slip out (it's no wonder some of us make such fabulous spies, and actors). Out there was always the sense of being an alien in my own country, which I never felt was my own; hampered, squeezed in upon myself behind my thick-walled fortress of a closet, fortified with paranoia grounded in actual fear, often for my very life, which was in no way unreal or imagined, both in my home and in the streets. I knew, daily, what enemies were out there to kill me, mentally, spiritually or physically, if they only had the chance.

I grew increasingly uncertain and depressed at the thought of leaving the relative safety of that unusual enclave in the hills of western North Carolina, and that old Black Mountain problem rearing its head once more, was lonely too. With so few students around, with only two or three highly competed for women students, myself the only out student left since John Wieners had gone, amorous life was pretty scarce once again for everyone, and since Jake had departed abruptly, just about zilch for me.

My needs and emotions were made extreme, even bizarre, I think, because of that scarcity, but more than that because of a tremendous immaturity, coupled with a fantastically romantic turn of mind. Put simply, my feelings and affections, my thinking, even most certainly my sexuality, were still in a stage of fetal development, a realization, unbeknownst to me at this time, that Olson himself had been owning up to in letters to Frances Motz Boldereff on his own amorous confusions regarding Connie and other women, not to mention the odd speculation over homosexuality.

I was now just 23, about the same age as Richard when I first met him. He seemed the only likely one around to give me what I needed. Perhaps I could give him back something, too. He insisted he liked women, but I persisted, my needs imperative, like those of the incipient alcoholic, out of control now, needing him with an unquenchable thirst, sensing that glimmer in him, in his patient, listening kindness, and magnifying it into a full-fleshed potentiality. "The heart wants what it wants," sighed Emily Dickinson (and no-nonsense nature wants us to want it). I was trusting, for better or worse, as D. H. Lawrence had enjoined, as Olson himself had come to, the evidence of my senses. Surely Richard would come to have affection for me, just as I had believed with Olson when, that day in the dining hall kitchen early on, he had told me flatly, "I can't teach you anything because I don't love you." And hadn't I, through hard work and persistent effort in my writing, not only gained respect from him but also a measure of the affection I craved?

Although it wasn't quite the same situation, I was sure I would succeed as well with Richard, make him love me, too, so foolishly green I was in matters of amour, then realizing at 23 what Charles himself was realizing at 43.

Considering what he knew of it, which was mostly the stereotypical nonsense extant about faggots and dykes then, a fantastic people as bizarrely imagined as creatures from outer space, often even by gay people themselves, Richard was fairly understanding, even sympathetic, patient (or so I wanted eagerly to believe)—which only served to increase my expectations all the more and fed my hope that he would eventually have some feeling for me.

I suppose he took a lot of razzing about it, about my not so circumspect wooing of him, especially from his Art Institute cronies, and it must have caused him some embarrassment and confusion. But he was, for the most part, at least in the beginning stage, decent with me, much of it, I think, due to his respect for me as a budding young writer; plus the fact that I'd become, as I intimated earlier, one of Olson's "favorites," and that meant a lot at Black Mountain, as far as acceptance and prestige went. He only became more tense and annoyed with me toward the end of that summer when I began to make a pest of myself, usually when drunk, usually appearing unannounced in his upstairs room at Black Dwarf late at night, the booze making me lose all timidity, giving me the phony courage to make it up the hill to talk to him, foolish, burbling talk. It was enough for me, really, simply to be in the same room with him. The heart, especially a tipsy one, doesn't understand the word No. Mine didn't, with Richard, even when sober. Without wanting to be, I expect I was very obnoxious, a real pain in the ass, my obsession increasing with his every refusal, politely, quietly given; as baffled as he was by my insistence and preoccupation (nature's trick again, to have its way, of robbing us of reason, of even the basic courtesies, in infatuations of the heart).

He would say things to try to make me feel better, to perhaps cool my ardor. Once he said to me, with that sheepish, appealing grin of his, "You wouldn't like it anyway—I don't have too much to brag about." Then he would recount some anecdote to emphasize his point, often remarking on guys he'd seen in high school locker rooms, telling me that once in a bar john he was amazed to see the man standing at the next urinal, Richard's eyes behind his glasses bugging wider as he described it, his hands making a continuous unwinding motion, "Unzipping his fly and taking it out and taking it out, trolling it out like a fire hose. And I'm standing there with mine just about hanging out of my pants, and he's still trolling it out and trolling it out. Unbelievable."

When I looked particularly glum, he would clown sometimes to try to cheer me up, and, corny as it was, would flick out and twirl on the tip of his tongue the false pivot tooth that made up one of his front teeth, and then, smiling impishly, pretend to swallow it.

As my obsession for him increased, I thought less and less of having sex with him, not that that prospect was any the less attractive but because, for most of that spring and early summer, I had what I can only describe as a *clean* feeling, a feeling of somehow being purified, a quiet and profound energy that was like sexual energy turned inward and contained, that strengthened and quieted me, made me content. It filled me for a time with calm, the source of this unforeseen happiness being located in the realization of his presence beyond the pine trees and across the distant mountain road, up in his pine-paneled room in Black Dwarf, which made me feel curiously secure and fed that inner serene light like the finest of oil.

Seeing the light on in his window through the pine boughs late at night was a strong and reassuring sight, sending me into a deep and refreshing sleep with the loveliest dreams, usually starring the two of us. The awareness of him only increased that strange sense of feeling safe. It was enough for me just to think of him painting or reading or sleeping not very far away. No matter where he was he was always with me. It strengthened my urge to write, to work on my graduation project with renewed will.

The difficulty was I had no one to talk to about any of this (or at least thought I hadn't). And what words did I have anyway? In those days, there were no words. And yet, and yet . . . despite all those twisted words I'd ever heard or read about, there persisted that dumb, bare whisper of doubt that all those words were lies . . . in the arms of a beloved, even a beloved stranger met only moments before, or in those just-right times with Merrill and Jake at Black Mountain, that whisper grew the most insistent so that I, frightening as the thought was afterwards, could no longer ignore it: How could anything so right as this be wrong? (let alone criminal, immoral or sick?) Today there is no question.

Graduations were individual ceremonies at Black Mountain—and as noted, painter Jorge Fick and poet Ed Dorn were also scheduled to receive diplomas at the same time, a 1955 class of three, the last graduates of the school. Each of us would have an outside examiner (painter Franz Kline was Jorge's) and oral questions from the entire faculty on any subject related, or unrelated, to our field, the prospect of which, as I confided in my June 5th letter to Charles, so unnerved me. By the end of summer, shortly before graduation, I can say now I don't think I was quite all there, so distorted in the extreme were my perceptions and feelings. Besides my continuing frustration with Richard, there was also the added strain of completing the projects in Shakespeare and the Greeks that Olson, as my adviser, had set up with me for my graduation project. I was also concerned about what kind of report my outside examiner, poet Robert Duncan (who was still living in Mallorca, Spain, with his lover, painter Jess Collins) would give in his evaluation of my work to the faculty. And as for that outside world—Black Mountain really was, for many of us, an enclave, a tiny bastion of protection against all the hostility lying just beyond the gates. Not only was I concerned about that world's terrifying and paralyzing homophobia, but in addition to that was my concern about finding work: a recession was on in 1955 and there was a scarcity of jobs; also would I have difficulty "passing"? Would a prospective employer see on my face traces of the Black Mountain rebel and misfit, not to mention the results of three years of relative freedom? And then there was the draft. I still had a 2-S student deferment, and since they were still drafting young men even after the Korean War, would I have the guts to tell them at my induction I was a faggot (oh, the shivery fears at that thought!) and risk becoming 4-F? Would I be able to bear that stigma on my draft card in looking for jobs, having to explain why I was rejected by the draft; that is, would I have the wits and cool to make up believable stories? Storyteller that I was, and slippery liar, of necessity, simply to survive, still, I was worried I wouldn't be capable of pulling it off. And, ironically, would the military psychiatrists at the induction center believe I was homosexual, or would they think I was, again, just trying to pass, paradoxically, to get out of the service, as so many guys who weren't really queer were doing then, as Ed Dorn had done? So much so that the Pentagon brass was really getting tough on that.

All these preoccupations were draining my energies away, wearing me down.

And on top of all these worriments was my overriding preoccupation with Richard, a weight burdening the stress of all my other concerns to such a degree that I could feel myself going increasingly dark with depression, and my nerves becoming so jittery I found myself drinking every chance I got. That was difficult, with money and transportation scarce now that Tom's Buick was in the repair garage. But I managed to drink, despite the hardships.

Much of this was certainly egocentric preoccupation with self—What's going to happen to poor little me? But many of my concerns were real enough and grounded in actuality.

Then one night, sitting in the kitchen of Meadows Inn, drinking beer with Tom, who was now off his crutches, and Jorge and Joe and Mary Fiore, idly listening to their talk, and the more beer I drank the more morose I got. I tried to follow the conversation but felt distanced from it, even bored, finding the same old talk from the same old mouths, after three, close, intense years of it, tedious. I became more and more agitated, and drank faster, several times getting up and walking out through the lobby to the wide grassy area in front of the house and staring up into the moonless dark August sky, then marching back into the house again and plunking myself down once more in my chair at the kitchen table, sullen, inarticulate (who was always so gabby, especially after a few brews), trying to listen and unable to follow their thread of talk. Perhaps picking up on my mood and not knowing how to deal with it, no one paid much attention to me and, as the evening wore on and a poker game was started, in which I did not join, not being clever enough at cards, I felt increasingly cut off, isolated. The long-gathering effects of that summer of frustration and resentment and projected fear, and the conclusion of three years of work, of leaving the nest Black Mountain had become, gathered in me that night in a smouldering knot of restlessness, which was also, curiously, paralytic in its tightness. In my tangled thoughts I remembered something Wes Huss had said in acting class one morning, about a man in despair who had cut his wrists and, seeing his own blood, the brightness of it, then knew he was *alive*. Over and over in my brain ran the line in Marlowe's *Faust*, "See, see, where Christ's blood streams in the firmament!"—which I'd heard Olson quote in his powerful voice in his writing class one evening and which had impressed itself so deeply in my mind. I was certainly in no shape to make the connection then; I could see later that, unconsciously, I had put myself up on a cross, had driven in my own spikes, had made myself the crucified, had become my own crucifier, had done this, not for the first time with Richard, but many times before, repeatedly, in twisted penance filled with disgust and shame of flesh, somnambulistically fulfilling the sacrificial destiny of the voices of the fathers within me, impaling my body again and again over their altars of blood, their chalices bottomless, their thirst unslakeable, demanding more and more sons and daughters to eat and drink—unable to love my mother, forbidden to—mothers are the origins of all, women are the origins of all, and the end, and therefore hated and feared by all men who are mere sparks, half creatures on endless journeys of completion, myself as well, my journey to and through Black Mountain a process to connect up with that starveling other self, those shriveled and neglected selves, a journey Charles and other males were certainly also on within the ring of the Seven Sisters.

Suddenly, in that kitchen, surrounded by others, I sensed an enormous, terrifying silence surrounding me—I had a tremendous need to speak out of this vacuum and be heard, but had no words, I, the apprentice writer, mute, even on paper, effectively silenced now in my voice about this central fact of my life and all that impacted on it.

I got up and went outside into the night again, leaned against the front fender of the Fiore's Jeep station wagon which was parked a little distance off in front of Meadows Inn in the shadow of the pine trees. I lit a cigarette and stared back at the lighted windows of the cottage, feeling shut out, feeling a huge and heavy sadness in my chest, convinced now that nothing would ever change, that I would always be as I was, and everything around me the same, feeling, underneath it all, very sorry for myself.

It wasn't a planned thing. I flipped away the cigarette and, in a quick, deliberate walk, determining to resolve it once and for all, crossed the yard, went up the steps and back into the house, marched straight for the bathroom just off the kitchen, oblivious to their laughter and talk in the poker game, turned on the bathroom light, yanked open the medicine cabinet and, taking up a metal pack of razors, pushed out a fresh, dark blade, sliding it carefully, calmly out of the pack, making sure to avoid touching that tiny smudge of oil on the flat of the blade so that, at the crucial moment, my fingers wouldn't slip, one of those Gillette blue blades that guaranteed you in those days any number of shaves. I was amazed at my calm, my head feeling more clear and logical than it had in months. I snapped off the light and, without even glancing in the direction of the kitchen doorway, marched up the hall, across the lobby, and out into the mild, warm night again.

I retraced my steps to the Fiore's Jeep, leaned back as I had before against the front fender, facing the house, and squeezing the paper-thin razor tightly between thumb and forefinger, tipped it, and with the point of the edge, knowing, surgically cool, that that would be the sharpest part, dug as deeply into my left wrist as I could in three, clean, precise sawing motions. Then I switched the blade to my left hand, pleased and amazed at my efficiency, and did the same to the other wrist, clumsily this time, being right-handed, the incisions more ragged.

I held both arms up in the weak light filtering through the pines from the upper floor of the house and watched the blood coursing down my forearms and spattering onto the white cotton trousers I was wearing, surprised not to feel pain, feeling instead curiously content, rocking back and forth on my heels. Then I slumped back against the grille of the car, reverting now to a woozy state, and waited to bleed to death. Although I fiercely wanted to die, yet in that instant I also wanted to live, and hoped someone would find me; in actuality, that someone would save me; secretly, what I had always wanted, not knowing how to save myself.

I felt bathed in a warm and pleasurable ecstasy, as warm and bright as the blood running out my wrists; as satisfying, although it seemed in that moment sacrilege to think it, as a good shit or an orgasm, in its intense and gratifying sense of relief, of release; was discovering what Wes had quoted was true: I hadn't felt so alive in a very long time.

I don't know how long I had been lying there, but it was Jorge, leaving the poker game early, found me. I could hear his heavy motorcycle boots (that he had constantly worn in idolization since seeing Marlon Brando in *The Wild One*, had even bought his own motorcycle in tribute, which he eventually crashed on a back road near the college), Jorge clumping toward me across the grassy expanse in front of the house. When I heard him cry out I opened my eyes and saw his eyes and mouth wide in surprise, then closed my eyes again as I heard him go off at a fast run, back to Meadows Inn.

I pressed myself back against the vertical slits of the Jeep's grille, curious to find there was a sensation of heat in the metal, even though the engine had been shut off some time before.

I was suddenly very tired and drowsy and began to slide down the radiator onto the bumper when I heard the commotion of feet running toward me and, opening my eyes a little saw Tom and Mary and Joe hurrying closer, with Jorge following behind. They had the same surprised, excited look on their faces that Jorge had had. In my grogginess it pleased me, made me feel special, that I had broken up their game, playing one of my own, perhaps; to get their attention, to make them see, to have someone, anyone, hear me at last, incapable of utterance, letting my blood serve as speech.

Tom, instantly again the army medic in Korea, was now all bustling efficiency, taking over immediately, directing Joe and Jorge to give him a hand. The three of them half carried, half dragged me into the house. I must have passed out because I don't remember much of what happened next except, in a momentary blur of awakening, felt the sting of antiseptics as Tom washed my wounds, and then fading out again (whether from booze or loss of blood, or both), only to awaken once more, hearing Tom say in a quiet voice, as if to reassure the others, "He didn't cut any tendons." Then, his voice loud and angry, his flushed, contorted face shoved up against mine, he jolted me awake with, " *Why did you do it, you idiot!*" Foggy as I was I could hear in his tone more fear than anger. "We don't need to take him to the hospital," I heard him say in a softer voice, and then I felt myself lifted and helped to my room and put into bed, their voices whispering like voices in a sick room, then the light was switched off and the door closed and the room was utterly silent and dark.

I awakened during the night, the hovering presence of the wide wings of a great dark bird flapping over me, alighting on my chest, its claws digging into my breastbone, pulling at me, pulling me up, wanting to carry me away, or to pull something out of me, the squeeze and pinch of its talons lifting me from the bed.

Terrified, I sat up in a cold sweat, stared around baffled at the inky shadows in the corners of the room, wondering at first where I was, searching frantically for the eagle-like bird. For the first time, I felt my wrists beneath their swathes of bandages really beginning to sting with pain. But even more unbearable than that, my face burned with shame. What had I done? I turned my face on the pillow, the room blacker than I had ever seen it in the night, and clamped my eyes shut against its darkness, waiting for morning.

I heard Tom call softly at my door late the next day, but kept silent, unable to face him, shuddering to think how I would face the others. I lay in a comatose state, unwilling to move, a weight of inertia pressing me down against the mattress.

Around midafternoon there was another quiet knock on the door, starting me up from a fitful doze. "Michael?" It was Olson's voice from the other side of the door, tactfully soft, hesitant. I shriveled inside. What could I possibly say to him, who of all the others might have understood, my confession of failure to the father, failing to measure up. He, who earlier that spring had had to deal with another suicide attempt of a troubled fey youth from the South who said he was related to Tennessee Williams and had come to study acting, but had ended up taking an overdose of pills in his upstairs room at Streamside and had to be rushed to the hospital in Asheville to have his stomach pumped. And, now, again . . .

Charles called my name once more but I kept still, hardly daring to breathe, hoping he'd go away, too ashamed to answer, to let him see me, too proud, too sick to see anyone, too sick of myself.

After a few moments of standing there, the floorboards under his tall, huge weight creaking in uncertainty—I pictured him listening intently at the door, that great balding head with its owl-like eyes behind horn-rimmed glasses cocked intently, another kind of bird—I heard him turn and go slowly up the steps on tiptoe, cross the lobby and go out the front door.

I wanted to call him back but I heard the door close quietly and knew it was too late. I wouldn't have been able to say anything to him anyway, my throat constricted, the disloyal son who had deeply betrayed (with no thought then of my own betrayal).

That evening Tom, whose own marginal androgyny had earlier that summer brought him trouble, in the very same spot out in front of Meadows Inn, when he'd deliberately wrecked his car, bathed and redressed my wounds, saying they were healing nicely. But I could see by his grimace I'd done an ugly job of it. I refused to look, turning my head away. I didn't try to talk to Tom about what had happened, knowing already, knowing him, reading it in his expression, his eyes, that he'd be fussily impatient, unable to comprehend how I could get so worked up over someone like Richard. Richard . . . I didn't even want to think about what his feelings were when he heard about it.

My first evening out of bed was the time one of Ed and Helene Dorn's young sons decided to play a prank while I was sitting outside my bedroom door on the top step leading into the lobby with its great stone fireplace, talking quietly with Tom, who was standing down in the hall by the kitchen, preparing a light meal to coax me to eat. Abruptly, the front door to the lobby was quickly opened and slammed shut hard, and I had only an instant to glimpse the bright tow head of what looked to be Paul Buck (Helene's youngest son by her first marriage) racing away in the dusk.

It happened so fast I wasn't sure what had occurred except that, my nerves still strung taut, it caused me to leap up in alarm. What frightened me even more in the next instant was suddenly seeing a half dozen or more pencil snakes, those small black snakes with the yellow collars, scattered slithering over the floorboards, most of them heading directly for the mouth of the fireplace, where I'd heard they liked to live in the cracks and crannies of the fieldstone.

Tom saw me jump up and he came forward, after the noise of

the door slamming, and asked what was the matter. When I pointed to the snakes, he looked puzzled, knitting his brow in surprise. I told him, in a shaky voice, I'd seen one of the Dorn kids yank open and shut the door as a prank, and that maybe he'd flung in a handful of snakes as well. Tom wondered if possibly the hard slam hadn't startled the snakes out of their hiding places in the cracks of the hearthstones. He shook his head in annoyance.

Although the snakes were harmless, compared to the numerous copperheads and rattlesnakes up in the hills and which could be found on occasion not far beyond our front door, the tiny black snakes really unnerved me, exacerbating my already frayed sensibilities. In my heightened paranoia, where everything was becoming symbols, allegory, they came as a sign, as omens, like the great dark bird in the night clawing at my chest, as if the Buck boy had been sent by some dark vengeful force to further harass and intimidate me, so coiled in was I upon myself. And in such an egocentric tightness, I distortedly perceived that perhaps, after all, my ritualistic attempt at sacrifice was an unconscious impulsion to appease the forces then destroying Black Mountain (as Tom's slamming into the front of Meadows Inn with his Buick had been, in my mind); a victim already, in extension—just as I had wanted to offer myself to Jake to quiet his rage—I was once more a voluntary lamb in appeasement.

I stood there, half risen, staring at the snakes, hypnotized by their elegant sinuosity, wanting to run back into my room, but instead stood paralyzed and put my hands to my face, terrified that what I had done had unleashed jarring and demonic energies scurrying all around in the air, air that had a chattering sharpness of blades.

Tom told me to quiet down and with an exasperated look, started rounding up the remaining snakes that hadn't yet crawled up into the chimney, and opening the lobby door, tossed them out in the darkness into the high grass beyond the front steps.

In a few days time I only had to wear smaller bandages on my wrists. My major concern now was how what I had done was affecting Richard, concerned that it had probably embarrassed him, put him in an uncomfortable position, perhaps even one of guilt and remorse (was that secretly what I hoped for, what I longed to see in his face?). My impulse, masochistically enough, was to go to him at the first opportunity, when my wounds had sufficiently healed, and apologize.

I don't know how long it was after the wrist-slashing when I faced him again, or what the circumstances of our meeting were, or where it occurred; I only remember the look of controlled anger in those usually mild eyes. They appeared uncustomarily waspish and displeased as they looked directly into mine. My eyes, unable to meet his, darted either side of his face.

I apologized, stammering and stuttering, totally abject. When I lapsed into silence, no longer knowing what to say, he asked me, "Why did you do it?" And it wasn't until some time after, recalling the tone in his voice and that piercing, injured look in his eyes, that I realized the question he was actually asking was, Why did you do this to *me*?

Soon after, on the evening of September 5th, I graduated, still wearing my bandages, though they were now reduced to the size of large bandaids. It was an informal ceremony and party (Richard of course was not there) held at the Fiore's Minimum House up along the road to the farm. Joe, as art instructor, was designated by Olson, as rector, to hand-letter a diploma for me, an Honors Degree "In the Field of Writing," and Joe was ticked off because Charles had asked him to do it only that very afternoon and complained it wouldn't give him enough time to do a really good job. I was still in such a highly over-touchy state I was a little put out by Joe's annoyance which made me feel that, in my graduating, I, as one more Black Mountain kook, was making myself a nuisance again to him.

But in spite of that, everyone was being very good-humored and talkative and tactfully considerate at the party later, which spared me the necessity of having to talk. Charles, as he handed me the diploma, with a grand flourish and his biggest grin, showman to the end, proudly announced he'd had Joe include "*Summa cum laude*" in blue letters, and looked into my eyes as he said it in a way as if he wanted it to make up for something. I sat glumly silent for the most part, exhausted, my nerves so whipped it was all I could do to keep from screaming for them all to shut up, particularly Wolpe, whose voice, usually inventive and delightfully noisy with his spontaneous atonal musical phrasings, seemed particularly shrill and piercing to my ears that night. I had to hold myself in my chair to keep from bolting out of the place.

It was definitely time to leave Black Mountain.

Meanwhile, over in Spain, Robert Duncan began writing the following letter to Olson and Creeley, the day after my graduation:

Banalbufar, Mallorca
September 6, 1955

Dear Charles : For both of you as it might be of an evening to talk of
Dear Bob : what concerns us three here as we go. A letter to accompany my letter of recommendation on Rumaker and how I see the questions I had about that occasion when you, Bob, first sent his work. I knew quite clearly and delighted in the qualities that Rumaker shows, and by "knew quite clearly" I mean that I imagine, whether he realizes it that way, a Rumaker universe. Then I had other tasks on my mind, other prose that Rumaker isnt going to write, that maybe nobody isnt going to write; and there for the moment I wanted to exclaim, "But does this young writer know this business of writing

as the frontier of something, as a part of a science as well as an art." But I meant "the way I do" and was, I was aware but didnt want to see it out, impatient with the way he does. With having it go along as he, as any of us, will have it unfold for us. And its that adventure, the finding the way of it, thats the thing. So, my bon voyage to Rumaker. Its a bon voyage not unhaunted by the wreckage of F. Scott Fitzgerald nor without its promise from the trials of Mark Twain. I think the thing that eats away at me is the difference between writing like this having a "level, 'educationally' speaking", between the "does he write as competently, and as potentially well, as the average graduate from the usual college"—which he more than does—and something else. O hell, the difference between the colleges and universities are and the Learning, between literacy and the spirit of letters. And in the Learning, you and I are all students. But Pound is RIGHT that once it is the Learning one is at and not the college graduation or the teaching profession—a Kultur appears to challenge one. The challenge is not to conquer or to inherit (as I am often minded—and there is something to this inheritance business along the line of the "cultural conglomerate" as Dodds has it, or the "increment of association" as Pound's Social Credit has it), but to discover your Maximus, Charles. As I see it right now anyway, my "wisdom" is to do with this inheritance business, this more or less ness, and your "against wisdom as such" is the man who comes to be able to converse with Shakespeare or further back into time, with Homer or Plato. To be engaged that is. And this IS learning, seeking out. "I sought you out." The thing is I'm driving at that just so he converses with rocks, birds, and energy: a complex in which the "Brother Fire" of Saint Francis has a place and makes him a legendary poet, and the lore of physics, "heat is disordered energy," has a place and makes of the "scientist" who comes to such a *make*, who says this, a *makaris*.

= = = = = = = = = = =10/7= =

       "that I am so by the grace of technique, and work, and being able to give myself an absolute accounting of, what it is, a poem." (Lorca comes saying this thru Blackburn to me out of this ORIGIN that arrived yesterday) and I'll go back to it—that the grace, the work, the absolute accounting of, what it is, the Effort for me, that first of Kung's listed three joys, or roots of joy. I think thats the beginning of the *Analects*. And then the poem is engaged in just this, this effort, this absolute grace, work and accounting. And the story. And that you, Bob, have got this; and that Rumaker hasnt got it yet—clear—is a difference of kind before any measure. Yet nothing is clearer than that while "technique" may be taught, grace of technique can't, can't, can't. This other word associated with grace of technique, "vocation", calling. Is exact. For the way the writer has to listen for a calling out of the language; is nothing until he can hear again; has to be in tune, tuned in like a radio. Exacto. And just there, where he gets it, not passive at all, but alert, at the struggle with his energy pitted to discriminate and make tell this energy of the language. What a specialty! The Rumaker case! the Rumaker case! Let's take it—it's not far out of the question that he takes it straight, along the line of the fact that he can do it, get into a story with gusto, has his keen sense of how they talk, and how they are, has this engagement with the time of living, and writes it. Sit down with the volume of Ring Lardner. This is what I have in mind. Or say, not as grim as Lardner but a step over to William Saroyan with an easy does it, difficult falls sense of being a writer. Part of this picture is a living, money coming in, and repute rewards, disrepute or no repute punishes. How well he knows life! the reader is moved to exclaim, where he is moved. But say a disturbance begins—a disturbance of time sense; and he begins to move out not from the journalistic center, the center of dailiness or rather of today. Say he finds himself as he is, not in his life but, in his race's life or—he is already then on the brink—in man's life. Everything changes and "Can you tell the down from the up?" Pound asks.

It needs a great innocence to live a lifetime without need of the Learning. And all about Rumaker I can see the wreckage of the break of innocence—of those like Hemingway who couldnt write eventually, or of those like Fitzgerald who drove the car wild like the innocents do in Rumaker's story. The point is that when innocence is out, then one really has to know or crash. There is no renigging [sic] on a question of a grace. A man's work is like his marriage, his friendships, his pleasures—he's got to know it for sure when he ain't innocent and then he has to search out the facts, the sphinx of it, to face them—or he goes back into that other thing of innocence—ignorance; lives in a wishes he didn't or hadnt, or a what he could have. It's in this absence of innocence in writing that the man has to tackle, take under and over the job as it appears once the journalistic, the daily, gives way to larger areas of time. Then he's got to go to just those works which have opend up this time; he's got to learn out of them how [to] live in time and how to keep at it . . . .

Perfectly posed questions, and a perfectly posed declaration Duncan enunciated in his last sentence; and imperfectly poised as I was to set out upon its exploration, I was ready and willing, and underneath it all, in spite of all that had happened (including Duncan's synchronistically intuited connection of "crashes"), I was eager for it, the "bon voyage," unbeknownst to me, that Duncan had wished for me.

That night, just after my graduation ceremony, I took down from the shelf over the door of my study all three stacks of foot-high manuscripts I'd written before and during my stay at Black Mountain and that I'd been saving for so long, took them out to the old rusty oil-barrel trash can outside the Stables, where the painters' studios were, and burned them, the sparks flying up against the sky more vivid and more exciting than any of those crudely written words of mine, emblems of my long and green apprenticeship—a ritualistic burning that was also a cleansing.

As I walked back up the hill to Meadows Inn in the dark—no need for a flashlight anymore, knowing now after three years, every stone, every tree root in the path—I felt suddenly unburdened, lighter in my step. I would pack that night and be gone by morning, hitchhiking north for the last time. I would stay temporarily, till I found a job, with friends in Philadelphia in their tiny "Father-Son-Holy Ghost house," as such 18th century former servant quarters were called—three little rooms built on top one another on the back-alley streets of Center City—and begin again. As I crossed over the wooden bridge, knowing intuitively where it was in the dark, I stopped a moment to listen one last time to the unseen mountain stream rushing under my feet down in the ravine below.

Yes, it was time to move on.

1956

Postscript:

I returned to Black Mountain one more time in the first week of August 1956, on a vacation visit from a job I'd gotten, after a long search in that recession year at, of all places, a financial advertising agency, Doremus-Eshleman at 15th and Locust Streets in Philadelphia, writing copy in the public relations department. The job enabled me to move from the tiny top room of my friends' Father-Son-and-Holy Ghost house on St. James Street to a place of my own. One of the reasons I got the job was that the boss who hired me, a middle-aged, Irish-Catholic, native Philadelphian, an active alcoholic who was also deeply closeted and still living with his mother (a not unusual circumstance in that city), overlooked my incompetencies because, as I learned later, he'd taken a shine to me (he even kept me on after a bout with pneumonia, undoubtedly brought on by the stress of my more harried life in the city, that landed me for a month in Pennsylvania Hospital on Lombard Street). We became no closer than drinking buddies, he introducing me to the dry martini in some of the tonier watering holes in Center City, such as local golf champ Helen Siegal's on Walnut Street that catered to the Main Line crowd, and where Grace Kelly's family hung out. As Woodie had done earlier in New York, my new boss even gave me one of his old, and expensively cut, gray flannel suits, only slightly threadbare, that fit fine once he had it altered for me, just so I'd fit in better in the gray flannel world of 1950s advertising.

Quite an unforeseen changearound from my life at Black Mountain, my days, and especially my nights, now even more so, very much like Pound's question that Duncan quoted in his September 6th letter from Mallorca to Olson and Creeley: "Can you tell the down from the up?"

This was literally so when one evening after work, after a number of martinis at Helen Siegel's with my boss, I literally crawled, in my camouflage drag of business-suit-and-tie, across Rittenhouse Square, a gay cruising park at night, back to my little basement apartment at 21st and Spruce.

What would Olson have thought?

After a number of such episodes, which sometimes led to my innocently picking up dangerous hustlers who preyed on queers—an old blue-collar Catholic, South Philly tradition—and being robbed and roughed up and, on one occasion, raped, I realized by August of 1956 that I desperately needed to touch base again with the gains I had gotten at Black Mountain and that I seemed to be rapidly losing in the alleged City of Brotherly Love. That, perhaps most importantly, included my inability, in spite of a brand-new olive-green portable Olympia typewriter, purchased at $121 on time with my new $70 a week wages, to turn out any writing of substance, except bleak poems and horror stories, essentially reflective of my life then. I thought, What better chance to go back to see Olson, to get in touch again with what was important, and perhaps be put by him, as he had so often done in the past, back on the right track.

The very first day of my vacation, able now to afford a ticket, I caught the Pennsylvania Railroad train at 30th Street Station south for Washington, as on my first rail trip down in 1952, where I switched to the Southern Railway (the difference now being the Jim Crow coaches were gone), for the journey back to North Carolina—thinking of it as going home, really, thinking of the return trip as maybe being able to "save" me in some way, where Olson, my father, waited for me to set me right. That included Betty Kaiser, now Betty Olson, newly married to Charles, and with new son, Charles Peter, the three of them living now under the Olson roof (a strange realignment to make now in myself, with Connie and Kate gone), in that vast, mountainous, near-wilderness I thought of, in spite of all the bleak happenings of my last few months there, as sanctuary, and that I needed at that moment more desperately than ever.

Coincidentally enough, I was put up again in Meadows Inn, with all its chilling reminders, but I was so glad to put my feet again on Black Mountain soil and to breathe in again the clean mountain air, after the booze and grime and confusion of Philly, the grim experiences of the summer of 1955 receded.

Not long after I'd unpacked, Charles caught me outside the cottage as he was passing, greeted me warmly, and invited me to supper that night with him and "Bet" and to get a look at his new son. He insisted, almost desperately it seemed, his tone suggesting he didn't think much of his new writing students, that I, "an old hand," attend his writing class after supper, "to show them a thing or two." I was, of course, immediately filled with unease, wondering if I had anything to share, nervous that Charles expected me to perform, and dreading that I would not be up to it after all that had happened in the intervening year. Still, I said I'd do the best I could.

At the time, I had several bad front teeth, from neglect due to poverty, coupled with a fear of dentists. (The emergency visit to the dentist in Black Mountain with Charles was the last time I'd seen one.) I was self-conscious about it, so much so, that, unconsciously, I had taken to putting my hand to my mouth when I spoke (just as my mother had when I was a child, ashamed of her own bad teeth, caused by the poor diet of poverty and certainly no money ever for any dentists).

Olson of course caught my gesture of concealment right away, asking with a slight grin, "What's the matter with your mouth?"

I was embarrassed, but took my hand away. I should have known I couldn't hide anything from Charles, not only bad writing but even bad teeth.

It was wonderful to see Betty again, quietly gracious as ever but now with an added incandescence in her smile and voice, as she proudly, before seeing to dinner, showed me baby Charles Peter, born in May 1955. I also saw, after all she'd been through, living in a cheap room in Manhattan and having the baby alone (she was so poor and unable to afford a crib, she kept her newborn in a bottom bureau drawer at first), that now all her attention was on her new baby, and on Charles, her thoughts of music and acting in abeyance. Charles made drinks and we all got quite merry. Charles, who was plainly annoyed with the shenanigans, and quality, of the current crop of students, gleefully suggested the handful of remaining faculty should vote to take down the Black Mountain College sign over the Gatehouse entrance and "run up a bright red flag that says 'SECONAL' on it in big letters!"

I was so glad to see Charles and Betty again I couldn't shut up, and, fueled by the booze, went burbling happily on and on, Charles so amused at my antic mouth, he leaned over to Betty at one point and slyly, jokingly, with an ironic touch of mockery, whispered, "See? Genius." That braked me for a moment, but only for a moment, seeing Charles' humor, and I was off again, Betty and Charles joining in, the three of us gabbing away through dinner till it was time to go to Charles' class.

Probably because it was cooler down there in the dog days, Charles was holding his writing class in the Conference Room on the lower level of the Studies Building. There were perhaps a half dozen or more students present around the big square table, just about the entire student population it seemed, since the number of those enrolled was even more drastically reduced than when I left. There were a few familiar faces: Jerry Van de Wiele, Eric Weinberger, Basil King, and Jonathan Williams, Jonathan there on a brief visit, like myself. Jerry told me later the behavior of some of the students, especially when they were drinking or on drugs, and even sometimes when they were not, was so unpredictable, he took to hiding his wood-chopping axe whenever someone knocked on his door up at Next-to-Last-Chance, where he now lived, in the apartment Merrill and I had shared, for fear of possible violence.

As "guest of honor," and with lavish praise—some of it, I suspected, booze-induced ham—Charles asked me to comment on a student's squib of a poem, a pot-smoking, Seconal-swallowing, boyishly handsome blond youth with black-rimmed glasses who putted into Asheville several afternoons a week on his little Lambretta scooter to see his shrink, and who later informed me that he was "18th in line for the throne of England," a prime example of the "new student" Charles had been complaining about over dinner. I of course, not exactly the picture of mental health myself, got an immediate, terrific crush on him. But at that moment, equally besotted from Olson's generous drinks, and probably more likely, after almost a year in Philly working in that financial advertising agency, I had not only lost my way but my edge as well, since all I could come up with was a comment that criticized the student's British spellings. (I believe Gavin, for that was his name, had attended a public school in England for awhile.) Olson, I could plainly see, was disappointed by my limp response. But I was not only out of practice but also nervous and more than a little fearful, being put on the spot that way, especially after Charles' exaggerated and embarrassing buildup.

I saw little of Charles or Betty the rest of my stay. Given, I suppose, the glum and unpredictable atmosphere of the campus, Charles preferred to hole up behind the walls of his house. I was also disappointed not to meet Robert Duncan who, though teaching that summer, was away for a few days, but I would meet him later in September when he hitchhiked up to Philadelphia to stay at my apartment. Jerry, still a lively source of pointed gossip, informed me that things were a bit strained between Charles and Duncan since the performance earlier that summer session of Duncan's satirical play on Olson, "The Origin of Old Son," starring muscular ex-marine Jerry Van de Wiele himself, in baby hat and clothes in a baby carriage, playing Charles, a further wicked declaration of independence by

Duncan from Olson.

As a result, I spent some of my time trying to get reacquainted with some of the old hands; I say "trying" because they seemed also holed up in their study or studio lairs. Hence, most of the time I spent mooning over The Pretender to the Throne, Gavin, my latest obsessive "love," even once riding precariously on the back of his motor-scooter all the way into Asheville, and dutifully waiting outside his psychiatrist's office during one of his sessions, the payoff, coming and going, being that I could wrap my arms tight around him and could occasionally snuggle close to his shoulder blades, in a pretense to shield myself from the wind.

Mary Fiore photographed me sitting astride the Lambretta in front of Meadows Inn where Gavin also roomed.

Black Mountain, though, to all appearances, was even more rapidly continuing its downward spiral. I knew now there was nothing there for me anymore. It was truly time to push on. It was then I began to think of hitchhiking to San Francisco to join Tom Field and the other Black Mountaineers who had recently settled out there.

Jonathan Williams and I took the train back north together. He was heading to New York City on some business and put some records and manuscripts for his Jargon Press on our seats to save them, while we spent most of the trip to Greensboro, where we'd change trains for Washington, in the bar car. On returning to our seats, we found two sodden farmer types in overalls and plaid shirts sitting not only in our seats but also on Jonathan's records and manuscripts. Apparently unaware they were sitting on anything, the two men refused to budge and Jonathan was stiffly furious as he forcibly recovered his property from under them. But I was secretly, tipsily amused, seeing the incident somehow as a fitting end to my last visit to Black Mountain.

Hungover when I left Jonathan and got off at 30th Street Station in Philly early next morning, I also realized the end of Black Mountain College was really now close at hand—realized that that was my last time there when it held even less so the bare remnants of a college, was now a truly shadowy pretense of what it once was—that it was finally not only the end of it for me, but for all who were still there vainly sticking it out; and for all those who had gone. Still, underneath all that, I knew wherever I went in the days ahead, what I got there would go with me.

I could see Philadelphia was an end for me as well, and after I settled with the draft (later, at the Newark, New Jersey, Induction Center, I finally screwed up the nerve to check off the box admitting my homosexuality, and was made a 4-F reject), I began making plans in earnest to hitchhike to San Francisco, to get away from my deadening and deadend job, from all the boozing and all the dangerous midnight cruisings in Rittenhouse Square, to be with Tom and Duncan and the others—another new beginning out West.

The last time I saw Charles was in Provincetown in the summer of 1958. I was at this time holing up rent-free in Denise Levertov and Mitch Goodman's apartment on West 15th Street in Manhattan while they were away for the summer in Maine with young son Nick. I was feeling very down and depressed, broke, unable to work or write, and drinking too much and downing too many amphetamines to cover it up. Don Allen, thinking a change would do me good, arranged with poet Robin Blaser that I spend some time visiting Blaser and his partner, Jim, in their apartment on Beacon Hill, so I reluctantly took the train to Boston. Jim, a chemist, sneaked home beakers of gin he secretly manufactured in the lab he worked in, the potency of which helped me get through some dark evenings.

One weekend, Robin suggested the two of us take the boat to Provincetown and meet with Charles and Betty and baby Charles Peter, who were vacationing there. They were now living up in Gloucester, after everything at Black Mountain College had been sold, the college's affairs having been settled and the place finally officially closed, leaving them free to head north to live in their large, drafty apartment on Fort Square facing the sea.

They met us at the boat, and we walked the streets crowded with summer tourists, Charles gabbing excitedly all the way, asking what Robin was doing and what I was up to, at which I hemmed and hawed, embarrassed to say that it wasn't much. We ended up at a table in the back of a packed, smoky bar where Charles continued to hold forth, Betty, clasping Charles Peter in her lap, smiling contentedly, Robin and I listening as best we could over the din, Charles' enthusiastic energy, as always, lifting my spirits, which was also helped by seeing Betty so apparently quietly happy. Of course, the endless pitchers of beer which Charles kept ordering from the bar helped too, but none of it did much to quiet an overriding queasiness that I was headed for trouble.

When it was time to catch the late afternoon boat back to Boston, the five of us walked down to the pier, Charles chattering ever more lively after having quaffed a number of brews. After we all embraced and said our goodbyes, Robin and I climbed the gangplank, then stood at the dockside railing to wave as the boat eased away from its moorings. Suddenly, startling the crowd of onlookers as well as Robin and me, Charles, in his exuberance, began to climb one of the tall, rotting pilings of the dock, hugging it with his heavy thighs, his long arms going up hand over hand over his big head, splinters flying, Betty watching, smiling indulgently, as she held baby Charles Peter, who stared as round-eyed as Robin and myself at the antics of his father, I, fearful the decaying piling would crumble

9293

under his weight, dropping Charles into the drink. But he reached the top all right where, with the biggest grin creasing his flushed face, he waved and waved at Robin and me, the piling waving back and forth with him, and he kept on waving until the boat pulled out to sea, before it turned in the direction of Boston, and we could no longer see him.

That was the last time I saw Charles, the last time I saw all three of them together.

The last time I spoke to Charles was in 1965 on the telephone in Grove Press and *Evergreen Review* editor Don Allen's room at the Hotel Grosvener on 5th Avenue. Don, who had published three of my early stories in *Evergreen Review*, had by that time started up his own independent Four Seasons Foundation and Grey Fox Press, was in town from Bolinas, California, on some business and we'd gotten together for drinks and dinner, *coq au vin* at a French restaurant on 6th Avenue in the Village. He'd placed a call to Charles in Wyoming, New York, where Olson was then living, and after he'd finished his business with him, handed me the phone, saying, "Here's an old friend of yours."

Charles sounded excited, in an elated mood. He thanked me for the "You" poem (which had recently appeared in *Evergreen Review* just after Betty's death in the car crash on that icy road just outside Wyoming), mistakenly thinking it had been written as a kind of in memoriam for her. The poem was actually my thinking of Rimbaud, intensely and briefly alive and so quickly dead, an unconscious reflection perhaps on my own fate if I kept on drinking and drugging. I didn't, out of respect for his feelings, correct him. No matter; the poem could have applied to Betty as well. So I kept quiet.

I asked him if he'd gotten my letter expressing my sympathy about Betty's dying, and he, typically Olson, chided me for its being such a measly note. He told me to write to him "more, and more open"—and gave me his address at the University of Buffalo, where he was then teaching. I got confused on the abbreviation "SUNY" for State University of New York, never having heard it before, and he said, "Just write it down like that— SOONYEE— and write me there."

It was the last time I heard his voice.

Even so, Charles, to this day is still in my dreams, enthroned often in the underworld, sending up cryptic messages, scoldings, about my life, my writing, I, still, the perennial apprentice—he, even on top, down there. He will always be.

Michael Rumaker is the author of ten books.

A graduate of Black Mountain College in
North Carolina and Columbia University,
he teaches at City University of New York.

A study of his life and work by Leverett T.
Smith, Jr., was published by Black Mountain
College Museum & Arts Center as
Black Mountain College Dossier No.6.

He lives in Nyack, New York.

The Black Mountain College Museum & Arts Center
has published the following *Dossiers* on students
and teachers of Black Mountain College:

No. 1	*Joseph Fiore*
No. 2	*Fannie Hillsmith*
No. 3	*Lore Lindenfeld*
No. 4	*Susan Weil*
No. 5	*Ray Johnson*
No. 6	*Michael Rumaker*
No. 7	*Gwendolyn Knight*

as well as:
Remembering Black Mountain College

AEI-3642

Gramley Library
Salem Academy and College
Winston-Salem, N.C. 27108